# RUSSIAN
# HISTORY

Neil M. Heyman, Ph.D.
San Diego State University

## McGraw-Hill, Inc.

*New York   St. Louis   San Francisco   Auckland   Bogotá   Caracas
Lisbon   London   Madrid   Mexico   Milan   Montreal   New Delhi
Paris   San Juan   Singapore   Sydney   Tokyo   Toronto*

**Neil M. Heyman** is a professor of history at San Diego State University, where he has taught Russian and European history since 1969. He received a B.A. summa cum laude from Yale University and M.A. and Ph.D. degrees in history from Stanford University. Professor Heyman was Visiting Professor of History at Concordia University in Montreal during the academic year 1988–1989. He is the coauthor (with Holger H. Herwig) of the *Biographical Dictionary of World War I*. His articles and reviews on Russian history have appeared in the *Journal of Modern History*, *Studies in Comparative Communism*, the *American Historical Review*, the *Russian Review*, the *Los Angeles Times*, and the *San Diego Union*. An honor graduate of the U.S. Army Language School in the study of Russian, Professor Heyman is proficient in five other languages. He is a frequent guest lecturer on Russian affairs.

*Sponsoring Editor*, Jeanne Flagg
*Production Supervisor*, Leroy A. Young
*Editing Supervisor*, Patty Andrews
*Front Matter Editor*, Maureen Walker

Russian History

2 3 4 5 6 7 8 9 10 11 12 13 14 15 16 17 18 19 20 DOC   DOC   9 8 7 6 5 4 3 2

ISBN 0-07-028649-3

Library of Congress Cataloging-in-Publication Data

Heyman, Neil M.
   Russian history / Neil M. Heyman.
      p.    cm.
   Includes index.
   ISBN 0-07-028649-3
   1. Soviet Union—History.  I. Title.
DK37.H49  1993
947—dc20

92-10670
CIP

# Preface

This volume examines the history of Russia from the prehistoric era to the closing months of 1991. It was written during a turbulent time for the people of the Soviet Union and completed just before the empire fell. The final chapter has been extended to reflect the dramatic events following the failed coup of August 1991.

The book was designed to present in concise but readable form the main facts and issues in Russian history, incorporating social, intellectual, religious, and artistic trends. Since the Russian Empire to 1917 and the Soviet Union thereafter contained numerous minority peoples, this account frequently considers the relationship between the central authorities (in Moscow or St. Petersburg) and the most important non-Russian groups.

Students will find this book helpful as a review to a course in Russian history or as a supplement to any of the standard texts. For both the student and the general reader, it can also stand alone as an introduction to the Russian past.

Every chapter contains a time line, an overview and a summary, and a list of recommended readings. Clearly drawn maps appear throughout.

Important terms are defined as soon as they appear in the text. Dates of birth and death have been provided for most of the individuals mentioned. For monarchs and religious leaders the dates given indicate their reign and are preceded by ''r.''

The dates of the Russian calendar, adopted in the early eighteenth century and used until the end of 1917, lagged behind those used in the rest of Europe by several days. In the interest of simplicity and clarity, this text gives all dates according to the European rather than the Russian calendar. In most cases, there is no significant difference between the Russian and European dates. When the problem arises in an important way, concerning the Bolshevik Revolution, for example, the text explains the variation in dates.

The Russian language is written using a Cyrillic alphabet very different from ours. There are several accepted ways of transferring (transliterating) names or words from the Russian to the English alphabet. Thus authors of books about Russia can use a variety of English spellings in presenting the same Russian names. This text presents Russian proper names in the form employed by the most popular college textbooks. Even the textbooks often differ, however, and in those cases I have picked a form likely to look familiar to an American reader. Where a Russian name varies sharply from any English equivalent, as in the case of Vasili and Basil, the text presents both.

# Acknowledgments

I wish to thank my students at San Diego State University and Concordia University in Montreal for their interest in Russian history. I have long admired their enthusiasm for this subject, their appreciation when it is presented with color and clarity, and their willingness to challenge my interpretations.

Jeanne Flagg at McGraw-Hill has been a consistently helpful and sympathetic sponsoring editor. Dr. Samuel C. Ramer of Tulane University and Nancy Cone reviewed an initial draft of the manuscript. Their extensive comments and criticisms saved me from errors of fact, errors of omission, and countless examples of stylistic awkwardness.

The staff of the Love Library at San Diego State University, in particular Mr. Phillip White, came to my rescue on numerous occasions.

Finally, my family tolerated with good humor my sometimes frenzied schedule as I combined teaching responsibilities with long hours in the library and in front of my computer. To my wife, Brenda, and my sons, Mark and David, my loving thanks.

Neil M. Heyman
San Diego, California
September 1992

# Contents

# Maps

# CHAPTER 1

## The Geographic Basis of Russian History; Early Peoples of Russia

### Time Line

| | |
|---|---|
| 1000–700 B.C. | Cimmerian era |
| 700–200 B.C. | Scythian era |
| 200 B.C.–<br>A.D. 200 | Sarmatian era |
| A.D. 200–370 | Gothic era |
| A.D. 370–558 | Era of the Huns |

| | |
|---|---|
| A.D. 558–650 | Avar era |
| | Arrival of first Slavs? |
| A.D. 600 | Establishment of the Khazar state |

*The physical setting of Russian history has created both opportunities and problems for the Russian people and the governments that have been established there.*

*From their beginnings to the present, the Russian people have lived in a vast land with a harsh climate. They have had no natural features like mountains and oceans to protect them against powerful, hostile neighbors. Moreover, Russia has been far removed from the centers of both European and Asian civilization.*

*Russia's governments have faced the problem of establishing internal order in such circumstances. They have also needed to find ways both to protect themselves from outside threats and to develop useful ties with other societies.*

*Starting more than 6000 years ago, the region that would become Russia contained a number of different peoples. It has been hard to date the arrival of the Slavic tribes who populated the first Russian state, with its center at Kiev. By the ninth century, however, these tribes could be found along the Dnieper Valley, in the northern forests, and in the prairies close to the Black Sea.*

## European Russia

The main events of Russian history have been concentrated in the region west of the Ural Mountains, the area known as "European Russia." An understanding of the physical setting of this area is a necessary starting point for a study of Russian history.

### The Great Plain

European Russia is dominated by a vast plain or flatland. It begins in Eastern Europe, in present-day Poland, and it stretches into Asia. One important consequence of this flatland has been the absence of natural defenses to protect Russia from outside invasion. Another consequence is that Russians themselves have been able to expand over the flat plains without facing natural barriers.

### The River System

A number of important rivers flow across the flatland of European Russia. Most begin in the Valdai Hills, a plateau in northwestern Russia halfway between the present cities of Moscow and St. Petersburg (formerly Leningrad).

The rivers have connected different regions of Russia with one another. For much of Russian history, only travel by river allowed Russians to overcome the vast distances the country contained.

The most important rivers of European Russia are the Volga, which flows southward for 2300 miles to the Caspian Sea, and the Dnieper, which flows southward for 1400 miles into the Black Sea. One of the reasons for Moscow's rise to the center of Russian life was that Moscow won control over the region between these major waterways.

### The Climate

Most of European Russia is located as far to the north as Canada or Alaska. Even the southern resort center of Yalta is on the same latitude as Minneapolis. Thus, European Russia has a harsh climate featuring extreme cold in wintertime. Storms frequently appear out of the Arctic; without mountains to stop them, their impact can carry as far as the Black Sea. Summers can bring extreme heat. The difficult climate has combined with poor soil to make farming impossible in much of Russia. Even where farming is possible it remains difficult. A short growing season and an unreliable supply of rain have often produced severe droughts.

## Non-European Russia

Starting in the sixteenth century, Russia expanded east of the Urals. Thus, to study the history of Russia over the last four centuries requires an understanding of the physical setting of non-European Russia.

### The Great Plain

The flatlands of European Russia extend east of the Ural Mountains and across much of Siberia. The plain narrows and ends east of the Yenisei River in a series of plateaus and mountain ranges.

## The Desert

Non-European Russia contains one important feature absent west of the Urals: a vast desert and semidesert that stretches southward from the plains of western Siberia. It ends in a series of mountain ranges that separate Russian territory from Afghanistan, China, and India.

## The Rivers

Most of the rivers of Siberia—the Ob, the Irtysh, the Lena, and the Yenisei—run northward to empty into the Arctic Ocean. The tributaries of these great rivers often run eastward or westward. Thus, as Russian explorers moved eastward after 1580, they found that the river systems provided routes for their advance. But only the Amur, which runs eastward and empties into the Pacific, connects Russia with the outside world.

## The Climate

The climate of Siberia is a harsher version of the one to be found in European Russia. Parts of Siberia have the coldest weather to be found anywhere in the world, but Siberia also has a brief, warm summer.

The climate of Central Asia becomes drier as one moves southward. Much of the region consists of desert in which a few oases and rivers have made it possible to establish cities like Tashkent and Samarkand.

# Growth of the Russian State

The history of Russia is marked by the expansion of territory under the control of Russia's rulers. Political and social upheavals caused this process to stop at times and even to go into reverse. Nonetheless, the growth of the Russian state is a basic theme in the country's history.

## Russia in the Era of Kiev

Historians consider the year 1054, at the death of Grand Prince Iaroslav the Wise (r. 1036–1054), to be the political peak of the

Kievan era. At that point, 400,000 square miles of territory were under the control of the Kievan state. This was approximately the size of Texas and New Mexico combined.

## Moscow

### *Moscovite State in the Era of Ivan I (Kalita)*

As Moscow began its rise to prominence in 1326, Prince Ivan Kalita (r. 1326–1341) controlled only 600 square miles. This was half the size of the state of Rhode Island.

### *Moscovite State in 1462*

When Ivan III (or Ivan the Great, r. 1462–1505) came to the throne, the Moscovite state covered about 15,000 square miles. It was about the size of Massachusetts, Connecticut, and Rhode Island combined.

### *Muscovite State in 1700*

By the early reign of Peter the Great (r. 1689–1725), the absorption of Siberia had increased the size of the tsar's realm to 5.9 million square miles. This was ten times the size of Alaska.

## The Russian Empire on the Eve of World War I

From the era of Ivan III to the start of the twentieth century Russian territory grew at the rate of 50 square miles a day! Much of this territory, of course, consisted of the relatively unpopulated expanses of Siberia and the Far East.

By 1913, the Russian Empire covered approximately 8.5 million square miles. Thus, Tsar Nicholas II (r. 1894–1917) ruled an empire two and a half times as large as the United States.

## The Soviet Union until August 1991

The twentieth century saw the transformation of the Russian Empire into the Soviet Union. Territory under the control of the Soviet government both increased and diminished during the seven and a half decades following the Bolshevik Revolution of 1917. In August 1991 when the political system linking the components of the Soviet

Union collapsed, the country covered about 8.5 million square miles. This was the approximate size of the Russian Empire in 1913.

# Topography of the Soviet Union

Geographers identify five major zones that stretched across the Soviet Union as it existed in early August 1991. The zones are defined by the type of soil and nature of the vegetation to be found in each.

### Tundra

The tundra was located along the northern fringes of the Soviet Union, mostly within the Arctic Circle. It is a wasteland where the climate and soil conditions are too harsh to support the growth of trees. Before the Soviet era, the tundra region was almost uninhabited.

### Forest Zone

Almost half the Soviet Union's territory consisted of a vast belt of forests stretching from European Russia to the Pacific. The forest zone, occupying approximately 3 million square miles, equals the size of the entire United States.

The northern portion of the forest zone is called the *taiga*. It contains great stands of pine and fir trees, but the soil is not rich enough to support successful farming. In the southern part of the forest belt, called the "mixed forest zone," much of the land has long been used for farming. Although far smaller than the *taiga*, it now contains three times as many people.

### Steppe

South of the mixed forest zone, a steppe, or prairie belt, extended across the European area of the Soviet Union. It covered a part of non-European Soviet territories up to the Altai Mountains.

The northern part of the steppe contains wooded areas. The southern part is mostly level grassland. The entire steppe region occupies 1.25 million square miles, twice the size of the state of Alaska.

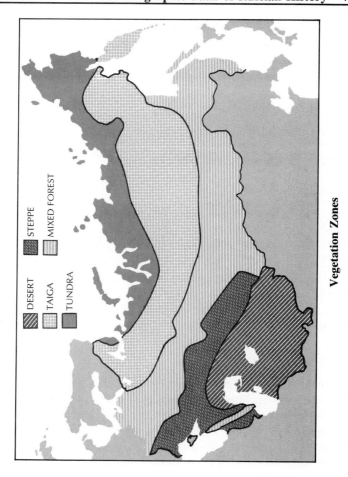

The steppe contained the country's richest agricultural regions. The best farming land in the Soviet Union, the "black earth" *(chernozem)* area, was located in the wooded steppe and the northern portions of the grasslands, stretching from the west-central Ukraine to southwestern Siberia. Its center was the Ukranian city of Kiev.

## Desert

The Soviet Union also contained a belt of desert and semidesert located south of the steppe. Beginning northwest of the Caspian Sea, it stretches eastward to the Tian Shan Mountains of Turkestan.

This dry region is the same size as the steppe: 1.25 million square miles. Its distance from European Russia and its harsh climate help explain why much of it did not come under Russian control until near the end of the nineteenth century.

# The Impact of Geography

Russia's dramatic geographic character has had a sharp effect in many areas of historical development.

### Foreign Invaders

The harsh climate and vast distances have served to protect Russia from outside invasion. The country's lack of natural geographic barriers to guard the frontiers has thus been counterbalanced.

One example of the way geography has sheltered Russia can be found in the failure of the German invasion in 1941 when the Soviet Union was drawn into World War II. Like the Mongols centuries earlier, the Germans occupied vast stretches of Russian territory only to find it impossible to turn these regions into permanent conquests.

### Domestic Expansion

The flat character of European Russia aided the expansion of Moscow's power. Many historians consider domestic expansion and the existence of an unsettled frontier within Russia to be crucial elements in shaping the country's development.

The similarity in climate and topography between European and Asian Russia made it easier for Russian explorers to move eastward than in other directions. The system of Siberian rivers also aided the march eastward, providing ways through the wilderness. Thus, Russian explorers and fur traders covered 6000 miles from the Urals to the Pacific between 1580 and 1640.

### Economic Backwardness

Distance and a harsh climate have made it difficult to reach many of Russia's raw material resources. Thus, the development of industry in recent centuries has suffered as a result of geographic factors.

Only part of the land is rich enough to be cultivated. The climate creates a short growing season, and no farming area can rely on sufficient rainfall. These factors have combined to keep Russia poor. All too often, they have combined to produce famine. Famines having grave political effects mark Russian history, for example, in the periods 1601–1603 and 1891–1892.

## The Problem of Access to the Sea

Russia was a landlocked country throughout most of its past. Some historians believe that an important theme in Russian history has been the effort to obtain good coastal ports and thus to open sea routes to the outside world. The reign of Peter the Great presents the example of successful expansion to the Baltic Sea.

# Early Peoples of Russia

The early history of the Eurasian steppe north of the Black Sea is filled with the movements of various peoples and the establishment of empires. Without natural defenses, the region was helpless in the face of powerful invaders. Onetime conquerors found themselves overcome by later powers.

The key issue for students of Russian history concerns the establishment of the immediate ancestors of the Russians: At what point did the first Slavic tribes settle in this region?

## Pre-Slavic Period

The region that became European Russia has been inhabited for at least 6000 years. Our information about the first peoples who lived here is based upon the findings of archaeologists, and useful information from them can tell us only about the period after 1000 B.C. Most scholars believe that non-Slavic peoples lived here long before that date. The arrival of the first settlers we can identify as Slavs came after, possibly long after, 1000 B.C.

### *The Earliest Known Settlers*

*The Cimmerians.*   The Cimmerians, a people who may have originated in Thrace, reached the steppes north of the Black Sea around 1000 B.C. The Cimmerians apparently set up control over earlier inhabitants here.

*The Scythians.*   A second people, the Scythians, whose ethnic origin remains uncertain, arrived from Central Asia. They conquered the Cimmerians around 700 B.C., and their control over the Eurasian plain continued until about 200 B.C. Archeological evidence like weapons and ornaments uncovered from burial mounds tells us they were militarily powerful nomads.

### The Greek Presence

The written record of events in the region north of the Black Sea begins around 650 B.C. At this time, the Greeks founded cities on the Crimean Peninsula and in nearby regions along the coast of the Black Sea. Greeks recorded their impressions of the Scythians. The Greek historian Herodotus, for example, vividly described the ability of the fierce Scythians to fight off the powerful Persian empire and to dominate a vast area north of the Black Sea.

### Invasions of the Sarmatians and Goths (200 B.C.–A.D. 370)

*The Sarmatians.*   The open plains of the region drew in other groups. Around 200 B.C., the Scythians were conquered by the Sarmatians, nomadic warriors of Iranian origin from Central Asia. For several centuries, the Sarmatians had close trade ties and even intermarried with the Greeks. Some historians consider this "Graeco-Iranian culture" a high point in the early history of the Black Sea steppe.

*The Goths.*   Around A.D. 200, a new wave of invaders came from a different direction. The Goths, a Germanic tribe, pushed in from Scandinavia and destroyed the control of the Sarmatians.

### Invasions of The Huns and Avars (A.D. 370–650)

*The Huns.*   The pattern of invasions from nomadic tribes moving westward across the plains from Asia continued. The Huns swept through the region around A.D. 370, driving on to Western Europe.

*The Avars.*   The Avars followed in A.D. 558. They created a huge state stretching from the Volga River westward to the Elbe.

## The Arrival of the Slavs

Historians are uncertain about the date when Slavs first settled in the Dnieper Valley. There are two views to note.

### The Traditional Interpretation

A theory to which some scholars hold states that Slavs arrived from somewhere in Central Europe, perhaps from what is now

Czechoslovakia, during the sixth century A.D. Records kept by writers in Byzantium, the capital of the Greek empire in the eastern Mediterranean, mention Slavs serving with Avar armies around A.D. 581.

*East Slavs.*    The Slavs who arrived from Central Europe became known as the East Slavs. They are considered the ancestors of the Great Russian, Ukrainian, and White Russian peoples who developed on Russian territory in the centuries that followed.

*Other Slavs.*    In the traditional view, the East Slavs are tied historically and by language to other Slavic peoples. Those Slavic peoples, like the Poles and Czechs, who remained in Central Europe became the West Slavs. Those who moved southward developed into South Slavs, like the Serbs and Bulgarians.

### Another Interpretation

Some recent historians claim that immediate ancestors of the Slavs lived on the Eurasian plain as early as the Scythian period (700 to 200 B.C.). In this view, the Scythians and later conquerors like the Avars ruled over a largely Slavic population.

### The First Slavic Tribes

Before the establishment of the first Russian state, with its center at Kiev, a number of East Slavic tribes lived in independence. They were scattered from the Baltic to the Black Sea.

*Poliane.*    The Poliane tribe was probably the largest. Their name means "people of the plain." Located south of Kiev, they farmed the rich black soil of that region.

*Drevliane.*    The Drevliane (sometimes called Derevliane) tribe was located northwest of Kiev. Their name means "forest people." Living in a barren region, they were less economically developed than the Poliane.

*Other Major Tribes.*    The Ulichi and Tivertsi were located in areas west of the Poliane along the valleys of the Bug and Dniester rivers.

The Radimichi and Severiane were southern tribes driven northward into the forest zone by the attacks of steppe nomads.

In northern Russia, the Krivichi lived near the Valdai Hills. The

Slovene were located near the town of Novgorod. These two tribes spread eastward into the region between the Volga and Oka rivers.

### The Khazar State

The period just before the founding of a Kievan state saw the rise of another power in the region. The Turkic Khazars established themselves north of the Black Sea and the Caspian Sea. The Khazars established trade ties to the Slavic tribes that had settled in the Dnieper Valley. They may also have had some political control over some of these Slavic tribes.

*The region that we call Russia began as an unsettled area in which the flat steppe offered an open door to invaders. The fertile but exposed regions of the south offered vast spaces for farmers, herders, and nomads. The poorer forest zones of the north offered greater protection against outside attack. By the ninth century the territory had seen a number of peoples who invaded and settled it at various times and places.*

### Recommended Reading

Adams, Arthur E., et al. *An Atlas of Russian and East European History* (1967).

Bater, James H., and R. A. French, eds. *Studies in Russian Historical Geography,* 2 vols. (1983).

Chew, Allen F. *An Atlas of Russian History: Eleven Centuries of Changing Borders* (rev. ed., 1970).

Dunlop, D. M. *The History of the Jewish Khazars* (1954).

Parker, W. H. *An Historical Geography of Russia* (1968).

Parker, W. H. *The Soviet Union* (1969).

Rice, Tamara Talbot. *The Scythians* (1957).

Rolle, Renate. *The World of the Scythians* (1989).

Rostovtzeff, Michael. *Iranians and Greeks in South Russia* (1922, reprint 1969).

Vernadsky, George. *Ancient Russia* (1943).

# CHAPTER 2

## The Kievan State (to 1054)

### Time Line

| | |
|---|---|
| 882 | Legendary arrival of Oleg at Kiev |
| 907 | Oleg attacks Byzantium |
| 913 | Death of Oleg |
| 913–945 | Era of Prince Igor |
| 941 | Igor attacks Byzantium |
| 945–962 | Reign of Olga |
| 955 | Olga converts to Christianity |
| 962–972 | Reign of Sviatoslav |
| 964–967 | Sviatoslav's eastern campaign |

| | |
|---|---|
| 967–971 | Sviatoslav's campaigns in Balkans |
| 980–1015 | Reign of Vladimir |
| 988 | Conversion of Kievan Russia to Christianity |
| 1019–1054 | Reign of Iaroslav: peak of Kievan power |
| 1036 | Iaroslav begins undivided rule |
| | Completion of Cathedral of St. Sophia |
| 1037 | Iaroslav defeats the Pechenegs |
| 1054 | Death of Iaroslav the Wise |

*Between 882 and 1054, the first Russian state, with its center at the city of Kiev, was founded and reached its peak of wealth, power, and stability. Located in the steppe region of the south, Kiev came to control a vast region stretching from the Baltic, along the Dnieper Valley, and southward toward the Black Sea.*

*This chapter deals with the way in which the Kievan state took shape. Between 882 and 980 the grand princes of Kiev accomplished two basic tasks. One was extending their control over the Slavic tribes of the forest and the steppe. The other was establishing links with the advanced cultural and economic center at Byzantium.*

*This founding era was followed by a second phase, stretching from 980 to 1054. In these years, Kievan Russia adopted the Christian religion, dealt effectively with the threat of attack by steppe nomads (the Pechenegs), and established important links with Central and even Western Europe.*

*We have only limited records from the Kievan era, and historians differ about many issues. An important controversy, with implications that come down to the present, has been the controversy between "Normanists" and "anti-Normanists" over the founding of the first Russian state.*

## Origins of the Kievan State

A sharp controversy has divided historians over the question of how the Kievan state was formed. The controversy centers on the role of the Vikings. Did these Scandinavian warriors play the leading role in organizing a Russian state drawn from the Slavic tribes scattered from the Baltic to the regions north of the Black Sea?

### The Norman Theory

The Norman theory argues that Vikings (also called Norsemen or Normans) united the squabbling Slavic tribes of the region around Novgorod. In this view the first Russian state was formed by outsiders who were invited to take control of some of the disorganized natives. That is, civilization had to be brought into Russia by foreigners.

Supporters of the Norman theory rely upon the *Primary Chronicle* (see p. 22), which records the arrival of a group called "Rus" from Scandinavia in 862. The group was led by a Varangian named Rurik.

### Modified and Opposing Views on the Norman Theory

Some historians now stress that the Vikings played only a limited role in the first stages of the Kievan state. Thus, Norse warriors may have formed the first ruling elite, but they quickly became Slavicized.

Opponents of the Norman theory question the accuracy of the *Primary Chronicle*. Some suggest that the term "Rus" refers to a Slavic tribe. Many "anti-Normanists," including recent Soviet historians, point to the advanced culture of the early Slavic tribes and deny any need for foreigners to bring order.

## The Founding Fathers (882–980)

The formative era of Kievan history lasted from 882 until approximately 980. Basic themes include Kiev's growing control over the Slavic tribes of the Dnieper Valley and series of expeditions against Byzantium. The influence of the Byzantine Empire on Kievan Russia is seen in the penetration of Christianity from Byzantium and in the Byzantine barrier to Russian expansion in the Balkans.

By the close of the first century of Kievan history, Kiev had become an important state in Eastern Europe.

## Oleg (r. 882–913)

Information about Oleg is skimpy and uncertain. A relative of Rurik, he succeeded Rurik as ruler of Novgorod and northern Russia. Oleg moved southward from Novgorod to establish himself at Kiev. This was an important change in Russian political affairs, since it shifted the political center to the middle regions of the Dnieper Valley.

### Kievan Expansion

Oleg's reign features Kievan expansion. He began the process of bringing the East Slavic tribes near Kiev under control. Nonetheless, their resistance continued, and Oleg left this task for his successors to complete.

### Relations with Byzantium

His second great achievement was in establishing a close trading tie with Byzantium. In 907, Oleg led a military expedition to attack the Greek capital. The attack probably went well, since in 911, the Kievan ruler obtained a favorable trade treaty with the Byzantines.

## Igor (r. 913–945)

Historians have more definite information about Igor. His reign may be characterized by his unsuccessful pursuit of Oleg's principal policies.

### Relations with Byzantium

Like Oleg, Igor sought an advantageous relationship with Byzantium. In 941, he led an unsuccessful military campaign against the imperial city. As a result, Igor's trade treaty with the Byzantines was marked by a loss of privileges for Kievan traders.

### Kievan Expansion

Igor also tried to spread Kievan authority over neighboring Slavic tribes and, like Oleg, faced their frequent rebellions. He was killed collecting tribute from the Drevliane, one of the Slavic tribes the Kievans attempted to control.

## Olga (r. 945–962)

Since when Igor died his son was too young to rule, Igor's widow, Olga, led the Kievan state as regent. She was the first woman to serve as ruler of Russia.

### Destruction of the Drevliane

Olga began her years in power by wiping out much of the Drevliane, the tribe that had killed her husband.

### Conversion to Christianity

The most notable event in Olga's reign was her conversion to Christianity around the year 955. As the first member of the ruling family to accept that religion, she helped prepare the way for the conversion of the entire country.

Olga died in 969 and was later proclaimed a saint by the Russian Orthodox Church.

## Sviatoslav (r. 962–972)

Sviatoslav's era was marked by two major military campaigns.

### Kievan Expansion

Between 964 and 967, Sviatoslav successfully expanded Kiev's control eastward and northward. Nearby Slavic tribes along with the Volga Bulgars and the Khazars were defeated. The Volga route to the Caspian came under Kievan control.

### Failure of Balkan Campaign

Sviatoslav's second campaign was directed into the Balkans. In 967, he reached the Danube Valley. He then fought and defeated the Bulgarians in several campaigns over the following years. However, he was forced out of the Balkans in 971 after an unsuccessful war against the Byzantines.

# Era of Vladimir (r. 980–1015)

The reign of Vladimir began a period of unprecedented power and development for Kievan Russia. It started, however, with a new burst of unrest.

The death of Sviatoslav (972) was followed by a disruptive civil war among his sons. The conflict indicated a problem that would

**Kievan Russia, circa 1000 A.D.**

continue to threaten political stability in the Kievan era: the absence of an accepted means of succession.

Sviatoslav's youngest son, Vladimir, emerged the victor in 980. His reign began a period of unprecedented power and development for the Kievan state.

### Conversion to Christianity

The central development in Vladimir's reign was his conversion to Christianity as practiced in Byzantium. Unlike the personal conversion of his grandmother Olga, Vladimir adopted Christianity as the religion of his subjects as well.

#### *The Cultural Consequences of Conversion*

Eastern Christianity became the basis for much of Russian art and culture. It linked Kievan Russia to the highly advanced society of Byzantium. At the same time, it hampered ties between Russia and the rest of Europe, where Western Christianity, with its center at Rome, held sway. The formal break between the Eastern and Western churches (1054) heightened Russia's isolation from the peoples of Central and Western Europe.

#### *The Organization of the Russian Church*

The Russian church was led by a metropolitan bishop located at Kiev. These bishops were appointed by the patriarch at Byzantium, and most of the early metropolitan bishops were Greek rather than Russian.

### Kievan Expansion

A second development in Vladimir's reign was the continued expansion of territory under Kievan control. Vladimir restored Kievan authority westward over areas lost to Poland during the recent civil war. He also extended Kievan authority northward to reach the Baltic.

## Era of Iaroslav the Wise (1019–1054): Kiev at Its Peak

The reign of Iaroslav began badly. In 1015, as in 972, the death of the ruler led to civil war among his sons. Iaroslav needed four years to defeat his brothers. Even then, he had to split control of Kievan territory with one brother until 1036.

Nonetheless, Iaroslav presided over Kievan Russia at its peak of power and prestige. Geographically Kievan Russia extended from the Black Sea to the Baltic and westward to the Carpathians. Ties with Central and Western Europe were strengthened in a series of marriage alliances with rulers there.

### Defeat of the Pechenegs

Since the era of Olga (945–962), Kievan rulers had faced a threat from the Pechenegs, warlike nomads living between Kievan lands and the Black Sea. Iaroslav administered a decisive defeat to the Pechenegs in 1037. For a brief time thereafter, Kievan Russia was free from the threat of nomads in the steppe.

### Ties with Europe

Iaroslav established strong relations with other countries by marriage alliances with members of their ruling houses. His sister married the king of Poland, and three of his daughters married foreign monarchs: the kings of Hungary, Norway, and Poland.

### Kiev as a Cultural Center

Iaroslav was known as "the Wise" even in his own lifetime. Under his leadership, Kiev became one of the great cities of Europe. Signs of Kiev's cultural prominence included the new churches, schools, and libraries.

### Art and Architecture

The Kievan era marks the start of a Russian artistic tradition. Early Russian art was strongly influenced by Byzantium and focused on religious themes.

#### *Churches*

Cathedrals like those named for St. Sophia in Kiev and Novgorod brought Byzantine architectural forms to Russia. These buildings had the shape of a cross and were highly decorated with frescoes and mosaics.

inting tradition that was ious pictures painted on churches and in private

## Economic Life

economy was based upon both trade and agriculture. Historians disagree over which was the more important element in pulation, however, was ure. Trade tended to be dominated by the princes, and wealthy merchants.

### Trade

that trade occurred both among regions under the Kiev and between the Kievan state and the outside world.

#### Domestic Trade

the Kievan state included both steppe and forest between northern centers like Novgorod and southern cities like Kiev probably involved exchanging the grain and cattle from the south for furs and timber from the north.

tant trading relationship with Byzantium. The grand prince of Kiev gathered tribute from the regions under his control. Each spring he led a trading expedition down the Dnieper and across the Black Sea to Byzantium. Private merchants from all over Kievan Russia traveled along under the prince's protection.

The Kievans traded raw materials such as furs for finished goods like weapons and luxuries such as spices and jewelry.

**Agriculture**

There were two regional types of farming. In the steppe, where land was abundant and easy to cultivate, farmers moved frequently as fields became worn out. The basic crop was wheat. In the zones farther north, farmers could get new land only by laboriously clearing away the forest. Thus, they were more settled, alternately using a part of their land or letting it rest fallow. The basic crops were rye, barley, and oats.

# Development of Culture

## Written Language

Kievan Russia acquired a written language, Old Church Slavonic, with the conversion of the population to Christianity in 988 and the arrival of the Cyrillic alphabet. That alphabet had been developed in the ninth century by two Byzantine missionaries, St. Cyril and St. Methodius, to aid them in translating the Bible for the conversion of the Southern and Western Slavs.

A Kievan literature in the form of religious documents now appeared using Old Church Slavonic, the language of church services. A secular literature of poetry and historical chronicles in Old Church Slavonic developed as well.

### *Primary Russian Chronicle*

The controversial *Primary Russian Chronicle* (see p. 15) stands as the basic document recording the history of Kievan Russia. It was probably written early in the twelfth century. A copy of the *Chronicle*, made by the monk Lavrentii in 1377 and known as the *Laurentian Chronicle*, has survived to the present.

### *Lay of Igor*

The *Lay* is an epic poem, the most famous literary product of the Kievan era. Written by an unknown author, it describes the defeat of Kievan forces at the hands of the Polovtsy nomads of the steppe in 1185. The poet argues that tragic conflict among Russia's selfish princes was causing the decline of the mighty Kievan state. He pleads for a restoration of Kievan unity.

## Literacy and Education

While the mass of the rural population remained illiterate, Kievan society contained educated groups. Schools and monasteries educated some of the urban population. Monasteries contained the first libraries in Russia. Some princes and members of their families may have been highly cultured, as the *Testament* of Vladimir Monomakh (see p. 30) suggests.

## Kievan Society

The population of the Kievan state was divided into a number of social classes. Though most people were peasants, the population ranged from powerful princes to slaves.

### The Upper Level

#### *The Royal Family*

The top level of Kievan society consisted of the prince and his family, supposedly descended from the Varangian Rurik. The growth of the princely family made this a numerically substantial group.

#### *Muzhi*

Just below the prince's family stood members of the *druzhina*, which composed the prince's aristocratic retinue. They were known as *muzhi*. Other aristocrats included dignitaries whose power and prestige were based on their regional prominence. They stood on the same social level as the *muzhi*.

#### *Boyars*

During the Kievan era, the difference between the two kinds of aristocrats gradually faded. Both aristocrats by virtue of serving the prince and aristocrats by virtue of their local power merged into a single noble group known as "boyars."

(A note of caution about the term "boyar." In the period *following* the Kievan era, the term took on a different meaning. At that time, a boyar was an extremely powerful and wealthy aristocrat, usually a large landowner.)

### The Middle Groups

Two groups of free citizens existed in both the cities and the countryside. Historians refer to both groups as a social class called the *liudi*.

### Urban Middle Class

An urban middle class consisted of merchants and small entrepreneurs such as carpenters and tanners. This class of free citizens was a significant part of the population in a society that was partly based on commerce.

Merchants engaged in long distance trade with Europe and Byzantium traveled together for safety. This cooperation led in turn to the formation of merchant *guilds* in Kiev similar to those in Western and Central Europe.

### Small Estate Owners

There was also a group of middle-class landowners, possessing small estates but without the privileges of boyars.

## Laborers

### Smerdy

Laborers in the lower classes made up the majority of the population. In rural areas, they were called *smerdy*. Though historians remain uncertain about the status of the *smerdy,* it seems clear that most of them were not yet serfs tied to the land.

### Slaves (*Kholopy*)

Beneath the *smerdy* there were groups tied down by firm obligations. Kievan society included slaves (*kholopy*). These were usually prisoners of war or formerly free laborers who were penalized for violating the law.

### Zakupy

*Zakupy* were indentured servants, held in a form of temporary servitude until they had discharged a debt.

# The Political System

## Princes

Kievan political life differed from one city to another. The grand prince in Kiev dominated the system, especially through the era of

Iaroslav the Wise (r. 1019–1054), but other princes emerged in other cities.

## Limits on the Prince's Power

No matter how powerful a prince in the Kievan era, he had to work with other institutions. The mixture of power among the prince, boyars, and the elected town assembly (or *veche*) varied from one place to another.

### The Boyar Duma

Senior members of the prince's *druzhina* became accustomed to advising him. The Boyar Duma grew out of that tradition. As members of the Duma, boyars, especially those who held large hereditary estates, consulted with the prince on important decisions. With the decline of princely power after the death of Iaroslav, a Boyar Duma could play a major role in running the government.

### The Veche

The town assembly, or *veche*, held public meetings. All freemen could attend, but decisions were made by the votes of male heads of households. The *veche* normally dealt with local matters, but it sometimes did so dramatically. On occasion princes were driven from office by the action of the *veche*.

*The Kievan state established political stability and permitted the development of a large and diverse society. By the standards of the eleventh century, Kievan Russia was on a par with the most advanced areas of the rest of Europe.*

*By the standards of later Russian history as well, this was an unusual interlude. Kievan Russia was linked to other parts of Europe. Kiev's government institutions placed limits on its princely rulers. The country was more or less secure against attack from the outside. In a short time after 1054, these features of the Kievan era faded, then disappeared.*

## Recommended Reading

Boba, Imre. *Nomads, Northmen and Slavs: Eastern Europe in the Ninth Century* (1967).

Chadwick, Nora. *The Beginnings of Russian History: An Inquiry into Sources* (1946).

Cross, Samuel Hazzard, and Olgerd P. Sherbowitz-Wetzor, trans. and eds. *The Russian Primary Chronicle: Laurentian Text* (1953).

Fedotov, G. P. *The Russian Religious Mind: Kievan Christianity* (1946).

Grekov, B. *Kiev Rus* (1959).

Obolensky, Dimitri. *Byzantium and the Slavs: Collected Studies* (1971).

Paszkiewicz, Henryk. *The Making of the Russian Nation* (1963).

Paszkiewicz, Henryk. *The Origin of Russia* (1954).

Vasiliev, Alexander A. *The Russian Attack on Constantinople in 860* (1946).

Vernadsky, George. *Ancient Russia* (1943).

Vernadsky, George. *Kievan Russia* (1948).

Volkoff, Vladimir. *Vladimir: The Russian Viking* (1983).

Wieczynski, Joseph L. *The Russian Frontier: The Impact of the Borderlands upon the Course of Early Russian History* (1976).

# CHAPTER 3

## The Decline of Kiev (1054–1240); Appanage Russia

### Time Line

| 1153–1187 | Reign of Iaroslav Osmomysl as prince of Galicia |
|-----------|--------------------------------------------------|
| 1169 | Prince Andrei Bogoliubskii captures Kiev |
|      | Transfer of capital to Vladimir |
| 1185 | Defeat of Prince Igor of Novgorod-Seversk by Polovtsy |
| 1203 | Prince of Smolensk captures Kiev |
| 1212 | Death of Vsevolod III and partition of principality of Vladimir-Suzdal |
| 1240 | Prince Alexander of Novgorod defeats Swedes |
| 1242 | Prince Alexander of Novgorod defeats Teutonic knights |

*The third phase of the history of the Kievan state presents a picture of growing disorder. Russian life no longer centered on a grand prince at Kiev who governed and defended vast regions stretched from the Baltic toward the Black Sea. While the decline was halted at times by capable leaders like Vladimir Monomakh (r. 1113–1125), the period after 1054 was dominated by civil war, social unrest, economic decline, and renewed external threats.*

*This chapter will show how a new and fragmented political system emerged as different parts of the Kievan state became independent and developed in their own way. It will also consider how Russia descended to a lower economic level, far different from the system that had featured extensive trading ties with the outside world.*

## Era of Decline

The era after the middle of the eleventh century was marked by the collapse of political unity within the Kievan state. The old problem of political succession became unmanageable, and civil wars raged. Power shifted from the grand prince at Kiev into the hands of a dozen local rulers who warred against one another.

Difficulties struck from outside as well. The Polovtsy continued to threaten Kievan territory with invasion. The decline of Byzantium undercut the importance of Kiev's historic Dnieper trade route from the Baltic to the Black Sea.

## Iaroslav's Flawed Legacy

Iaroslav failed to establish a stable system to maintain the unity of the Kievan state. Before his death in 1054, he divided the state among his five sons, the eldest of whom was to rule Kiev and act as senior prince.

As vacancies in ruling principalities came up, the sons were to shift to new locations based on seniority. The senior brother was to become grand prince in Kiev. Upon his death, the next senior brother would move from Chernigov to Kiev, the next senior would move to Chernigov from Pereiaslavl, and so on. In theory, the Kievan state was to be ruled by the collective will of the princes.

This complex method of succession, called by historians the "rota" or "ladder" system, failed to work as Iaroslav had hoped.

## Collapse of Political Order

### Civil War

A period of prolonged civil war broke out among the heirs of Iaroslav after 1054. Princes increasingly concentrated on local concerns. Their internecine rivalry is a major characteristic of the era.

### Settlement of 1097

The Russian princes met in 1097 at Liubech in an effort to settle their differences. Kievan Russia was being shattered by civil war. Meanwhile, the threat of steppe nomads (see below) was growing.

The conference led to an agreement to abandon Iaroslav's "rota" system. Henceforth, princes would rule their own principalities and pass them on to their sons. This decision was an important step in transforming Kievan Russia into an aggregation of loosely linked, independent states.

However, the agreement at Liubech did not end political conflicts among the princes. Nor did it push them to form a united defense against the Polovtsy.

## Danger from the Polovtsy

Disunity at home made it difficult to defend Kievan society from outside attack. Starting in 1061, the Turkic tribe known as the

Polovtsy (or Cumans) began to raid Kiev's territory. After 1100, the nomadic Polovtsy tightened their control by establishing settlements in the steppe.

The Polovtsy stood as a constant threat to Kievan Russia for nearly two hundred years. Their raids disrupted Russian life, devastating the frontier settlements in regions like Pereiaslavl and Chernigov.

## Kievan Revival under Vladimir Monomakh (r. 1113–1125)

Order returned briefly when Vladimir Monomakh, Iaroslav's grandson, became grand prince in 1113.

### Campaigns against the Polovtsy

As prince of Chernigov, Vladimir had won fame for his victory over the Polovtsy at the Battle of Salnitsa in 1111. Vladimir's reign was distinguished by his constant campaigning in defense of Kievan territory against the Polovtsy threat.

### Restoration of Russian Unity

Vladimir restored the prestige of the prince of Kiev as grand prince and effective ruler of all the Russian principalities. He was the last leader to hold together all the territories of Kievan Russia under the authority of an effective grand prince.

Vladimir made an important contribution to Russian literature in his *Testament*. It combined a description of his life with a set of precepts by which he hoped his sons would rule. He urged them, for example, to become educated men and to follow the tenets of Christianity.

## Factors in the Decline of Kievan Russia

Division and civil war ensued after Vladimir Monomakh's death in 1125.

Several ominous trends dominated the remainder of the century. First, Kievan Russia became a group of about a dozen virtually independent principalities. Second, raids by the Polovtsy remained a terrifying part of Russian life. (The defeat of Prince Igor by the Polovtsy in 1185 became the basis for the epic poem *The Lay of Igor's Campaign* [see p. 22].) Third, power shifted northward. Principalities like Suzdalia and Smolensk emerged as the most potent contenders out to dominate Kievan Russia.

Apart from civil war and foreign invasion, historians have suggested social and economic reasons for the fall of Kievan Russia.

## Invasions

Kiev itself was besieged and captured twice by northerners: in 1169 by Prince Andrei of Suzdalia (r. 1158–1187) and in 1203 by the prince of Smolensk.

## Social Unrest

Kievan society developed serious internal conflicts. Starting in the eleventh century, members of a prince's *druzhina* were often rewarded with gifts of landed estates. Peasants found their rights, including the right to move freely, increasingly restricted by these landowners. Unrest also developed as a result of clashes between the urban poor and affluent groups like town merchants.

## Economic Decline

The economic role of the Dnieper Valley and the city of Kiev changed for the worse starting in the eleventh century.

### Decline of Trade

Trade through Byzantium, Kievan Russia's major commercial outlet, declined after Byzantium was captured and pillaged in 1204 during the Fourth Crusade. At the same time, Kiev's trade links to the Black Sea were endangered by the continuing power of the Polovtsy.

### Shifting Trade Routes

The increasing commercial power of the cities of northern Italy and of north German cities on the Baltic Sea cut into the significance of trade through the Dnieper Valley.

Cities in the Russian north like Novgorod and Smolensk prospered as a result of these shifts. Their prosperity increased their tendency to ignore the authority of Kiev and to act as independent states.

# The Appanage Era

The decline of the Kievan state, which began after the middle of the eleventh century, gave rise to a new *appanage* system. This system was characterized by tremendous political fragmentation and the virtual disappearance of any effective central authority.

The appanage era lasted for more than four centuries, ending around 1500 when the rulers of Moscow established a newly unified Russian state.

### Definition

The term "appanage" means a separate parcel of land held by a prince. The term "appanage Russia" refers to the period starting with Iaroslav's death in 1054 in which Russia was politically fragmented. A prince became linked to a single principality, and upon his death his land was further divided among his sons. Whatever political unity had existed under Kiev now disintegrated, and territorial holdings tended to become smaller and weaker.

### Characteristics of the Appanage Era

The appanage era developed from the period of the Kievan state. Though institutions like the church continued to unite the population, a number of new and different trends emerged.

#### *Foreign Invasion*

One consequence of political division was weakness, sometimes catastrophic, in the face of external enemies. Up to the thirteenth century, the chief threat was from the Polovtsy. After 1200, vastly more dangerous foreign invaders appeared: the Teutonic knights from the west and the Mongols from the east.

#### *Migration and Ethnic Division*

Population shifts took place as well. As migrants fled the exposed regions of the south, regions of the southwest, the north, and the northeast emerged as centers of Russian life.

The distinction grew between Great Russians, living in the region around Moscow, and groups like the Ukrainians and White Russians. The latter two developed in the west and southwest under both Polish and Lithuanian influences. The Ukrainian and White Russian languages and cultures showed marked differences from those of the Great Russians.

### Economic Stagnation

Domestic and foreign trade declined in much of the territory of the old Kievan state. Appanage era economics revolved around a system of agriculture in which communities depended upon what could be grown locally.

## Appanage States

### Moscow

The most important state to develop out of the appanage era was the principality of Moscow (see Chapter 5). But Moscow rose by absorbing other states that had risen to prominence earlier in the appanage era.

### Novgorod

Novgorod was an important economic and political component of the Kievan state. As a trading center, it connected northwestern Russia and the Baltic with the Dnieper trade route to Kiev and the Black Sea.

Novgorod was often under the rule of sons of the grand prince at Kiev. The most important characteristic of the city's political life, however, was the power of the *veche* (the town council). After a popular revolution ousted the ruling prince in 1136, princes were highly restricted by the *veche*.

Novgorod was active in exploring and settling northeastern Russia as far as the Urals. It maintained an economic level, based on commerce, that was disappearing elsewhere.

At a time when foreign invaders threatened Russia from several directions, the prince of Novgorod, Alexander (r. 1236–1263), won spectacular victories. In 1240, he defeated the Swedes at Neva River, and in 1242, he defeated the Teutonic knights at Lake Peipus.

**Russia before the Mongol Invasion**

Thus, while most of appanage Russia was declining economically and politically, Novgorod maintained important features of the Kievan past.

### States of the Northeast

The principality of Vladimir-Suzdal became the seat of the grand prince after Andrei Bogoliubskii (r. 1158–1175) captured Kiev in 1169. Nonetheless, in this northern forest region, the disintegration typical of the appanage era soon appeared. In 1212, for example, upon the death of Grand Prince Vsevolod III of Vladimir-Suzdal (r. 1176–1212), his principality was repeatedly divided.

Like Novgorod, the appanage states of this region extended their control and their territory to the north and to the east.

The political system that emerged here was marked by the concentration of power in the hands of the local prince. There were no firmly established institutions like the *veche*. Instead, the harsh political and economic environment created by life in the northern forests seemed to encourage one-man rule.

### States of the Southwest (*Volynia and Galicia*)

The development of the regions bordering on Poland and Hungary resembled conditions elsewhere in the Kievan state. As Kievan authority declined, powerful local leaders like Iaroslav Osmomysl (r. 1153–1187) of Galicia emerged as independent rulers.

In other ways, Volynia and Galicia were special. Both had powerful and long-established boyar landowners who limited all but the strongest princes. Moreover, powerful and advanced neighbors like Poland and Hungary were poised to intervene in the Kievan regions. Such outside intervention was sometimes invited by rebellious boyars. Between 1205 and 1235, as boyar power in Galicia reached its peak, boyars deposed and even executed princes who displeased them.

*The decline in the Kievan state system produced a weakened and divided Russian political order. At its height, the Kievan state had provided a framework for order and unity. By the beginning of the thirteenth century, that framework had disappeared.*

*Russian life was now organized around dozens of appanages. These individual princely states tended to become weaker as they were subdivided among the prince's heirs. In such a system most economic life took the form of primitive local farming.*

*Fading unity brought increased dangers from the outside. Civil war weakened Russia's princes and prevented their cooperation for mutual defense. The growing threat of the Polovtsy, who now controlled the steppes and the route to Byzantium, illustrated this trend. Soon, the greater peril of the Mongol invasion would expose Russia's vulnerability even more clearly.*

## Recommended Reading

Birnbaum, Henrik. *Lord Novgorod the Great: Essays in the History and Culture of a Medieval City-State* (1981).

Cross, Samuel Hazzard, and Olgerd P. Sherbowitz-Wetzor, trans. and eds. *The Russian Primary Chronicle: Laurentian Text* (1953).

Dmytryshyn, Basil, ed. *Medieval Russia: A Source Book, 850–1700* (3rd ed., 1991).

Fennell, John. *The Crisis of Medieval Russia, 1200–1304* (1983).

Grekov, B. *Kiev Rus* (1959).

Presniakov, A. E. *The Formation of the Great Russian State* (1971).

Thompson, W. W., ed. *Novgorod the Great: Excavations at the Medieval City* (1967).

Vernadsky, George. *Kievan Russia* (1948).

# CHAPTER 4

## The Mongol Conquest;
## The Lithuanian State;
## Appanage Russian Society

### Time Line

| | |
|---|---|
| 1211 | Mongols invade China |
| 1223 | Mongol armies raid southern Russia |
| 1237–1238 | Mongol attacks on northeastern Russia |
| 1240 | Mongols conquer southern Russia |
| | Fall of Kiev |
| 1241 | Battle of Liegnitz |
| | Succession crisis in Mongolia |

| | |
|---|---|
| 1242 | Grand Prince Iaroslav confirmed in office by Mongols |
| 1252 | Alexander Nevsky of Novgorod made grand prince |
| 1262 | Rebellion in Suzdal |
| 1282–1283 | Leaders of the Golden Horde adopt Islam |
| 1294 | Death of Kublai Khan; decline in unity of Mongol Empire |
| 1316–1341 | Reign of Gedymin of Lithuania |
| 1349 | Galicia annexed by Poland |
| 1386 | Dynastic union of Poland and Lithuania |
| | Volynia annexed by Lithuania |
| 1471 | Novgorod comes under the control of Moscow |
| 1485 | Tver comes under the control of Moscow |
| 1569 | Union of Lublin |

*In the early part of the thirteenth century, Russian history turned in a sharply new direction. Almost all of the old Kievan lands came under foreign control. The Mongols invaded Russia from the east and placed most of the Russian lands within their extensive empire. This chapter will examine the different views of historians about the effect of this Mongol control.*

*At the same time, the western regions of Russia came under the control of the Lithuanians and the Poles.*

*In the midst of these foreign incursions, the different parts of appanage Russia continued to develop in various ways. Here again historians disagree. Did Russia in this period resemble the society of medieval Europe?*

## The Mongol Conquest

### Origins of the Mongols

The Mongols originated as a group of nomadic tribes in northeastern Asia. Neighbors of the Chinese, they roamed a region including modern Mongolia and nearby areas of Manchuria and Siberia.

## Conquests of Genghis Khan

The Mongol tribes became a formidable aggressive force when they were unified by a tribal leader named Temuchin (1167–1227) in 1206. Using the title of Genghis (or Jenghis) Khan, which meant "Universal Ruler," Temuchin created a huge empire with extraordinary speed.

### *The Conquest of China*

The first great display of Mongol power started in 1211 when Mongol armies penetrated the Great Wall and invaded China. Peking fell in 1215. By 1216, much of China had come under Mongol control.

### *The Conquest of Persia and Raid into Southern Russia*

The Mongol forces next turned westward. They swept through Persia, and, in 1223, crossed the mountains of the Caucasus to raid southern Russia. The Mongols returned home in 1223, and the Russian princes assumed, incorrectly, that this threat from the east had now passed.

### *Military Superiority*

The total Mongol population was approximately one million. Relatively small Mongol armies were enlarged by Turkish auxiliaries.

Mongol military successes were due to the superior organization and tactics of their army. Based upon mounted archers, Mongol forces moved rapidly in widely dispersed columns. Keeping contact by means of messengers or smoke signals, the columns moved in a coordinated campaign to surround the enemy's main army.

*Use of Siege Warfare.*   In their early campaigns, the Mongols learned the art of siege to take fortified cities. By the time they attacked Russia, the Mongols were skilled in assaulting their enemies' strongholds as well as in maneuvering on horseback.

*Use of Psychological Warfare.*   Mongol campaigns included psychological warfare. Moving ahead of their armies, Mongol agents stirred up social and religious tensions to weaken the enemy population's will to resist.

## The Mongol Conquest of Russia

The Mongol conquest of Russia came under Batu (?–1255), a grandson of Genghis Khan. Under Batu's field commanders, Mongol forces drove through Russia and penetrated Eastern Europe, briefly reaching the Adriatic and the eastern regions of Germany in 1241. In the aftermath of these campaigns, almost all of Kievan Russia found itself under effective Mongol control.

### *The First Assault, 1237*

In December 1237, the Mongols made their first conquest in Russia in the northeast. They launched a successful attack in two stages on the principality of Riazan. First, the army of this eastern principality was defeated on the battlefield. Next, the city itself was taken after a short siege.

The conquest of the principalities of the north, the strongest areas in Russia, continued throughout the winter of 1237–1238. The Mongols had the advantage of a divided enemy. Individual princes defended their own holdings, and the Mongols never had to encounter a united Russian force.

### *The Deluge, 1240–1242*

The second major wave of Mongol conquests began in 1240. It took the southern regions of Russia, including the city of Kiev, which was completely destroyed. The Mongols then continued westward toward Poland and Hungary. On the way, they drove through Galicia and Volynia, the westernmost principalities of Kievan Russia.

## The Mongol Withdrawal

The Mongol advance into Central Europe halted as a result of a political crisis back in Mongolia. After occupying Hungary and defeating a combined force of Poles and Germans at Liegnitz (1241) in Silesia, Batu received news of the death of the Khan Ugedei. Realizing that he could not influence the election while campaigning so far from home, Batu returned to Mongolia in the spring of 1242.

## The Rule of the Golden Horde

The Mongols did not attempt to occupy Russia directly. Instead, they pulled back to the Volga.

The Mongol state established to rule Russia and the nearby steppes was called the Golden Horde. It developed in two ways. First, the Mongols of the Golden Horde, relatively small in number, were submerged in the Turkic population in which they found themselves. Second, in the early part of the thirteenth century, the rulers and part of the population of the Golden Horde converted to Islam.

The Russian term for the Mongols is "Tatar." The oppression of Russia under the Mongols is called the "Tatar Yoke."

### Sarai

Immediately after their conquest of Russia, the Mongols established their headquarters at Sarai. From this city on the lower Volga (near the location of today's city of Astrakhan), they supervised their newly won imperial holdings in Russia.

## Mongol Government

In most areas, the Mongols did not attempt to rule directly over Russia, though they put down open rebellions like the one in Suzdal in 1262. The Mongols governed for the most part with the cooperation of native Russian princes.

### Indirect Rule

The Mongols permitted Russia's princes to keep their thrones in return for accepting Mongol control. The grand prince was required to travel to Sarai to pledge his loyalty to the Mongols in person. The Russians were expected to pay taxes to the Mongols and to provide recruits for the Mongol army.

### The Duties of the Grand Prince

The duties of the grand prince came to include collecting taxes and tribute for the Mongols. Thus, a friendly grand prince could hope for Mongol political support. Within the divided Russian political system, a grand prince had the best chance of eventually emerging as the nation's leader.

**The Mongol Impact on Russian History**

Historians differ sharply over the influence that Mongol rule (the "Tatar Yoke") had on Russian history. The disagreement centers on two questions. First, did the Mongol conquest have a serious and lasting effect on Russian life? Second, was the effect a positive or a negative one?

### The Positive View

This interpretation stresses the role of the Mongols in the creation in Russia of a powerful, centralized monarchy. Thus, the Mongols are seen as a crucial element in ending the divided and squabbling appanage era.

Historians who credit the Mongols with a positive influence on Russia's development point to the Russian adoption of Mongol methods in military affairs, taxation, and the administration of government. They see the princes of Moscow, who eventually united Russia, as leaders who imitated the Mongols.

### The Negative View

Most historians are persuaded by a more critical assessment of the Mongol impact on Russia. This view argues that the Mongols had a limited effect in some areas of Russian life and a negative effect in others.

Defenders of this view note that the Mongols themselves were a relatively backward people with little to offer Russia. Moreover, the Mongols did not settle in Russia nor did they rule directly.

Historians of this opinion stress the loss of life and property during the Mongol conquest and the heavy tax burden placed on the Russian population. Moreover, Russia's existing ties to the Western world were disrupted for centuries by the Mongol conquest while Russian ties to Asia increased. Isolation and the strains of the long struggle to defeat the Mongols meant that Russia had no contact with European developments like the Renaissance.

# The Lithuanian State

While Russia was under Mongol control, a powerful Lithuanian state emerged to the west. Unified under Prince Gedymin (r. 1316–1341) and his successors, the Lithuanian state incorporated large areas that had been part of Kievan Russia, including the entire Dnieper Valley. Some ambitious Lithuanian leaders hoped to rule all of Russia.

### Russian Component

For several reasons this Lithuanian state can be considered one of the successors to Kievan Russia. First, most of its population consisted of Russians. Second, Russian culture, the Russian church, and even local Russian princes remained unaffected.

### Merger with Poland

In 1386, the situation changed drastically with an intermarriage between the ruling families of Lithuania and Poland. This began a process in which Polish and Roman Catholic influences came to dominate Lithuania. The ties between Poland and Lithuania grew, culminating in 1569 in the merger of the two states by the Union of Lublin.

#### *Russian Conflict with Poland-Lithuania*

As a result of these events, the western regions of the Kievan state were no longer under Russian control. With the growth of a new center of Russian power at Moscow (see Chapter 5), regaining lost Kievan territories became a major goal for Russia's leaders. This meant a prolonged political conflict with Lithuania and especially with Poland.

#### *Linguistic and Ethnic Changes*

"Polonization"—the growing influence of the Polish language, culture, and Roman Catholic religion—first affected the Lithuanians. In time, it also came to affect parts of the Russian population.

Over the centuries of Lithuanian, then Polish, influence, the language and culture of Russians in the west changed. This influence contributed to the present-day distinction between the Ukranians and White Russians on the one hand, and the Great Russians on the other.

## Appanage Russia: Political and Social Development

In the decades after the Mongol conquest, the different parts of Russia continued to evolve. The fact that Russia was now a part of the Mongol empire, which stretched from Poland to the Pacific, did not prevent various principalities of Russia from going off in diverse directions.

A crucial element in the development of appanage Russia—the emergence of a new power center at Moscow—will be considered in the next chapter.

## Novgorod

### *Alexander Nevsky*

Under the leadership of Alexander Nevsky (r. 1236–1263), Novgorod accepted Mongol control. This submission permitted Nevsky to concentrate on defending Novgorod against German and Swedish invasions.

The Mongols granted Nevsky the position of grand prince in 1252. Hence Novgorod at the middle of the thirteenth century became the center through which the Mongols exerted their control over the Russian people.

### *The Importance of Novgorod*

Novgorod continued to play an important role during the rest of the appanage period. Relatively untouched by the Mongol invasion, it remained a wealthy commercial city with close ties to the west. Novgorod also expanded its control of large stretches of land in northern Russia.

The northern city-state preserved its independence by good diplomacy. The rise of powerful neighbors like Lithuania and the principality of Moscow gave Novgorod the opportunity to turn for help first to one, then to the other. In 1471, however, Novgorod finally lost its independent status and came under the authority of Moscow.

## The Northeast

### *Recovery from Mongol Invasion*

Though devastated by the Mongol invasion, this region showed signs of political recovery. Distance and their location in the northern forest zone offered the principalities here some protection against further Mongol military intervention. From the middle of the thirteenth century on, the position of grand prince was held regularly by rulers of such northern principalities as Tver.

### Conflict in Moscow

Political rivalries in the northeast featured a prolonged struggle between Moscow and Tver. In 1485, Tver was forced to accept Moscow's political domination.

## The Southwest (Galicia and Volynia)

The two southwestern states of the Kievan era fell into foreign hands in the century following the Mongol conquest. In 1349, Galicia was annexed by Poland. By 1386, all of Volynia had been taken by Lithuania.

## Appanage Russian Society

As in other areas of early Russian history, scholars came to different conclusions about the society of the appanage era. The continuing question of whether or not Russia is a European country with a history similar to other European countries appears again here.

Another important social development is the decline of Russian stability. This disintegration can be seen in such factors as depopulation and increased migration.

### The Question of Feudalism

Some historians think that Russia went through a period dominated by feudalism, in much the same way as happened in Western Europe. Others consider Russia's experience in this period sharply different from what occurred in the West.

*The Case for Russian Feudalism.*   The view that Russian society resembled the feudal society of countries such as France is supported by several factors. The land was divided and held by local strongmen. Much of the land was held by boyars in return for service, usually military service, to a prince. The term for such an estate is *pomestie.* In this system, boyars in turn often gave land to individuals below them on the same basis of land for service.

*The Case against Russian Feudalism.*   Other historians cite differences between Russia and the West. They reject the idea that most boyars got land in the form of *pomestie*. Instead, they believe that Russian landlords at this time normally inherited their land. Boyars could shift their loyalty from one prince to another. Moreover, Russian peasants were not yet laborers tied to the land as serfs were in the feudal West.

*A Midway Position.*    While there are obvious differences in the Russian and the Western European experiences, Russia in the appanage era has a general resemblance to Europe of the Middle Ages. This can be seen in the fact that power was held mainly at the local level and in the way economic life was organized around large landed estates.

### Social Disruption

The difficult years following the Mongol conquest brought the abandonment of large parts of the country. An important feature of Russian life after the middle of the thirteenth century was the flow of people from south to north. Another significant change was the growing difficulty faced by landowners in maintaining a force of rural laborers. In later centuries, the solution to this problem would emerge in the form of a system of serfdom.

*By the middle of the fourteenth century, the old Kievan lands were divided between those under indirect Mongol rule and those coming under the direct control of Poland and Lithuania.*

*The destruction from the Mongol conquest had sent much of Russia's population fleeing to the northern forest zone. The various appanage states, encouraged by the Mongols, continued to squabble and contend among themselves. The prospects for the revival of a Russian state comparable to the one centered on Kiev seemed dim.*

### Recommended Reading

Dmytryshyn, Basil, ed. *Medieval Russia: A Source Book, 850–1700* (3rd ed., 1991).

Fennell, John. *The Crisis of Medieval Russia, 1200–1304* (1983).

Halperin, Charles J. *Russia and the Golden Horde: The Mongol Impact on Medieval Russian History* (1985).

Halperin, Charles J. *The Tatar Yoke* (1986).

Paszkiewicz, Henryk. *The Rise of Moscow's Power* (1983).

Prawdin, M. *The Mongol Empire: Its Rise and Legacy* (2nd ed., 1967).

Presniakov, A. E. *The Formation of the Great Russian State* (1971).

Vernadsky, George. *The Mongols and Russia* (1953).

# CHAPTER 5

## The Rise of Moscow; The Russian Church

### Time Line

| | |
|---|---|
| 1147 | Moscow first mentioned in chronicles |
| 1237 | Moscow destroyed by the Mongols |
| 1276–1303 | Daniel Nevsky as prince of Moscow |
| 1318 | Iurii Danilovich becomes first Muscovite to be made grand prince |
| 1328 | Ivan Kalita (Ivan I) appointed grand prince |
| | Metropolitan Theognost settles in Moscow |
| 1359–1389 | Era of Dmitrii Donskoi |
| 1368–1372 | Lithuanian attacks on Moscow |

| | |
|---|---|
| 1378 | Russian victory over Mongols at Vozha River |
| 1380 | Russian victory over Mongols at Kulikovo Pole |
| 1382 | Mongol counterattack takes Moscow |
| 1389–1425 | Era of Basil I (or Vasili I) |
| 1395 | Tamerlane advances against Moscow |
| 1408 | Mongol punitive expedition attacks Moscow |
| 1425–1448 | War of succession for Moscow's throne |
| 1430–1466 | Division of Golden Horde into successor khanates of Crimea, Kazan, and Astrakhan |
| 1439 | Council of Florence: temporary union of Byzantine and Roman churches |
| 1447 | Renewed union of Poland and Lithuania |
| 1448 | Council of Russian bishops chooses new metropolitan |
| 1452 | Mongol prince of Kasimov places himself under Moscovite authority |
| | Moscow stops regular tribute payments to the Golden Horde |
| 1453 | Fall of Constantinople to Turks |
| 1462–1505 | Era of Ivan III: "the gathering of the Russian lands" |
| 1472 | Ivan III marries Byzantine princess Sophia |
| 1478 | Moscow acquires Novgorod |
| 1480 | Formal independence of Moscow from Mongol control |
| 1485 | Moscow acquires Tver |
| 1493 | Ivan III takes title of "Sovereign of All Russia" |
| 1497 | Law Code Established |

| 1500–1503 | War with Lithuania |
| 1505–1533 | Era of Basil III (or Vasili III) |
| 1511 | Annexation of Pskov |
| 1512–1522 | War with Lithuania |
| 1514 | Capture of Smolensk |
| 1521 | Crimean khanate's forces reach Moscow |

*Starting in the fourteenth century, the principality of Moscow grew to become the center of a new and increasingly centralized Russian state. An advantageous location, good political leadership, and the support of the church as well as a friendly tie to the leaders of the Golden Horde combined to lift Moscow above competitors like Tver.*

*Two signs of Moscow's success were fully visible in the era of Ivan III (r. 1462–1505), whom historians recognize as "Ivan the Great." First, with most of the old Kievan principalities under Moscow's control by the middle of the fifteenth century, the appanage era had ended. The rulers of Moscow now claimed to be the successors to the grand princes of Kiev. Second, Russia led by Moscow was now independent of the Mongols.*

*But Muscovite Russia was far different from Kievan Russia. It featured a ruler with effective power that was far more sweeping, a nobility based on service to the ruler, and a peasantry increasingly tied to land owned by the nobility.*

## The Rise of Moscow

### Early History (to 1389)

The small town of Moscow was founded sometime before the middle of the twelfth century. (It was first mentioned in the chronicles in the year 1147.) The Mongols attacked and destroyed the city in 1237.

In the aftermath of the Mongol assault, Daniel Nevsky (r. 1276–1303) established his family as the hereditary rulers of Moscow.

Daniel began the process of expanding the principality's territory along the Moscow River.

### Conflict with Tver

Around 1300, Moscow began a prolonged rivalry with Tver, a city that had developed in northern Russia during the years when Kiev's authority was declining.

Muscovite leaders like Iurii Danilovich (r. 1303–1325) competed for Mongol favor and the title of grand prince that the Mongols had to award. Since Tver seemed more powerful and a greater threat to Mongol control, the Mongols tended to back Moscow. Frequently Mongol actions diminished Tver's power and thus aided Moscow's ambitions. In 1327, for example, the Mongols sent a punitive expedition against Tver and sacked the city.

### Ivan I (r. 1326–1341)

*Services to Mongols.*    Moscow's power began to grow substantially during the reign of Ivan I (Ivan Kalita). Good relations with the Mongols played an important role in Ivan's success. Ivan traveled to Sarai nine times over the course of his life, and he served in the Mongol punitive expedition against Tver in 1327. Among his services rendered to the Mongols, Ivan collected tribute from other Russian princes.

In 1328 the Mongols confirmed Ivan in the position of grand prince. His close tie to the Mongols meant that his son succeeded him as grand prince without difficulty. His nickname "Ivan Kalita" or "John Moneybag" indicates his success in raising revenues and buying more land.

*Move to Moscow by the Orthodox Church.*    One of Ivan's greatest successes was in attracting the head of the Russian Orthodox Church to settle in Moscow. The Metropolitan Theognost (r. 1328–1353) made Moscow his residence in 1328. This decision provided Moscow with increased prestige throughout Russia.

A later powerful church leader, the Metropolitan Alexis (r. 1354–1378), helped to fill a political leadership vacuum when Moscow was ruled by the underage Prince Dmitrii from 1359 to 1367.

### Dmitrii Donskoi (r. 1359–1389)

Dmitrii continued Moscow's bitter rivalry with Tver. He fought both against Tver and against Tver's ally, Lithuania, whose armies attacked Moscow in 1368 and again in 1372. In the end, however, Dmitrii was able to defend his city against the combined attacks of Tver and Lithuania. In 1375, he forced Prince Michael of Tver (r. 1365–1399) to acknowledge for a brief time Tver's subservience to Moscow.

*The Defeat of the Mongols.*    The most significant event in Dmitrii's reign was his military victory over the Mongols in 1378 at the Vozha River. This was the first time a Russian force was able to defeat a Mongol army. Thus, it showed a change in the old pattern of Mongol power and Russian subordination.

Following Dmitrii's defeat of a Mongol army, the Mongol leader Mamai launched a joint attack on Moscow in alliance with Lithuania. Dmitrii managed to defeat the Mongol forces at Kulikovo Field (or Kulikovo *Pole*) south of Moscow in September 1380. The battle was won by a large Russian force estimated at 30,000 men before the Lithuanians arrived to aid their Mongol allies.

During the campaign Dmitrii received the support of about twenty other Russian princes. This was not only a sign of the willingness of Russian rulers to cooperate against the Mongols but also indicated Moscow's growing role as the leader of the Russian people.

*Aftermath of Kulikovo Pole.*    The effect of Dmitrii's victory was soon weakened. In 1382, a Mongol force captured Moscow and massacred 24,000 of its inhabitants. Dmitrii was forced to restate that he was the subordinate of the Mongol khan. On the whole, however, the long-range effect of Kulikovo was to weaken the Mongol hold over Russia.

### Basil I (r. 1389–1425)

The era of Dmitrii's son Basil (or Vasili) saw the continuation of both Moscow's territorial growth and its long military struggles.

Moscow meanwhile remained vulnerable to attack from powerful outside forces from the east. In 1395, the Central Asian warlord Tamerlane (1336–1405) advanced close to Moscow. In 1408, a Mongol punitive expedition raided the outskirts of the city.

### Basil II (r. 1425–1462)

The reign of Basil II (or Vasili II) brought both substantial dangers and substantial advantages to the rising Muscovite state. Conflict over who would hold the position of prince of Moscow led to prolonged civil war. Mongol power began to disintegrate, but danger grew elsewhere as Poland and Lithuania joined again to form a powerful state.

The military and political forces Russia had to face in the east and west went through substantial changes during Basil's reign. In the area of Russia's religious ties to the outside world, equally important changes occurred.

### The War of Succession

Basil's right to the throne was challenged by his uncle and cousins. The result was a civil war in which Basil was blinded by his opponents. Finally, in 1453, Basil won with the death of his last serious rival.

### Foreign Relations

*The West.*   In 1447, the two states of Poland and Lithuania were reunited under a common ruler. With the decline of the Mongol threat (see p. 56), relations with Poland-Lithuania now became the most important concern for Moscow's foreign policy.

*The East.*   Starting in Basil's reign, Mongol power declined sharply as the Golden Horde split apart. The Crimean khanate took the lead, becoming an independent state in 1430 and coming under the control of the Ottoman sultan in 1475. Kazan became an independent state in 1436, and Astrakhan followed in 1466.

### Independence of Moscow

In 1452, Moscow stopped its regular payment of tribute to the Golden Horde. That same year, the Tatar khanate of Kasimov was established southeast of Moscow under Russian control. This was another sign of the shift in power away from the Golden Horde and toward Moscow.

The failure of military campaigns launched against Moscow by the Golden Horde from 1451 to 1461 was one more sign that Moscow had achieved independence in all but name.

### Changes in Church Relations

In 1439, at the Council of Florence, the leaders of the Greek church in Byzantium agreed to recognize the authority of the pope and the doctrines of the western church. The union of the eastern and western churches was not widely accepted in the Byzantine Empire, and it quickly became meaningless when the Turks took Byzantium in 1453. Basil II and principal figures in the Russian church, however, assumed in 1439 that the union would be a lasting one and vigorously objected to the decision.

In 1448, for the first time, a council of Russian bishops chose the new leader of the Russian church. From this point, the Russian church no longer looked to the Greek church even for nominal leadership. Thus the uproar over religious policy helped to break the longstanding cultural link between the Russians and Byzantium.

### Ivan III (r. 1462–1505)

During the reign of Ivan III (or Ivan the Great), Moscow reached a position dominating the Russian people. The power of the ruler of Moscow was expressed in new titles and authority. Moscow's successes included absorbing numerous other Russian principalities and waging successful wars with its neighbors.

#### *The End of the Appanage Era*

By various means Ivan acquired one formerly independent principality after another. This ''gathering of the Russian lands'' is best understood as the expansion of the Moscow dynasty. Ivan purchased some regions like Iaroslavl (1463), conquered others like Perm (1472) and Viatka (1489), and inherited still others like Riazan (1500). By the time of Ivan's death, only a few principalities remained independent even in name, and these were in fact satellites of Moscow. The division of Russia into small, separate principalities— the basic characteristic of the appanage era—now ended.

*The Conquest of Novgorod.*    Caught between Moscow and Lithuania, Novgorod had become a dependency of Moscow in 1456 during the reign of Basil II. In 1471 after a revolt sponsored by the boyars of Novgorod, Ivan's forces conquered the city.

A final revolt took place in 1478. In the aftermath, Ivan responded with exile and executions for his opponents. Novgorod became part of the Muscovite state. In a symbolic blow to the memory of Novgorod's independence, Ivan's forces removed the bell used to call together the town assembly (*veche*).

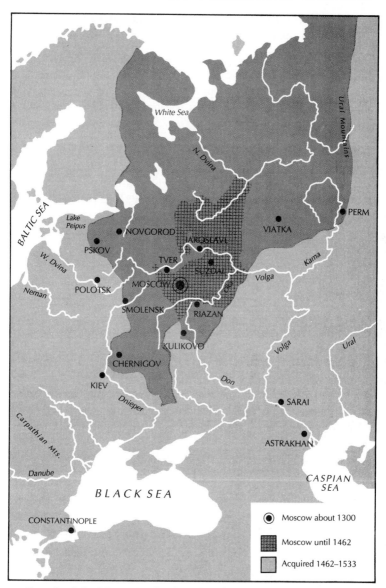

**Growth of the Muscovite State, 14th through Early 16th Centuries**

The addition of Novgorod's vast land holdings nearly doubled the size of the territory under Ivan's control.

*The Conquest of Tver.*    The old rivalry between Moscow and Tver ended with a decisive victory for Moscow. In 1485, Ivan III attacked the city, forcing its prince to flee to Lithuania, where he died without leaving an heir. Tver became a part of the Muscovite state.

### Defeat of Lithuania

Ivan's success in taking over formerly independent appanage states led to confrontation with Russia's neighbor to the west. In Ivan's view Lithuania had taken advantage of Russia's long period of weakness to seize lands belonging to the Kievan state. Seeing himself as heir to the grand princes of Kiev, Ivan claimed the right to regain those regions.

At the same time, Ivan's successes in winning Novgorod and Tver removed buffer states between Moscow and Lithuania. The two now stood face to face.

*The War with Lithuania (1500–1503).*    War broke out in 1500. The immediate issue was the action of Russian appanage princes once loyal to Lithuania who switched their allegiance to Moscow.

*Gains from Peace Treaty.*    Ivan's forces won a decisive military victory. The peace treaty that followed gave Ivan large areas around Smolensk, Polotsk, and Chernigov.

### End of Mongol Control

Mongol control over the Muscovite state had been growing weaker for decades. Ivan took the final, dramatic step of ending all formal loyalty to the Golden Horde in 1480. The ruler of the Golden Horde responded with a military campaign in alliance with the Lithuanians. In the end, however, the Mongols broke off their advance without choosing to fight. Their claim to be the overlords of Russia thus became meaningless.

### Ivan III's Claim to Authority

Ivan pursued a policy of surrounding his political and military power with theoretical justifications, for example, his claim to be the rightful heir to all the lands of the Kievan state. He supported this claim by taking the title of "Sovereign of All Russia" in 1493. In addition Ivan used titles that implied great power and authority: for example, the Greek term "autocrat" and the Russian term *tsar*, drawn from the Roman *caesar*.

Following his marriage to a Byzantine princess in 1472, Ivan adopted ceremonies and decorations (like the double-headed eagle) copied from the old Byzantine imperial court.

### Government under Ivan III

Ivan pursued a policy of centralized control over the territories he acquired. He even took over lands held by his brothers. The idea that Russia was a loose collection of lands ruled by independent princes faded as Ivan's authority grew.

*Muscovite Administration.*  Ivan placed the new regions he obtained under his own officials. In a system called "feeding," his governors received part of the taxes they collected. To restrict the governors from abusing their power, Ivan granted charters to various areas setting the amount of taxes they were to pay.

A crude central administration developed at the grand prince's court in Moscow.

*Law Code of 1497.*  Moscow's expansion led to the establishment of a new *Sudebnik* or law code in 1497. This was the first collection of Russian law since the rise of Moscow, and it established uniform judicial procedures over Moscow's extensive territories. Its features included the death penalty for armed rebellion, thus strengthening the position of the grand prince against potential rivals. It also set down detailed rules for the conduct of trials.

An important provision in the code limited the right of peasants to move from one landowner's estate to another. Peasants could make such a move only during a period of two weeks in late November. This confirmed the increase in the rights of landowners over their laborers, who now moved toward the status of serfs.

### Social Developments

*The Nobility.*  Ivan depended heavily upon noblemen for administrative and military services. In return for service, he granted a nobleman a parcel of land (called a *pomestie*); most of these were from newly acquired regions like Novgorod and Tver. Thus, the nobility increasingly included nobles whose status depended upon an obligation to aid the grand prince.

The nobility included the boyars. In the era of Ivan, *boyar* meant a member of the top part of the nobility, someone who was traditionally a landowner without necessarily providing service to the prince.

*The Boyar Duma.*    A center of boyar power was the Boyar Duma. It was the highest authority in the government for passing laws and running the administration, and it advised the prince on major decisions. The Boyar Duma was appointed by the prince, but tradition required him to choose its members from old, established boyar families.

*The Peasantry.*    The era of Ivan III marked a decline in the status of the peasant and a further step toward serfdom. A land grant (*pomestie*) had little value unless there was a guaranteed supply of labor. To aid the service nobles in keeping such a labor supply, the Law Code of 1497 (see p. 57) sharply reduced the right of peasants to move from one estate to another.

### Basil III (r. 1505–1533)

Basil III (or Vasili III) continued the policies of his father. In domestic affairs he consolidated the power of the grand prince of Moscow over the Russian people. In foreign affairs, he pursued a warlike policy against Lithuania.

#### Domestic Affairs

Basil asserted his authority as his father had done by using the dramatic new titles of ''tsar'' and ''Sovereign of All Russia.'' However, the Muscovite ruler still found himself surrounded by individuals who might challenge his authority. The dissolution of independent appanages drew members of former princely families to the court at Moscow. Basil continued to consult with the Boyar Duma and to rely on the support of important boyars.

#### Foreign Policy

Basil acquired most of the appanages that had maintained some independence so far. For example, Pskov was annexed in 1511.

*Acquisition of Smolensk.*    New fighting broke out with Lithuania. During this major conflict, which extended from 1512 to 1522, Basil obtained the important city of Smolensk (1514), a prize Ivan III had tried without success to win.

*Turkish Threat.*    This period brought the first in a series of armed conflicts between Russia and Turkish power based in the khanate of the Crimea. The danger posed by this new enemy was evident in 1521 when the khan's forces approached Moscow.

## Explanations for the Rise of Moscow

Historians have disagreed over interpretations of the emergence of Moscow as the new center of Russian life. Some have seen this development as a smooth and even inevitable process stemming from Moscow's role as the natural leader of the Russian people. Others have stressed the aggressive policies of Moscow's leaders.

### *Moscow's Advantages*

*Geography.*    Those who claim that Moscow was destined to lead Russia point to geography. For example, Moscow is close to the headwaters of several key Russian rivers, including the Volga and the Dnieper. Its location in the northern forest zone helped protect Moscow from invaders. Some scholars have claimed that Moscow is located at the geographic center of the Great Russian population.

*Religion.*    Moscow became the religious capital of Russia in 1328 when the Metropolitan Theognost settled there.

*Economy.*    In the realm of economics, some historians suggest that Moscow was a center of progress in agriculture and trade during the poverty of the appanage era.

*Leadership.*    Moscow enjoyed the additional advantage of capable leaders like Ivan III. Fortuitously, several lived long enough to provide stable leadership over a long time. In the early years of their dynasty, Moscow's princes had displayed decisive political skill in holding the support of the Mongol khans.

### *Moscow as Ruthless Conqueror*

Other historians see Moscow's rise as a brutal campaign of conquest. In this view Moscow's success began with aiding the Mongols against its fellow Russians. It continued with the acquisition of one independent appanage after another, often by means of war. In each case, subordination to Moscow meant oppression of the population and wiping out existing traditions of government.

# The Russian Church

The church played an important role in unifying the Russian people during the appanage era. An important monastic movement spread the Christian religion into remote regions of the north. With the Russian metropolitan located at Moscow, the Orthodox religion also aided the rise of Moscow to political domination.

During the reigns of Ivan III and Basil II, several serious disputes shook the church. At the same time, theologians developed a new and ambitious description of Russia's central position for the Christian religion.

## St. Sergius and Russian Monasticism

St. Sergius of Radonezh (1322–1392) founded the Trinity Monastery north of Moscow around 1350. It became a gathering place for pilgrims and an important religious and cultural center in the era of the Tatar Yoke. Sergius lent his prestige in support of Dmitrii Donskoi's successful campaign against the Mongols in 1380 (see p. 52).

Disciples of St. Sergius spread the monastic movement throughout northern and northeastern Russia.

## Disputes

### *The Judaizers*

The "Judaizers" formed a heretical group that rejected the New Testament and thus the existing Orthodox Church. The arrival of their beliefs has been linked to Moscow's growing contact with Lithuania and other parts of Europe.

Led by Joseph Volotskii (1440?–1515), the church condemned the Judaizers. Church officials pushed Ivan III to repress the movement by executing its leaders.

The successful campaign against the Judaizers helped maintain the dislike and suspicion many Russians felt toward Europe and the entry of European influences.

*Possessors and Non-Possessors*

A second controversy revolved around the policies of the church itself. Led by Nil Sorskii (1433–1508), an Orthodox theologian, a group within the church challenged the church's possession of landed wealth. The "Non-Possessors" also objected to the close relationship between church and state that dated back to the fourteenth century.

*Volotskii's Case for Possessors.*   Joseph Volotskii again led the church's successful attack. As spokesman for the "Possessors," Joseph made the case that wealth was necessary for the church to carry out its religious role. Joseph was also a strong defender of the tsar's autocratic political power.

*Role of Ivan III.*   Ivan III played an important role in the victory of the "Possessors." He abandoned his ambition of seizing church lands, considering it more important to back the church faction that favored cooperation with the monarch. Ivan's participation in the controversy indicated how vital the support of church leaders remained for a tsar.

## Moscow as "The Third Rome"

The idea that Moscow was the legitimate center of Christianity emerged in the aftermath of two events. In 1439, church authorities at Byzantium (Constantinople), facing intense danger from the Turks, temporarily accepted the authority of the pope at Rome (see p. 53). Secondly, in 1453 Byzantium was captured by the Turks, leaving Russia the largest independent Orthodox state.

In the early sixteenth century, a church official presented to Basil III the concept of "the Third Rome": that is, the falls of Rome and Byzantium had made Moscow the third and last center of Christianity. The idea corresponded with Moscow's growing role as a great political and military power.

# The Arts

Artistic development flourished in the years following the Russian victory at Kulikovo. The outstanding artist of the time was Andrei Rublev (1370?–1430). A monk who was influenced by the monastic movement led by St. Sergius, Rublev produced icons that are considered the greatest Russian masterpieces in the visual arts. Rublev's most renowned icon was the Old Testament Trinity, which he produced around 1411 for Trinity Cathedral.

Rublev's work is distinguished by his delicate drawing style and his use of intense and sharply contrasting colors.

*By 1533, The Muscovite State had emerged as a significant power in Eastern Europe. Its religious claim to be "the Third Rome" went hand in hand with its military and political strength.*

*The defeat of the Mongols was followed by a conflict with Lithuania to regain the lands lost during the centuries following the Mongol conquest. The outcome was still uncertain, but leaders like Ivan III and Basil II had been successful in their campaigns along Russia's western border.*

*Meanwhile, great changes had taken place within Russia. The independent appanage states had been brought under control by Moscow. A new group of nobles, service gentry based upon land grants from the tsar, existed side by side with the traditional boyars. The peasantry was increasingly hemmed in by restrictions imposed by the state.*

## Recommended Reading

Backus, Oswald. *Motives of West Russian Nobles in Deserting Lithuania for Moscow, 1377–1514* (1957).

Billington, James. *The Icon and the Axe: An Interpretive History of Russian Culture* (1966).

Cherniavsky, Michael. *Tsar and People: Studies in Russian Myths* (1969).

Crummey, Robert O. *The Formation of Moscovy, 1304–1613* (1987).

Dmytryshyn, Basil, ed. *Medieval Russia: A Source Book, 850–1700* (3rd ed., 1991).

Fennell, John. *The Crisis of Medieval Russia, 1200–1304* (1983).

Fennell, John. *The Emergence of Moscow, 1305–1359* (1968).

Fennell, John. *Ivan the Great of Moscow* (1961).

Grey, Ian. *Ivan III and the Unification of Russia* (1964).

Kollmann, Nancy Shields. *Kinship and Politics: The Making of the Muscovite Political System, 1345–1547* (1987).

Meyendorff, John. *Byzantium and the Rise of Russia* (1981).

Presniakov, A. E. *The Formation of the Great Russian State* (1971).

Vernadsky, George. *The Mongols and Russia* (1953).

Vernadsky, George. *Russia at the Dawn of the Modern Age* (1959).

# CHAPTER 6

## The Era of Ivan IV
## (1533–1584)

### Time Line

| | |
|---|---|
| 1533 | Ivan inherits throne at age of three |
| 1538 | Death of regent, Ivan's mother |
| 1547 | Ivan crowned tsar |
| 1550 | New Law Code Established |
| 1551 | Church reform |
| 1552 | Conquest of Kazan |
| 1553 | Ivan's illness |
| | English merchants reach Russia via White Sea |

| | |
|---|---|
| 1554 | Conquest of Astrakhan |
| 1558 | Start of Livonian War |
| 1560 | Death of Ivan's wife, Anastasia |
| 1563 | Death of Metropolitan Macarius |
| | Russians capture Polotsk |
| 1564 | Flight of Kurbsky |
| | Ivan's trip to Alexandrovsk |
| 1565 | Formation of *oprichnina* |
| 1569 | Union of Lublin: Poland and Lithuania join forces |
| 1570 | Reign of terror in Moscow |
| | Terror in Novgorod |
| 1571 | Crimean Tatars take Moscow |
| 1572 | Purge of *oprichnina* leaders |
| 1581–1583 | Ermak conquers Western Siberia |
| 1581 | Ivan kills his eldest son |
| 1582 | End of Livonian War: treaty with Poland |
| 1583 | Peace treaty with Sweden |
| 1584 | Death of Ivan |
| 1584–1598 | Reign of Theodore |
| 1587 | Rise of Boris Godunov as de facto ruler |
| 1589 | Russian patriarchate established |
| 1590 | Outbreak of war with Sweden |
| 1591 | Death of Prince Dmitrii |
| 1595 | Peace of Teusin ends war with Sweden |

*Russian history in the sixteenth century was dominated by the reign of Ivan IV ("Ivan the Dread" or "the Terrible"). A complex and violent individual, Ivan brought major changes to Russian life. Like rulers elsewhere in Europe at this time, he solidified the power of his monarchy by striking brutally at high-ranking members of his country's aristocracy. His attack on the boyars and his establishment of a personal tool of repression in the* oprichnina *made Russia's ruler more of an autocrat (an unlimited monarch) than ever before.*

*Ivan displayed equally grand ambitions toward the outside world. His attacks on the khanates along the Volga opened the way for Russian expansion eastward and southward, and individuals like the Stroganovs soon pushed forward into Siberia. On the other hand, Ivan's moves westward led to the prolonged and unsuccessful Livonian War.*

## Ivan's Character and Early Life

The force and brutality of Ivan's rule over Russia have stimulated interest in the roots of his personality. His background includes a troubled and insecure childhood. Ivan displayed emotional instability from an early age.

### Succession to the Throne

When Basil III died in 1533, his son, the future Ivan IV, was a child of three. Five years later, the boy was orphaned when his mother, the regent Elena Glinsky, died.

### Boyar Power

From the age of nine, Ivan found himself surrounded by competing boyar families, including the Shuiskys and Belskys, who acted as regents after his mother's death. The violence of their quarrels and the disruption it caused in Russian life made the boyars unpopular with groups like Russia's merchants and the lower (or service) nobility. For Ivan, boyar rule meant that he was treated with disdain by these powerful members of the upper nobility.

### Cruelty

From an early age Ivan displayed a streak of cruelty (for example, toward his pet animals). His mistreatment at the hands of the boyars stimulated a deep hatred toward that group. In 1543, at the age of thirteen, Ivan ordered the execution of boyar leader Prince Andrei Shuisky.

# Ivan's Reign

Ivan was crowned in 1547. The first prince of Moscow to be crowned with the title of "tsar," Ivan used this title regularly along with the equally striking title of "autocrat." Both reflected his belief that he held complete power as a sovereign ruler at home and abroad.

That same year he married Anastasia Zakharin-Koshkin (1531?–1560). She was the daughter of an obscure boyar family, and more prominent boyars objected to the tsar's marriage to someone they considered their social inferior.

## First Phase (to 1560)

During the first portion of his reign, Ivan remained a conventional ruler. He left the conduct of government largely in the hands of his Chosen Council composed of aristocrats and important church leaders.

### Domestic Affairs

*Increased Government Power.*    An important feature of this period was the trend to increase the power of the central government, often at the expense of the boyars. The lesser nobility or gentry were a driving force behind this policy, which included promoting the power of the bureaucracy.

*Church Council.*    A church council convened in 1551 (the Hundred Chapters Council or *Stoglav*). It reformed the organization of the church and restricted in theory the church's rights to hold land and avoid taxation. In reality, however, the church kept most of its privileges intact.

*New Law Code.*    A new law code (or *Sudebnik*), which modernized court procedures, was put into effect in 1550. Its most important feature allowed some localities, chosen on the basis of the size of their tax revenues, to put elected officials in place of appointed governors. Where appointed governors continued to rule, those officials were made responsible for the misconduct of their subordinates.

Like the Code of 1497 (see p. 57), the Code of 1550 restricted peasants from leaving the estates on which they worked, except for a brief period in late November.

*Military Reforms.*   The army was reshaped into a stronger and more reliable force for the tsar. Restrictions were placed on *mestnichestvo,* which forbade high-ranking nobles to serve under someone of lesser social status. Regularly paid infantry units (musketeers or *streltsy*) formed a loyal core of the army at the tsar's disposal.

A law put in effect in 1556 required military service for all ablebodied nobles above the age of fifteen. This was a sign that the government was moving to end the distinction between those who held a hereditary estate (*votchina*) and those who held an estate based on service (*pomestie*).

*Conflict with Boyars.*   When Ivan became seriously ill, many boyars refused his directions to name his infant son as heir to the throne. This crisis sharpened the hostility between the tsar and the boyars.

The boyars reacted in particular to the centralization of power in the tsar's hands. They also disliked Ivan's demand that they perform military service.

### Foreign Policy

Ivan enjoyed substantial success during this period in expanding Russian territory and power.

*Advance to the East.*   In 1552, Ivan's army stormed the city of Kazan, and the Moslem khanate of Kazan was annexed. Four years later, the khanate of Astrakhan further south on the Volga likewise fell into Russian hands.

Religious hostility toward Islam and the desire to expand Moscow's territory combined to promote Ivan's offensive eastward.

*Results of Ivan's Conquests.*   The results of Moscow's success are noteworthy. First, Russia could now move to control the entire course of the Volga River. This was achieved in 1556 when Ivan conquered the khanate of Astrakhan. These conquests opened routes eastward to the Urals and Siberia and southward to the Caspian Sea and Persia. Second, the Muscovite state now took on a strong multiethnic character, as non-Russian peoples like the Bashkirs came under the tsar's authority.

*The Baltic War.* In 1558, Ivan invaded the Baltic region known as Livonia in pursuit of the major Russian goal of obtaining ports on the Baltic. Political authority in Livonia was sharply divided. The Livonian Order, the descendants of a medieval order of knights who had conquered this part of the Baltic coast in the thirteenth century, controlled much of the region. But parts of Livonia were ruled by the archbishop of Riga and by the governments of individual cities.

The war went well for Russia initially. Ivan's forces took a number of important towns, including Narva and Dorpat. Even when the Lithuanians entered the conflict, Russian successes continued for a time, but the war dragged on into the second, more unstable part of Ivan's reign.

*The English and the White Sea.* In 1553, the English sea captain Richard Chancellor landed on the White Sea coast. Chancellor had set out to reach China via the Arctic. The result of his voyage was to establish an important trade route connecting Russia and Western Europe via the White Sea.

## Second Phase (1560–1584)

From 1560 on, Ivan pursued a new domestic policy, featuring a reign of terror against groups like the boyars, and indeed against everyone the tsar suspected of being an enemy.

### *Personality Crisis*

Some historians see a sharp personality change in Ivan IV after 1560. A number of events occurred to disturb the tsar's emotional stability. He now displayed a new degree of cruelty and an intention to make sweeping changes in Russian life.

*Death of Ivan's Wife (1560).* The death of Anastasia may have contributed to changes in Ivan's personality. Nonetheless, Ivan had moved toward a more radical policy even before her death.

*Death of Macarius (1563).* The leader of the Russian church, Metropolitan Macarius (r. 1542–1563), had been a trusted adviser to the tsar since Ivan was a boy. His death in 1563 removed an important restraining influence on Ivan.

*Treason of Prince Kurbsky.*    In 1564, a prominent boyar, Prince Andrei Kurbsky (1528–1583), deserted the Russian side in the Livonian war. Kurbsky was one of several boyars who also went over to the Lithuanians. He may have feared punishment from Ivan following a recent defeat on the battlefield. From these desertions, Ivan's long-standing hatred and distrust for the upper nobility received a new stimulus.

*Flight from Moscow (1564).*    In a mysterious series of events, Ivan left Moscow in 1564, fled to the town of Alexandrovsk, and announced his abdication. Since the political system revolved around the tsar, this action aroused a wave of confusion and alarm. The tsar received pleas to return from both the boyars and other groups in the population.

*The Conditions of Ivan's Return.*    Ivan agreed to return to Moscow as tsar, but he set down a number of conditions. The effect of those conditions was to permit him to strike at his enemies.

The first condition was easy to comprehend. Ivan got the power to punish his opponents and enemies of the state as he saw fit. The second condition was more unusual. Ivan demanded that the Muscovite state be split. One part, to be called the *zemshchina*, kept traditional institutions. The second part, the *oprichnina* ("the areas set apart"), was to be ruled by a special administration responsible only to the tsar.

*Oprichnina.*    The term *oprichnina* is also used to indicate the special corps of bodyguards Ivan created to carry out his wishes. The *oprichniki* or members of this corps eventually numbered 6000. Their uniforms included terrifying symbols of death and revenge: brooms to sweep Russia free of traitors, a model of a dog's head to indicate their ferocity in hunting down the tsar's opponents.

### Domestic Affairs

*The Reign of Terror.*    Boyar and gentry members were evicted from the regions of the *oprichnina*. The Metropolitan Philip (r. 1566–1569) was murdered after he criticized *oprichniki* brutality. The terror quickly spread beyond the boyars. It struck all groups of society and extended beyond the lands of the *oprichnina* to the *zemshchina* territory.

*Reduction of Novgorod.*    In the winter of 1569–1570, the *oprichniki* were dispatched to Novgorod when Ivan came to believe reports of treason there. They spread terror on the way: for example, murdering thousands of people in Tver. They then proceeded to slaughter tens of thousands of inhabitants in Novgorod. This crushed the life from one of Russia's oldest and most prosperous regions.

*Tatar Attack on Moscow.*    The devastation and disruption created by *oprichnina* terror against Russia's population brought problems from outside Russia's borders. In 1571, the disorganized Russian army was unable to defend Moscow from foreign invasion. Crimean Tatars devastated the suburbs of the capital.

*The Abolition of the Oprichnina (1572).*    Ivan turned as well on his own band of ruthless servants. He abolished the *oprichnina* organization in 1572, slaughtering the leaders of this band of his personal servants.

### Foreign Affairs

*Livonia.*    Ivan's most important foreign policy effort, the Livonian War, dragged on for decades. In the end, Ivan's ambitions led to complete failure of his attempted conquest.

*Poland-Lithuania.*    From 1569 onward, Russia faced the opposition of the combined Polish-Lithuanian state. The following year, Sweden joined Ivan's opponents. With the Crimean Tatars threatening Russia from the south, the crisis deepened.

Ivan launched a final offensive in 1577. When it failed, Russia faced a counterattack into its own territory. In 1582, Ivan accepted a settlement with Stephan Bathory (r. 1575–1586), the monarch of Poland-Lithuania. Peace was established with the Swedes the following year.

After a quarter century of warfare along its northwestern border, Ivan's state was no closer than before to having an outlet to the Baltic.

### Siberia

During the last years of Ivan's reign, Russian expansion reached into Siberia.

*Ermak and the Cossacks.*    In 1581, the Stroganov family hired a band of Cossacks (see p. 73) under the command of Ermak (?–1584) to strike at the khanate of Western Siberia beyond the Urals. At the time, the Livonian War occupied the attention of the tsar, and the defense of territory near the Urals had to be left to private landholders.

This privately sponsored expedition brought extraordinary results. With fewer than 1000 men, Ermak began the Russian conquest of the crumbling Moslem states east of the Urals. The path was now clear for Russian fur traders and explorers to race eastward toward the Pacific.

*Government Presence.*    Ivan accepted the gains brought by this local initiative. Government authority began to follow the trail of the successful Cossack raiders across Siberia. The important government fort at Tobolsk, east of the Urals on the Irtysh River, was built in 1587.

### The Death of the Heir

Ivan's violent personality and brutal behavior left an immediate problem for Russia: the absence of an effective successor. In 1581, the tsar struck and killed his eldest son.

The tsar's remaining family consisted of two sons who seemed unlikely candidates for the succession. One, the future Tsar Theodore (r. 1584–1598), was in poor health, uninterested in governing, and, according to some historians, mentally defective. His younger brother, Dmitrii, was still a two-year-old child.

## Social Change during Ivan's Reign

Two important shifts should be noted during the reign of Ivan IV. The financial demands of the Livonian War and the opening of new lands following the conquest of Kazan and Astrakhan promoted increased peasant migration. At the same time, large communities of those who fled began to form along the frontiers.

### New Moves toward Serfdom

Ivan's government and his military establishment depended upon the cooperation of the service gentry. But land grants for them were useless without a stable supply of labor.

In 1581, the government added an important limit to the right of peasants to leave the estates where they lived. The new restriction deprived some peasants of their traditional right to leave during the two-week period around St. George's Day, the holiday marking the end of the harvest season. From 1581 onward, the areas to which the limitation applied were increased each year.

### The Cossacks

The Cossacks were groups of runaway peasants and other fugitives. They formed warlike, free communities, principally in the steppe regions between the Dnieper and the Don.

The first reference to the Cossacks appears in the chronicles of the middle of the fifteenth century. The dislocation brought by Ivan's domestic and foreign policies helped draw fugitives to these Cossack communities.

The Cossacks were becoming a significant force as the sixteenth century ended. They resisted government control and rejected the powerful, centralized state that had taken shape around Moscow.

## Ivan's Successors

Ivan's death in 1584 placed the crown in the hands of his son Theodore (1557–1598). However, the boyar Boris Godunov (1552?–1605), brother-in-law of the tsar, became the effective ruler of Russia soon after Theodore took the throne.

### The Reign of Theodore and Godunov

During these years, Godunov seemed to be an effective leader in both domestic and foreign affairs. Nonetheless, serious problems were developing both for the country and for him as an individual.

### Domestic Affairs

*Consolidation of Government.*    Godunov reduced the power of prominent and ambitious boyar families like the Shuiskys. He promoted the expansion of government authority into Siberia, following the trailblazing journeys of explorers and fur traders. He continued government efforts to limit the right of the peasants to escape their positions on the estates of the service gentry.

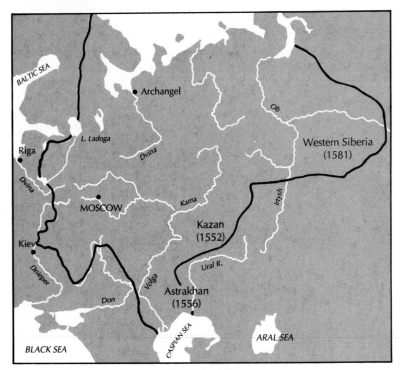

**Russia in 1584**

*Ascendancy of Patriarch.*   In 1589, the patriarch of Constantinople ordained the metropolitan of the Russian church as a patriarch.
Although the metropolitan of Moscow had been independent since
1448, the patriarch at Constantinople had remained his nominal superior. Now the head of the Russian church was placed on the same
level as the highest-ranking Orthodox leaders elsewhere.

### Foreign Policy

Under Godunov's leadership, Russia began to restore its weakened position along the Baltic. Following a successful war against
Sweden (1590–1595), Russia regained territory from Sweden lost in
the Livonian war.

## Growing Tensions

### Threat of Dynastic Extinction

In 1591, the death of Prince Dmitrii (1582–1591) at Uglich brought the Muscovite dynasty closer to extinction. Dmitrii, the heir to the throne, died under mysterious circumstances. Theodore was childless and in poor health. Thus, rumors spread that Godunov had murdered Dmitrii to put himself in position to take the throne. Suspicions of Godunov's ambition were fed by the fact that he had established something resembling a tsar's court and entourage and was acting the part of tsar already.

### Social Unrest

Popular unrest and political difficulties were also evident. Peasants continued to resent the burdens the government imposed, and many of them attempted to flee. Boyar families like the Shuiskys harbored ambitions of regaining the positions they had enjoyed before the attacks on them by Ivan IV.

*By the close of the sixteenth century, Russia had become a larger and more powerful country. Under Ivan IV, the authority of the tsar had grown at the expense of the boyars.*

*But Ivan had left a troubled legacy. The strains of growth and change had embittered groups throughout Russian society. For example, Russia was predominantly a country of impoverished peasants who resented the growth of a system of serfdom.*

*Even the position of the tsar, the center of the political system, was now in question. Ivan's family, which could trace its origins back to Ivan Kalita at the start of the fourteenth century, was about to die out. With no recognized and accepted leader, Russia threatened to collapse into disorder.*

---

## Recommended Reading

Anderson, M. S. *Britain's Discovery of Russia, 1553–1815* (1958).

Berry, Lloyd E., and Robert O. Crummey. *Rude and Barbarous Kingdom: Russia in the Accounts of Sixteenth Century English Voyagers* (1968).

Bobrick, Benson. *Fearful Majesty: The Life and Reign of Ivan the Terrible* (1987).

Cherniavsky, Michael. *Tsar and People: Studies in Russian Myths* (1969).

Crummey, Robert O. *The Formation of Moscovy, 1304–1613* (1987).

Dmytryshyn, Basil. *Medieval Russia: A Source Book, 850–1700* (3rd ed., 1991).

Emerson, Caryl. *Boris Godunov: Transpositions of a Russian Theme* (1986).

Grey, Ian. *Boris Godunov: The Tragic Tsar* (1973).

Longworth, Philip. *The Cossacks* (1969).

Perrie, Maureen. *The Image of Ivan the Terrible in Russian Folklore* (1987).

Platonov, S. F. *Boris Godunov* (1973).

Platonov, S. F. *Ivan the Terrible* (1974).

Platonov, S. F. *The Time of Troubles* (1970).

Staden, Heinrich von. Edited by Thomas Esper. *The Land and Government of Muscovy* (1967).

Vernadsky, George. *Russia at the Dawn of the Modern Age* (1959).

Vernadsky, George. *The Tsardom of Muscovy, 1547–1682*, Part I (1969).

Willan, T. S. *The Early History of the Russia Company, 1553–1603* (1968).

Yanov, Alexander. *The Origins of Autocracy: Ivan the Terrible in Russian History* (1981).

# CHAPTER 7

## The Time of Troubles (1598–1613)

### Time Line

| | |
|---|---|
| 1606–1607 | Rebellion under Bolotnikov and Shakhovskoy |
| 1608–1610 | Rebellion under Second False Dmitrii |
| | Poles intervene to aid Second False Dmitrii |
| 1609 | Swedish intervention on behalf of Shuisky |
| 1610 | Shuisky deposed by Muscovite population |
| | Murder of Second False Dmitrii |
| 1610–1613 | Interregnum |
| 1611 | National Revival begins: Minin and Pozharsky |
| 1612 | Russians capture Moscow from Poles |
| 1613 | *Zemskii sobor* chooses Michael Romanov as new tsar |

*At the start of the seventeenth century, Russia entered a period of dev-astation and crisis. The building of the Muscovite state and the re-sulting changes in Russian society had created an unstable situation.*

*Large parts of the population at all social levels were angry and even prepared to rebel. Boyars hoped to regain the power that they had lost in the era of Ivan IV. Peasants resented the restrictions that were turning them from free agricultural laborers into serfs. Cos-sacks resisted the growing authority of the government and its at-tempts to subordinate them to state control.*

*This chapter will show how the crisis began with the end of the dynasty that had ruled Russia for over two centuries. The absence of an accepted ruler combined with economic problems like famine to create a political catastrophe. This in turn led to a massive social upheaval.*

*Finally, since Russia was weakened by its internal problems, powerful neighbors like Poland found an opportunity to invade and intervene.*

## The Dynastic Crisis

The calamity that struck the Muscovite state at the beginning of the seventeenth century began at the top of the political system. The

Moscow government depended upon a strong and accepted figure as ruler, and now such a figure was missing.

## The Reign of Boris Godunov

The death of Ivan IV's son Theodore in 1598 set the stage for political crisis. The legitimate ruling family had now come to an end.

The regent, Boris Godunov, took the throne as tsar. He was elected to that office by a *zemskii sobor,* an assembly dominated by members of the church, boyars, and members of the gentry.

Godunov had the advantage of experience; he had been ruler in all but name during his time as regent for Theodore. Initially popular, he soon faced serious opposition, most strongly from the boyars.

The new tsar pursued unpopular policies, many of which involved closer contact with the West. He attempted to bring more Western experts to Russia; he sent young Russians to study abroad; and he even tried to found a university with a faculty of German scholars. Godunov reacted to opposition by repressing and silencing his opponents, and he struck with particular force against the boyars.

### Economic Crisis

The new tsar faced a series of droughts and crop failures from 1601 through 1603. Mass starvation resulted. The economic tragedy saw the rise of bands of desperate runaway peasants who turned to robbery.

### Accusations and Rumors

Godunov found his authority undercut by rumors that he had murdered Ivan IV's son Dmitrii, the true heir to the throne. An equally damaging rumor, that Dmitrii was alive and ready to reclaim the throne, spread as well.

The onset of the famine was tied to the assault on Godunov's personal reputation: Russia was allegedly being tormented because of the sins of this usurper.

## The First Pretender

In 1603, a young man claiming to be Dmitrii surfaced in Poland. He found a number of sources of support. The Jesuit Order, Lithuanian and Polish aristocrats, and perhaps boyars in Moscow as well encouraged him. Since the start of the famine, Godunov's distrust of the boyars had grown. He had taken violent measures against them, and some may have retaliated by backing the pretender, whom historians have labeled the "False Dmitrii."

### False Dmitrii's Invasion

False Dmitrii (1582?–1606) invaded Russia with a tiny army in 1604. He received a friendly reception in many areas. This can be explained by considering the suffering that Russian society had experienced. The famine, the extension of serfdom, and Godunov's harsh treatment of his opponents had made the tsar unpopular. Some Russians probably accepted Dmitrii as the rightful tsar. Others surely saw him as a rallying point against Godunov.

Godunov's death in April 1605 allowed Dmitrii to reach Moscow and to become tsar.

### False Dmitrii in Power

The young tsar soon aroused bitter opposition on two grounds. First, he seemed more Polish than Russian. He surrounded himself with Polish followers, and he prepared to marry the daughter of a Polish aristocrat. Second, his efforts to rule rather than to serve merely as a figurehead brought clashes with leading boyars.

### Overthrow of False Dmitrii

Boyars, including Prince Basil Shuisky (1552–1612), led an uprising against Dmitrii in May 1606. Dmitrii was killed, along with thousands of his Russian supporters and Poles who had come to Moscow for his wedding.

## Basil Shuisky as Tsar Basil IV

The new tsar was Basil Shuisky, who took the throne as Basil IV (or Vasili IV) after Moscow's boyars arranged for him to be chosen by a *zemskii sobor* (see p. 84).

Two elements hampered Shuisky's reign from the beginning. First was his identity as a boyar and his dependence upon the boyars of Moscow. Second, Shuisky quickly found himself facing a country torn by bitter social divisions.

# Civil Wars

With the start of Shuisky's reign as tsar, the story of the Time of Troubles grows even more complicated.

For one thing Shuisky found that he lacked the authority to govern or even to control the country. At the same time, rebellions sprang up among different groups and in various regions. Shuisky faced serf uprisings, local rebellions, and challenges from other members of the nobility.

The complicated tangle of events can be divided into three parts: (1) the rebellion in the south (1606–1607); (2) the revolt led by the Second False Dmitrii (1608–1610); and (3) the crisis of 1610.

## The Bolotnikov-Shakhovskoy Rebellion (1606–1607)

### Ivan Bolotnikov

The most serious challenge to the new tsar came from a lower-class rebellion led by Ivan Bolotnikov (?–1608). Historians think that Bolotnikov's followers consisted primarily of serfs, Cossacks, and runaway slaves. His proclamations stressed the injustice of serfdom and called for attacks on boyars.

### Prince Gregory Shakhovskoy

The Bolotnikov rebellion was complicated by his cooperation with Prince Gregory Shakhovskoy (?–?). A governor of the southern city of Putivl, Shakhovskoy, like many other local officials, revolted against Shuisky. Shakhovskoy added urban and more prosperous groups to the lower-class rebellion headed by Bolotnikov.

### Defeat of Bolotnikov and Shakhovskoy

The rebel forces, which now included members of the gentry, were strong enough to attack Moscow in the fall of 1606. Their diverse forces fell apart after being defeated at the capital. Shakhovskoy and Bolotnikov were captured (1607) after retreating to Tula. The prince was exiled, but Bolotnikov was imprisoned and then executed in 1608.

## Rebellion under the Second False Dmitrii (1608–1610)

A second individual claiming to be the Tsar Dmitrii appeared in the summer of 1607. Following the defeat of Shakhovskoy and Bolotnikov, this Second False Dmitrii (?–1610) formed a force of Cossacks and other discontented elements of the population.

This phase of the Time of Troubles brought in a foreign element. Individual Polish noblemen and their private armies entered Russia to help the new False Dmitrii.

### The Second False Dmitrii at Tushino

The new pretender defeated one of Shuisky's armies, reached the outskirts of Moscow, and set up his royal court in the nearby village of Tushino (1608). From Tushino, he held at least nominal authority over southern Russia and many of the cities of the north.

### Swedish Intervention

The Time of Troubles began to take a dramatic new turn in 1609. To end the stalemate between Shuisky and the Second False Dmitrii, Shuisky asked for Swedish military help.

With the assistance of Swedish troops, Shuisky's forces retook northern Russia and forced the pretender to flee from Tushino.

## The Crisis of 1610 and the Start of the Interregnum

The year 1610 brought a cluster of critical events one after the other.

### The Polish Advance

The Swedish invasion of Russia brought further Polish intervention. This time the Polish army, rather than individual noblemen, entered Russia and advanced to Smolensk. The Polish king, Sigismund, began to weigh plans to take the Russian throne for his family.

One of Shuisky's armies was defeated by the Poles near Smolensk. The Poles then marched on Moscow. Much of the population they met along the way accepted Sigismund's son as their new tsar.

### The Return of the Second False Dmitrii

Encouraged by Shuisky's failures, the pretender again established himself near Moscow.

### The Fall of Shuisky and the Arrival of the Poles

In July 1610, Shuisky was forced to give up the throne upon the demand of most of the elements of Muscovite society. The boyars who held the power to choose the new ruler decided that the Polish Prince Wladyslaw (1595–1648) would be preferable to False Dmitrii and his radical followers. As a condition of his rule, Wladyslaw was required to abandon Roman Catholicism for Russian Orthodox Christianity.

### The Polish Betrayal

The crisis reached its peak when the Polish king reversed himself: His son would not be permitted to convert to the Russian religion. Sigismund seemed determined to seize the Russian throne for himself and to put Russia under Polish control.

Russia now had no tsar, and Moscow was under Polish occupation. For three years (1610–1613), an interregnum continued in which the country had no recognized monarchy.

## Liberation of Moscow

From 1610 onward, the Time of Troubles continued with dynastic conflicts and social tensions in evidence. But this final phase of the era was dominated by the confrontation between Russians and foreign invaders, especially the Poles. The death of the second pretender in late 1610 simplified the situation. It seemed that now Russians of different social levels could work in a common political cause.

### The National Armies and the War against Foreign Control

Upon the initiative of church leaders, an army formed in Riazan and marched on Moscow in early 1611. At first, it had considerable success against the Poles. However, tensions between groups within the army like the Cossacks and the service gentry soon caused it to disintegrate.

### The Second National Army and the Capture of Moscow

The church continued to serve as a national rallying point. A second army was put together in the city of Nizhnii Novgorod (1611). A key figure in organizing the army was a town butcher named Kuzma Minin (?–1616?), and the commander of the army was Prince Dmitrii Pozharsky (1578–1642).

Crummey, Robert O. *The Formation of Muscovy, 1304–1613* (1987).

Dmytryshyn, Basil. *Medieval Russia: A Source Book, 850–1700* (3rd ed., 1991).

Emerson, Caryl. *Boris Godunov: Transpositions of a Russian Theme* (1986).

Gordon, Linda. *Cossack Rebellions: Social Turmoil in the Sixteenth-Century Ukraine* (1983).

Grey, Ian. *Boris Godunov: The Tragic Tsar* (1973).

Platonov, S. F. *Boris Godunov* (1973).

Platonov, S. F. *The Time of Troubles* (1970).

Vernadsky, George. *The Tsardom of Moscow, 1547–1682*, 2 vols. (1969).

# CHAPTER 8

## The First Romanovs
## (1613–1682)

### Time Line

| | |
|---|---|
| 1648 | Moscow tax revolt |
| | Cossack revolt against Poland in the Ukraine |
| 1649 | New Law Code established |
| 1652 | German Suburb founded as required residence for foreigners |
| | Nikon elected patriarch |
| 1653 | Last meeting of *zemskii sobor* |
| 1654 | Agreement at Pereiaslavl: Russian authority established over the Ukraine |
| 1654–1667 | Thirteen Years War with Poland |
| 1656–1658 | War with Sweden |
| 1666–1667 | Church Council |
| | Nikon deposed as patriarch |
| 1667 | Treaty of Andrusovo with Poland |
| 1670–1671 | Stenka Razin revolt |
| 1676–1682 | Reign of Theodore III |
| 1682 | Execution of Avvakum |
| | End to practice of *mestnichestvo* |
| 1689 | Treaty of Nerchinsk with China |

*During the seventeenth century, Russia recovered from the Time of Troubles. Domestic order was reestablished even through popular rebellions continued to challenge the government. Russia began to play an increasingly important role in international affairs.*

*Individual tsars of the new Romanov dynasty were weak and unimpressive. Figures close to the throne played the key role in directing the policies of the government.*

*Important trends from earlier periods continued. The institution of serfdom was consolidated. Russian penetration of Siberia extended to the Pacific and reached China. Contact with the West grew*

from the Turks and offered it to Russia, but Michael would not risk war with Turkey.

*Military Modernization.*    Military weakness led to increased contact with the West. In order to modernize Russia's military power, Filaret brought 400 experts from all over Europe.

This began a process of borrowing from the West (see p. 95) that continued on an increasing scale during the remainder of the century.

# Reign of Alexis (r. 1645–1676)

The reign of Alexis found Russia growing stronger in international affairs. Russia acquired much of the Ukraine and successfully defended its action. With the tsar taking the lead, contact with the West increased as well.

In domestic life, the country was shaken by periodic rebellions and a major religious controversy. The status of the peasantry, which had been falling for centuries, was legally defined by the establishment of serfdom.

## Character and Influences

Alexis was a quiet, religious individual who became tsar at the age of sixteen. Throughout his reign he depended upon advisers and favorites. They ranged in ability from capable individuals like Athanasius Ordyn-Nashchokin (1605?–1680) to reckless and divisive figures like Boris Morozov (1590–1661).

## Domestic Policy

The government continued to face problems like the lack of sufficient tax revenue and the flight of peasants from the estates of the service gentry. But during the reign of Alexis efforts to deal with these problems led to violent popular outbursts.

### Tax Rebellion in Moscow

Early attempts to raise money for the government included unpopular measures like a higher tax on salt. Promoted by Boris Morozov, such taxes led in 1648 to a violent rebellion in Moscow that soon spread to a dozen other cities.

### Establishment of Serfdom

Restrictions on the peasantry had been growing tighter for decades. These restrictions took two forms. First, the right to move from the position of laborer on an estate had been limited to a brief time each year, and such moves had been forbidden entirely in given years. Second, the period in which a landowner could legally force a runaway peasant to return to his former position had been lengthened.

In the *Ulozhenie* (law code) of 1649, restrictions on peasant freedom were confirmed. Serfdom was now established for all laborers on private estates.

After 1649, runaway serfs and their descendants could be hunted down indefinitely and returned to their former positions. Thus, peasants were now bound to the land and to the service of the nobles who owned the land. Moreover, serfdom was formally made hereditary.

### Stenka Razin Revolt

Popular discontent grew in reaction to developments like serfdom and the growing tax burden. A major revolt began in 1667 under the leadership of Stepan (or Stenka) Razin (1630?–1671), a Don Cossack. At its peak in 1670, Razin's movement advanced up the Volga, attracting thousands of runaway peasants, Cossacks, and religious dissidents.

Razin was defeated by the tsar's troops at Simbirsk. He was captured and executed in 1671.

### Schism in the Church

Two significant events took place in the Russian Orthodox Church during the reign of Alexis. Led by the Patriarch Nikon (1605–1681), the church successfully reformed and purified its rituals. This led to a split between those willing to accept the changes and "Old Believers" who rejected them. The second development saw Nikon challenge the political authority of the tsar.

The results were crucial for the future. The religious quarrel brought the most important split in the history of the Russian Orthodox Church. The political conflict produced a turning point in the establishment of government supremacy over the church.

### The Issue of Church Reform

Under the leadership of Patriarch Nikon, church authorities moved to reform the rituals and to cleanse the religious texts of the church. The changes were based on the view that errors had come into the Russian church's texts and rituals over the centuries. Nikon demanded corrections to be based on the model of the Greek Orthodox Church. For example, he wanted members of the Russian church to make the sign of the cross with three fingers, which was the practice in the Greek church. Russians had developed the custom of using two fingers.

### The Old Believers

The Church Council of 1666–1667 adopted the changes. But many members of the church, including the archpriest Avvakum (1620?–1682), refused to accept such changes. They insisted that if Moscow were the Third Rome, it had no need to copy the example of the Greek church.

Clinging to Russian traditions, the dissidents developed into a schismatic (separatist) movement, the "Old Believers." They survived government persecution, and the schism in the church became permanent.

### Nikon and the Tsar

Nikon succeeded in winning government approval for his religious reforms even at the cost of splitting the church. Nonetheless, he failed when he tried to promote a more sweeping claim to church political authority over the tsar's government. The theory that the church was supreme over the state roused Alexis' firm opposition.

Alexis blocked Nikon's ambitions in two steps. Nikon had acted as regent after 1654 while the tsar was away conducting war against Poland. In 1658, Alexis ended the regency. In 1666, Nikon was removed from his position as patriarch and banished from Moscow.

## Zemskii Sobor

The *zemskii sobor* met during the early part of Alexis' reign. It convened in 1649 to approve the new law code, and it met again in 1651 and 1653 to deal with the issue of the Ukraine (see p. 94).

After 1653, the government of Alexis did not call the *zemskii sobor* together. (Some historians think that a final *zemskii sobor* was convened as late as 1682.) This fact probably reflected increased stability and confidence of the government. No longer needing the support of the *zemskii sobor*, the government was unwilling to see its powers limited by such a body.

### Foreign Policy: Poland and the Ukraine

Russian foreign policy gained substantial successes during the reign of Alexis. Victory in war against Poland confirmed the incorporation of part of the Ukraine into Russia. This marked a turning point in the relations between Russia and Poland.

#### Rebellion in the Ukraine

Polish control over the Ukraine intensified by the beginning of the seventeenth century. It included the arrival of Polish nobles, their efforts to impose serfdom on the Cossack population, and Polish attempts to win converts from the Russian Orthodox Church to the Uniate Church. The Uniate Church, set up in 1596, followed the practices of Russian Orthodoxy but accepted the leadership of the pope at Rome.

In 1648, Cossack chief Bogdan Khmelnitsky (1595?–1657) began a Ukrainian rebellion against Polish authority. The success of the Cossacks encouraged the entire Ukrainian population to rebel.

#### Russian Involvement and the Pereiaslavl Agreement

Seeking help against Poland, the Ukrainians appealed to Tsar Alexis. By accepting Russian authority, the Ukrainians expected to receive the protection of an Orthodox nation against the Roman Catholic Poles.

Alexis hesitated, knowing that a decision to take the Ukraine would mean war with Poland. Finally, relying in part on the advice of a *zemskii sobor* called in 1653, he decided to risk the conflict.

The Ukrainians pledged their loyalty to the tsar and received a considerable degree of autonomy from the government at Moscow. For example, the Cossacks retained the right to conduct their own foreign relations, except with Turkey and Poland.

### Interpretations of Pereiaslavl

Russian and Ukrainian historians differ about the agreement at Pereiaslavl in 1654. The Russians claim the Ukrainians pledged their loyalty without condition, and, *only afterwards,* Russia granted considerable autonomy to the Ukraine. Ukrainians claim that they accepted Russian authority *on the condition* that Ukraine receive autonomy.

The different interpretations of Pereiaslavl became important in the eighteenth century when the Russians moved to end the special rights that had been enjoyed by the Ukraine. Bitterness over Pereiaslavl became particularly strong in the late nineteenth century as the Russian government tried to restrict the use of the Ukrainian language and the growth of Ukrainian culture.

### War with Poland (1654–1667)

The ensuing conflict with Poland lasted for thirteen years. After early victories against Poland, Russia turned to fight the Swedes (1656–1658). When the campaign resumed against Poland, it continued with heavy losses on both sides until 1667.

### Treaty of Andrusovo (1667)

The war ended with the Treaty of Andrusovo, negotiated by Alexis' talented adviser, Ordyn-Nashchokin. The Russians received the "left bank Ukraine," that is, the portion of the Ukraine east of the Dnieper River. The "right bank Ukraine," west of the Dnieper, was left in Polish hands.

Russia got control of the two prize cities along its western border: Smolensk and Kiev. Each was awarded temporarily to the Russians for a set term of years, but, as it turned out, both remained under Russian control.

## Westernization under Alexis

Alexis showed a greater interest in contact with the West than had any previous tsar. He encouraged foreign merchants and manufacturers to settle in Russia. Like Michael Romanov, he hired military experts to come to Russia to help modernize his armed forces.

### The German Suburb

In 1652, Alexis designated a village northeast of Moscow as the area in which foreigners were required to live. This "German Suburb'' was designed to keep foreigners isolated from the Russian population. But soon even Alexis shocked conservatives by visiting here frequently. The German Suburb may have contained nearly 18,000 foreigners—mainly Dutch, English, and Germans—by the close of Alexis' reign.

### The Vinius Father and Son

The Dutch entrepreneur Andrew (or Andrei Denisov) Vinius (?–1662?) and his son, Andrei Andreevich Vinius (1641–1717), present an important example of what foreigners brought Russia. The elder Vinius set up the first modern iron works and weapons factory in Russia in the 1630s. Thereafter, he served as a government official, purchasing military supplies for Russia in Western Europe.

The younger Vinius was a key government official in the era of Peter the Great. A close adviser to the tsar, he set up a postal system throughout European Russia. He also performed the vital task of developing a system for manufacturing modern artillery during the Northern War (see Chapter 9).

## The Reign of Theodore III (r. 1676–1682)

Following the death of Alexis, his son Theodore held the throne for six years. He died at the age of twenty. This brief interlude continued trends visible during the previous several decades. The new tsar was interested in the West, and he had received an education that included Western languages.

Incapable of ruling himself, Theodore relied on favorites. The policies of the time were set largely by court figures like Prince Basil Golitsyn (1643–1714). Golitsyn made an important advance in modernizing Russian government by abolishing *mestnichestvo*. This practice, which dated back to Ivan III, specified that members of senior noble families could not serve below those of lesser ancestry. It had long complicated Russian government and the Russian military system.

## Military Reform

Following the Time of Troubles, Russia had begun to set up a more effective military system. The gap between Russian and Western armies was evident by 1613. Raids northward from the khanate of the Crimea showed Russian weakness in the face of the Turks as well.

Starting in 1635 the Russians met the problem of the Turks by constructing border fortifications, the Belgorod Line, to defend central Muscovy. French and Dutch military experts were called in to help.

During the reign of Alexis, the army came to depend increasingly upon foreign advisers like the Scotsman Patrick Gordon (1635–1699), who arrived in 1661. These men trained and commanded Russian units and organized them on European lines.

# The Advance into Asia

## Settlement of Siberia

The seventeenth century saw the Russians continue their push eastward. Hunters, fur trappers, and adventurers used the river system of Siberia to speed their advance.

In 1639, an exploring party reached the Pacific. By 1645, 8000 peasant families had settled in the western regions of Siberia.

## Contact with China

### Military Conflict

The occupation of Siberia was followed by contact with the Manchu empire in China. Russian explorers began to reach Chinese outposts in the Amur Valley around 1640. Armed clashes followed in which the Russians found themselves facing superior Chinese forces.

### Treaty of Nerchinsk

In 1689, the Treaty of Nerchinsk regulated relations with Russia and China in the Far East. The Russians recognized Chinese possession of the Amur Valley. In return, the Russians got the right to cross the border to trade with China.

*By the last decades of the seventeenth century, Russia had emerged as a powerful and expanding country. Success in taking part of the Ukraine was accompanied by a dramatic advance to the Pacific Ocean. Confrontations with neighbors like Poland ended favorably. The expansion of state power over the peasantry and over the church reversed the decline seen during the Time of Troubles.*

*The most important trend to begin in the era of the early Romanovs was increasing contact with the countries of Europe.*

---

## Recommended Reading

Avrich, Paul. *Russian Rebels, 1660–1800* (1972).

Bushkovitch, Paul. *The Merchants of Moscow, 1580–1650* (1980).

Crummey, Robert O. *Aristocrats and Servitors: The Boyar Elite in Russia, 1613–1689* (1983).

Crummey, Robert O. *The Old Believers and the World of Antichrist: The Vyg Community and the Russian State, 1694–1855* (1970).

Dukes, Paul. *The Making of Russian Absolutism, 1603–1801* (1982).

Fisher, Raymond H. *The Russian Fur Trade, 1550–1700* (1943).

Fuhrmann, Joseph T. *The Origins of Capitalism in Russia: Industry and Progress in the Sixteenth and Seventeenth Centuries* (1972).

Fuhrmann, Joseph T. *Tsar Alexis: His Reign and His Russia* (1981).

Hellie, Richard. *Enserfment and Military Change in Muscovy* (1971).

Kliuchevskii, V. O. *The Rise of the Romanovs* (1970).

Lantzeff, George, and Richard Pierce. *Eastward to Empire: Exploration and Conquest on the Russian Open Frontier to 1750* (1973).

Longworth, Philip. *Alexis: Tsar of All the Russias* (1984).

Mancall, Mark. *Russia and China: Their Diplomatic Relations to 1728* (1971).

O'Brien, Carl B. *Muscovy and the Ukraine: From the Pereiaslavl Agreement to the Truce of Androsovo, 1654–1667* (1963).

Platonov, S. F. *Moscow and the West* (1972).

Vernadsky, George. *The Tsardom of Moscow, 1547–1682*, 2 vols. (1969).

# CHAPTER 9

## Peter I (1672–1725)

### Time Line

| | |
|---|---|
| 1672 | Birth of Peter |
| 1682 | Death of Tsar Theodore |
| | Peter becomes Co-Ruler |
| 1682–1689 | Regency of Sophia |
| 1686 | Treaty of Poland |
| 1689 | Revolt topples Sophia |
| 1689–1695 | Second regency under Peter's mother |
| 1696 | Victory over Turks at Azov |
| | Death of Ivan; Peter becomes sole tsar |

| | |
|---|---|
| 1697–1698 | The Grand Embassy: Peter's first trip to Europe |
| 1700–1721 | Great Northern War |
| 1700 | Defeat of Swedes at Narva |
| | Julian calendar adopted |
| 1701 | School of Mathematics and Navigation founded |
| 1703 | Founding of city of St. Petersburg |
| 1705–1706 | Revolt at Astrakhan |
| 1707 | Reform of provincial administration |
| 1707–1708 | Bulavin revolt |
| 1708–1709 | Swedish invasion of Russia |
| 1708 | Russian victory at Lesnaia |
| 1709 | Russian victory at Poltava |
| 1710–1711 | War with Turkey |
| 1711 | Russia defeated by Turks |
| | Azov surrendered to Turks |
| | Establishment of the Senate |
| 1712 | Peter's marriage to Catherine, his mistress |
| | St. Petersburg becomes Russia's capital |
| 1714 | Naval victory over Swedes at Hangö |
| 1715 | Naval academy opened |
| 1717 | Government colleges established |
| | Peter's second trip to the West |
| 1718–1722 | National census conducted |
| 1719 | Provincial reform |
| 1721 | Peace of Nystadt ends Northern War |
| | Peter named ''Emperor'' and ''the Great'' |

|  | Church reform and establishment of Holy Synod |
|---|---|
| 1722 | Table of Ranks established |
|  | New law of succession |
| 1724 | Head tax introduced |
|  | Catherine, Peter's second wife, crowned empress |
| 1725 | Death of Peter |

*The reign of Peter the Great brought rapid and intensive change to Russia. Peter was a restless and dynamic leader, far different from the mediocre tsars who had reigned after 1613. Ruling in an era dominated by constant war, he mobilized the population for military success and domestic reform in a way never seen before in Russian history.*

*The process of borrowing from the West increased enormously, spurred on by the tsar himself. As a result, Russia expanded its military power, defeated its old rival Sweden, and established itself as one of the Great Powers of Europe.*

*At the same time, Peter expanded the authority and influence of the Russian government over its own population. The church was subordinated to the state, and the gentry were placed under an effective obligation to provide either civilian or military service.*

*Opposition to Peter's reforms proved ineffective. By the close of his reign, Russia had been dramatically and permanently reshaped.*

## Character and Early Life

Peter was a physically powerful man, six feet nine inches tall, with a restless nature and unlimited energy. He traveled widely at home and abroad. From childhood onward, he showed a burning interest in many areas like technology.

The political turmoil during Peter's youth exposed him directly to scenes of extreme violence. As a result, his personality may have been affected. Historians point to Peter's cruelty, his extreme nervousness, and his impetuous nature as products of his boyhood experiences.

The tsar was uncomfortable with court ceremonies, and he set an example for other Russians by working with his hands. Russia had never before had a ruler interested in mastering trades like carpentry, shipbuilding, and dentistry.

## Accession and Minority of Peter

Peter spent his childhood as the nominal ruler of Russia. He was left to develop his own interests while court factions fought to control the throne.

Peter and his half-brother, Ivan (1666–1696), became co-rulers of Russia in 1682 after the death of Tsar Theodore. Each child's claim was backed by a separate faction linked to one of Theodore's wives. The faction around the Naryshkin family, the relatives of Peter's mother, supported Peter. The faction around the Miloslavsky family, relatives of Sophia and Ivan, supported Ivan.

## Sophia's Regency (1682–1689)

The regent who actually served as monarch from 1682 to 1689 was Ivan's half-sister, Sophia (1657–1704). Like other seventeenth-century Romanovs, Sophia depended on energetic court favorites like Basil Golitsyn, her lover and a Western-oriented boyar.

### Sophia's Policies

Under Golitsyn, Russia experienced both important success and failure in international affairs. A treaty of peace with Poland in 1686 gave Russia permanent possession of Kiev. Military campaigns against Turkey (1687, 1689), which Golitsyn led personally, resulted in major military defeats.

### Sophia's Fall

In 1689, Sophia tried to take the throne for herself. However, important groups, including the westernized military units under Patrick Gordon (1635–1699), defended Peter's succession. Sophia was forced to give up her position as regent, and Golitsyn was exiled. Peter's mother became the new regent.

## Peter's Early Life

Peter played only a ceremonial role, along with his half-brother, Ivan, during the years of his mother's regency. Much of the time he lived with her at the village of Preobrazhenskoe near Moscow.

### Military Affairs

While still a boy, Peter was drawn to military interests. He organized and drilled two military units, the Preobrazhensky and the Semenovsky regiments, which later developed into the first units of the imperial guards.

Peter immersed himself in naval affairs as well. He began to build small ships at Pereiaslavl in 1688. He visited the port of Archangel in 1693 and 1694 and saw the sea for the first time. At a time when Russia lacked a navy, these visits led him to begin the creation of a seagoing fleet.

### Foreign Contacts

Unlike most of his predecessors, the young tsar showed a personal interest in foreigners and foreign ways. He frequently visited the German Suburb (see p. 95), and some of Peter's early friends and tutors were foreigners—like the Scottish soldier Patrick Gordon.

## Peter in Power

### First Phase (1694–1699)

Peter took on an active role as monarch in 1694 upon the death of his mother. Although he was formally the tsar from 1689 onward, he had left governing to his mother while he pursued his military interests.

The first phase of Peter's rule reflected both his interest in military development and his desire to lead a strong, expansionist foreign policy.

### War with Turkey (1695–1696)

Peter's earliest adventure in foreign policy was a successful war against Turkey. Russia remained in a state of hostilities with Turkey since Golitsyn had directed foreign policy (see p. 102). Peace negotiations had begun between Turkey and Russia's allies, Poland and Austria, and Peter may have wished to strengthen Russia's position in a future peace settlement.

In the winter of 1695–1696, Peter built a fleet on the Don River. The following summer, his forces captured the strategic Turkish fortress at Azov, which was incorporated into Russia.

### *Travel to the West (1697–1698)*

For almost a year and a half, Peter traveled in Central and Western Europe. The journey had a diplomatic purpose: to form a grand alliance of European countries against the Turks. But Peter also wanted to gain personal knowledge of the West.

No Russian ruler had ever taken part in such a journey, and Peter displayed a remarkable openness to foreign ways. The tsar became acquainted with countries like Prussia and Holland. He studied the latest technology, even working as a laborer in a Dutch shipyard.

During this short time, Peter hired over 700 European experts (officers, mathematics teachers, engineers, and seamen) to work in modernizing Russia.

### *Early Westernization*

Peter returned to Russia and immediately tried to give his country a Western look (see p. 112). He demanded, for example, that upper-class men cut their beards off. This was a radical step, since beards had religious significance and were traditional for Russian men.

The tsar also insisted that members of his court and the bureaucracy adopt Western styles of clothing.

These measures served to demonstrate that Peter was committed to change Russia and showed his willingness to attack even the everyday routines of Russian life.

### Second Phase (1700–1721)

Peter's efforts to reform and westernize Russia grew more extensive during the Great Northern War against Sweden. Many changes, including a new recruiting system for the military and the expansion of Russian factories, were attempts to build up Russian military power during this serious crisis in foreign affairs.

### *War with Sweden: 1707–1709*

At the close of the seventeenth century, Sweden was the main power in the eastern Baltic. In 1700, Peter joined an apparently powerful anti-Swedish alliance with Denmark and Poland-Saxony. The alliance fell apart at once, however, and Russia found itself facing Sweden alone.

*Battle of Narva (1700).*   The first fighting between Russia and Sweden brought a disaster to Peter's forces. Led by their young king, Charles XII (r. 1697–1718), the Swedes defeated a much larger Russian army at Narva.

*Founding of St. Petersburg.*   Russian forces had their first successes between 1701 and 1703. Under Field Marshal Boris Sheremetev (1652–1719), Peter's troops conquered coastal regions along the Baltic and the Gulf of Finland.

In 1703, Peter began constructing a port city, St. Petersburg, from scratch in the newly won area. Thus, in the years after Narva, Russia secured its contacts from the West via the Baltic.

*Swedish Defeats at Lesnaia and Poltava.*   The course of the war turned decisively in 1708–1709. Charles XII attempted to invade Russia. His aim was to take Moscow in 1708, but he diverted his forces southward to rest in the Ukraine.

The Russians won a victory at Lesnaia in the fall of 1708. This prevented the Swedes from receiving supplies and reinforcements.

In the summer of 1709, Peter personally led his troops in the decisive victory at Poltava.

### War with Sweden: 1710–1721

The conflict with Sweden continued after Poltava. It was marked by a series of Russian successes. In 1713–1714, Russia captured most of Finland from Sweden. On the sea, Peter's Baltic Fleet defeated the Swedes near Hangö (1714).

After the death of Charles XII (1718), Russian forces invaded Sweden.

*Peace of Nystadt (1721).*   The two sides made peace by the Treaty of Nystadt in 1721. According to the peace terms, Russia got to keep present-day Estonia, Latvia, and southeastern Finland.

The immediate result of the treaty was to secure St. Petersburg's position as Russia's outlet on the Baltic. More important, Russia now replaced Sweden as the greatest power in northeastern Europe.

### Peter's Defeat by Turkey

The years of the Northern War brought an important defeat to Russia. Following the victory at Poltava, Russia went to war with Turkey in 1710. Surrounded by Turkish forces in the Balkans in

**Russia in 1725**

1711, Peter was forced to surrender the gains from his first conflict with Turkey. The most important loss was the fortress at Azov.

### Peter's Prestige

The rising status of Russia and its ruler can be seen in two areas. In 1721, following the Treaty of Nystadt, the Senate awarded Peter the titles of "Emperor" and "the Great." Starting with Prussia and Holland, the other countries of Europe recognized Peter's claim to be an emperor.

By the close of Peter's reign, Russia had established a series of marriage alliances with rulers of several states in northern Germany. These were the first such links with Europe since the era of Kievan Russia.

# Peter's Reforms

Peter made substantial changes in Russia during the period of the Northern War. Some reforms such as the reconstruction of the army were probably frantic measures to help him fight the war. Other reforms were more ambitious efforts to modernize Russia on the model of the advanced countries of Europe.

## Military Reforms

The shock of the defeat at Narva in 1700 stimulated Peter to move quickly to make Russia's military forces equal to those of Western powers like Sweden.

### The Army

Peter created a new army after the defeat at Narva. Previously, Russia had only a small standing army that was expanded in wartime by the call-up of nobles, together with a number of their peasants.

The new system was dramatically different. It featured compulsory military service for most of the Russian male population. Members of the nobility were expected to perform military service as required for life. The result was a powerful standing army.

Communities of serfs and peasants on state-owned land were made subject to conscription. Every group of seventy-five households was ordered to provide one conscript for military service. The required numbers of conscripts were called up annually and sometimes even more often. Over 300,000 men were conscripted between 1699 and 1714, giving Russia a far larger military force than ever before.

The second important change was in the form of the army. This meant introducing modern firearms and artillery as well as promotion on the basis of merit.

By 1725, Russia had a permanent army of 200,000. It was the largest such force in Europe.

### The Navy

Peter had been interested in naval affairs since boyhood (see p. 103). As tsar he created a Russian navy on the Baltic and instituted a Russian ship building industry. At the close of his reign, Russia had almost 50 major war vessels and a navy of nearly 30,000 men.

## Reforms in Government

Peter's reforms in government were designed to increase the efficiency of the system below the tsar. Some reflect Peter's continuing efforts to bring Western ways into Russian life.

### The Senate

Peter created the Senate in 1711. Designed to replace the old Boyar Duma, it supervised the main operations of the government (administration, courts, finances) in the name of the tsar.

As it developed during Peter's reign, the Senate worked mainly in drafting laws for the tsar and supervising the administrative colleges. It also became the country's supreme court.

### The Colleges

Starting in 1717, Peter set up central administrative colleges. These were modern government departments modeled on the system that existed in Sweden and other parts of Europe. Each college was run by a board of officials, and each dealt with a specific branch of government work such as war (the War College) or diplomacy (the Foreign Affairs College).

### Weaknesses in Government

Peter set up a more centralized and efficient system of government then Russia had ever had. But the system had two notable weaknesses.

The first weakness was that it required a ruler who was as capable and energetic a leader as Peter. In Peter's absence on military campaigns, the Senate and administrative colleges did not function effectively.

The second weakness had to do with provincial and local government. Here Peter's reign was filled with a series of confusing reorganizations.

Russia's territory was divided and redivided into provinces, counties, and districts. The result was disorder below the central government, causing difficulties in vital matters such as tax collection.

## The Church in Peter's Russia

Peter's most radical reform concerned the church, which occupied a central place in the traditional culture of Russia. This basic institution now came under the effective control of the government. Peter's model was the position of the Lutheran Church in Scandinavia and in northern Germany.

The main motive for this action by Peter was to combat the church hierarchy's opposition to his reform. This had been evident in the conspiracy (see p. 113) involving Peter's son, Alexis (1690–1718).

### The Blocking of Patriarchate

Peter's first blow at the church came in 1700, when he blocked the appointment to fill the vacant position of patriarch. Peter's concerns about the church included the fear that an ambitious patriarch like the seventeenth-century reformer Nikon (see Chapter 8) might emerge to challenge the tsar's program of change. Many of the patriarch's powers were taken over by state authorities, and the state also took over some church properties to help pay for the Northern War.

### The Spiritual Reglament

In 1721 Peter issued a document, the "Spiritual Reglament," which reorganized the church. The position of patriarch was abolished. The Holy Synod, consisting of a committee of church officials, became the governing body of the church. All Synod members were appointed by the tsar. In 1722 a layman, the Ober-Procurator, was added to supervise the Synod for the tsar.

The government now controlled church organization, as well as its property and policies. Some historians consider the church little more than an agency of the government from this time on.

## Tax Reforms

Peter's government put increasingly heavy tax burdens on the Russian masses. The cost of Russia's new military system pushed the government to demand more money from the population.

The most significant change in the tax system was the introduction of the head tax (also called the soul or poll tax) in 1724. This replaced the existing tax on peasant households. The new tax required every male serf to pay a set amount each year. Male state peasants and townsmen paid a set amount which was higher than that paid by the serfs.

The head tax placed a greater burden than before on each individual it affected. It was enforced in two significant ways. First, it was accompanied by a census that registered all members of the population subject to the tax. Second, landlords were responsible for the collection of head tax from their serfs.

## Reforms in Gentry Service

Peter made the old requirement that the gentry serve the state into a real one. The obligation, dating back to Ivan IV, now became heavier, and Peter enforced it vigorously.

Unlike their noble counterparts in other countries, the Russians' noble status depended upon compulsory service.

### The Call-up

Around the age of about sixteen, approximately two-thirds of the gentry were sent off to military service. The remainder were assigned to civilian branches of the government.

### The Gentry and Landholding

In 1714 Peter ended the theoretical distinction between the *votchina* and the *pomestie*. All noble estates were now to be passed down on a hereditary basis. The estates, however, were to be held in return for government service.

Peter also required that nobles leave their estates to only one son, thus preserving a family's estate. Other sons would thus be compelled to devote themselves entirely to government service.

### Table of Ranks

In 1722, Peter set up a hierarchy or ladder of fourteen ranks to regulate government service. It applied to military officers or their civilian counterparts.

A recruit to government or military service began at the fourteenth rank. This meant serving as an ensign or a junior lieutenant in the military or as an assistant councillor in the civil service. Individuals won promotion on the basis of merit.

In theory a commoner could acquire hereditary noble status by rising through the Table of Ranks to the eighth civil or twelfth military level. This was the rank of major in the army or its equivalent. Most individuals who entered the Table of Ranks were members of existing noble families, but the new system permitted at least a limited number of commoners to attain noble rank.

## Economic Reform

Peter pursued a mercantilist economic policy common in Europe at the time. This called for government action to build up industry, to promote economic self-sufficiency, and to expand exports.

### Aid to Industrialization

About 200 industrial enterprises were founded in Russia between 1700 and 1725. Russia's new entrepreneurs were often merchants by background. The government continued to help them with protective tariffs, tax exemptions, and direct subsidies.

### The Production of Armaments

The most pressing problem after the start of the Northern War was to produce weapons. The government itself founded armaments factories, then turned them over to private individuals. Some factories went to middle-class industrialists, but members of the nobility also got ownership of factories.

# Westernization

Peter put Russia into closer contact with the West, and he pushed consistently to import Western ways into his country and its society.

His reforms affected and transformed the upper levels of Russian society. Thus Peter set up a cultural wall between a secular westernized elite and the masses who remained bound by tradition and religion.

### Dress and Manners

Peter struck deeply into Russian life by demanding an end to beards and traditional clothing styles. He challenged the traditional seclusion of women. Under Peter's influence women were invited to attend mixed social gatherings, especially in the new capital of St. Petersburg.

### Education

Peter promoted westernized education in two ways. First, he sent Russian noblemen to schools in Europe. Second, Russia acquired schools like those to be found in the advanced countries of the West. These included a School of Mathematical and Navigational Sciences (established in 1701) and a Naval Academy (established in 1715).

### Academy of Sciences

Shortly before his death, Peter ordered the creation of a scientific institution then common throughout Europe. The Academy of Sciences was intended to encourage scientific studies. Moreover, by offering in addition courses in nonscientific subjects, it served as the framework of a university.

### Julian Calendar

In 1700 Peter replaced the existing Russian calendar with the Julian calendar formerly used in the West. This made Russian years correspond to those of Europe. Russian dates, however, continued to differ slightly from Western ones, since Europeans had already abandoned the Julian calendar for the Gregorian. The conventional Western calendar was not adopted until 1918. Thus, Russian dates lagged behind those in the West by eleven days in the eighteenth century, twelve in the nineteenth, and thirteen in the twentieth.

## St. Petersburg

Peter used the new city he constructed on the Baltic as a tool of westernization. He made St. Petersburg a center of trade and government, drawing activity away from more traditional Russian cities. For example, Peter required merchants to shift their trade route from the northern port of Archangel to St. Petersburg.

In 1712, the Baltic city was named Russia's new capital. Two years later Peter ordered the Senate and other government bodies to move to St. Petersburg from Moscow.

# Opposition to Peter

Opposition to Peter's reform was fierce and varied. Russia had never before been so open to strange Western ways that traditional Russians found offensive. Meanwhile, heavy new burdens were being placed on the mass of the population. Thus, opposition appeared at various levels: in plots connected with conservative members of the monarch's family and in new examples of popular upheavals.

## Alexis

Relations between Peter and his son Alexis (1690–1718) were never close. Alexis showed no support for Peter's reforms. In fact his strongest loyalties were directed toward the church. Therefore, opponents of Peter's reforms looked to Alexis as their champion.

### Alexis' Flight and Return to Russia (1716–1718)

Peter got Alexis to renounce his right to the throne, but the young man aroused his father's suspicions by fleeing abroad in 1716. Alexis returned to Russia in 1718, and an investigation of his flight uncovered a network of opposition to the tsar.

### Death of Alexis

Alexis was tried and condemned to death. He died, possibly from the effects of torture, in 1718.

### Alexis and the Church

The link between Alexis and church leaders stimulated Peter's efforts to subordinate the church to state control. Some church leaders had planned to burn the navy, drive out all foreigners, and abandon the new city of St. Petersburg.

## Popular Uprisings

### The Astrakhan Revolt

Significant revolts broke out against Peter's reforms and the increasing burdens of taxation and serfdom. The first came in 1705 in Astrakhan. It lasted until 1706, and a major military campaign was required before government control resumed there.

### The Bulavin Revolt

In 1707, a rebellion under the Cossack Conrad Bulavin (1660–1708) began near the Don River and spread over much of southern Russia. In order to put the rebellion down, Peter had to divert troops from the war with Sweden.

## The Succession Crisis

Peter's reign ended with the question of his successor unsettled. He had no living sons, but his family included his second wife Catherine (1684–1727), whom he crowned empress in 1724, several daughters, and a number of other relatives.

## Catherine

Peter's second wife was an illiterate Lithuanian peasant girl taken to Moscow in 1703 after the Russian conquest of her native region. She was the mistress of several of Peter's leading subordinates before Peter brought her into his household. She married the tsar, after being his mistress for several years, in 1712.

## The Succession Law

Peter set the stage for crisis with a new succession law in 1722. Based on his disappointment with his son Alexis, it removed the principle that the throne passed by hereditary right to the most senior relative of the deceased monarch. Under the new system, the tsar could appoint his successor.

Nevertheless, when Peter died in early 1725, he had not yet chosen anyone to succeed him.

## Evaluations of Peter

Controversy about Peter falls into two categories. First, a debate centers on the value of abandoning Russian traditions to borrow extensively from the West. During the nineteenth century in particular, some Russian thinkers criticized Peter for destroying an old and worthwhile society by his wave of reforms. Thus, while some praised Peter for founding a modern state, others criticized him for introducing Western materialism and for splitting the upper and lower levels of Russian society.

The second controversy focuses on the novelty of what Peter achieved. Did he take Russia in a completely new direction or not?

### Peter's Ties to the Past

Most historians find precedents for Peter's policies. The first Romanovs moved toward closer contact with the West, for example, during most of the seventeenth century.

Peter, however, caused the process to move much faster. He also put the resources of the government behind the effort to borrow from the West.

### Peter as Enlightened Despot

Most modern scholarship views Peter as a ruler who followed the eighteenth-century European ideal of "enlightened despotism" or "enlightened absolutism." This ideal presented the ruler as a figure who ruled without being tied by traditional institutions. Just as important, however, the monarch ruled in the interest of his subjects.

*Russia in 1725 had gone through vast changes and rapid changes. While Peter the Great did not begin the process of westernization, he forced it forward more rapidly than had any earlier Russian leader, and he made it irreversible.*

*The shift of Russia's capital to St. Petersburg was a symbol of closer ties to the West. Russia's victory over Sweden was an indi-*

*cation of Russia's new military strength and Russia's influential role in northern Europe.*

*Under Peter, the direction of Russian life had been dominated by an energetic and talented leader. In 1725, Peter died without naming an heir. This raised the question of how the system would operate when the future brought less talented monarchs.*

## Recommended Reading

Anderson, M. S. *Peter the Great* (1978).

Avrich, Paul. *Russian Rebels, 1600–1800* (1972).

Cherniavsky, Michael. *Tsar and People: Studies in Russian Myths* (1969).

Cracraft, James. *The Church Reform of Peter the Great* (1971).

Cracraft, James. *The Petrine Revolution in Russian Architecture* (1988).

Gasiorowska, Xenia. *The Image of Peter the Great in Russian Fiction* (1979).

Keep, John L. H. *Soldiers of the Tsar: Army and Society in Russia, 1462–1874* (1985).

Kliuchevskii, V. O. *Peter the Great* (1984).

Massie, Robert. *Peter the Great: His Life and Work* (1980).

Meehan-Waters, Brenda. *Autocracy and Aristocracy: The Russian Service Elite of 1730* (1982).

Muller, Alexander, trans. and ed. *The Spiritual Regulation of Peter the Great* (1972).

O'Brien, Carl B. *Russia under Two Tsars, 1683–1689* (1952).

Peterson, Claes. *Peter the Great: Administrative and Judicial Reforms: Swedish Antecedents and the Process of Reception* (1979).

Raeff, Marc. *Imperial Russia, 1682–1825* (1971).

Raeff, Marc. *Understanding Imperial Russia: State and Authority in the Old Regime* (1984).

Riasanovsky, Nicholas. *The Image of Peter the Great in Russian History and Thought* (1985).

Soloviev, S. M. *Peter the Great: The Great Reforms Begin* (1981).

Sumner, B. H. *Peter the Great and the Emergence of Russia* (1951).

Sumner, B. H. *Peter the Great and the Ottoman Empire* (1949).

Tolstoy, Alexei. *Peter I* (1959).

Waliszewski, Kazimierz. *Peter the Great* (1968).

Yaney, George L. *The Systematization of Russian Government: Social Evolution in the Domestic Administration of Imperial Russia, 1711–1905* (1973).

# CHAPTER 10

## 1725–1762

### Time line

| 1736–1739 | War against Turkey |
| 1740 | Reign of Ivan VI |
| 1741 | Coup places Elizabeth on the throne |
| 1741–1762 | Reign of Elizabeth |
| 1741–1743 | War against Sweden |
| 1746–1748 | Russia participates in War of Austrian Succession |
| 1755 | University of Moscow founded |
| 1756–1762 | Russia participates in Seven Years' War |
| 1762 | Reign of Peter III |
| | Compulsory gentry service ended |
| | Secularization of monastery lands |
| | Peter III removed by palace coup |

*Between 1725 and 1762, Russia went through a period of political instability. Rulers were weak, and there was uncertainty over who was the legitimate ruler. The imperial guards at St. Petersburg frequently intervened to change rulers, and imperial favorites often dominated policy.*

*Significant trends developed. In domestic life, the gentry were gradually freed from their obligation to do state service. At the same time, the peasants found themselves under heavier burdens of taxation and other restrictions.*

*In foreign affairs, the policies of Peter the Great continued. There was increased contact with the rest of Europe, and Russia moved to dominate its neighbors. Austria became Russia's chief ally.*

## The Interlude after Peter

Peter failed to designate a successor. Two of his relatives, his wife and then his grandson, ruled briefly between 1725 and 1730. A crucial change had taken place since Peter's rule. Direction of the government no longer rested in the hands of the monarch. Real power rested with several of Peter's lieutenants, and they were soon challenged by members of the aristocracy.

The imperial guard showed its political power during this period. Events indicated that these military units had the decisive voice in choosing the ruler.

## Catherine I (r. 1725–1727)

Peter had crowned his wife empress before his death, and she was probably the tsar's choice to succeed him. She had the support of one faction of Peter's lieutenants, including Alexander Menshikov (1673–1729), who expected her to safeguard their power and to preserve Peter's reforms. She also had the backing of the imperial guards regiments. Catherine took the throne in 1725.

### The Supreme Secret (or Privy) Council

The real center of power became the Supreme Secret Council, set up in 1726. Composed of six members, it was controlled by leaders like Menshikov.

### The German Presence

During Catherine's reign, the imperial court began to contain large numbers of influential Germans. Some came from the Baltic regions acquired during the reign of Peter the Great. Others arrived from the German principalities to which Peter had tied Russia by diplomatic marriages.

## Peter II (r. 1727–1730)

Following Catherine's death in 1727, Peter the Great's grandson became tsar. Only a child during his short reign, he depended on advisers to run the government. At the suggestion of prominent noblemen, Peter agreed to transfer the capital back to Moscow.

### The Fall of Menshikov

Menshikov was the first significant victim of intrigue in the new imperial court. In 1727, the former lieutenant of Peter the Great was deprived of his offices, and exiled to Siberia the following year.

Menshikov typified men of humble background who had risen to prominence under Peter the Great. His fall evidenced the ascendancy of several old aristocratic families.

### Death of Peter II

Peter II died in early 1730. Like Catherine and Peter I before him, he had failed to name a successor.

# The Reign of Anne (1730–1740)

In 1730 the throne went to Anne, the daughter of Peter the Great's half-brother.

## The Crisis of 1730

Anne was chosen by the leading noblemen of the Supreme Secret Council, whose power and ambition had grown during the reign of Peter II. They considered Anne someone they could dominate and manipulate.

Anne had to promise to get the Council's consent before making any significant state decisions: going to war, levying taxes, appointing high officials. The Council was to have control over the imperial guards.

## The Coup of 1730 and Its Aftermath

Anne threw off the limits on her power with the support of lesser members of the nobility and the imperial guards. Most of these members of the gentry had no trust in a government dominated by a handful of prominent noblemen. They were frightened, for instance, by the example of Poland, where rival aristocratic factions had promoted the collapse of effective central government.

Anne abolished the Supreme Secret Council, thus restoring the autocracy. Political life stabilized. A symbol of the reinvigorated monarchy was Anne's decision to make St. Petersburg the capital once again. The move took place in 1732. A small cabinet led by Andrew Ostermann (1686–1747) ran the government.

### Biron (or Biren)

The empress gave sweeping power to a number of foreign-born favorites. Some of these men were highly capable, but others were ignorant of Russian life and simply out to enrich themselves.

The most infamous of Anne's German favorites was Ernst-Johann Biron (1690–1772), who, as the empress's lover, enjoyed wide political influence.

Biron conducted a brutal policy of collecting taxes through the use of military expeditions. He arrested and exiled thousands of Russians, and thus became a natural target of public hostility. Biron seemed a symbol of tyrannical and ambitious foreigners ruling over the Russians. The term "Bironovshchina" was coined to refer to his widely known evil deeds.

A different interpretation argues that Biron lacked serious influence on the course of policy during Anne's reign.

## Foreign Policy

Foreign policy was conducted effectively under the direction of the German-born Ostermann. The basis of Ostermann's policy was drawn from the era of Peter I: that is, Russia acted the role of a great European power, concerned with all major issues arising on the continent.

### The Austrian Alliance

Austria was a traditional enemy of Russia's dangerous neighbors: Turkey, Poland, and Sweden. Austria was also a traditional enemy of France, whose influence Russia wanted to counter in those three countries.

Hence, between 1725 and 1762, all the wars in which Russia was engaged saw Russia allied with Austria.

### War of the Polish Succession

From 1733 to 1735, Russia fought successfully as Austria's ally against France. The victory prevented France's candidate from being elected king of Poland. During the fighting, there was a remarkable projection of military strength westward. A Russian army nearly reached the eastern border of France.

### War against Turkey

From 1736 to 1739, Russia fought in alliance with Austria against France and Turkey. Despite numerous military victories over the Turks, the war brought few immediate advantages to Russia. Russia was handicapped in the peace negotiations by the military failures of her ally Austria.

Nevertheless, Russia's string of military triumphs in these years was significant. It marked the start of steady Russian successes in the long confrontation with the Turks.

## Domestic Policies

### The Army

In the reform of the army, the crucial factor was General Burkhard Münnich (1683–1767), chief of military engineering and then president of the War Collegium (War Ministry). Münnich fitted out the army with new heavy artillery, and he organized the first Russian engineering and heavy cavalry units. Under Münnich, the first complete table of organization, listing all of the Russian regiments available for service, was compiled.

Münnich played an important role in the wars of the 1730s. He campaigned against the Turks throughout the years from 1736 to 1739, capturing the Crimea early in the war and advancing deep into the Balkans in 1739.

### The Gentry

The gentry made major gains during Anne's reign. Peter the Great's unpopular decree that noble estates had to pass undivided to a single heir was rescinded.

Under Münnich's initiative, a gentry cadet school opened in 1731. This permitted young nobles to obtain the rank of officer through their schooling and ended the traditional obligation to serve a term in the ranks first.

In 1736, the government limited gentry service to the state to a term of twenty-five years. Again at Münnich's suggestion, one son from each gentry family was freed from the obligation to serve the state in order to manage the family property. In fact, there was little effort to enforce service obligations at all.

### Serfdom

The position of the serfs declined as the status of the gentry rose. Starting in 1736, serfs had to get permission from their estate owners to leave for temporary work elsewhere.

Other restrictions also limited a serf's economic freedom. He was forbidden to buy land, to set up a factory, or to hold a government contract.

# Levels of Russian Society: Terminology

## Nobles, Aristocrats, and Gentry

Texts on Russian history are often unclear in using different terms to describe the privileged individuals at the upper levels of Russian society. The Russian term *dvorianstvo,* which refers to all such people, is translated as both "nobles" and "gentry." The same Russian term is sometimes also translated as "aristocracy."

### *Nobles and Gentry*

From the time of Peter the Great onward, it is correct to use "nobles" and "gentry" interchangeably. Both refer to individuals who had gained hereditary nobility, including the right to own land and serfs.

As indicated in Chapter 9, such status was won by rising through the Table of Ranks to a certain level. But even entering the Table of Ranks often required membership in an ennobled family.

Russia differed from other European countries precisely because its nobility (or gentry) was required to perform state service.

### *Aristocracy*

The term "aristocrat" tends to refer to extremely wealthy and powerful members of the nobility. Often they came from old families such as the Dolgoruky clan, and they frequently were significant members of the imperial court.

Thus, one can talk about a clash in 1730 between "the aristocrats," who wished to limit the power of Empress Anne, and "the gentry," who felt more comfortable with an autocratic monarch.

## State Peasants and Serfs

The distinction between serfs and state peasants is also important.

### *Serfs*

"Serfs" were the labor force bound to the land of individual noble landowners. Their condition tended to deteriorate steadily during the eighteenth century. A symbol of this decline was the absolute control the landowner had over his serfs. In practice, this meant that a serf could even be detached from the land and sold like a slave.

### State Peasants

"State peasants," whose status was defined in the era of Peter the Great, consisted primarily of peasants working on land belonging to the state. They were bound to their villages; they paid rent to the state treasury; and they were under the authority of government officials.

In the second half of the eighteenth century, the government or the monarch distributed large amounts of state land to individual landowners. Often huge estates went to favorites of the monarch. This meant that state peasants could find themselves transformed into serfs.

## The Succession Crisis of 1740–1741

### Biron

The death of Anne in 1740 set off a scramble for power. Since the empress had no children, she named her sister's grandson as her successor. Ivan VI (r. 1740–1741) was an infant, and the government remained under Biron's control.

### Münnich and Ostermann

The second stage in the crisis saw Anne's favorite, Biron, overthrown by another German, Münnich. In short order, Münnich was himself overthrown by Ostermann.

### The Imperial Guards Intervene

In the third and final stage, the imperial guards intervened decisively. They ousted the entire "German party" and gave power to Elizabeth (1709–1762), the daughter of Peter the Great. A complicating factor in the coup was the intervention of the French and Swedish ambassadors on behalf of Elizabeth.

## The Era of Elizabeth (r. 1741–1762)

Like Anne, Elizabeth was an ineffective ruler who let power fall into the hands of imperial favorites. She differed from Anne in one crucial respect: Elizabeth surrounded herself with Russian, not foreign, officials. Thus, she seemed to be returning power to her countrymen.

Elizabeth's reign was marked by the construction of the Winter Palace at St. Petersburg and the founding of the University of Moscow (1755). There were also numerous small-scale uprisings as serfs reacted against the deterioration of their status in Russian society.

## Domestic Policy

Under Elizabeth industrial growth encouraged by the government continued. Notable development took place in the iron industry in the Urals and in textile production around Moscow and Vladimir.

Elizabeth also promoted the eighteenth-century trend of growing privileges for the gentry and harsher conditions for the peasants.

### The Gentry

The status of the gentry continued to rise in a number of ways. In 1746, the right to hold serfs was formally restricted to the gentry. In 1758, anyone not a member of the gentry who held serfs was required to sell them.

Between 1758 and 1760, the government made it impossible for those who were not already nobles to reach the status of hereditary nobleman by climbing the Table of Ranks.

### The Peasantry

Elizabeth harshened the condition of the peasantry in several ways. She provided her favorites with generous gifts of state lands, thereby transforming the workers on those estates from state peasants into serfs. An individual who was shifted from state peasant to serf faced heavier burdens and closer supervision.

Moreover, the number of state peasants working in industry increased. Conditions for these "industrial serfs" were notoriously bad.

There were no major peasant revolts during Elizabeth's reign. But mass discontent was growing. It would explode in the Pugachev revolt in the late 1760s (see Chapter 11).

## Foreign Policy

The basis of Russian policy remained friendship with Austria. But, under foreign minister Alexis Bestuzhev-Riumin (1693–1766), fear and suspicion of Prussia emerged as a new force in Russian foreign relations. Prussia's rise to power in Central Europe and its successful attacks on Austria seemed threatening.

### War against Sweden (1741–1743)

In the early 1740s, Russia defeated Sweden, reaffirming the Russian domination of the Baltic that went back to the era of Peter the Great.

The customary pattern of Russian conflicts can be seen here: Russia fought in alliance with Austria, while Sweden was backed by France.

### War of the Austrian Succession (1746–1748)

Russia participated in a minor way in the closing years of the War of the Austrian Succession, when Russia and Austria fought the Prussians.

The conflict is important, however, because it showed Russia lining up for the first time against Prussia, though the usual pattern of a diplomatic tie to Austria held true.

### The Seven Years' War (1756–1762)

Russia stood once again with its customary partner Austria against the Prussians.

Several new elements emerged. France was now part of the Austro-Russian coalition. More important, Russia achieved its first great successes in Central Europe. In 1759, the Russians and Austrians defeated Prussia at Kunersdorf. The following year, the Russians occupied Berlin.

When Russia suddenly left the war at the command of the new tsar, Peter III (r. 1762), Prussia's power was exhausted. The Russians were on the verge of even greater military successes.

## The Reign of Peter III (1762)

Elizabeth died in 1762. She was succeeded by her young nephew, Peter, Duke of Holstein-Gottorp (1728–1762). Two themes dominated his brief reign: his personal friendship for Prussia and his hearty dislike of Russia and Russian institutions.

## Foreign Affairs

### Withdrawal from Campaign against Prussia

Soon after becoming tsar, Peter took the dramatic decision to remove Russia from the alliance against Prussia.

Prussia was then in desperate straits, and Peter's decision deprived Russia of the fruits of its military victories. The move reflected his personal admiration for the Prussian monarch, King Frederick the Great (r. 1740–1786).

### Plan for War with Denmark

Peter's unpopularity reached a peak when he prepared to send the Russian army to fight Denmark in the spring of 1762. He intended to use Russian forces against Denmark in order to gain territory for his native Duchy of Holstein. Such a campaign served no purpose for Russia, and it alienated the imperial guards who expected to be sent to fight in Germany. The war had scarcely begun when Peter was overthrown.

### The Lessons of Peter's Withdrawal from the War

Some historians consider Peter's withdrawal from the Seven Years' War as an example of two crucial elements in Russian political affairs in the eighteenth century. First, it indicates the extensive power of the tsar to shift the course of policy, in this case foreign policy. Second, it indicates the lack of ability, and even the frivolity, of Russia's rulers in the decades after Peter the Great.

## Domestic Policy

### Peter and the Orthodox Church

Peter carried out a number of provocative measures against the church.

*Clerical Clothing and Icons.* The tsar required priests of the Russian church to adopt a Western style of dress. He also ordered all icons removed from Russia's churches.

*Secularization of Monastery Lands.* The new monarch began to seize monastery lands and to place them under the control of the state. This process was completed under Catherine II (see Chapter

11), and it led to the transfer of one million serfs to the status of state peasants.

### Peter and the Gentry

Peter abolished compulsory service for the gentry, whose members could now decide whether or not to perform state service. The motives for this decision remain uncertain. Some historians consider it an example of Peter's frivolity. Others suggest that it reflected his desire to create a professional bureaucracy not dependent on gentry participation.

### Peter and the Army

The new tsar threatened to end the privileged status of the imperial guards, and he appointed foreigners as military advisers.

## The Overthrow of Peter III

Peter soon faced a number of enemies. His contempt for Russian customs and his apparent betrayal of Russian interests in the war with Prussia made him a target for powerful discontented elements.

The overthrow of Peter illustrated the continuing power of the imperial guards regiments to determine who would be tsar. In July 1762, Peter's wife, Catherine (1729–1796), used the support of the guards to depose her husband, who was murdered shortly afterward.

# Culture and Westernization

Russia continued and deepened its contact with the West in the decades following Peter the Great. New institutions of learning were founded in imitation of the West. A handful of individual Russians showed how Western ideas were penetrating Russia.

## The Academy of Sciences

Founded in 1725 under the orders of Peter the Great, the academy was designed to foster scientific study and progress. The academy also supported a Western style newspaper, the *St. Petersburg News*.

### The Academy's Membership

The slow pace of westernization can be seen from the fact that only a minority of its members were Russian during the eighteenth

*Enlightenment. However, the harsh conditions of Russian life and her need to safeguard her place on the throne set limits to her ability to implement reform. In fact, her reign brought increased restrictions on Russia's peasantry and increased privileges for Russia's noblemen.*

*Western ideas and instructions continued to enter Russia. With the outbreak of the French Revolution, however, Catherine found herself required to prevent new trends in Europe from affecting Russian life.*

# Catherine's Rise to Power

Catherine (1729–1796) came to power through a coup. She had no Russian blood and no legal title to the throne. On the other hand, she had used the years of her marriage in many ways to prepare to rule. She had learned Russian and converted to the Russian Orthodox Church. More important, she had linked herself to powerful groups at the top of Russian society.

### Influence and Character

Catherine was German by birth. Her father was the ruler of the tiny principality of Anhalt-Zerbst. The young princess grew up without wealth; financial pressure forced her father to serve as an officer in the Prussian army.

A crucial feature in her background was the influence of the French language and culture. Like many children of European monarchs in the eighteenth century, Catherine had an education based on the ideas of the French Enlightenment.

Her most important personal traits were intelligence, energy, ambition, and a legendary sexual appetite.

### Marriage to Future Tsar Peter III

Catherine arrived in Russia in 1744 to marry Duke Peter of Holstein-Gottorp (1728–1762), whom the Russian empress Elizabeth had designated as heir to the Russian throne.

### Birth of Son

The marriage was an unhappy one. In 1754, Catherine gave birth to the future Tsar Paul, but it is doubtful that Peter was the father.

Paul was taken from her immediately to be raised by the empress. Catherine kept her energies directed to learning the ways of her adopted country.

### Seizure of the Throne

Catherine took the throne in 1762 with the help of the imperial guards (see Chapter 10). Her son, Paul, had the strongest traditional claim to the throne, but Catherine only designated him as her heir.

#### Consequences of the Coup

Since Catherine lacked a convincing claim to the throne, she began her reign in a weak position. This meant, first, that other claimants posed a danger for her. Second, she was dependent on the good will of key groups: the imperial guards and the nobility.

#### The Death of Ivan VI

In 1764, Ivan VI (1740–1764) was murdered in prison, thereby eliminating one of Catherine's rivals for the throne. The young man had been tsar briefly while an infant, then imprisoned throughout his life. He was killed by his guards during a rescue attempt.

## The Role of Nikita Panin (1718–1783)

Catherine's key assistant and adviser during the first twenty years of her reign was Nikita Panin. Panin worked on domestic reform, but his most significant role was in shaping foreign policy.

Panin advocated a close tie with Prussia as part of a "Northern System." His aim was to concentrate Russian power on controlling events around the Baltic.

By the late 1770s, Catherine was turning her ambitions southward toward Turkey, and Panin was forced to retire in 1781.

## Domestic Policy

Despite her weak claim to the throne, Catherine consolidated her position. She publicized herself at home as a defender of Russian institutions after the harm done by the foreigner Peter III and abroad as a modern ruler with close ties to the French Enlightenment. She played one aristocratic faction off against another.

Catherine soon had an increasing impact on Russian life.

## Secularization of Church Lands

Under Catherine, the remaining lands of the Orthodox Church were put into the hands of the state. The program, begun by Peter III (see Chapter 10), was carried out in 1763 and 1764.

## Legislative Commission

An early example of considering ambitious change based on the Enlightenment was the calling of the Legislative Commission. The purpose of the Commission was to revise Russia's laws. The last such revision had been the *Ulozhenie* of 1649.

Though the Commission failed to produce substantial change, it did present the basic grievances of the population to Catherine.

### Catherine's "Instruction"

Catherine set the tone for the Commission in an "Instruction" that she wrote personally. It borrowed many of the ideas of the Enlightenment such as opposition to capital punishment and torture.

At the same time, Catherine avoided criticism of basic institutions such as serfdom and autocracy.

### The Membership of the Commission

Most of the deputies were elected. The largest delegations came from the townspeople and the nobility. There were also elected representatives from the state peasantry, Cossacks, and national minorities.

### Popular Ideas

Sets of instructions to the delegates from the voters gave a cross section of popular thinking. Common themes were an acceptance of the existing autocracy, a desire for lower taxes, and calls for a clear indication of what rights and obligations belonged to each social class.

### End of the Commission

The Commission had no immediate results. Bitter confrontations took place among delegates. For example, delegates from the peasantry differed sharply from gentry delegates over serfdom.

Catherine was probably disturbed by the quarrels that were surfacing among the delegates. She used the start of war against Turkey in 1768 as an excuse to dismiss the Commission.

## Local Government

In 1775, Catherine decentralized the system of local government. Russia was divided into provinces with about 300,000 inhabitants in each. Each province was subdivided into ten districts. It was at the district level that the local gentry played a key role.

The reform of local government reflected two important trends. First, it showed Catherine's alarm at the collapse of local authority during the Pugachev Rebellion (see p. 138). Second, it illustrated Catherine's principle of relying on the support of the gentry.

## Status of the Nobility

Catherine's reign brought a series of measures to increase the power of the gentry. At the same time, Catherine used a variety of measures to encourage the gentry to continue its service to the state.

### Charter to the Nobility (1785)

The charter Catherine granted to the nobility in 1785 elevated their status in an unprecedented way. The nobles in each district and province were recognized as a legally defined group with specific rights. Unlike other segments of the population, the nobles of a province could express their concerns to the monarch in petitions.

Nobles also got assurances that older rights like exemption from personal service and taxation remained in force. Limits on their control over their lands were now removed.

Nobles were permitted to meet every three years to choose local and provincial officials.

### Implications of Nobles' Rights

The rights guaranteed the nobility made them the first group in Russian society to enjoy protection against the autocracy. Thus, some historians see the Charter (like England's Magna Carta) as a step toward even greater limits on the power of Russia's monarchs over the population.

### State Service by the Nobles

Catherine used several methods to maintain the nobility's service to the state. Nobles who served well were rewarded with honors, decorations, and rapid promotions. Those who did not serve were deprived of a place in the noble assemblies that chose local and provincial officials (see p. 137).

### Immigration and Colonization

An effort to attract immigrants and colonists brought large numbers of Germans to Russia. Many such settlers were placed in regions of southern Russia that Catherine had recently won from the Turks.

Bringing in such immigrants provided Russia with energetic and skilled farmers. It also allowed the settlement of new regions without loosening the restrictions on the mobility of Russia's own peasants.

# The Pugachev Revolt (1773–1774)

Catherine's reign was strongly influenced by a widespread and violent rebellion led by the Don Cossack Emelian Pugachev (1742–1775). Pugachev claimed to be Tsar Peter III, and he offered a Russia free of burdens like serfdom and taxation. However, since Pugachev presented himself as Russia's true monarch, he was not assaulting the basic political system.

### Origins of the Revolt

The rebellion began among Cossacks in eastern European Russia along the Ural River. It drew support from a variety of groups: Old Believers, serfs, non-Russian minorities. All felt injured by the extension of serfdom and the growing power of the Russian state.

### The Course of the Revolt

The revolt spread widely. At its peak, Pugachev's forces controlled part of the Volga Valley, along with important cities like Kazan. The rebels killed 3000 landowners and government officials. It appeared that Pugachev might attack Moscow.

## Suppression of the Revolt

The end of war with Turkey (see p. 140) released troops to deal with this threat. Pugachev's forces were defeated by government armies in 1774, and Pugachev himself was captured and executed.

## Impact of the Revolt

The revolt was the last great peasant uprising in Russia until the start of the twentieth century. However, it created a constant fear among Russian landowners of another such upheaval. As a result, Empress Catherine was pushed toward a greater degree of conservatism and a reliance upon the support of the gentry.

# Foreign Policy

Catherine's most spectacular successes came in foreign policy. During her reign, Russia seriously weakened one traditional opponent, Ottoman Turkey, while eliminating a second traditional opponent, Poland. In both cases, Russia's success was marked by the acquisition of vast new territories.

The final years of Catherine's reign were concerned largely with the new problem posed by the French Revolution of 1789 and its consequences.

## Alliance with Prussia against Poland

The most important feature of Catherine's early foreign policy was Russia's diplomatic tie to Prussia. Following their alliance of 1764, the two countries cooperated closely to control Poland.

Poland was kept helpless by Russian pressure to ensure the election of a pro-Russian king. Russia and Prussia also worked together to prevent the reform of Poland's weak and divided government.

## Russo-Turkish War of 1768–1774

War between Russia and Turkey broke out in 1768. Austria and France had encouraged Turkey to declare war, hoping to distract Russia from gaining further control over Poland.

### Russian Military Victories

Russia was victorious in land fighting in the Balkans and in naval campaigns in the eastern Mediterranean.

### Treaty of Kuchuk Kainarji (1774)

Russia got territorial gains, notably coastal territory between the Bug and Dnieper rivers. For the first time since the Kievan era Russia now had a foothold on the Black Sea.

A second important provision made the Crimea into an independent principality. Surrounded by Russian territory, it was now likely to fall under Catherine's control.

Another significant part of the treaty gave Russia a vague right to protect Christians under Turkish control.

## First Partition of Poland (1772)

In a complex series of developments, Russia's victory over Turkey led to the partition of Polish territory among Russia, Austria, and Prussia.

### The Prussian Initiative

Tensions grew between Russia and Austria as a result of Catherine's Turkish victories. King Frederick the Great of Prussia (r. 1740–1786) proposed that the three countries share Polish territory.

### Territorial Gains

In the partition of 1772, Russia received 35,000 square miles of territory in eastern Poland, including Polish Livonia and parts of Belorussia. Russia's share of Poland turned her away for the time being from further attacks on Turkish lands.

Austria took Galicia in southern Poland and thus received compensation for Russian expansion in the Balkans. Prussia obtained gains in the lower Vistula valley that linked the hitherto separated Prussian regions of Brandenburg and East Prussia.

## Second Turkish War (1787–1792)

Russia's ambitions to expand southward led to a second clash with Turkey. The result confirmed Russia's new position on the Black Sea and demonstrated its growing military superiority over the Turks.

### Causes of the War

Russian power moved steadily southward after 1774. At times Catherine considered an ambitious "Greek Project." It was never carried out, but it envisioned throwing the Turks out of Europe, partitioning the Balkans with Austria, and placing her grandson in power in Constantinople.

The Russians annexed the Crimea (1783) and established a fleet on the Black Sea. Catherine's tour of her lands here in "New Russia" (1787) was another alarming sign to the Turks, who declared war in 1787.

### The Course of the War

Russia obtained spectacular victories over Turkish armies in the Balkans, notably under General Alexander Suvorov (1729–1800). Meanwhile, the new Russian fleet won naval victories on the Black Sea.

### Treaty of Jassy (1792)

The peace treaty expanded Russia's holdings along the Black Sea coast. Turkey no longer had territory on the northern shore of the Black Sea from which to threaten Russia.

## Second Partition of Poland (1793)

Russia grew alarmed by Polish efforts to establish a more stable political system. To preserve the old order, Russia invaded Poland in the spring of 1792.

The following year, Russia and Prussia agreed on a second partition of Polish land between them. Moreover, Russia got a protectorate over what remained of Poland.

## Third Partition of Poland (1795)

Inspired by the French and American revolutions, Polish patriots mounted a nationalist uprising against Russia in 1794. This revolt led to an invasion by Russia and Prussia.

In 1795, Poland disappeared as an independent state. The territory left over after the second partition was now divided among Russia, Prussia, and Austria.

**Russia in the 18th Century**

## The French Revolution

Catherine did not pay close attention to events in France when the revolution began in 1789. Russia was mainly concerned with its policy toward Poland and Turkey.

As the French Revolution grew more radical, Catherine broke relations with France (1793). Before her death three years later, she probably considered joining other conservative countries like Austria and Prussia to invade France.

# Social Change

Catherine's reign saw several important trends reach their peak. The status of the peasantry deteriorated in a number of ways to a new low.

At the same time (see p. 137), the gentry of Russian society enjoyed "a golden age."

### The Growth of Serfdom

Serfdom spread geographically in Catherine's era as the institution was established in the Ukraine. Moreover, Catherine herself made numerous state peasants into serfs by lavish land grants to her court favorites. The number of state peasants available to be given away grew as a result of the secularization of church property (see p. 136): Peasants on secularized church lands became state peasants.

At the close of Catherine's reign, serfs and state peasants amounted to more than ninety percent of Russia's population.

#### *Gentry Authority over Serfs*

During Catherine's reign gentry control over serfs grew tighter than ever before. A nobleman could send his serfs into the army or into exile in Siberia.

From 1792 onward, nobles had the authority to sell serfs away from the land on which they labored. This transformed the status of a serf into virtual slavery.

#### *Peasant Obligations*

Serfs faced increasing burdens in the last decades of the eighteenth century. Serfs who made money payments (*obrok*) to their landlord, a common practice in northern and central Russia where agriculture was not profitable, found themselves paying two and a half times again as much in 1800 as in 1760.

Those who owed labor service (*barshchina*) to their landlord saw their obligation rise from three to five days each week. *Barshchina* was common in the south, where fertile land made agriculture more profitable.

Many peasants owed a combination of *obrok* and *barshchina*.

## The Course of Westernization

Under Catherine, Russia adopted an increasing number of the features of European life.

### Criticism of Russian Institutions

The spread of Western ideas led to critical examinations of Russian life. Such developments seemed to have approval from the monarch. During much of her reign, Catherine presented herself as a supporter of the Enlightenment, an intellectual movement using reason to criticize European traditions.

### The Spread of Books and Publishing

As writers began to produce works based on Western models, ten times more books were published in the reign of Catherine II than in the era of Peter the Great.

### The Spread of Secular Education

Catherine was a pioneer in creating a network of government-operated schools. She formed a Commission for the Establishment of Popular Schools. A teachers college was established in St. Petersburg in 1783, and elementary and secondary schools were opened throughout many of Russia's provinces.

At the close of Catherine's reign, 22,000 students (out of a population of 26 million) were being educated in the new school system.

### The Russian Language

Foreign words and expressions entered the Russian language in large numbers by the close of the eighteenth century. In imitation of trends in Western and Central Europe, Russian authors became pioneers in producing grammars, dictionaries, and literary treatises on the Russian language.

By the end of the century, written Russian had dropped much of the formality of Old Church Slavonic.

## Literature

By the close of the century, Russian literature included works based on Western forms such as novels, drama, and poetry, as well as Western ideas and criticism.

### *Gabriel Derzhavin and Denis Fonvizin*

Notable authors during the reign of Catherine included Gabriel Derzhavin (1742–1816) and Denis Fonvizin (1745–1792). Derzhavin was a leading Russian poet. Fonvizin wrote comic dramas.

Some of Fonvizin's writing reflected the westernization of Russia by satirizing the way in which Russians imitated the French.

### *Alexander Radishchev*

Radishchev (1749–1802) was the first Russian writer to condemn the institution of serfdom clearly and publicly. His ideas appeared in vivid form in *Journey from St. Petersburg to Moscow* (1790), where he portrayed the injustices of serfdom and criticized Russia's autocratic government. In the light of the French Revolution, Catherine found such ideas highly dangerous. Radishchev was imprisoned and exiled to Siberia.

### *M. M. Shcherbatov*

Other writers critical of institutions and mores in Catherine's time presented a case for the values and practices of an older Russia. Prince M. M. Shcherbatov (1733–1790) was familiar with the ideas of the French Enlightenment. However, in such works as *Petition of the City of Moscow on Being Relegated to Oblivion* (1787), he criticized placing the capital in St. Petersburg, defended serfdom, and argued for a powerful aristocracy.

In a second work, *On the Deterioration of Russian Morals* (1787), not published until 1859, Shcherbatov attacked the empress's immorality. He contrasted the general corruption of the Russian court since the time of Peter the Great with the healthier era of the seventeenth century.

### Nicholas Novikov

Novikov (1744–1816) was a prominent publisher, journalist, and social critic. As editor of the University of Moscow press, he helped spread the ideas of the Enlightenment by publishing popularizations of the writings of the French *philosophes*. Nonetheless, several of his satirical journals, including *The Drone* and *The Painter*, criticized the way in which the Russian nobility unthinkingly adopted French ways.

Novikov was a member of the Masonic Order, a religious and charitable organization with ties to Western Europe. In 1792, as Catherine became concerned about the French Revolution and foreign influences on her subjects, Novikov was imprisoned. His career as publisher abruptly ended.

*By the close of Catherine's reign, Russia was larger and more powerful than ever before. Victories over Poland and Turkey had eliminated traditional opponents and expanded Russian territory. A German by birth, Catherine had raised Russia to the unquestioned status of a great European power.*

*At the same time, Russia remained different from the rest of Europe. At the end of the eighteenth century, the autocracy and serfdom were Russian, not European institutions.*

*The rapid changes begun in Europe with the French Revolution made it uncertain how Russia's growing contact with the West would affect Russian life.*

### Recommended Reading

Alexander, John. *Autocratic Politics in a National Crisis: The Imperial Russian Government and Pugachev's Revolt, 1773–5* (1969).

Alexander, John. *Bubonic Plague in Early Modern Russia* (1980).

Alexander, John. *Catherine the Great: Life and Legend* (1989).

Alexander, John. *Emperor of the Cossacks: Pugachev and the Frontier Jacquerie of 1773–1775* (1973).

Avrich, Paul. *Russian Rebels, 1660–1800* (1972).

Bartlett, R. P. *Human Capital: The Settlement of Foreigners in Russia, 1762–1804* (1979).

De Madariaga, Isabel. *Britain, Russia and the Armed Neutrality of 1780* (1962).

De Madariaga, Isabel. *Catherine the Great: A Short Life* (1990).

De Madariaga, Isabel. *Russia in the Age of Catherine the Great* (1981).

Dukes, Paul. *Catherine the Great and the Russian Nobility* (1967).

Dukes, Paul. *The Making of Russian Absolutism, 1613–1801* (1982).

Fisher, Alan. *The Russian Annexation of the Crimea, 1772–1783* (1970).

Gleason, Walter J. *A Kinship of Purpose: Moral Idealists in the Service of Catherine the Great* (1981).

Jones, Robert E. *The Emancipation of the Russian Nobility, 1762–1785* (1973).

Jones, Robert E. *Provincial Development in Russia: Catherine II and Jakob Sievers* (1984).

Jones, W. Gareth. *Nikolay Novikov: Enlightener of Russia* (1984).

Kahan, Arcadius. *The Plow, the Hammer, and the Knout: An Economic History of Russia in the Eighteenth Century* (1985).

Kaplan, Herbert. *The First Partition of Poland* (1962).

Lang, David M. *The First Russian Radical: Alexander Radishchev* (1959).

LeDonne, John P. *Ruling Russia: Politics and Administration in the Age of Absolutism, 1762–1796* (1984).

Longworth, Philip. *The Art of Victory: The Life and Achievement of Field Marshal Suvorov, 1729–1800* (1965).

McConnell, Allen. *A Russian Philosopher: Alexander Radishchev,* (1964).

Raeff, Marc. *Catherine the Great: A Profile* (1972).

Raeff, Marc. *Origins of the Russian Intelligentsia: The Eighteenth Century Nobility* (1966).

Ransel, David L. *Mothers of Misery: Child Abandonment in Russia* (1988).

Ransel, David L. *The Politics of Catherinian Russia: The Panin Party* (1975).

Rogger, Hans. *National Consciousness in Eighteenth-Century Russia* (1960).

Thomson, Gladys G. *Catherine the Great and the Expansion of Russia* (1947).

# CHAPTER 12

## The Reign of Paul
## (1796–1801)

### Time Line

| | |
|---|---|
| 1796 | Death of Catherine II |
| | Paul succeeds to the throne |
| 1797 | New law of succession |
| | Serfdom extended to southern Russia |
| | Restriction placed on serfdom |
| 1798 | Paul elected Grand Master of Knights of Malta |
| | Russia forms the Second Coalition against France |
| | War with France |
| | Suvorov's campaign in Italy and Switzerland |

| 1800 | Russia changes alliances, tie to France |
| 1801 | Russian expedition against India |
| | Palace coup |
| | Murder of Paul |

---

*The most important political developments at the close of the century took place in foreign policy. The spread of the effects of the French Revolution made Russia's relations with France vital.*

*Under the direction of Tsar Paul, Russia followed an inconsistent course of action concerning France. Russia took the lead in forming a European alliance against France, then deserted its allies and went over to the French side.*

*At home, Paul's policies seemed just as erratic. The offenses he directed at the nobility created deadly enemies for him and led to his overthrow and murder.*

## Paul's Rise to Power

### Influences and Character

Paul exhibited a violent and erratic personality, and many historians consider him mentally unbalanced. The circumstances of his childhood were emotionally difficult, and episodes during his years as an adult may have contributed to his mental problems.

#### Childhood Traumas

No one could be sure who Paul's father was. He was legally recognized as the son of Tsar Peter III, but it is more likely he was fathered by one of Catherine's lovers.

Paul was removed from Catherine soon after his birth and raised by the Empress Elizabeth. The dislike between Paul and Catherine stemmed in part from this early separation.

Paul's emotional difficulties appeared early in his life. They may have begun at the age of eight when he was shaken by the murder of Peter III, his official father, in 1762.

### *Paul at Gatchina*

From 1782 onward, Paul isolated himself at Gatchina outside St. Petersburg. Here his mental quirks became even more obvious. He compulsively immersed himself in training and disciplining a small private army.

### Paul's Claim to the Throne

An important factor shaping Paul's life was his frustration in waiting for decades to become ruler. As Peter's recognized son, he had a better claim to rule than did Catherine, who had taken power in a coup. However, Catherine refused to allow Paul any political role even after he had become an adult.

Catherine, who had the right to choose her successor (see p. 114), intended to keep Paul from becoming tsar. However, her death in 1796 came before she had carried out her purpose to name Paul's son, Alexander (1777–1825), as the next tsar. Hence, Paul succeeded to the throne.

### Political Philosophy

Paul had received a broad education from tutors familiar with the Enlightenment. As a boy, he was even encouraged to consider the benefits of a limited, constitutional monarchy.

By the time he became tsar, however, he was a convinced supporter of absolute monarchy. All social classes were to serve the state, and the tsar was to rule it as an autocrat.

## Domestic Policies

### Reversal of Catherine's Course

Paul pursued a domestic policy designed to end and even reverse the policies set down by Catherine. He gave early signs of this in two acts. First, he released political prisoners, including Alexander Radishchev. Second, he moved the body of his murdered father, the deposed Tsar Peter III, to the Peter-Paul Fortress. Peter III was buried there with public honors alongside Peter the Great and the other Russian monarchs of the eighteenth century.

### Campaign against the Nobility

A key theme of Paul's reign was his distrust of the nobility. He wished, in particular, to reverse Catherine's policy of securing their privileges.

In several ways, Paul undercut the rights Catherine had awarded the nobles in 1785. For example, nobles were once more required to perform military service, and their right to petition the monarch was eliminated.

### Succession Law

As part of his campaign to reverse Catherine's policies, Paul changed the law of succession. He considered that the existing system, by which the monarch chose a successor, placed too much influence in the hands of the nobility. They had shown their influence throughout the eighteenth century in staging palace coups (see Chapter 10).

Determined to diminish noble power, Paul decreed in 1797 that the crown was to be passed to the oldest male heir.

## Policy toward Serfdom

Paul pursued a contradictory policy toward serfdom. He extended it geographically but placed limits on the duties serfs owed their gentry landowners.

### The Spread of Serfdom

Under Paul, serfdom was extended to the newly acquired territories north of the Black Sea. In addition, Paul transferred numerous landed estates to private owners. More than 500,000 state peasants became serfs in this way.

### Limitation of Landowners' Power

Paul limited the number of days that serfs could be required to perform labor service (*barshchina*) for their landlords. The maximum was set at three days. In addition, he refused to allow the breakup of peasant families by the selling of serfs.

Down through the reign of Catherine the Great, the burdens of serfdom on the peasantry had been increasing. Thus, Paul's action is significant as the first example of state action to limit the institution of serfdom. However, Paul was more concerned to strike against the gentry than to aid the serfs, and the limitation was impossible to enforce.

# Foreign Policy

Like the other traditional powers of Europe, eighteenth-century Russia found its most pressing problem to be its relation with France. By the 1790s, French power was expanding eastward, and Russia needed to decide on a response.

## War with France

Paul entered the conflict against France in 1798. He took the lead in forming the Second Coalition with Britain and Austria against Napoleon. The war was fought on both land and sea.

### Causes of the War

Paul reacted to the expansion of French power in the Mediterranean. Napoleon (1769–1821) captured Malta, the Ionian Islands off the coast of Greece, and Egypt.

Paul was particularly concerned about the island of Malta. In 1798, he had been persuaded by the Maltese Order of the Knights of St. John, the rulers of the island, to become their protector. His link to the island played a large role in his decision to take up arms against Napoleon.

Another factor in Russian hostility toward France was the rumor that Napoleon intended to restore Polish independence.

### Naval Campaigns in the Mediterranean

For once, Russia and Turkey were allies. Russian naval power could thus move easily into the Mediterranean, and Russia seized the Ionian Islands from France.

### The Land Campaigns

At first, Russia had major successes with its army. General Suvorov won spectacular victories in northern Italy in 1798–1799.

The tide of the land war turned, however, because of Austrian defeats. Suvorov was forced into a dangerous retreat through Switzerland to southern Germany.

**Reversal of Alliances**

Paul left his partners of the Second Coalition, Austria and Britain, in 1800. He now became an ally of France.

### Paul's Antagonism toward Britain

An important reason for the shift was friction between Russia and Britain.

Britain grew alarmed at Russian naval power in the Mediterranean. Paul was offended when Britain recaptured the island of Malta but refused to hand it over to Russia.

### Russia's Threat to Britain

Paul tried without success to conduct a land campaign against Britain by sending a Cossack expedition across Russia to attack India.

# The Murder of the Tsar

Paul was murdered in early 1801. By this time his policies had antagonized numerous powerful elements such as high officials and military officers, while members of the nobility resented Paul's continuing attack on their privileges.

The conspiracy was led by Count Peter Pahlen (1745–1801), the military governor of St. Petersburg. Many of the conspirators, as well as the small group that actually killed the tsar, were officers in the imperial guards.

## Role of the Imperial Guards

The overthrow of Paul was the last time the imperial guards interfered successfully in deciding who would rule Russia.

## Role of Britain

Paul's antagonism toward Britain was an important factor in his overthrow. His policies threatened to break Russia's important economic tie to that country. The conspirators were pro-British, and the British ambassador may have encouraged their action.

### Role of Alexander, the Heir to the Throne

Paul's son Alexander was aware of the plot against his father. It is uncertain, however, whether or not he knew that Paul would be murdered.

# Historians' Views of Paul

### Traditional View

Historians disagree about Paul's reign. A traditional and critical view stresses Paul's mental illness, holding that his policies were inconsistent and ineffective.

### Recent View

A more recent view rejects the idea of Paul as mentally unbalanced. It stresses the positive achievements of his reign, such as the limitation on serfdom and the new law of succession.

# Russian Society at the Close of the Eighteenth Century

Russia in 1800 differed in substantial ways from its situation a century earlier. The country was larger, more heavily populated, and increasingly tied to other parts of Europe.

On the other hand, some features of Russian life remained the same. Russia was still a poor country with a predominantly agricultural economy and rural population.

### The Russian Population

#### Growth

Russia had about 13 million inhabitants in 1725. By the end of the eighteenth century, territorial expansion and the growth of the indigenous population had increased the number to more than 36 million.

#### Ethnic Diversity

Russia's population included highly westernized groups such as the German landlords in the Baltic region and the German farmers whom Catherine the Great had attracted to settle in southern Russia. At the same time, the country included such relatively primitive groups as the tribal societies of northern Siberia.

### Religious Membership

Lutherans were brought under Russian control by the acquisition of the Baltic regions, many Jews by the partitions of Poland, and Moslems by expansion southward to the Black Sea and eastward toward Central Asia. A substantial Jewish population was a new feature in Russian life, since there had been almost no Jews in the Russian state prior to 1772.

However, about sixty percent of the population still belonged to the Russian Orthodox Church.

### Social Groups

Almost ninety-five percent of the Russian population were peasants living in the countryside, almost as many as at the close of Peter the Great's reign. Serfs comprised about fifty-three percent of the peasant population, the rest being state peasants.

Urban groups consisted of merchants, artisans, and town workers. They were still a small and unimportant segment of Russian society.

## Westernization and Social Division

During the eighteenth century, a significant gap developed between Russians who absorbed Western culture and those who did not.

The nobility was the most westernized group in Russian society. French was often their everyday language, and many of them traveled extensively abroad. The vast majority of the population, however, remained ignorant of the world away from their own rural communities.

*The brief reign of Paul had seen turmoil in both domestic and foreign policy. Despite some positive changes carried out under Paul, the tsar's period of four years on the throne illustrates the way in which an erratic monarch could make sudden, and unpopular, turns in Russian policy. Paul showed what autocratic power could mean.*

## Recommended Reading

Dukes, Paul. *The Making of Russian Absolutism, 1613–1801* (1982).

Klier, John Doyle. *Russia Gathers Her Jews: The Origins of the "Jewish Question" in Russia, 1772–1825* (1986).

Longworth, Philip. *The Art of Victory: The Life and Achievement of Field Marshal Suvorov, 1729–1800* (1965).

Ragsdale, Hugh. *Detente in the Napoleonic Era: Bonaparte and the Russians* (1980).

Ragsdale, Hugh. *Tsar Paul and the Question of Madness: An Essay in History and Psychology* (1988).

Ragsdale, Hugh, ed. *Paul I: A Reassessment of His Life and Reign* (1979).

Ransel, David L. *The Politics of Catherinian Russia: The Panin Party* (1975).

Rodger, Alexander B. *The War of the Second Coalition* (1964).

Saul, Norman E. *Russia and the Mediterranean, 1797–1807* (1970).

# CHAPTER 13

## Alexander I (1777–1825)

## Time Line

| | |
|---|---|
| 1801 | Alexander takes the throne |
| | Extension of right to own land to nongentry |
| | Formation of Unofficial Committee |
| 1802 | Formation of government ministries |
| 1803 | Law on voluntary emancipation of serfs |
| | Annexation of Georgia begun |
| 1804–1813 | War with Persia |
| 1805 | War of Third Coalition |
| | Russian defeat by Napoleon at Austerlitz |

| | |
|---|---|
| 1806–1812 | War with Turkey |
| 1807 | Russian defeat by Napoleon at Friedland |
| | Treaty of Tilsit |
| | Grand Duchy of Warsaw established |
| 1808–1809 | War with Sweden |
| 1809 | Speransky's plan for a constitution presented |
| | Grand Duchy of Warsaw Expanded |
| | Conquest of Finland |
| 1810 | Council of State established |
| | Annexation of Georgia completed |
| 1812 | Fall of Speransky |
| | Treaty of Bucharest with Turkey |
| | Napoleon's invasion of Russia |
| 1813 | Battle of Leipzig |
| 1814–1815 | Congress of Vienna |
| 1816–1821 | Arakcheev's military colonies |
| 1816 | Union of Salvation founded |
| 1819 | University of St. Petersburg founded |
| 1820 | Constantine renounces right to the throne |
| 1821 | Start of Greek revolt against Turkey |
| 1823 | Nicholas designated heir-apparent |
| 1825 | Novosiltsev's *Constitutional Charter* presented |
| | Death of Alexander |
| | Decembrist revolt |

*Two developments make the era of Alexander I a crucial one in Russian history. First, success in defeating Napoleon in 1812 and leading the westward advance against France made Russia the most powerful and respected country on the continent. Only a century after Peter the Great had led Russia into the European diplomatic community, Alexander brought Russia to its peak of prestige and influence.*

*The other development saw Alexander as the first tsar to address seriously the twin problems of serfdom and autocracy. In the end, however, Alexander made only minor changes in the system of serfdom. He feared noble opposition and the social disruption that sweeping change would bring.*

*Similarly, he stopped short of political reforms that would infringe on his rights as autocrat.*

*Confirming the fact that the issue of reform would not disappear, these years produced the Decembrist conspiracy. Its participants are considered the first in a series of revolutionary plotters who drew their inspiration from the political systems of Western Europe.*

## Character of Alexander

The character and motivations of Alexander I stand as one of the great mysteries of Russian history. He seemed at different periods to be either a political liberal or a fanatic conservative.

Educated in the tradition of the eighteenth-century Enlightenment, at times Alexander considered radical reforms such as establishing a constitution or abolishing serfdom. But he never made these schemes into reality. Moreover, he spent the last years of his life presiding over a harsh Russian scene dominated by fanatics like Alexis Arakcheev (1769–1834). In international affairs, the last part of his life saw Russia as one of the most conservative forces in Europe.

### Early Influences

Alexander was raised by his grandmother, Catherine the Great. A major influence on his childhood, promoting a respect for the ideas of the Enlightenment, was his Swiss tutor, Frédéric-César de LaHarpe (1754–1838). But Alexander was also influenced by the military atmosphere and autocratic ideas of his father's court at Gatchina.

### Rise to Power

Alexander took power in 1801 after his father, Tsar Paul, was assassinated. He had taken part in the plot to depose Paul, but it seems doubtful that he was responsible for the murder of his father.

# Domestic Policy (to 1812)

Alexander began his reign with a series of measures to ease the tensions that Paul had created. Thousands of people who had been unjustly imprisoned by Paul were freed, and the privileges enjoyed by nobles under the Charter of 1785 were restored.

There were two periods in which reforms were concentrated in Alexander's reign. The first, from 1801 to 1805, came in his first years on the throne. The second, from 1807 to 1812, featured reforms promoted by the liberal minister Michael Speransky (1772–1839).

The results of the reforms were limited. Nonetheless, Alexander was the first tsar to consider serious reform of basic Russian problems, notably serfdom and autocracy.

### Advisers

Alexander quickly formed a small committee of four close friends to consider long-range policies. With the help of such figures as Prince Adam Czartoryski (1770–1861) and Count Paul Stroganov (1772?–1817), Alexander considered a program that included an end to serfdom and a more enlightened absolutism.

### The Issue of a Constitution

Alexander's reputation as a liberal comes largely from several times when he seemed to consider a constitution. One occasion came in 1809, and a second in 1820.

However, Alexander and the members of the "Unofficial Committee" did not push for a constitutional monarchy. Instead, Alexander may have considered possibilities like turning the Senate into a real legislature. But even here, once his position as monarch was secure, he showed an unwillingness to dilute his authority.

## Administrative Reform

### New Ministries

In 1802, Alexander abolished the administrative colleges (see p. 108) that had existed since the time of Peter the Great. In their place he established Western-type ministries headed by a single responsible official.

### Role of Ministers

Alexander was careful to keep his ministers from forming a cabinet that might limit his powers. Instead, each minister dealt individually with the tsar to report and to receive orders. Alexander did, however, meet regularly with his Committee of Ministers. The tsar kept the power to decide issues, but he found it useful to hear the Committee discuss those issues first.

## Free Agriculturalists Law

Alexander took one step toward dealing with serfdom in a law passed in 1803. This permitted landowners to free their serfs voluntarily. Although the number of serfs affected turned out to be small, the measure signified that serfdom was no longer a dynamic and expanding social institution.

## Education

A concern to extend education added to the liberal coloration of Alexander's first years on the throne.

### Founding of Universities

New universities were founded at Kharkov, Kazan, and St. Petersburg.

### Entry to Universities

All Russians with academic qualifications could enter a university. Thus, the Russian university became an institution where the customary privileges awarded to the nobility did not mean that others were excluded. Enrollments at Russia's universities remained small, but the student body included both nobles and commoners.

### Speransky and the New Government System

Michael Speransky, the son of a priest, came from a humble background, but he rose through the Table of Ranks to become the principal figure in the government between 1807 and 1812.

#### The Speransky Reforms

In 1809, Speransky presented the tsar with a program for major political reform under which the government would have separate branches: legal, executive, and legislative.

Speransky wanted to maintain a powerful monarchy. At the same time, he desired a system that would include local self-government, civil rights for all members of the population, and a national legislative assembly.

*Civil Rights.*    Civil rights would include freedom to own property; freedom from forced service, i.e., an end to serfdom; and freedom from punishment without trial.

*Political Rights.*    Political rights were to go to all members of the gentry and middle-class property owners such as merchants with a specified amount of wealth. One version of Speransky's plan included political rights for state peasants. Political rights would include the rights to vote and to hold public office.

#### The Possibilities in Speransky's Program

Parts of Speransky's new system were modest in their original form, but they opened the way to further developments. The legislative assembly, in particular, was to play only a limited role in national affairs, but over time it might have developed into a powerful institution.

#### The Rechtsstaat Model

One way that historians characterize the Speransky reforms is as the Russian equivalent of the *Rechtsstaat* system already to be found in Germany. In such a system, the main features were an efficient and orderly administration carried out under a clearly established set of laws.

Such a system would not impinge on the tsar's autocratic power. It would, however, prevent cruel and arbitrary acts such as those carried out by Tsar Paul.

### Outcome

The tsar did not put Speransky's project into effect, apparently believing that it would limit his power as autocrat.

Speransky himself fell from power in 1812. He had been opposed by the gentry and government bureaucrats. Since war with France was imminent, he was also weakened by his reputation as a Francophile.

# Foreign Affairs (1801–1815)

The first half of Alexander's reign was dominated by the figure of Napoleon (1769–1821) and Russian policy toward France. The basic theme of Russian policy was a desire to limit France's power. Nonetheless, Russian military defeats at the hands of Napoleon compelled Russia to maintain peaceful relations with France from 1807 to 1812.

From 1812 through 1814, Russia played a vital role in the defeat of Napoleon. Along with Alexander's vast military power, this made Russia the strongest country on the continent after Napoleon's fall.

### Ties to Britain

After becoming tsar, Alexander sought closer ties to Britain. He moved at once to stop the Cossack force Paul had sent to attack India. His fear about French ambitions was heightened by the pro-English feelings among the members of the Unofficial Committee.

### Third Coalition against Napoleon

In 1804, French incursions into Germany stirred Russian concern. In early 1805, an Anglo-Russian alliance was formed. Austria was the other major member of the new Third Coalition.

### Battle of Austerlitz (1805)

The Russians fought alongside the Austrians and suffered their first defeat at Napoleon's hands at Austerlitz in Bohemia. Following the battle, Austria made peace with the French, and the Third Coalition fell apart.

### War with Turkey

In 1806 Russia tried to block the spread of French influence in the Balkans, primarily by means of Russia's Mediterranean fleet. Napoleon responded by persuading the Turks to go to war with Russia late in the year.

### The Defeat of Prussia

The Russians suffered a second humiliation in central Europe at French hands. France crushed Prussia, Russia's last ally, at Jena in the fall of 1806.

### Battle of Friedland

Russian and French armies fought several times in East Prussia. The campaign ended with a decisive French victory at Friedland in mid-1807.

### Treaty of Tilsit

Immediately following the Russian defeat at Friedland, Alexander and Napoleon met at Tilsit. Russia agreed to accept Napoleon's dominant power in Western and Central Europe. In addition, the Russians pledged to cooperate in France's continuing struggle with England.

### Breakdown of the Franco-Russian Alliance (1807–1812)

The tie between Russia and France was based upon France's military power, not on common interests. Several factors put stress on the relationship and led to the French invasion of Russia in 1812.

#### The Continental System

France wanted Russia's cooperation in blockading British trade with Europe. Russian economic interests, however, were hurt by this "Continental System," as Britain had been a traditional trading partner for Russia since the sixteenth century.

#### French Policy in Central and Eastern Europe

As France tightened its control over much of Europe, it seemed to threaten Russia. By the end of 1807, the French had annexed substantial parts of Germany and reduced the remaining parts to the status of satellite states.

*France and Poland.*   The French victories of 1806 and 1807 compelled Prussia to give up its Polish holdings. These were transformed (1807) into the Grand Duchy of Warsaw. To the Russians this seemed a direct threat for several reasons. First, it offered the Poles a base from which to retake Polish lands held by Russia. Second, it gave the French a foothold in Eastern Europe from which Napoleon could launch an assault on Russia.

### France and the Mediterranean

France's ambitions in the Mediterranean collided with those of Russia. The French objected to Russian expansion in the Balkans and to Russian efforts to gain control of Constantinople and the Turkish Straits.

## War with France (1812)

Napoleon invaded Russia in June 1812. The French reached Moscow, but in the fall they were forced to retreat. Most of the French army was destroyed in the campaign.

The Russian victory over France was the first great defeat for Napoleon's army. It set the stage for Russia to emerge from the war as the dominant country in Europe.

### Reasons for the Russian Victory

The Russian people rallied to the defense of their country. The size of Russia and the manpower the government could call upon made it impossible for Napoleon to strike a knockout blow. Even Russian defeats like the great battle at Borodino in September weakened the French, who suffered heavy casualties.

Moreover, Alexander refused to consider a peace treaty with Napoleon. When the city of Moscow burned down, destroying French supplies and equipment, Napoleon had no choice but to retreat from Russia. Historians disagree about whether the fires were an accident or deliberately set by Russians.

During the retreat, the Russian army, the action of Russian guerrilla forces, and the harsh winter destroyed most of Napoleon's forces.

### The Russian Offensive (1813–1814)

In the war against the French, Russian forces did not stop at their own border. In two years of fighting, they advanced westward.

There was one clear sign of Russia's new power throughout the continent: the entry of the tsar and his army into Paris in the spring of 1814.

## Congress of Vienna (1814–1815)

Russia played an important role at the peace conference following the defeat of Napoleon. The main purpose of the Congress of Vienna was to establish a post-war international order.

Russia's most visible gain from the conference was the control over a newly established Kingdom of Poland, although Russia's former allies Britain and Austria joined with France to limit the size of Russia's gains in Poland.

## Other Russian Gains

The Napoleonic era brought other rewards as a result of Russia's growing power.

### Acquisition of Georgia

Russia established itself south of the Caucasus Mountains when Alexander obtained control of Georgia between 1803 and 1810. The Georgians were willing to become a part of the Russian empire in order to shelter themselves from their Islamic neighbors, Turkey and Persia.

To secure its gains here, Russia had to fight both Persia (1804–1813) and Turkey (1806–1812).

### The Balkans

In its war with Turkey, Russia won possession of Bessarabia.

### Finland

Besides the Kingdom of Poland, Russia's most important gain in Europe was control over Finland. This was the result of a successful war with Sweden (1808–1809).

## A Summary of Russia's New Power

By 1815, Russia had acquired territory that put it in a commanding position in Eastern Europe and Scandinavia. Its gains in the Transcaucasus set the stage for future advances at the expense of Turkey and Persia.

Apart from territory, Russia had won an enormous political and military reputation as a result of its part in defeating Napoleon. A key theme in Russian and European history up to the Crimean War (1854–1856) is that other countries took Russian power and influence for granted.

# Domestic Policy (1812–1825)

After the fall of Speransky, Russian domestic policy took a largely conservative direction.

There were echoes of the liberal years. Alexander promoted one new constitutional draft and carried out an experiment in emancipating serfs. Speransky himself received a new government post in 1819 and returned to St. Petersburg in 1821.

But the basic tendency was to avoid considering serious change or even criticism of the status quo.

### Novosiltsev and the Constitutional Charter

Alexander considered a reform project similar to that of Speransky late in his reign. Nicholas Novosiltsev (1762–1838), a member of the Unofficial Committee, presented his *Constitutional Charter of the Russian Empire* to the tsar in 1820, which is significant for two reasons.

First, the proposed charter shows the complexity of Alexander's mind and character. Even in an era dominated by his own conservative policies, the tsar kept in touch with reformist thinking.

Second, the project, unlike Speransky's, stressed the autonomy of Russia's provinces rather than concentrating power at the center of the system.

In the end, however, Alexander refrained from putting the constitution into effect.

### Serf Emancipation in the Baltic

Between 1811 and 1819 Alexander freed the serfs of the Baltic provinces. However, the freed peasants received no land and soon sank into poverty.

This may have been an experiment in preparation for a larger emancipation. If so, Alexander did not carry the plan forward.

### Arakcheev and Golitsyn

Alexis Arakcheev, Alexander Golitsyn, and similar conservatives dominated domestic affairs during the last decade of Alexander's reign.

#### *Military Colonies*

Since Arakcheev was an agent in carrying out the conservative designs of the tsar, he can be considered a symptom of Alexander's effort to block change. Arakcheev is best known for implementing the tsar's scheme to establish military farming settlements. The settlements were intended to lower the cost of maintaining a large military force.

In the colonies, soldiers and their families lived on state land, farming while they carried out their military training. The colonies featured severe discipline, and conditions there sparked numerous revolts among the inhabitants.

#### *Golitsyn and the Ministry of Education*

As minister of education, Alexander Golitsyn (1773–1844) instituted a severe regime designed to establish a religious outlook among the students and faculties of Russia's few universities.

# Foreign Affairs (1815–1825)

In the last decade of Alexander's reign, Russia's chief role in international affairs focused on preventing new revolutions.

### The Quadruple Alliance

The alliance that defeated Napoleon consisted of Great Britain, Russia, Austria, and Prussia. In late 1815, the four countries pledged to continue their alliance for twenty years and to consult periodically.

Thus, the conservative leaders of Europe hoped to prevent a repetition of the events following 1789 when revolution in one country, France, had spread and disrupted the entire continent.

### The Congress System

Starting in 1818, the four allies, soon joined by France, began to hold congresses. The main concern of this "Congress System" was to put down European revolutions.

Russian foreign policy supported the actions of Prince Klemens von Metternich of Austria (1773–1859). Metternich was the most active leader conducting political and military intervention against revolution on the continent.

## The Decembrist Conspiracy (1816–1825)

A novel development in Alexander's reign was a liberal conspiracy among circles of aristocratic Russians.

### The Character of the Conspirators

Many of the plotters were officers in elite guards regiments who had been educated in the ideas of the Enlightenment. They had served in Western Europe during the Napoleonic wars, and their awareness of Russia's economic and political backwardness had shocked them.

Several of the plotters were members of the tsar's court and military entourage. Nonetheless, all the Decembrist conspirators were disillusioned and frustrated with Alexander I. He had apparently lost his early interest in domestic reform, and thus change from above under his stimulus seemed impossible.

### Origins

The Decembrists formed their first organization, the Union of Salvation, in St. Petersburg in 1816. Over the next nine years, several branches were established in other parts of Russia.

### Objectives

All of the Decembrists wanted changes in Russian government and society. They were opposed in particular to autocracy and serfdom.

### Political Changes

Some Decembrists were willing to stop with a constitutional monarchy. Others, notably Colonel Paul Pestel (1793–1826), favored a radical political revolution producing a republic. Pestel took the position that a temporary dictatorship would be needed to preserve order and to defend the revolution. In this view he anticipated the system that Vladimir I. Lenin (see Chapter 21) would put into effect in the twentieth century.

### Agricultural Reform

All Decembrists favored an end to serfdom. They called for an end to the military colonies and for the distribution of land to the peasantry.

Pestel offered the most specific plan for land reform. The land was to become state property. Half of it was to be held and cultivated by individuals such as the former serfs. The other half was to be rented, and eventually sold, to large-scale entrepreneurs.

## Northern and Southern Centers

The movement developed at two centers: one was St. Petersburg; the second, where Pestel was located, was at Second Army headquarters in the south, at the city of Tulchin.

## The Decembrist Revolt

News of Alexander's death came in December 1825. The line of succession was in doubt (see Chapter 14). The conspirators in St. Petersburg staged a demonstration for the candidacy of Grand Duke Constantine (1779–1831) and against the candidacy of Grand Duke Nicholas (1796–1855). The plotters managed to win over several regiments of troops by disguising their revolutionary intentions.

The mutineers were crushed in St. Petersburg. Shortly afterward, Pestel and the plotters in the south were captured or killed.

## Alexander's Death

The death of the tsar in 1825 was surrounded by mystery. He died suddenly in southern Russia at the age of forty-eight. Some histori-

ans have given credence to rumors that he abandoned his responsibilities to live the life of a religious hermit.

   *Russia had changed substantially between the start of the century
and 1825. It was no longer a large country confined to the eastern
fringes of Europe. Instead, it was a powerful presence at the center
of European life. Alexander I's decision to support Metternich in
stifling revolution had an effect all over the continent.*
   *At home, Russia was still a land of serfdom and autocracy. But
the tsar himself had considered reform proposals, even if he decided
finally not to implement them. Meanwhile, men the tsar knew, aristocrats and officers of the imperial guards, had become revolutionaries out to overturn the social and political system.*

## Recommended Reading

Almedingen, Edith M. *The Emperor Alexander I* (1964).

Cate, Curtis. *The War of Two Emperors: The Duel between Napoleon and Alexander, Russia, 1812* (1985).

Duffy, Christopher. *Borodino and the War of 1812* (1973).

Jenkins, Michael. *Arakcheev: Grand Vizier of the Russian Empire* (1969).

Kennedy, Patricia Grimsted. *The Foreign Ministers of Alexander I* (1969).

Kukiel, Marian. *Czartoryski and European Unity, 1770–1807* (1960).

Lobanov-Rostovsky, Andrei. *Russia and Europe, 1789–1825* (1947).

Lotman, Iurii M. "The Decembrist in Daily Life," in Nakhimovsky, Alexander, ed. *The Semiotics of Russian Cultural History* (1985).

Mazour, Anatole. *The First Russian Revolution, 1825: Its Origins, Development, and Significance* (1937).

McConnell, Allen. *Tsar Alexander I: Paternalist Tsar* (1970).

Palmer, Alan. *Alexander I: Tsar of War and Peace* (1974).

Raeff, Marc. *Michael Speransky: Statesman of Imperial Russia* (1957).

Saul, Norman. *Russia and the Mediterranean, 1797–1807* (1970).

Seton-Watson, Hugh. *The Russian Empire, 1801–1917* (1967).

# CHAPTER 14

## The Era of Nicholas I (1825–1855)

### Time Line

| | |
|---|---|
| 1825 | Decembrist revolt |
| 1826 | Third Department established |
| 1826–1828 | War with Persia |
| 1827 | Battle of Navarino |
| 1828–1829 | War with Turkey |
| 1830–1831 | Revolutions in France, Belgium, and Germany |
| | Uprising in Poland |
| 1831 | Pushkin completes *Eugene Onegin* |

| 1832 | Organic Statute makes Poland part of Russian Empire |
| 1833 | Doctrine of "Official Nationality" proclaimed |
| | Treaty of Unkiar Skelessi |
| | Convention of Berlin |
| | Uvarov becomes minister of education |
| 1836 | Chaadaev's *Philosophical Letter* |
| 1837 | Pushkin killed in duel |
| 1841 | Straits Convention |
| 1842 | Gogol publishes *Dead Souls* |
| 1844 | Agreement with Britain over partition of Turkey |
| 1846 | Russians occupy Cracow |
| 1848 | Revolutions throughout Europe |
| 1849 | Russian military intervention in Hungary |
| | Arrest of Petrashevsky circle |
| 1850 | Olmütz Agreement |
| 1853 | Menshikov ultimatum to Turkey |
| | War with Turkey |
| | Russian naval victory over Turks at Sinope |
| 1854–1856 | Crimean War |
| 1854 | Allies land in Crimea |
| 1855 | Allies take Sevastopol |
| 1856 | Treaty of Paris |

*Between 1825 and 1855, Russia was ruled by a committed conservative. Nicholas I sought to preserve the existing order at home and in the rest of Europe.*

*Serfdom and autocracy remained untouched. Russia's political and military influence played a vital role limiting the effect of the 1848 revolutions in Central Europe. Only with the calamity of the Crimean War did Russia's international prestige fall sharply.*

*Within Russia, however, lively debates broke out in the 1840s. "Slavophiles" and "Westernizers" considered the nature of Russia's past and the proper course for its future.*

## The New Tsar: Nicholas I

As the third son of Tsar Paul, Nicholas was not expected to become the monarch. He had only a narrow military education, which gave him a passion for order and stability. Confronting the Decembrist revolt at the start of his reign confirmed his strong, conservative beliefs.

The most important influence on Nicholas' early years was his service in the army during and after the Napoleonic wars. He came to see military behavior, with its harsh discipline, as an ideal for himself and others.

### Confusion over the Succession

In the confused circumstances following the death of Alexander I, the question of his successor remained unresolved. In the midst of the confusion, the Decembrist conspirators (see Chapter 13) staged their rebellion.

#### *Constantine's Position*

Constantine was Alexander's oldest brother and the legitimate heir to the throne. However, in 1820 he had renounced his right to become tsar after divorcing his wife and marrying a Polish noblewoman.

Constantine was in Poland at the time of Alexander's death.

#### *Nicholas' Position*

The actions of Nicholas in St. Petersburg brought on a crisis. He doubted he would be accepted as tsar and remained convinced that Constantine had the legitimate claim to the throne. He swore allegiance to Constantine.

During several weeks of hesitation and confusion, Nicholas waited for Constantine to renounce the throne in a clear and formal announcement. In the end, Nicholas was pushed to take the throne quickly in late December 1825. He had received information that a group of conspirators had decided to overthrow the autocracy.

### The Decembrist Revolt

The Decembrists used the confused situation to stir up mutiny among regiments in the St. Petersburg garrison. They told the troops that Nicholas was taking away the throne that belonged by right to Constantine. The conspirators did not wish to back Constantine, but instead sought a way to appeal to rank and file soldiers who would not otherwise follow them.

Nicholas' first important act as tsar was to crush the rebellion.

The revolt confirmed Nicholas' early conservative beliefs. He showed the effects of the revolt in several ways. First, he personally followed the investigation of the Decembrists. Second, he established a study commission (see below) to examine the condition of the Russian empire. Third, he became an enemy of serious political and social reform both inside and outside Russia.

## Domestic Policy

Nicholas pursued a policy of maintaining the status quo in Russia. In several ways, however, he introduced some novel elements into Russian life.

### New Institutions

Nicholas did not depend upon the official parts of the Russian government such as the Senate or the Committee of Ministers. Instead, he used personal assistants, often military officers, for special missions.

#### Ad Hoc Committees

Nicholas used special commissions including such eminent figures as Michael Speransky and Count Victor Kochubey (1768–1834). One was established in December 1826 to examine all the problems of Russia. Ten separate committees were set up during Nicholas' reign to consider the issue of serfdom.

The committees produced no results. They turned away from recommending substantial change in major Russian institutions like serfdom. Nicholas himself admitted the gravity of Russia's problems, but he insisted that trying to solve them would be too disruptive.

### The Chancery

The center of Russian government became the tsar's chancery, originally established to run the imperial family's household.

At Nicholas' direction, sections of the chancery were set up to deal with important areas of Russian life such as internal security and codifying Russia's laws.

### The Third Department (or Third Section)

The best-known part of the chancery was the Third Department (or Third Section). Set up in 1826, it was designed to prevent revolution by controlling the actions and behavior of Russians. A major task of the Third Section was enforcing Russia's rigid censorship laws.

## Peasants

Although Nicholas recognized the bad effects of serfdom, his government took no important steps to reform that institution.

The only significant change dealt with the state peasantry. Count Paul Kiselev (1788–1872), head of the Ministry of State Domains, moved to improve the status of the state peasantry after taking office in 1837.

State peasants were freed from the soul tax, and poorer peasants received additional land. The reforms for the state peasantry also included limited self-government along with medical and educational assistance.

## "Official Nationality"

The Russian government sponsored the doctrine of "Official Nationality" that was designed to maintain political order and social stability. The doctrine was announced by the minister of education, Serge Uvarov (1786–1855), in 1833. It had three components.

### Orthodoxy

One component proclaimed the essential role that the official Orthodox Church and its teachings occupied in Russian life.

### Autocracy

The second component proclaimed that Russia needed an absolute monarch as the central element in its political system. The tsar was not merely an absolute ruler but one whose authority was derived from God.

### Nationality

The final component proclaimed the special character and value of the Russian people who, it was suggested, had a special role to play in the world.

## The Law Code

Under the direction of Michael Speransky, a new law code was produced and put into effect in 1835. It was the first clear and complete statement of Russian law since the *Ulozhenie* of 1649, and, with supplements inserted, it remained in force until 1917.

One effect of the codification was to show how the status of serfs had deteriorated over the last two centuries.

# Foreign Policy

The foreign policy of Nicholas I centered on two issues. First, there was the "Eastern Question," the relationship between Russia and the declining state of Ottoman Turkey. As Turkish power waned, Russia pushed farther and farther into the Balkans. This advance concerned other countries, including Britain, France, and Austria.

The second issue was Nicholas' effort to preserve stability in Europe in the face of growing pressures for revolutionary changes.

## Relations with Turkey

Russia's problems with Turkey ran through Nicholas' entire reign. Russia had ambitions of expanding into the Balkans at Turkey's expense. Moreover, Russia had to consider whether or not to promote a partition of Turkish territory if, as many observers expected,

Turkey's government collapsed. Finally, Russia was concerned for the Orthodox Christian populations under Turkish control.

### Russia and the War for Greek Independence

A Greek insurrection against Turkish control had begun in 1821 during the reign of Alexander I. Russians were sympathetic to the Greeks as fellow Orthodox Christians, but conservative Russian governments hesitated to give aid to any revolutionary movement.

Unlike Alexander, Nicholas intervened. Before war was formally declared, Russia, along with France and Britain, defeated the Turkish navy at Navarino (1827).

### Russo-Turkish War of 1828–1829

Russia defeated Turkey after a series of land campaigns in the Balkans.

At this time, Russian policy favored the preservation of the Turkish state. The Russian government considered Turkey a vital part of the European power balance.

### Treaty of Adrianople (1829)

The peace settlement signed at Adrianople, while expanding Russian influence, was a moderate one. First, Russia acquired territory in the Balkans and Caucasus. Second, Russia got the right to send merchant ships through the Turkish Straits into the Mediterranean. Third, the Turkish provinces of Moldavia and Wallachia in the Balkans received autonomy under a Russian protectorate.

### Crisis in Near East (1832–1833)

Russia's influence over Turkey reached its high point in the first years of the 1830s, when the Russians took advantage of a conflict between Turkey and Egypt.

With Turkey being invaded by Egyptian forces, Nicholas sent ships and troops to defend Constantinople. The Russians withdrew after the major powers of Europe arranged a settlement between the Turks and Egyptians.

The incident led to the Treaty of Unkiar Skelessi (1833) between Turkey and Russia. It established an alliance between the two countries, and it recognized Russia's special influence over the Turkish government. The treaty also recognized Russia's exclusive right to send ships through the Bosporus and the Dardanelles.

### London Straits Convention of 1841

A renewed conflict between Turkey and Egypt led to another intervention of the major powers into Turkish affairs in 1840.

Russia's special rights in Turkey, established in the Treaty of Unkiar Skelessi, were ended by the London Straits Convention of 1841. Turkish security, especially its control over the Straits of the Dardanelles, was now guaranteed by all five of the major powers of Europe: Britain, France, Austria, Prussia, and Russia.

### Agreement with Britain on Partition (*1844*)

Talks in 1844 led to a controversial agreement between Russia and Britain regarding Turkey. It had two basic components. First, Russia and Britain would try to maintain Turkey's independent existence. Second, if this effort failed, the two would cooperate in partitioning Turkey.

The agreement led to future difficulties. The Russians considered it an arrangement upon which they could rely: There would be no controversy with Britain if Russia wanted to partition a collapsing Turkey. The British did not agree.

Thus the stage was set for the Crimean War (see p. 181).

## Russia's Opposition to European Revolution

Throughout his reign, Nicholas used Russian power to combat revolutions in other parts of Europe.

### Revolution in France (*1830*)

Nicholas regarded the French Revolution of 1830, which spread to Belgium and western Germany, as a threat to the entire European order.

Nicholas considered military intervention in Western Europe. The major factor that prevented him was the outbreak of revolution in Poland that required Russia's urgent attention.

### Revolution in Poland (*1830–1831*)

*Constitutional System in Poland.*   The kingdom of Poland was placed under Russian control at the close of the Napoleonic wars. The tsar ruled Poland as a constitutional monarch. Poland was granted a constitution guaranteeing freedom of the press and freedom from arbitrary arrest. The kingdom had its own army, and Polish was the official state language. A two-house Diet had the right to consider legislation proposed by an executive council appointed by the king.

*Polish Rebellion and Results.*    Despite Poland's relatively privileged position under Alexander, resentment of Russia remained high and erupted in 1830.

The Russians put down the rebellion with a major military campaign that lasted until the end of 1831. Following the Russian victory, Poland lost its constitutional protections and special status, and it was incorporated into the Russian empire.

### Ties to Austria and Prussia

The shock of the revolutions of 1830 led Russia to agreements with the other conservative powers, Austria and Prussia.

In two meetings in 1833, at Münchengrätz and Berlin, Russia, Austria, and Prussia pledged to cooperate to protect the existing political order in Europe.

### Revolutions of 1848

Starting in France in February 1848, a wave of revolutions swept Europe. Nicholas saw this development as a threat that Russia had to combat.

Russia's response to the revolutions of 1848 marked the high point of its influence as the leading defender of the old order.

*Russia as a Conservative Bastion.*    Russia urged Austria and Prussia to resist the revolutionary movements that threatened to establish constitutional monarchies in those countries. Nicholas pressured the Prussian king, Frederick William IV (r. 1840–1861), not to accept an offer to become monarch of a united Germany.

Russia also supported Austrian efforts to prevent the various peoples within the Austrian empire from breaking away to form independent states.

*Russian Military Intervention in Hungary.*    Russia intervened directly in Hungary in 1849 at the invitation of the Hapsburg emperor, Franz Joseph (r. 1848–1916). His Austrian forces were not strong enough to put down an uprising against Hapsburg authority in Hungary, and Russia was not willing to tolerate a successful national revolution in Eastern Europe. Nicholas' troops suppressed the Hungarian revolution.

### Intervention against Prussia

When Prussia challenged Austria following the revolutions of 1848, Russia supported Austria as the country preserving the existing order.

At Olmütz in 1850, Russian influence pushed the Prussians to accept Austrian domination over German affairs. This agreement promoted Russia's consistent policy of maintaining the traditional political order in Europe.

# The Crimean War

The Crimean War was Russia's most important conflict during the century following the Napoleonic wars. It resulted in a humiliating defeat that not only shattered Russia's international prestige but also highlighted its need for sweeping domestic reforms.

## Origins

The war resulted from Russia's moves to exert an influence over Turkey and the opposition of other powers to these Russian initiatives.

The immediate issue was trivial: Russia objected to Turkish policy toward Christian shrines in Palestine and to the French emperor's claim to be protector of these places. The tsar sent Turkey an ultimatum by personal emissary, Prince Alexander Menshikov (1787–1869). In the next step escalating the crisis, Russia carried out a military occupation of Moldavia and Wallachia.

## War with Turkey (1853)

The first fighting broke out between Russia and Turkey in late 1853. The Russians won a decisive naval victory over the Turks in the Black Sea near Sinope.

## War with Britain, France, and Sardinia

In early 1854, Britain and France, joined by the Italian kingdom of Sardinia, went to war with Russia in defense of Turkey. The

Russians also faced potential opposition from Austria, which was neutral at the war's beginning.

### The Crimean Campaign and the Siege of Sevastopol

The major fighting in the war took place after the allies landed in the Crimea. Following a number of battles, the war centered on the allied siege of the Russian port of Sevastopol. The siege lasted from October 1854 until the Russians abandoned the port in September 1855.

### Treaty of Paris

The peace settlement reflected Russia's defeat in the war. First, it required the surrender of territory: Turkey received from Russia the mouth of the Danube and part of Bessarabia.

The treaty also included the humiliating surrender of Russian rights, including the right to have naval forces or coastal defenses on the Black Sea. Russia also had to give up its claims to be the protector of Orthodox Christians living under Turkish control.

## Implications of Russia's Defeat

Russia was shown to be militarily inferior to the more industrialized countries of Western Europe. Unlike their stand in 1812, the Russians had not been able to defend their own territory against outside invasion.

Thus, the era of Russian power and prestige, begun with the defeat of Napoleon, was over. The expansion of Russian territory, dating back to the era of Peter the Great, had now come to a halt and even been reversed.

# Culture in the Era of Nicholas

The reign of Nicholas saw the development of major Russian literary figures. Their writings and careers often reflected the problems of Russian life and society.

## Alexander Pushkin (1799–1837)

Pushkin is considered to be Russia's greatest poet and a major prose writer. One of his most important works, *Eugene Onegin,* examines Russia's upper-class society. Another, *The Captain's Daughter,* is set in the time of the Pugachev rebellion. A third, *The Bronze Horseman,* raises the question of the role of Peter the Great in Russian history.

Pushkin was an early and prominent target for the harsh censorship that began in the final period of the reign of Alexander I and continued under Nicholas. His writings and sympathy for the Decembrists got him banished to the countryside several times. He was killed in a duel in 1837.

### Michael Lermontov (1814–1841)

A poet and writer of prose, Lermontov is best known for his novel *A Hero of Our Times* (1840). Set in the Caucasus, the novel reflected Lermontov's own military service in this newly won part of the empire.

Critics see the novel partly as a picture of an expanding Russia. They also consider its depiction of freedom in the frontier wilderness as an implied criticism of the harsh and artificial world of the Russian court and bureaucracy.

### Nicholas Gogol (1809–1852)

Gogol's literary masterpieces include a play, *The Inspector General;* his story *The Overcoat;* and his great novel, *Dead Souls.* Published in 1842, *Dead Souls* is a harsh attack on serfdom and a bitterly satirical picture of the Russian countryside and its provincial landowners. Gogol's incorporation of the fantastic and the grotesque in his writing anticipates much of modern literature.

## New Ideologies and the Intelligentsia

Despite the rigor of censorship under Nicholas I, his era saw the development of a sweeping debate about Russia's future. It centered on the significance of Peter the Great and the desirability of following the West or of retaining Russia's special traditions and characteristics.

The issue of Russia's past and future was raised with great force by Peter Chaadaev (1794?–1856) in the 1830s. During the following decades, the debate expanded as groups of "Slavophiles" and

"Westernizers" argued the merits of tradition versus change on the model of Western Europe.

## Chaadaev

Chaadaev presented a negative picture of Russia's past in his *Philosophical Letter* (1836). He insisted that Russia had never been a part of either the West or the East, and he denied any Russian contribution to civilization.

Chaadaev argued that Russia was different from the West, and he challenged the notion that catching up was even a possibility.

## Slavophiles

Led by writers like Alexis Khomiakov (1804–1860), Constantine Aksakov (1817–1860), and Ivan Kireevsky (1806–1856), the group known as the Slavophiles glorified traditional Russian life. They extolled the Orthodox religion, the peasant commune, and historic institutions like the *zemskii sobor*.

They were the first group to challenge the westernizing orientation of Russian culture since the time of Peter the Great.

### The Slavophile View of Peter the Great

Slavophiles condemned Peter for importing Western ideas and institutions, which in their view had destroyed the historic harmony and cooperative spirit of Russian life.

### The Slavophile Program

Slavophiles favored the continuation of the autocracy. On the other hand, they also advocated freedom of speech, limits on the power of the bureaucracy, and the abolition of serfdom.

## Westernizers

The diverse group known as Westernizers rejected the view that Russia was unique. They thought that Peter the Great had played a positive role in beginning to westernize Russia, and they wanted the process to continue.

### Vissarion Belinsky (1811–1848)

Belinsky was a significant figure in the development of the Westernizers' position. He equated progress with westernization and stressed the positive role of Peter the Great in Russian history.

Belinsky set a pattern for future Russian writers. First, as a literary critic, he advanced the influential theory that one must evaluate literary works in part on the basis of their political message. Second, Belinsky used his literary essays to get around the system of censorship. Comments on literature became a means to criticize aspects of Russian life.

Belinsky was the most radical spokesman for the Westernizers' position, and he called for specific, sweeping changes in Russian life. These included an end to serfdom, the disestablishment of the Russian Orthodox Church, and the creation of a democratic government.

### Alexander Herzen (1812–1870)

Herzen was a leading member of the Westernizers in the 1840s. He left Russia in 1847 and spent the remainder of his life in exile in the West.

Following the failure of the Revolution of 1848 in France, Herzen came to question whether Western Europe was breaking a path that Russia should follow. His ideas changed, and he eventually advanced the theory of a Russian brand of socialism founded on the peasant commune.

### Petrashevsky Circle

Members of the Petrashevsky circle met for the discussion of Western ideas during the late 1840s. Beginning with an interest in the French socialist Charles Fourier (1772–1837), the group conducted discussions critical of the existing system in Russia. In 1849 its members were rounded up by the police.

The group is best known for one member, Fedor Dostoevsky (1821–1881), who survived a term of imprisonment in Siberia to become one of Russia's greatest novelists.

## The Economy and the Society

In contrast to that of Western Europe, Russia's economy evolved slowly in the decades up to the middle of the nineteenth century.

Russia saw nothing like the great industrial revolution that began in Britain and spread to the continent of Europe. In agriculture, the institution of serfdom and the inability of most landowners to modernize their estates blocked any major change.

Meanwhile, Russia's population grew rapidly.

## Economic Development

Some signs of economic progress were the establishment of Russia's first railroad line and the growth of an export trade in grain.

### *Railroad Development*

The first major Russian railroad, linking St. Petersburg and Moscow, went into operation in 1851. Compared to leading industrial countries like Britain and Belgium, Russia lagged behind in the size of its railroad network and the speed of railroad construction.

A painful sign of Russia's backwardness was the difficulty the government found in trying to send men and supplies to defend Russian territory during the Crimean War. At the end of the war, there was a total of only 660 miles of track in the entire country.

### *Foreign Trade*

An important sign of trade growth was the shipment of wheat from southern Russia through the Black Sea. Russia thus became an important supplier of food to the industrializing countries of Western Europe.

### *Kankrin and Official Anti-Industrialism*

Some historians attribute Russia's lack of industrial growth in part to the policies of Count Egor Kankrin (1774–1845), the finance minister from 1823 to 1844.

Kankrin saw no value in railroad construction and objected to state loans for industrial development. His policy of high tariffs, which protected new industries, was designed instead to raise money for the government.

## Social Change

### *Population Growth*

Between the end of the eighteenth and the middle of the nineteenth century, the Russian population increased from 36 million to 67 million.

### Urban Life

Russia became a more urbanized society over this period, although it kept its basically rural character. In 1800, about 1.5 million out of a population of 36 million inhabitants of the Russian empire lived in a city. In 1850, some 5 million out of a population of 67 million were city dwellers.

### The Nobility

Many members of the nobility could not maintain their economic position. A number of factors combined to produce the growing indebtedness of gentry landowners: inefficient farming methods, a lack of capital with which to modernize, and a competitive world market for grain exports.

The nobility became increasingly dependent on income from state employment, e.g., as military officers or government officials.

### The Peasantry

At the close of Nicholas' reign, the peasantry still made up eighty-four percent of the population. They were divided almost equally between serfs and state peasants.

The status of the peasantry had scarcely changed since 1825, and Russia was now the only major country of Europe with an extensive system of serfdom.

*By the close of Nicholas' reign, the picture of a powerful Russia, dominating the international order, had disappeared.*

*The Crimean War had demonstrated Russia's military and economic weaknesses. A large agrarian country with a poor peasant population had been invaded and defeated by the smaller but industrialized countries of Western Europe.*

*The persistence of traditional institutions, starting with serfdom, now seemed to place Russia behind other countries of the continent.*

---

## Recommended Reading

Blackwell, William L. *The Beginnings of Russian Industrialization, 1800–1860* (1968).

Curtiss, John Shelton. *The Russian Army under Nicholas I* (1965).

Curtiss, John Shelton. *Russia's Crimean War* (1979).

Evans, J. L. *The Petrashevsky Circle, 1846–1848* (1974).

Gleason, Abbott. *European and Muscovite: Ivan Kireevsky and the Origins of Slavophilism* (1972).

Hoch, Steven L. *Serfdom and Social Control in Russia: Petrovskoe; A Village in Tambov* (1986).

Lincoln, W. Bruce. *In the Vanguard of Reform: Russia's Enlightened Bureaucrats, 1825–1861* (1982).

Lincoln, W. Bruce. *Nicholas I: Emperor and Autocrat of All the Russias* (1978).

Malia, Martin. *Alexander Herzen and the Birth of Russian Socialism, 1812–1855* (1961).

Monas, Sidney. *The Third Section: Police and Society in Russia under Nicholas I* (1961).

Palmer, Alan W. *The Banner of Battle: The Story of the Crimean War* (1987).

Pintner, Walter. *Russian Economic Policy under Nicholas I* (1967).

Riasanovsky, Nicholas. *Nicholas I and Official Nationality in Russia, 1825–1855* (1959).

Riasanovsky, Nicholas. *A Parting of the Ways: Government and the Educated Public in Russia, 1801–1855* (1976).

Riasanovsky, Nicholas. *Russia and the West in the Teachings of the Slavophiles: A Study of Romantic Ideology* (1952).

Rich, Norman. *Why the Crimean War?: A Cautionary Tale* (1985).

Roosevelt, Priscilla Reynolds. *Apostle of Russian Liberalism: Timofei Granovsky* (1986).

Seddon, J. H. *The Petrashevtsy: A Study of the Russian Revolutionaries of 1848* (1985).

Simmons, Ernest J. *Pushkin* (1937).

Squire, P. S. *The Third Department: The Establishment and Practices of the Political Police in the Russia of Nicholas I* (1968).

Stanislawski, Michael. *Tsar Nicholas I and the Jews: The Transformation of Jewish Society in Russia, 1825–1855* (1983).

Walicki, Andrzej. *The Slavophile Controversy: History of a Conservative Utopia in Nineteenth-Century Russian Thought* (1975).

Whittaker, Cynthia. *The Origins of Modern Russian Education: An Intellectual Biography of Count Sergei Uvarov, 1785–1855* (1984).

# CHAPTER 15

## The Era of Alexander II
## (1855–1881)

### Time Line

| | |
|---|---|
| 1855 | Alexander takes throne |
| 1856 | Treaty of Paris ends Crimean War |
| | Secret committee formed to plan emancipation of serfs |
| 1858–1860 | Russia acquires Amur-Ussuri region from China |
| 1861 | Peasant emancipation |
| 1863 | New university statute |
| 1863–1864 | Polish revolt |

| | |
|---|---|
| 1864 | Reform of local government; establishment of the zemstvos |
| | Judicial reform |
| 1865 | Reform of censorship system |
| 1866 | Assassination attempt on tsar |
| 1867 | Sale of Alaska to United States |
| 1868 | Russians take Samarkand |
| 1870–1874 | Miliutin military reforms |
| 1870 | Russia renounces the Black Sea military restrictions |
| 1873–1874 | The movement "to the people" |
| 1873 | Three Emperors' League |
| 1875 | Russia obtains Sakhalin from Japan |
| 1876 | "Land and Liberty" founded |
| 1877–1878 | War with Turkey |
| 1878 | Treaty of San Stefano |
| | Congress of Berlin |
| 1879 | "People's Will" founded |
| 1880 | Loris-Melikov appointed minister of interior |
| 1881 | Alexander assassinated |

The reign of Alexander II brought rapid and intensive change to Russian life. Events moved in marked contrast to the immobility seen during the era of Nicholas I.

The tsar himself took the lead in one sweeping reform: the emancipation of the serfs. Meanwhile, disappointment over the limits of change led to the development of a widespread radical movement calling for change from below. "Populism," with its call for peasant revolution, became a permanent part of Russian political life.

In international affairs, Russia found its role sharply diminished.

*The rise of a powerful Germany was one sign of Russia's declining role in Europe. So too was the way in which Britain and Austria blocked Russian expansion in the Balkans. Meanwhile, in Central Asia and the Far East, Russian territory and Russian influence expanded notably.*

## The New Tsar: Alexander II

### Background and Personality

Unlike his father, Alexander had been trained carefully to become tsar. He had been well educated, and he had traveled widely both inside Russia and in the rest of Europe. Nicholas gave him extensive experience in government affairs.

The new tsar was a political conservative by nature, and as a young man had not shown himself to be more liberal than his father. On the other hand, he had a clear understanding that changes—even sweeping ones—were necessary in some areas of Russian society.

### Reform Initiatives

Alexander initiated a wave of reform beginning with the emancipation of the serfs. His motives in promoting a reform era, whether his own beliefs or his realization of the need to avert revolutionary upheaval, remain uncertain.

## The Problem of Serfdom

Alexander II's personal decision to emancipate the serfs initiated the reform process. Though he never specifically stated his reasons, his decision represented a change in his earlier views. A number of factors had led many Russians, including the tsar, to conclude that serfdom must be eradicated.

### Crisis of the 1850s

By the 1850s, the labor of serfs was no longer economically efficient. As free labor became more common, it was clear that serfdom had become a drag on Russia's economy.

But there were events outside the realm of economics that discredited serfdom.

### Peasant Rebellions

Peasant rebellions were becoming a common feature of Russian rural life. Some historians think that the frequency and destructiveness of these rebellions had been getting steadily worse in the first half of the nineteenth century.

### Moral Concerns

Moral objections to serfdom as cruel exploitation of Russia's peasantry were increasing. Writers like Ivan Turgenev (1818–1883) in his *A Sportsman's Notebook* (1852) portrayed the serfs as suffering human beings.

### Military Weakness

The defeats of the Crimean War led to reexamination of Russian institutions. Serfdom could be blamed for the backwardness of Russia's military industry as well as the ignorance and poor health of the army's rank and file, who were conscripted serfs.

## Reform from Above (1858–1861)

Soon after his coronation, Alexander pushed the gentry to consider ways of emancipating the serfs. The tsar shaped the debate over serfdom by stating that emancipation of the serfs with allotments of land for their use was government policy.

### The Moscow Gentry Address

Alexander first made his intentions clear in an address to the nobility in Moscow in 1856. He told them that it would be preferable to abolish serfdom "from above" than to wait for upheaval from below.

### Study Commissions

In 1858 committees composed of members of the gentry were established in all provinces to study emancipation. An Editing Commission, set up in 1859, examined the individual plans and produced an overall plan that was quickly adopted by the government.

### Emancipation Proclamation (1861)

The manifesto proclaiming the emancipation was signed in March 1861. The major figure in pushing the plan through to approval was the tsar himself.

### Emancipation Provisions

The emancipation was a complex process carried out over a period of several years.

*Allotment of Land.*    Serfdom was abolished for both landowners' serfs and state peasants. Russia's land was split between the gentry landowners and the serfs. The amount of land allocated to the peasants varied from one part of Russia to another.

The serfs were expected to pay for the land they received. The government paid the landowners at once, and the serfs were to repay the government—with "redemption payments"—over a period of forty-nine years.

*The Mir.*    In most parts of Russia, the peasants' land did not go directly into the hands of individual peasants. Rather it was held by the *mir,* the local commune running the affairs of each peasant village. The *mir* was responsible to the tsar's authorities for the tax and redemption payments of all members of the village. In many parts of Russia, the commune redivided the land under cultivation every ten years. Peasant households that had grown in size would get more land at the expense of other households.

### Persistent Problems

The form of the emancipation created difficulties that became increasingly severe over time.

*Loss of Land.*    According to the terms of the emancipation, numerous peasants were entitled to receive half the total land in their region. In practice, many received far less. They were deprived of some of the land they had been tilling themselves, and they often lost the right to use formerly open woods, pastures, and meadows.

*Redemption Payments.*    The need to make redemption payments to the government became a burden peasants could not carry. The debt for unmet redemption payments grew heavier until the payments were ended in 1905.

*Inefficiency.*    Granting land to the communes instead of to individual peasants hindered the development of modern farming. Peasants were unlikely to work efficiently when they might lose part of their farms when the commune redivided all of its land holdings every ten years.

*Difficulty of Leaving the Commune.*    The terms of the emancipation settlement made it difficult for peasants to leave the commune (village organization).

The commune was responsible for the payment of the taxes to the government and for the supply of military recruits. Therefore, it was unlikely to permit members to sever their legal ties to the commune and to cease to fulfill their corresponding obligations. Peasants who succeeded in doing so would leave a heavier burden on those remaining behind.

# Post-1861 Reforms

The emancipation of the serfs required other reforms. Much of Russian life had been constructed around the institution of serfdom. Its abolition required changes in areas including local government, the judicial system, and the military.

## The Zemstvos

The zemstvos were organs of district and provincial government set up by law in 1864. They represented an attempt to solve the longstanding problem of bringing effective administration below the level of the central government. They were also intended to replace the judicial and administrative power that the aristocracy had earlier wielded over their serfs.

### Elections to the Zemstvos

The district zemstvo representatives were elected indirectly and in a way that favored the gentry. District zemstvos, in turn, elected mainly gentry delegates to the provincial zemstvos. In one dramatic way, however, the zemstvos were a new development. Here for the first time elected representatives of all classes worked together.

### Limits on the Zemstvos

The work of the zemstvos was restricted to local activities. Their taxing power was restricted, and they were carefully watched by police and government officials.

### Significance of the Zemstvos

Despite their limitations, zemstvos had an important effect on Russian life. For example, they set up schools and brought doctors and agronomists to help rural communities. However, the most important achievement of the zemstvos may have been to serve as a training ground for political leaders. Some members of the gentry used the success of local self-government to argue for a national representative assembly.

## The Legal System

### New Provisions

The abolition of serfdom led to a new legal system that featured an independent judiciary, trial by jury, and the development of a large class of lawyers.

### Separation of Peasants

In principle, all Russians were equal before the law, but an important exception was made for the peasantry. Cases between peasants were decided by a system of special courts. Separating peasants from the regular judicial system kept up the old distinction between free citizens and serfs.

## The Military

Emancipation meant change in the military, since the old military system had conscripted men from the serf population only and required them to serve for twenty-five years.

Under Minister of War Dmitrii Miliutin (1816–1912), Russia set up a system of conscription modeled on the successes of modern Prussia.

The new system was put in effect in 1874. It made all Russian men liable for conscription, but it reduced the maximum term of service to six years. It also set up reserve forces drawn from men who had completed their active service.

## Education

The early years of Alexander's reign brought liberal trends in education.

### The Universities

The universities regained their autonomy according to the university statute of 1863. In general, the close supervision placed over the universities that had prevailed in the era of Nicholas I was now lifted.

### Elementary Education

Following the institution of the zemstvos, numerous elementary schools were established in European Russia. By 1880, there were more than 22,000 such schools with more than a million students. Most of these schools had been founded as a result of the zemstvo reform of 1864.

## Minorities

### Non-Russian Peoples

Alexander pursued a liberal policy toward the non-Russian half of the empire's population. In Finland, the Diet was allowed to meet and Finnish autonomy was generally respected.

### The Jews

The Jews received markedly better treatment under Alexander than under Nicholas I. The practice of taking disproportionately large numbers of Jewish boys away for military service was ended. Moreover, the government loosened living restrictions on Jews. Educated and prosperous Jews could now leave the western region called the "Pale of Settlement," where formerly they had been required to reside. The Pale consisted of twenty-five provinces: the ten provinces that made up the kingdom of Poland, and fifteen provinces in western and southwestern Russia. The legal restrictions governing where Jews could live, first set down by Catherine the Great in 1791, were strictly enforced. All but five percent of Russia's Jews remained permanent residents of the Pale down to World War I.

# Declining Pace of Reform

Alexander's leadership stimulated the reform movement most effectively in the early 1860s. His energies were directed particularly toward the abolition of serfdom.

However, several events took place following the emancipation of the serfs that seemed to alarm the tsar. These included peasant riots and calls by members of the gentry for a constituent assembly. Soon Alexander faced other unwelcome developments that turned him in a more conservative direction.

## Poland

### Revolt of 1863–1864

Under Alexander Poland regained much of its previous autonomy. Nonetheless, discontent with Russian rule led to a rebellion that broke out in 1863 and was suppressed only the following year.

### Renewed Russian Control

Following the revolt, Poland once again lost its autonomy. The emancipation of serfs here included a generous land settlement for Polish peasants that was designed to penalize Polish landowners. A process of Russification was initiated featuring the use of the Russian language at the University of Warsaw.

## Assassination Attempt on the Tsar (1866)

In 1866 Alexander escaped an assassination attempt at the hands of a crazed student. An investigation of the student's writings revealed him to be a radical democrat who hoped that assassinating the tsar would bring down the entire political order.

## Conservative Trends

Following 1866, Alexander's policies mixed reformist and conservative elements. In areas like the military (see p. 195) and municipal reform change continued. In most respects, however, the government slowed down—and even reversed—earlier moves toward liberalization.

The change was evident in restrictions on the press and in removing politically sensitive cases from the jurisdiction of the regular courts.

# Economic Development

Russian industrial growth continued to be weak in comparison with that of Western European countries.

## Theories of Industrial Development

### A Marxist Interpretation

Soviet Marxist historians have claimed that the emancipation of the serfs set the stage for the rapid expansion of Russian industry. This occurred primarily because the former serfs were now free to become industrial workers.

### An Opposing View

It seems more accurate to say that emancipation had only a limited effect. Peasants were not free to move from the commune, and they did not seem to leave the countryside in large numbers.

Industrial growth was slow, and it was often tied to government efforts.

## The Railroads

An example of government encouragement for industry was the railroad construction policy of Minister of Finance Michael Reutern (1820–1890). Working through private companies, the government provided subsidies and guarantees to promote the construction of railroad lines selected by the government.

# The Revolutionary Movements

During the reign of Alexander II, open opposition to the existing political and social system became more widespread than ever before. The reforms of the 1860s raised expectations for further change, but those expectations were disappointed as the tsar turned in a more conservative direction.

In part, this dissension was due to the freer intellectual atmosphere permitted under Alexander. There was now enhanced scope for the open exchange of opinion. This included discussion of political and economic issues.

## Beginnings in the 1860s

### Gentry Liberalism

During the 1860s, the example of the peasant emancipation encouraged groups among the gentry to call for a limited, constitutional monarchy. After the establishment of the zemstvos in 1864, this "gentry liberalism" found a base in those organs of local government.

### Conspirational Cells

The 1860s also saw the development of cells of more radical opponents of the status quo. A member of one such cell, Serge Nechaev (1847–1882), developed the concept of the dedicated, professional revolutionary working within a system of iron discipline to overthrow the established order.

### Student Protest in the 1860s

During the early 1860s, student disorders appeared for the first time in Russia. Strikes and street demonstrations became common protest devices at the universities of St. Petersburg, Kazan, Kharkov, and Kiev.

Most protests concerned the regulations imposed on student life by university officials. But some protests, even in 1861, had a direct political goal. At St. Petersburg, students demonstrated against the limited character of the government's policy to emancipate the serfs. As the decade continued, political protests became increasingly common.

### Radical Intellectuals of the 1860s

Several young writers in the 1860s set down guidelines for future radical movements.

*Nicholas Chernyshevsky (1828–1889).*   Chernyshevsky, the son of a priest, had a brief career as a journalist and literary critic. He was openly critical of Tsar Alexander's limited policy of changing the status of the serfs and called for revolutionary, not reformist, changes in Russian society.

He was arrested in 1862 and sent off to Siberian exile. In a widely read novel that he wrote in prison, *What Is To Be Done?*, Chernyshevsky called for a new generation of intellectuals who would dedicate themselves to overturning the existing order. Chernyshevsky presented a model of educated and politically engaged revolutionaries out to create a revolution for the benefit of the mass of the population.

*Nicholas Dobroliubov (1836–1861)*.    Dobroliubov, like Chernyshevsky, was a priest's son who took up a career as a writer and literary critic. He echoed Chernyshevsky's call for revolutionary change rather than reform. Dobroliubov's most important contribution to the radical movement in Russia was his insistence that literature must serve political ends.

### Fathers and Sons

Some historians interpret mid-nineteenth century Russian radicalism in terms of different generations, one more radical than the next. In this view, members of the generation of the 1840s were the fathers. They were idealists like Alexander Herzen, reluctant to use violence and hoping for reform from above.

The sons were the generation of the 1860s, personified by Chernyshevsky and Dobroliubov and especially the literary critic Dmitrii Pisarev (1840–1868). They were influenced by modern science and materialism, and they rejected traditional morality. They were attracted to extreme remedies for Russia's failings, and they were willing to use extreme, violent means.

## Revolutionary Populism in the 1870s

The decade of the 1870s witnessed the new development of a broad revolutionary movement. Centered among the educated young people of urban Russia, this "populism" aimed at stimulating a great peasant revolution.

### Herzen

Alexander Herzen was an important theorist behind Revolutionary Populism. Herzen had abandoned the westernizing position (see

Chapter 14) of his younger days. Direct contact with the West had convinced him that Russian socialists would do better to rely on Russian institutions as the basis for a new society.

From exile in London, Herzen called for a Russian socialism based upon the existing institutions of the peasant commune. He appealed to young Russians to go "to the people." It was an ambiguous message that could be interpreted as a call to educate the peasants or to rouse them to revolution.

### Student Movement

In 1873 and 1874, more than 3000 young Russians, many of them students, followed Herzen's call and went "to the people." Some participants in this movement hoped to prepare the peasantry for a future rebellion in which the peasants would be the driving force.

The effort got no effective response. The peasants remained politically passive, and they even handed over to the police many of the students who had come to promote revolution.

### The Role of Women

Women made up a substantial part of the group that went to the countryside in the early 1870s. Despite legal restrictions, many women had managed to attend Russian universities in the 1860s. Others had obtained a higher education abroad, notably in Switzerland.

### The Shift to Terrorism

In the late 1870s following the failure of the movement "to the people," radical attacks on the political and social situation centered in smaller underground organizations.

*"Land and Liberty."* One of these organizations was "Land and Liberty," founded in 1876 and including a diverse group of radicals. Some members wished to continue a campaign of educating and arousing the peasantry. Others favored direct action against the government such as terrorism.

*The "People's Will."* In 1879, "Land and Liberty" split apart over the issue of terrorism. Nonviolent actions had had no effect. The "People's Will" was a small group that broke away to follow a program of assassinating major political leaders. Their members believed that the murder of Russia's leaders would create chaos and bring on mass revolution.

"People's Will" was successful in murdering high government officials and, in 1881, the tsar himself (see p. 205). It was not, however, effective in its larger goal: to arouse popular revolution and bring down the existing political system.

### Anarchism

Another variety of political radicalism was anarchism. Its main spokesmen were two exiles, Michael Bakunin (1824–1876) and Peter Kropotkin (1842–1921).

Bakunin called for the total destruction of the Russian state and an end to all centralized political authority. He wanted a Russian society organized as a federation of peasant communes.

## Foreign Affairs

Compared to what it had done during the period from 1815 to 1855, Russia now played a modest part in international affairs. Its foreign policy was aimed at recovering from the Crimean War, expanding in Central Asia and the Far East, and rebuilding Russia's position in the Balkans.

The crucial diplomatic event during Alexander's reign was the unification of Germany. In this development, Prussia's leader, Otto von Bismarck, successfully manipulated the Russians.

### Russia in Europe

Russia was weakened by its territorial losses and humiliated by the restrictions placed upon its military power in the Black Sea.

#### *Austrian Hostility*

Relations with Russia's longtime ally, Austria, had deteriorated. Austria had taken a hostile position, barely disguised as formal neutrality, against Russia during the Crimean War.

#### *The Polish Problem*

Russia's suppression of the Polish revolt in 1863–1864 (see p. 197) led to further isolation for the tsar's government. The major countries of Western Europe—Britain and France—were openly sympathetic to the Poles.

### German Unification

Russia had a longtime interest in German affairs dating back to the era of Peter the Great. No Russian leader could consider a strong, unified Germany to be a favorable development. But Bismarck skillfully prevented Russia from intervening in his successful move to unify Germany. The Prussian prime minister took two important steps. First, he supported Russian policy in putting down the Polish rebellion. Second, he accepted Russia's move (in 1870) renouncing the restrictions on Russian military power in the Black Sea.

### The Three Emperors' League

*Formation of Alliance.*   A new alliance, the Three Emperors' League (1873), renewed the old tie between Russia and the conservative monarchies of Central Europe: Germany (dominated by the old kingdom of Prussia) and Austria.

*Collapse of Alliance.*   Friction between Russia and its two partners soon ended the alliance. First, Russia took the side of France against Germany during a war scare in 1875. Second, Russian support for Balkan Slavs—Bulgarians, Serbs, and Montenegrins—rebelling against Turkish authority aroused Austrian concerns.

### War with Turkey

The rebellion of Balkan Slavs against Turkish rule pulled Russia into a new conflict with Turkey.

*The Balkan Crisis of 1875–1877.*   Rebellion against the Turks began in Bosnia and Herzegovina in 1875. It led to war against Turkey by Serbia and Montenegro in 1876. The defeat of these Slavic peoples by the Turks roused popular anger inside Russia.

*Aims of Pan-Slavism.*   Pressure for Russian intervention came in particular from followers of Pan-Slavism. These ideologues considered Russia linked as a ''big brother'' to the weaker Slavic peoples of Eastern and Southern Europe.

Some Pan-Slav thinkers like Nicholas Danilevsky (1822–1885) looked to the creation of a great Slavic confederation. Its center would be in Constantinople, and Russia would be its natural leader.

*Practical Effect of Pan-Slavism.*   Pan-Slavs encouraged Russian support for the rebelling Slavic peoples of the Balkans. Russian volunteers, as well as Russian medical and financial aid, entered the Balkan conflict. All these factors reduced official Russian resistance to a new war with Turkey.

*Victory and the Treaty of San Stefano.*   War broke out in the spring of 1877. After a year of hard fighting, Russia won a clear military victory.

The Treaty of San Stefano, signed in March 1878, reshaped the Balkans to reflect Russian wishes. The chief feature of the treaty was the creation of a large, autonomous Bulgarian state.

*Great Power Objections and the Congress of Berlin.*   The treaty seemed to European powers like Britain and Austria to be a plan for Russian domination of the Balkans with the new Bulgaria as a base for spreading Russian influence.

British and Austrian protests led to a congress of the great powers at Berlin in 1878. The Treaty of San Stefano was revised. Much of the territory promised to Bulgaria was left under Turkish control.

*Russian Reaction.*   Like the results of the Crimean War, the results of the Congress of Berlin were viewed as a humiliation for Russia. Once again, more advanced and powerful countries like Britain had forced a Russian retreat.

### Russia in Asia

The reign of Alexander II saw enormous territorial gains in Asia for the Russian empire. An initial success was to establish firm military control over the Caucasus region, which Russia had acquired earlier in the nineteenth century.

#### Central Asia

During these decades, Russian military forces penetrated the desert regions of Central Asia. The Russian empire grew by the addition of territory twice the size of France.

By 1885, the advance had reached and conquered the desert khanates of Kokand, Khiva, and Bokhara. The legendary city of Samarkand fell to the Russians as early as 1868.

### Eastern Siberia and China

The major factor promoting Russian gains in East Asia was the declining power of the Chinese empire.

Led by ambitious officials like Count Nicholas Muraviev (1809–1881), the Russians advanced beyond the border set down in 1689 by the Treaty of Nerchinsk. By 1860, Russia had acquired the left bank of the Amur River and the Ussuri region from China.

### Sale of Alaska

In 1867 the Russian government sold Alaska, where there had been Russian settlers since the middle of the eighteenth century, to the United States. Alaska's economic value seemed small as fur-bearing animals there grew scarce, and the region seemed indefensible against a British attack from Canada.

The American government purchased the region from Russia for approximately $7,000,000.

## The Assassination of the Tsar

Alexander narrowly escaped several assassination attempts by members of the "People's Will." Repressive measures against the conspirators were unsuccessful, and it even seemed that much of the educated public sympathized with some political goals of the radicals.

In the last year of his life, the tsar took up the idea of political reform.

### Loris-Melikov Program

Under Minister of the Interior Michael Loris-Melikov (1825–1888), plans were drawn up to establish a nationally elected body of representatives. They would not have the right to make laws, but they were to have an advisory role on government policy. Some historians see this measure as a step toward the establishment of a parliament and a constitutional monarchy.

### Death of Alexander II

In 1881, the tsar was assassinated after giving tentative approval to Loris-Melikov's proposals. The "People's Will" had condemned

Alexander to death before Loris-Melikov began his work. Nonetheless, the prospect that Russia might move toward gradual reform may have energized the terrorists to remove the tsar as quickly as possible. They saw mild change as a bar to the great national uprising for which they were working.

It remained to be seen whether Alexander II's successor would put the reforms into effect.

## The Arts in the Era of Alexander II

These years brought the emergence of Russia's most famous and influential writers. Dostoevsky and Tolstoy are considered two of the world's greatest novelists. Along with Pushkin and Gogol (see Chapter 14), they are the stellar figures in a "Golden Age of Russian Literature" extending from the 1820s to the late 1880s.

### Leo Tolstoy (1828–1910)

A Russian aristocrat, Tolstoy established himself as a noted writer at an early age. In *War and Peace,* he explored with great psychological insight numerous levels of Russian society at the time of the Napoleonic wars. His other masterpiece, *Anna Karenina,* focuses on personal crisis in a single aristocratic family, but encompasses events like the decline of the nobility and the Russo-Turkish War of 1877–1878.

In his last decades, Tolstoy underwent a religious conversion, retired to his estates to live the simple life of a peasant, and became a bitter critic of modern society.

### Fedor Dostoevsky (1821–1881)

A member of the Petrashevsky circle, Doestoevsky was a noted writer before his arrest and exile to Siberia in 1849 (see Chapter 14). He resumed his writing upon his return, and his greatest novels were published between 1866 (*Crime and Punishment*) and 1880 (*The Brothers Karamazov*).

Dostoevsky's works take place in a Russian setting and often deal with typical questions like the development of terrorist organizations in the 1860s. His renown as a writer, however, comes from his exploration of human psychology, his deep interest in the sources of good and evil, and his belief in the redeeming power of religion.

## Ivan Turgenev (1818–1873)

A less distinguished novelist than Tolstoy or Dostoevsky, Turgenev was a talented writer whose work had wide political ramifications. *A Sportsman's Notebook* (1852) helped promote the idea of emancipating the serfs (see p. 192). *Fathers and Sons* (1862) presented the new, scientifically minded Russian intellectual who was open to radical change and perhaps open to revolutionary activity.

*Russia in 1881 had changed substantially from Russia in 1855. The government had finally addressed the problem of serfdom, and it seemed willing to consider limits on autocracy as well.*

*Nonetheless, difficult problems remained. The abolition of serfdom had left the peasantry impoverished and discontented. The emergence of radical groups, capable of assassinating even the tsar, was a sign of deep domestic divisions. Diplomatic humiliation at the Congress of Berlin was only the latest in a series of indications of how far the advanced countries had outstripped Russia.*

## Recommended Reading

Acton, Edward. *Alexander Herzen and the Role of the Intellectual Revolutionary* (1979).

Billington, James. *Mikhailovsky and Russian Populism* (1958).

Emmons, Terence. *The Russian Landed Gentry and the Peasant Emancipation of 1861* (1968).

Emmons, Terence, and Wayne Vucinich, eds. *The Zemstvo in Russia: An Experiment in Local Self-Government* (1982).

Field, Daniel. *The End of Serfdom: Nobility and Bureaucracy in Russia, 1855–1862* (1976).

Field, Daniel. *Rebels in the Name of the Tsar* (1976).

Gleason, Abbott. *Young Russia: The Genesis of Russian Radicalism in the 1860s* (1980).

Hardy, Deborah. *Land and Freedom: The Origins of Russian Terrorism, 1876–1879* (1987).

Kropotkin, Peter. *Memoirs of a Revolutionist* (1962).

Lampert, Evgenii. *Sons against Fathers: Studies in Russian Radicalism and Revolution* (1965).

Lincoln, W. Bruce. *The Great Reforms: Autocracy, Bureaucracy, and the Politics of Change in Imperial Russia* (1990).

Lincoln, W. Bruce. *Nikolai Miliutin: An Enlightened Russian Bureaucrat* (1977).

Mackenzie, David. *Lion of Tashkent: The Career of General M. G. Cherniaev* (1974).

Mackenzie, David. *The Serbs and Russian Pan-Slavism, 1875–1878* (1967).

Miller, Forrestt A. *Dmitrii Miliutin and the Reform Era in Russia* (1968).

Miller, Martin A. *Kropotkin* (1976).

Owen, Thomas C. *Capitalism and Politics in Russia: A Social History of the Moscow Merchants, 1855–1905* (1981).

Petrovich, Michael. *The Emergence of Russian Panslavism, 1856–1870* (1956).

Pierce, Richard. *Russian Central Asia, 1867–1917* (1960).

Rieber, Alfred, ed. *The Politics of Autocracy: Letters of Alexander II to Prince A. I. Bariatinskii, 1857–1864* (1966).

Starr, S. Frederick. *Decentralization and Self-Government in Russia, 1830–1870* (1972).

Thaden, Edward C. *Conservative Nationalism in Nineteenth-Century Russia* (1964).

Venturi, Franco. *Roots of Revolution: A History of the Populist and Socialist Movements in Nineteenth Century Russia* (1960).

Zelnik, Reginald. *Labor and Society in Tsarist Russia: The Factory Workers of St. Petersburg, 1855–1870* (1971).

# CHAPTER 16

## Russia under Alexander III (1881–1894)

### Time Line

| | |
|---|---|
| 1881 | Alexander III becomes tsar |
| | "Temporary Regulations" issued |
| | Three Emperors' League |
| 1881–1882 | Anti-Jewish rioting in Pale of Settlement |
| 1883 | Plekhanov founds first Russian Marxist organization |
| 1884 | New university statute |
| | Three Emperors' League renewed |
| 1885 | Gentry Land Bank created |

| | |
|---|---|
| 1885–1886 | Bulgarian crisis |
| 1887 | Reinsurance Treaty with Germany |
| | Restrictions on Russian borrowing in Germany |
| | Failed conspiracy to assassinate tsar |
| | Quotas established for admission of Jews to secondary, higher education |
| 1889 | Office of Land Captain established |
| 1890 | New restrictions on rural zemstvos |
| | German government refuses renewal of Reinsurance Treaty |
| 1891 | Trans-Siberian Railroad begun |
| | Jews expelled from Moscow |
| | Franco-Russian Treaty |
| 1892 | New restrictions on urban zemstvos |
| | Sergei Witte appointed minister of finance |
| 1894 | Franco-Russian Military Agreement |

*Alexander III came to power following the death of his father at the hands of revolutionaries. He made his primary goals the repression of revolutionary groups and the preservation of order. The dominant force of his reign was political and social reaction.*

*Alexander III tried to stabilize the countryside by returning power to the gentry. Many of the reforms of the 1860s were curtailed. A policy of ''Russifying'' non-Russian groups also aimed at maintaining a stable, conservative order.*

*But the picture was complicated by government efforts to sponsor industrial growth. This was seen as necessary to keep up Russia's status as a great power, but it tended to promote social and political change.*

*In foreign affairs, the key event was the end of Russia's alliance with Germany. This was followed by a new link to France.*

*An important change also took place in radical circles. Side by side with older groups looking to a peasant revolution, Marxist revolutionaries now appeared as a rival movement to challenge the existing order.*

## The New Tsar: Alexander III

The new tsar was a powerfully built, intellectually limited individual. Until the age of twenty, he had been trained for a military career. Then he became heir to the throne upon the death of his older brother. An important influence on his political education had been Constantine Pobedonostsev (1827–1907), a conservative professor of law who now became one of his key advisers.

## Domestic Policy

After a brief period of hesitation, Alexander III moved to halt pending reforms. Under the influence of Pobedonostsev, he stated his desire to maintain Russia's autocratic form of government.

In particular, the new tsar rejected a proposal to establish a consultative assembly. Such an assembly, envisioned by Alexander II, would have brought together officials and elected representatives to help draft legislation.

### Departure of Liberal Ministers

Four ministers who had served under Tsar Alexander II resigned in May 1881. They included Minister of War Dmitrii Miliutin and Minister of the Interior Michael Loris-Melikov. Advocates of reform, they resigned after Alexander issued an imperial manifesto in which the new tsar committed himself to maintaining the autocracy.

### "Temporary Regulations"

In the summer of 1881, the tsar issued temporary regulations to combat terrorist activity. The regulations gave sweeping powers to provincial governors and the minister of the interior. These included the authority to prohibit public gatherings and to try in military courts individuals considered politically dangerous.

The regulations were renewed regularly and remained in force until the March Revolution in 1917.

## Education

The government tightened controls on education, with rules stringently applied by Minister of Education I.V. Delianov (1818–1897). A law of 1884 ended the autonomy of universities. Rectors and deans were now chosen by the minister of education.

### Restrictions on Students from Poor Families

Students from humble social backgrounds were discouraged from seeking higher education. They faced increased fees to attend secondary school, and university admissions officials were instructed to bar students whose family origins were unsuitable.

### Role of the Orthodox Church

The Orthodox Church was encouraged to expand its role in providing primary education. Church parish schools taught approximately 100,000 pupils in 1881, nearly a million by 1894.

## The Gentry and the Countryside

Alexander III sought to promote the role of the gentry in order to maintain stability in the countryside.

### State Gentry Land Bank

The government created the State Gentry Land Bank in 1885. Its purpose was to provide loans at low rates of interest to members of the nobility to enable them to maintain possession of their land.

### Land Captains

In 1889, the government established the new office of "land captain" to help restore the local powers of the gentry that had been lost in the reforms of the 1860s.

Land captains were to be chosen from the local nobility. They received sweeping powers to control the peasant population. For example, the land captains replaced elected justices of the peace in deciding civil disputes and minor criminal cases.

## Attack on the Zemstvos

The government distrusted the potential autonomy of both rural and urban zemstvos. In 1890, it sought to make the rural zemstvos more reliable by increasing the influence in them of the gentry. Two years later, the urban zemstvos were changed as well. The right to vote was restricted to large property owners. In both cases, the government intended that the zemstvos would now be dominated by reliably conservative social groups.

## Russification of Minorities

The era of Alexander III was marked by a policy of "Russification." In part, this meant eliminating any special political status enjoyed by groups like the Finns within the empire. Russification also included promoting the authority of the Russian Orthodox Church in areas like Poland and the Baltic which were inhabited by members of other religious groups.

### *Promotion of the Russian Language*

The use of the Russian language was imposed in schools, courts, and government offices in non-Russian areas. Centers of minority cultures, like theaters and publishing houses, were shut down.

### *Motives for Russification*

One cause of Russification was growing concern about defending sensitive border areas like the Baltic provinces against powerful neighbors like Germany. Russian leaders feared the territorial ambitions of Imperial Germany, especially in an area like the Baltic. There the German-speaking population was openly attracted to the unified Germany created by Bismarck. A German move to annex some of Russia's Baltic regions seemed a plausible threat after 1871.

Russian concern about a rising sense of national identity in regions like the Ukraine and Armenia also promoted official Russification.

### *The Jews*

The minority group hit hardest by Russification was the Jewish population of the empire. They were restricted to the western provinces (the "Pale of Settlement"), and, in 1891, Jews living in Moscow were expelled to the Pale.

Most Jews were barred from higher education through a rigid quota system. Violent popular attacks on the Jews, called "pogroms," began in 1881. The government took no steps to stop them.

Many Jews reacted to the growing difficulty of their situation by emigrating to other parts of Europe or to the United States. They were the only ethnic group to leave Russia in large numbers during this period.

# Foreign Policy

During these years, Russia pursued an active policy of expanding its influence in Southeastern Europe (the Balkans) and Central Asia. This policy resulted in confrontations with Austria and Great Britain.

Alexander's reign saw the end of Russia's formal diplomatic tie to another conservative monarchy, Germany, in 1890. Soon afterwards, Russia reluctantly turned to the alternative of a link with republican France.

## Three Emperors' League

In 1881, the tie among the three conservative monarchies of Eastern Europe—Russia, Germany, and Austria-Hungary—was reestablished after breaking down in the Balkan crisis three years earlier. The Three Emperors' League was renewed in 1884, and it remained Russia's most significant foreign alliance for most of the decade.

The League rested on such mutual interests as restricting the growth of nationalism in Poland. Nonetheless, clashes between Russia and Austria brought unmanageable strains.

## The Balkans

An important development in the Balkans during these years was the confrontation between Russia and Austria-Hungary. As the power of Ottoman Turkey faded, the two conservative empires of Eastern Europe moved to fill the vacuum.

### The Bulgarian Crisis

Russia's most serious defeat in the Balkans came in Bulgaria starting in 1885. Attempting to dominate the ruler of that country— Prince Alexander (r. 1879–1886)—the Russians roused a storm of ill will. Prince Alexander was forced to abdicate in 1886, but the Bulgarians replaced him with a new monarch favorable to Austria.

### The End of the Three Emperors' League

Russia's recent humiliation at the hands of Austria made it impossible to renew the Three Emperors' League. Russia, however, maintained its link to Germany with a secret agreement, the Reinsurance Treaty of 1887.

## Central Asia

The Russian advance into Central Asia (see Chapter 15) alarmed the British government. War seemed possible in 1885 when Russian troops reached the border of Afghanistan at Pendjeh. London was concerned about the establishment of a Russian controlled region close to India.

In 1886 the two countries agreed to establish a compromise border in Central Asia.

## Break with Germany

Despite Russian efforts, the important diplomatic tie with Germany was broken in 1890. Otto von Bismarck, the architect of the Reinsurance Treaty, was forced from office in early 1890. His successors refused Russian requests to renew the treaty.

The new leaders of German foreign policy thought it would be impossible for Germany to maintain treaty ties with both Russia and Austria-Hungary. Considering the link with Austria-Hungary to be crucial, they decided to let the treaty with Russia lapse.

## Entente with France

Over the next several years, Russia placed France in the position of its chief ally. Russian conservatives, notably the tsar, disliked a tie with Europe's largest republic, but France was an attractive partner after Russia's break with Germany.

### Advantages of an Alliance with France

France offered military cooperation against Germany. In addition, Russia wanted to tap the French money market for financial support for Russian industrialization.

### The Formation of the Alliance

The basis of the alliance was set with a loose agreement in 1891. By the beginning of 1894, the two countries were tied more tightly by a military convention. The link with France remained Russia's most important diplomatic friendship down to the outbreak of World War I.

## Social and Economic Developments

Although Alexander III's government held to a policy of political conservatism, it could not freeze the social and economic status quo. Under three ministers of finance—Nicholas Bunge (in office, 1881–1886), Ivan Vyshnegradsky (in office, 1887–1892), and especially Sergei Witte (in office, 1892–1903)—economic change accelerated as the government promoted industrial growth.

### Witte's Program

Witte insisted that Russia was doomed to political weakness on the world stage unless it industrialized. Far more than his predecessors, he was motivated by a desire to maintain Russia as a great power.

The most significant sign of expanding industrialization was the growth of a system of railroads. Under Witte, the expansion of the railroads became the central element in a general plan for establishing a network of heavy industries.

#### Government Sponsored Industrialization

Witte realized that only government action could speed the process of industrial growth. Therefore, he taxed the peasants heavily in order to provide the necessary financial resources and set up tariffs against foreign manufactured goods. Domestic manufacturers sold rails to the government at two or three times the price asked by foreigners.

#### Results of Witte's Policy

Witte's policy of stimulating the economy by railroad construction led to annual growth rates of seven or eight percent. The most important single railroad project was the construction of the Trans-

Siberian Railroad, which was begun in 1891 (see Chapter 17). With the aid of massive foreign loans (see Chapter 17), Russia's industrial surge continued throughout the 1890s.

## The Countryside: Peasants and Gentry

In the aftermath of the reforms of the 1860s, the position of both the gentry and the peasantry changed substantially.

### The Decline of the Gentry

The gentry found themselves losing their traditional role at the top of the society. Many of them were unable to adjust to new systems of agriculture based on free labor and modern technology. Trained bureaucrats increasingly replaced members of the gentry in the central government.

A clear sign of a declining place for the gentry in rural areas was transfer of land to others. Between the era of the reforms and the eve of World War I, the gentry lost over forty percent of their land.

### Hardships for the Peasantry

Peasants in the countryside faced a number of severe problems. Agriculture organized on a communal basis was backward and inefficient. The economic well-being of the peasantry was also shaken by a vast increase in the size of the population.

The tax burden on the peasants included redemption payments for land received under the emancipation. Moreover, government policy under Sergei Witte added a hidden tax. Witte required the peasants to make tax payments right after harvest time. Thus, they were compelled to sell their grain to the government at an artificially low price.

## Urban Workers

The growth in industry drew substantial numbers of peasants into the industrial cities. Russian factory workers usually kept a strong tie to their native village, and they were still a small social group compared to factory workers in such countries as Britain and Germany. Nonetheless, the urban factory workers were already an important element in Russian life. One sign of their influence was the set of labor laws instituted by Nicholas Bunge as minister of finance. An-

### Plekhanov's Brand of Marxism

Plekhanov tried to apply classic Marxist ideology directly to Russian circumstances. But Russia was behind the rest of Europe: It had not yet had a revolution equivalent to the French Revolution of 1789. This meant that Plekhanov had to plan for two revolutions, or, as he put it, a revolution in two phases.

*The First Phase of the Revolution.* In the first phase, the workers would aid the bourgeoisie to overthrow tsarism. This would set the stage for a long period of capitalist development during which Russia would become an industrialized country. The factory workers would grow in numbers and would organize.

*The Second Phase of the Revolution.* Eventually, the second phase of the revolution would take place. The workers would revolt, seize political power from the capitalist owners of industry, and create a proletarian state.

*The Development of Russia during the Revolution.* A key element in Plekhanov's thinking was the long interval between the two phases of the revolution. This meant that the workers' efforts to promote change would not bring them to power until far in the future.

## The Populists

### The "People's Will"

Following the assassination of Tsar Alexander II (see Chapter 15), the revolutionary populists of the "People's Will" were hunted down. The entire Populist movement faded as a factor in Russian political life.

### The Assassination Plot of 1887

Nevertheless, one action by a small group of Populists helped keep the tsar concerned about his personal safety. A small number of students, including Lenin's elder brother, Alexander Ulianov (1866–1887), made an unsuccessful attempt to murder the tsar. Several of the participants, including Ulianov, were executed.

*The pace of official political change slowed dramatically during the reign of Alexander III. While the tsar promoted an official policy of conservatism, the evolution of Russian radicalism continued. Marxist revolutionaries, who based their plans on the revolutionary potential of the factory workers, emerged alongside the older Populists with their plans for peasant revolution.*

*In two ways, the government itself moved toward radical change. In foreign policy, the end of an alliance with a conservative Germany led to a new tie with France, one of the liberal countries of Western Europe. In economic life, the government began to sponsor rapid industrial growth, a process certain to put new strains on Russian society.*

---

## Recommended Reading

Alston, P. L. *Education and the State of Tsarist Russia* (1969).

Baron, Salo. *The Russian Jew under Tsars and Soviets* (2nd ed., 1976).

Baron, Samuel, *Plekhanov: The Father of Russian Marxism* (1963).

Billington, James. *Mikhailovsky and Russian Populism* (1958).

Byrnes, Robert. *Pobedonostsev: His Life and Thought* (1968).

Katz, Martin. *Mikhail Katkov: A Political Biography, 1818–1887* (1966).

Kennan, George. *The Decline of Bismarck's European Order: Franco-Russian Relations, 1875–1890* (1979).

McKay, John. *Pioneers for Profit: Foreign Entrepreneurship and Russian Industrialization, 1885–1913* (1970).

Naimark, Norman. *Terrorists and Social Democrats: The Russian Revolutionary Movement under Alexander III* (1983).

Offord, Derek. *The Russian Revolutionary Movement in the 1880s* (1986).

Pearson, Thomas S. *Russian Officialdom in Crisis: Autocracy and Local Self-Government, 1861–1900* (1989).

Robbins, Richard G. *Famine in Russia, 1891–1892: The Imperial Government Responds to a Crisis* (1975).

Rogger, Hans. *Russia in the Age of Modernisation and Revolution, 1881–1917* (1983).

Seton-Watson, Hugh. *The Russian Empire, 1801–1917* (1967).

Thaden, Edward C. *Conservative Nationalism in Nineteenth-Century Russia* (1964).

Thaden, Edward C., ed. *Russification in the Baltic Provinces and Finland, 1855–1914* (1981).

Von Laue, Theodore. *Sergei Witte and the Industrialization of Russia* (1963).

Whelan, Heide W. *Alexander III and the State Council: Bureaucracy and Counter-Reform in Late Imperial Russia* (1982).

Wildman, Allan. *The Making of a Workers' Revolution: Russian Social Democracy, 1891–1903* (1967).

Zaionchkovskii, P. A. *The Russian Autocracy under Alexander III* (1976).

# CHAPTER 17

## The Era of Nicholas II
## (to 1906)

### Time Line

| | |
|---|---|
| 1894 | Nicholas II becomes tsar |
| 1897 | Witte establishes gold standard |
| 1898 | First Congress of Russian Marxists |
| 1901 | Formation of Socialist Revolutionary Party |
| 1902 | Lenin writes *What Is To Be Done?* |
| 1903 | Second Congress of Russian Marxists |
| 1904 | Outbreak of Russo-Japanese War |

| January 1905 | Surrender of Port Arthur |
| | Bloody Sunday |
| February–March 1905 | Battle of Mukden |
| May 1905 | Battle of Tsushima |
| June 1905 | Mutiny on *Potemkin* |
| August 1905 | Government offers "Bulygin Duma" |
| September 1905 | Treaty of Portsmouth |
| October 1905 | General strike |
| | St. Petersburg Soviet formed |
| | October Manifesto |
| December 1905 | Repression of Moscow Uprising |

*At the turn of the twentieth century, Nicholas II and his government struggled against growing problems at home and abroad. The new tsar tried to maintain the existing political and social order, but he faced increasing opposition.*

*The government itself promoted trends that produced deep change. Under the guidance of Minister of Finance Sergei Witte, Russia's government followed a policy of rapid industrialization, certain to shake the existing system.*

*A nationwide revolution exploded as a result of the military disasters and strains on the home front in the Russo-Japanese War. The revolution reached its peak in the final months of 1905. Faced by a threat to the monarchy itself, Nicholas reluctantly issued the October Manifesto, which seemed to pledge a constitution and a representative body or "Duma."*

# Nicholas II (1868–1918)

The last Tsar of Russia came to the throne upon the sudden death of Alexander III in 1894 (see Chapter 16). Only twenty-six years old, the new tsar soon proved as rigid a conservative as his father. Unlike Alexander, Nicholas was weak as well as narrow minded. He also showed himself to be dogged and stubborn.

## Marriage and Family

In 1894, Nicholas married Alexandra of Hesse-Darmstadt (1872–1918). They had several daughters before Alexandra gave birth to a son, Alexis (1904–1918), first in line to inherit the throne.

Nicholas' family influenced him in two crucial ways. First, his wife proved even more reactionary than the tsar himself and supported his instincts against reform. Second, Alexandra's unsavory associates helped to undercut the prestige of the imperial family and the monarchy itself. The poor health of Alexis, who suffered from hemophilia and faced death from uncontrolled bleeding as the result of even a slight injury, opened the doors of the imperial family to a parade of charlatans and sleazy faith healers, most notably Rasputin.

## Political Philosophy

Like Alexander, Nicholas saw no justification in calls for political change. He considered himself the divinely appointed and unlimited monarch ruling over the empire and its people. The tsar was unable or unwilling to see the difference between proposals for moderate reform presented by respectable members of society and the subversive plotting of irreconcilable revolutionaries.

## A Policy of Reaction

The main lines of domestic political policy remained unchanged under the new tsar. Like his father, Nicholas barred moves toward a constitution or representative institutions that would limit the monarchy. Nicholas also pursued a policy of harsh Russification of minority groups.

### Gentry Liberalism

In 1895, Nicholas received representatives of the zemstvos, who requested a modest consultative role in the national government. Nicholas dismissed the idea without reservations, calling even these suggestions ''senseless dreams.''

The tsar's unwillingness to consider even moderate plans for reform pushed liberals to the left. Without hope for peaceful change, they found themselves more sympathetic to the radical groups that called for violent opposition to tsarism.

### The Nationalities

Like his father, Nicholas pursued a policy of ''Russification'' against the non-Russian peoples of the empire. Particular targets included the Jews and the Finns.

*Jews.*    Jews were subject to tightened requirements to live in the Pale of Settlement. Their educational opportunities were curtailed. Worst of all, the government stood aside when popular anti-Semitism erupted in the form of mass violence.

*Finns.*    Finland's special status within the Russian empire came under direct attack. Finland's political autonomy was restricted in 1898. Three years later, Finland lost the right to maintain a separate army.

## Witte and Industrialization

While Nicholas tried to halt political change, he was persuaded to permit the government to sponsor massive economic development.

The guiding figure in the program of speedy industrialization was Sergei Witte. Minister of finance under Alexander III (see Chapter 16), he remained in that post until 1903.

Witte used political arguments to keep the tsar's support. Unless industrialized, he insisted, Russia would be unable to maintain its position as one of the great powers of Europe.

### Railroad Construction

Witte's effort to promote industrial growth centered on the building of railroads. A good railroad network connecting the different regions of the empire aided industrial production at the same time that it provided mobility for the army to defend the country. Most important, railroad construction stimulated the growth of other industries.

The railroad network expanded rapidly. Over 10,000 miles of

new track were laid in the years 1896–1900 alone. In all, Russia's railroads had grown from 14,000 miles in 1881 to 35,000 at the turn of the century.

The showpiece project in Witte's construction program was the Trans-Siberian Railroad. Completed just before the Russo-Japanese War, it permitted a million new settlers to move to Siberia by 1902. The railroad promoted Russia's penetration of northern China, thus heightening the tensions with Japan that led to war in 1904 (see p. 231).

### High Protective Tariffs

Witte was willing to pay high prices for rails produced in Russian factories rather than buy such goods abroad. Behind high tariff barriers, Russia's new iron and steel industries grew on the basis of producing supplies for the rail system.

### Foreign Capital

Heavy taxes on the Russian people paid only some of the costs of industrialization. Witte's policies depended on borrowing large sums abroad, especially in France, Britain, Belgium, and the United States.

An important step in attracting foreign capital was putting Russia's currency on the gold standard in 1897.

### Social and Political Consequences of Industrialization

By the time Witte left the post of minister of finance in 1903, Russia had made impressive progress in becoming an industrialized country. It had a substantial iron and steel industry and textile centers such as Moscow and Lodz. Oil was being drawn from wells in the Caucasus.

The number of factory workers grew rapidly, notably in major cities like Moscow and St. Petersburg. The census of 1897 showed that more than 2.5 million Russians now labored in factories. Their harsh working conditions and poor housing made them a potentially dangerous political force.

#### *Danger to the Political Order*

Since much industrialization had taken place around important government centers like St. Petersburg, unrest among factory workers meant violence at the country's political heart. Mass industrial unrest directly threatened the political order, and the concentration of workers in cities facilitated group action.

### Effects on the Peasantry

Rapid industrialization put strains on the rural population as well. Peasants were hit by heavy taxes designed to pay for industrial growth. At the same time, industrial expansion offered the peasants no immediate gain. Until industry began to produce inexpensive consumer goods, average Russians could expect no rise in their standard of living.

# The Revolutionary Movements

The first half of Nicholas' reign saw important developments among radical opponents of the monarchy and the existing social system.

## The Marxists

The industrialization of Russia and the spread of Marx's writings stimulated the development of a number of underground Marxist organizations. These emerged in both Russian areas and non-Russian areas, including Poland, the Baltic provinces, Georgia, and Armenia.

Three important questions confronted these Marxist groups. First, could they construct a single party as a center for the Marxist movement? Second, what kind of program would serve best to attract the support of the proletariat and to promote revolutionary change? Third, how could the doctrines of Marxism, which presupposed an overwhelmingly urban society, be adapted to agrarian Russia?

### Congress of 1898

The first meeting of Marxists hoping to create a united movement took place at the White Russian city of Minsk in 1898. It was sponsored by the Jewish Bund, an organization based on Jewish proletarians in Lithuania, Poland, and Russia.

This meeting proclaimed the founding of a single party, the Russian Social-Democratic Workers' Party or RSDWP.

Shortly afterwards, most of the delegates were arrested. Thus, this first Marxist organizing effort failed to produce permanent results.

### Legal Marxism

An important development within Russian Marxism was "Legal Marxism" as formulated by thinkers like the economist Peter Struve (1870–1944) and the philosopher Nicholas Berdiaev (1874–1948).

Such figures were influenced by the German Marxist Eduard Bernstein (1850–1932), who played down the need for violent revolution in bringing victory to the proletariat. Struve's favorite theme from Marx was the inevitability of industrial development, even in Russia. Struve hoped the establishment of capitalism in his country would lead logically but peaceably to socialism.

### Emergence of Lenin

A far more radical variety of Russian Marxism developed around Vladimir Lenin (born Vladimir Ulianov) (1869–1924). The brother of a Populist executed in 1887, Lenin offered a brand of Marxism based on an elite political party.

In his book *What Is To Be Done?*, published in 1902, Lenin argued that an effective Marxist organization in Russia had to consist of dedicated full-time revolutionaries.

### Lenin's Concept of a Revolutionary Party

The party for which Lenin called was to be secret, disciplined, and set up in a strict hierarchical organization.

Lenin's party was not designed to represent the wishes of the factory workers. Lenin believed that the workers, left to their own instincts, would choose reforms in wages and working conditions over political revolution. Thus Lenin stressed the leading role of the party. It was the party that must mobilize and direct the workers toward the goal of overturning the existing political and economic order.

### Congress of 1903

In 1903, Russian Marxists gathered for a second time in an attempt to organize a united movement. About fifty delegates met in Brussels; however, they were compelled by the police to move their meeting to London.

The congress saw bitter clashes between Lenin and rival leaders, including Julius Martov (1873–1923), over questions of organization and policy. Lenin maintained his view that the party must consist of a disciplined elite. Martov favored a broad party open to all who accepted Marx's principles.

### Division between Bolsheviks and Mensheviks

Though Lenin failed to gather a majority of the delegates to back him on the concept of an elite party, he used his success on other issues to label his followers "the majority faction" or "Bolsheviks." The group around Martov came to be called "the minority faction" or "Mensheviks."

The factions that emerged and clashed in 1903 never eliminated their disagreements. Thereafter, Bolsheviks and Mensheviks developed sharply different organizations, programs, and expectations for a future revolution.

## The SRs

Radicals who based their hopes on peasant revolution formed a new organization, the Socialist Revolutionary Party (or SRs) in 1901.

Heirs to the peasant radicalism of the nineteenth-century Populists, the SRs appealed specifically to the rural masses who were the majority of the Russian population.

In addition to educational work among the peasantry, some SRs resorted to terror against tsarist officials.

# Foreign Affairs

## Expansion in the Far East

Tensions between Russia and Japan developed over a decade before the outbreak of war in 1904. Russia's growing interest in the Far East collided with Japanese expansion on the continent of Asia.

### The Collapse of China

The first direct encounter between Russia and Japan took place in 1895 following Japan's successful war against China. Japan demanded and received substantial territorial gains in the peace settlement, the Treaty of Shimonoseki (1895).

Russia, along with France and Germany, prevented Japan from profiting fully from the treaty. The Japanese were forced to return to China the Liaotung Peninsula with its valuable seaport, Port Arthur. Two years later, the Russians infuriated the Japanese *by taking* for themselves much of the Liaotung Peninsula, including Port Arthur, from China.

### The Boxer Rebellion

Tensions increased in 1900 when an antiforeign Chinese organization called the Boxers attacked foreigners. Troops from several European nations occupied portions of China in response to the Boxers. The Russians placed their troops in Manchuria, a highly industrialized part of northern China where Russian interests owned the East China Railway.

### The Manchurian Problem

An important cause of war was Russia's refusal to evacuate Manchuria. Japan was establishing itself on the nearby Korean peninsula. At the same time, Russian business interests, including close associates of the tsar, were trying to penetrate the region of Korea around the Yalu River.

The Japanese repeatedly sought a Russian withdrawal from Manchuria. Russian stubbornness on this issue may have been based in part on a belief that Japan was only a weak military adversary.

## War with Japan

During the Russo-Japanese War of 1904–1905, the Russians suffered an unbroken string of military defeats both on land and on sea. Despite its larger population, Russia proved to be inferior to Japan in both military leadership and military technology.

That the conflict ended with a relatively mild peace settlement for the Russians was due to two factors. First, the Japanese as well as the Russians were exhausted after a year and a half of fighting. Second, Sergei Witte, the former minister of finance, proved a skilled and successful diplomat.

### The Assault on Port Arthur

The war began with a successful attack (February 1904) by the Japanese navy against the main Russian fleet then stationed at Port Arthur. The Japanese attacked before war had been formally declared. Nonetheless, Russian commanders in the Far East had not evaluated the tense diplomatic situation, and they failed to set up proper defenses.

The Japanese army soon lay siege to Port Arthur, which fell in January 1905.

### The Campaigns in Manchuria and Northern Korea

With control of the sea assured, Japanese forces poured into Korea and Manchuria. Russian forces fought tenaciously, and some battles, like the Battle of Mukden (February–March 1905), lasted for weeks. But the course of the war saw the Russians pushed backward.

The land war brought encounters between huge armies accompanied by heavy losses for both sides, foreshadowing the First World War. For example, in the Battle of Mukden, each side put more than 300,000 men into combat. The Russians suffered 60,000 casualties, the Japanese at least 40,000.

### Expedition of the Baltic Fleet

In a desperate move to regain the initiative in the Far East, the Russian government sent its Baltic Fleet under Admiral Zinovii Rozhdestvensky (1848–1909) on an eight-month voyage around Africa to the war zone. The fleet's mission was to relieve Port Arthur. But even after news had come that Port Arthur had fallen in January 1905, the fleet was ordered to continue its voyage.

Its mission uncertain and its ships slow and poorly armed compared to those of the Japanese, this was what historian Richard Hough called "the fleet that had to die."

### Battle of Tsushima

The fleet suffered the final military catastrophe of the war. In May, it was thoroughly defeated by the Japanese at the Battle of Tsushima, in the strait between Korea and Japan.

## The Peace Conference

Peace negotiations were held at Portsmouth, New Hampshire, under the auspices of President Theodore Roosevelt.

### The Role of Theodore Roosevelt

Roosevelt was interested in promoting a balance of power in the Far East. He had long admired the Japanese and favored Japanese expansion at Russian expense, but he did not want to see the Russians crushed. He had indicated to the Japanese as early as June 1904 that he would make diplomatic efforts to end the war in a way favorable for them.

### The Role of Witte

Witte had been appointed, against his will, to lead the Russian delegation. Accompanied by well-informed Russian military leaders, he knew that the Japanese forces were worn down despite their land and naval successes. In the end he was able to arrange a decent settlement from the Russian point of view.

### Treaty of Portsmouth (September 1905)

Russia was forced to accept a Japan that was larger and more influential than it had been before the war. The Japanese got effective control of Korea. They also obtained the Russian lease on the Liaotung Peninsula along with Port Arthur.

The Russians, however, escaped without paying an indemnity to Tokyo. The only Russian territory lost to Japan was the southern half of Sakhalin Island, which Russia had obtained in 1875.

## Revolution at Home

The Revolution of 1905 developed partly from the strains of the Russo-Japanese War on Russia's population and the government's loss of prestige as its forces suffered a string of defeats. These elements combined with longstanding discontent within Russian society. Even before war broke out, signs of severe problems in the country could be seen in rural unrest in Kharkov and Poltava provinces. Indications of mass unrest in the cities appeared in events such as the general strike in Rostov in 1902.

In some ways, the revolution was violent from the start. Terrorists carried out spectacular assassinations early in the war. For example, Minister of the Interior Viacheslav Plehve (1846–1904) was killed in July 1904. But during that year, the most important opposition to the government came from the liberal, educated groups of Russian society. In 1905, however, the revolution became a mass movement touching a large part of the empire's population.

## 1904 Rumblings: Liberal Protests

A clear sign of discontent with the tsarist system came in the fall of 1904. Educated Russians gathered in banquets and professional meetings to demand political reform. Their most important objective was an elected body of representatives to limit the power of the monarchy.

There were signs that such moderate protests were inciting the factory workers. By the start of 1905, strikes with political goals took 140,000 workers in St. Petersburg away from their jobs.

## 1905: Mass Unrest

The crucial trend in 1905 was the spread of political protest to the mass of the population. For the first time the tsarist system faced a simultaneous challenge in urban and rural areas.

### Bloody Sunday

One event began the waves of popular protest that marked the year.

On January 22, 1905, thousands of factory workers in St. Petersburg set off to petition the tsar to ease their difficulties with unemployment and wartime inflation. They were led by Father Gapon (1870–1906), an Orthodox priest who had sponsored workers' organizations for several years with government approval.

The massacre of hundreds of workers as they approached the Winter Palace set off a wave of strikes and demonstrations.

### Reform Efforts: Bulygin

The government no longer held fast against all political reform. In a hesitant and grudging way, it offered a series of concessions such as increased religious freedom.

The most important of these concessions came in August when the government offered to permit a limited national assembly. This "Bulygin Duma," named after Russia's minister of the interior, Alexander Bulygin (1851–1919), had no effect in quieting the country.

### Potemkin Mutiny

The mutiny of the crew of the battleship *Potemkin* in Odessa harbor (June 1905) was a memorable sign of the decline of government authority. The crew seized the vessel, put out to sea, and sailed to Romania.

### St. Petersburg Soviet

The maximum danger to the government arose when opposition elements gathered under a single center of authority. This was the significance of the St. Petersburg Soviet.

The Russian word *soviet* means "council." The St. Petersburg Soviet was originally a council of elected workers' representatives chosen to direct a spontaneous general strike. The strike began in October and spread through much of the empire.

*Role of Leon Trotsky (1879–1940).* The St. Petersburg Soviet found a colorful and effective leader in its vice-chairman, the young Marxist Leon Trotsky. Neither a Bolshevik nor a Menshevik, Trotsky was an independent, highly talented orator and organizer. He had returned to Russia from exile in Western Europe at the start of 1905.

# The Settlement

The general strike pushed the tsar to make concessions. He did so with reluctance, having been unable to find a capable figure willing to assume the dictatorial powers needed to repress the revolution. The logical candidate for dictator, the tsar's uncle, Grand Duke Sergei (1857–1905), had been assassinated by terrorists in February.

Thus Nicholas grudgingly issued the October Manifesto, which seemed to grant the longstanding demands of Russian liberals.

## The October Manifesto

The manifesto promised Russians civil liberties and an elected Duma based upon universal suffrage. No law was to be passed without the approval of the Duma.

## The Aftermath

The October Manifesto satisfied the political demands of moderate supporters of the Revolution.

With the revolutionary coalition now weakened, the government arrested the leaders of the St. Petersburg Soviet.

A final outburst of revolutionary activity in the cities took place in Moscow in December. It was harshly repressed by elite guards regiments of the Russian army.

*Nicholas began his reign with the intention of maintaining the conservative political status quo. Nonetheless, events escaped his control.*

*The course of Russian foreign policy led to a disastrous confrontation with Japan in the Far East. The strains of industrialization created mass discontent at home. The desire for political change became evident in groups ranging from middle-class and gentry liberals to Marxist and Populist revolutionaries.*

*Following the Revolution of 1905, the tsar was forced to promise a constitution and a national parliament. Thus, the first phase of Nicholas' reign seemed to end with Russia pointed toward the model set by Western Europe.*

## Recommended Reading

Ascher, Abraham. *The Revolution of 1905: Russia in Disarray* (1988).

Bushnell, John. *Mutiny and Repression: Russian Soldiers in the Revolution of 1905–1906* (1985).

Charques, Richard. *The Twilight of Imperial Russia* (1958).

Edelman, Robert. *Proletarian Peasants: The Revolution of 1905 in Russia's Southwest* (1987).

Engelstein, Laura. *Moscow, 1905: Working-Class Organization and Political Conflict* (1982).

Esthus, Raymond A. *Double Eagle and Rising Sun: The Russians and Japanese at Portsmouth in 1905* (1988).

Glickman, Rose L. *Russian Factory Women: Workplace and Society, 1880–1914* (1984).

Haimson, Leopold. *The Russian Marxists and the Origins of Bolshevism* (1955).

Hamburg, Gary. *Politics of the Russian Nobility, 1881–1905* (1984).

Harcave, Sidney S. *First Blood: The Russian Revolution of 1905* (1964).

Hough, Richard. *The Potemkin Mutiny* (1961).

Johnson, Robert E. *Peasant and Proletarian: The Working Class of Moscow at the End of the Nineteenth Century* (1979).

Judge, Edward. *Plehve: Repression and Reform in Imperial Russia, 1902–1904* (1983).

Keep, John. *The Rise of Social Democracy in Russia* (1963).

Mehlinger, Howard, and John Thompson. *Count Witte and the Tsarist Government in the 1905 Revolution* (1972).

Pipes, Richard. *Struve: Liberal on the Left* (1970).

Reichman, Henry. *Railwaymen and Revolution: Russia, 1905* (1987).

Rogger, Hans. *Jewish Policies and Right Wing Politics in Imperial Russia* (1986).

Sablinsky, Walter. *The Road to Bloody Sunday* (1976).

Seregny, Scott. *Russian Teachers and Peasant Revolution: The Politics of Education in 1905* (1989).

Suhr, Gerald. *1905 in St. Petersburg: Labor, Society, and Revolution* (1989).

Theen, Rolf H. W. *Lenin: Genesis and Development of a Revolutionary* (1973).

Verner, Andrew M. *The Crisis of Russian Autocracy: Nicholas II and the 1905 Revolution* (1990).

Von Laue, Theodore. *Sergei Witte and the Industrialization of Russia* (1963).

Weissman, Neil. *Reform in Tsarist Russia: The State Bureaucracy and Local Government* (1981).

Wolfe, Bertram. *Three Who Made a Revolution* (1948).

# CHAPTER 18

## The Era of Nicholas II
## (1906–1914)

### Time Line

| | |
|---|---|
| May 1906 | Fundamental Laws promulgated |
| | First Duma opens |
| July 1906 | Stolypin becomes premier |
| | Vyborg Manifesto |
| November 1906 | Initiation by decree of Stolypin land reforms |
| March 1907 | Second Duma opens |
| June 1907 | Stolypin changes the election law |
| August 1907 | Treaty with Britain |

| 1907–1912 | Third Duma |
| --- | --- |
| 1910–1911 | Stolypin land reform laws passed by Duma |
| June 1910 | Stravinsky's *Firebird* presented in Western Europe |
| January 1911 | Western Zemstvo Bill defeated |
| September 1911 | Assassination of Stolypin |
| January 1912 | Prague conference of Lenin's Bolsheviks |
| November 1912 | Fourth Duma opens |
| October 1912–May 1913 | First Balkan War |
| July–August 1913 | Second Balkan War |
| June 1914 | Tsar considers abolition of Duma |

*After 1905, Russian history was marked by significant developments in government and dramatic trends in foreign affairs.*

*The decisive trend of the period came in foreign affairs. Russia solidified its ties to France. At the same time, the Russians collided repeatedly with Austrian power in the Balkans.*

*At home, the major event was the establishment of the Duma and a limited constitution. A number of political parties like the Cadets led by Paul Miliukov operated openly, a first in Russian history. The most significant leader of the time, Prime Minister Peter Stolypin, pursued an imaginative program of rural reform.*

*The tsar remained at heart an unlimited monarch. Meanwhile, Lenin's Bolsheviks continued to work to overthrow the existing political and economic system. Thus, important elements on both the right and the left maintained the positions they had held prior to 1905.*

## The New Political Order, 1906–1907

The new political order faced severe difficulties from the start. The tsar was reluctant to concede any legal authority to the Duma. He not only regretted the concessions he had made in 1905 but also moved repeatedly to cancel their effect.

On the other hand, even though the Duma was elected in a complex way designed to restrain popular control, representatives of the people presented a call for political and social change.

Several parties now appeared. Most notable was the Cadet party, which was committed to create a parliament on the British model. This meant a government cabinet and prime minister responsible to a majority in the Duma. Others, particularly the Octobrists, were satisfied with the concessions given in the October Manifesto.

Even a politically moderate party like the Cadets called for the redistribution of noblemen's landed estates.

### The Fundamental Laws

The new political order was most clearly defined in the Fundamental Laws, issued by the government in May 1906.

The tsar's autocratic power was confirmed. For example, he appointed and dismissed ministers and conducted foreign policy. The government, moreover, had extensive power to govern by decree.

In contrast, the Duma's power was highly restricted. The tsar could dismiss it whenever he chose. Its laws could be blocked by the tsar or by the partly appointed State Council. Its authority over financial legislation was severely limited.

### The First Duma, 1906

Elections to the First Duma began in March, and the Duma met in May 1906. Dominated by the Cadet party, the Duma clashed with the government at once over the issue of land reform. It quickly became clear that the government wanted the Duma to occupy only a minor role in Russian affairs. The Duma, on the other hand, was out to initiate major changes.

After less than three months, the Duma was dismissed.

### The Vyborg Manifesto

Following their dismissal, several hundred Duma deputies gathered in Finland and issued the Vyborg Manifesto. The document reflected the bitter political divisions between the Duma and the government. The deputies called on the people to refuse to pay taxes or obey the conscription laws until the Duma was called back into session.

## The Rise of Stolypin

After the dissolution of the First Duma, Peter Stolypin (1862–1911) took over the post of premier from Ivan Goremykin (1839–1917).

A tough and energetic leader, Stolypin from his first months in office brought tightened government control over the country. Punitive expeditions, featuring military courts and numerous executions by hanging, were directed against centers of peasant unrest in the Baltic region.

Stolypin also tried to manipulate elections to the Second Duma to produce a more conservative assembly.

## Rural Reform

Stolypin moved at once to stabilize the countryside by freeing the peasant population from the burden of the commune. Under the Stolypin reforms, a peasant could consolidate the strips of land he held under the commune into a single parcel. He could then leave the commune entirely, setting up as an independent farmer.

Stolypin hoped to create a class of prosperous conservative farmers who would be a barrier against rural revolution.

## The Second Duma, 1907

Despite the government's effort to influence the elections, the Second Duma, which opened in March 1907, was even more radical than the first. Disputes with the government over how to deal with terrorism led Stolypin to dissolve this Duma. Like the first, the second met for less than three months.

## The Coup of June 1907

Following the dissolution of the Second Duma, Stolypin altered the election law without the Duma's consent. This violated the Fundamental Laws, but Stolypin hoped the change would produce a Duma that the government could more readily control.

The new election law reduced the number of deputies representing the peasantry and non-Russian minorities. It increased the number of deputies representing more conservative groups like the gentry.

# The Dumas, 1907–1914

## The Third Duma, 1907–1912

The Third Duma was the only one to complete its full five-year term. It avoided controversies such as those that had brought the first two dumas to an early end. Instead, it produced important results in the field of education. A law passed in 1908 vastly expanded the opportunities for Russian children to get a primary education. It set the goal of eliminating illiteracy by 1922.

### Interpellation

Even the conservative Third Duma took on a critical role at times. It used its power of "interpellation" against government ministers. This let the Duma officially and publicly interrogate figures like the minister of the interior over their official conduct.

### Stolypin's Decline

Stolypin's position weakened as Tsar Nicholas came to feel more secure with the return of peace and quiet to the country. The tsar had no desire to maintain a talented and perhaps ambitious chief minister in office.

*Western Zemstvo Law.*    The relationship between the monarchy and Stolypin was severely shaken by the 1910 crisis over the Western Zemstvo Law. The law was intended to establish zemstvos in six provinces of the western part of the empire. Such local representative institutions would cut down the power of the Polish landowners in the region. The measure passed the Duma, the lower chamber of the country's two-chamber representative body, but Russian conservatives blocked the measure in the State Council, the upper chamber.

Stolypin insisted that the tsar put the law into effect by decree. He backed up his demand by threatening to resign. The tsar gave in, but he never forgave Stolypin for pressing him in this manner.

*Stolypin and Rasputin.*    Stolypin suffered as well for his criticism of Grigory Rasputin (1864?–1916). Rasputin was the latest and most influential of the disreputable faith healers who had gathered around the imperial family.

*Assassination of Stolypin*

In September 1911, shortly before the conclusion of the Third Duma, Stolypin was assassinated. By the time of his death, he had lost the favor of the tsar. Nevertheless, he was the last leader of notable talent to serve Nicholas II.

## The Fourth Duma, 1912–1914

The Fourth Duma had no record of substantial activity before the outbreak of war in 1914. During the conflict, however, it came to play a significant role in national life (see Chapter 19).

## The Tsar's Opposition to the Duma System

In 1913 and 1914, the tsar, encouraged by several of his ministers, considered returning Russia to the political system that had existed before the Revolution of 1905. Another possibility that was seriously considered was to end the Duma's authority in making laws. This would leave a Duma with only the power to advise the tsar.

Thus, as Russia approached World War I, the tsar continued to see the Duma as an unnecessary and even dangerous institution.

# Revolutionary Movements

During the Duma period, Russia's revolutionary parties entered a time of apparent decline. The government effectively restored order, and Stolypin's agrarian reforms threatened to create permanent stability in the countryside.

## Lenin's Revisions of Marxism

Though Russian Marxists spent the years after 1905 in a series of internal conflicts, there were two important developments. First, a formal split occurred between Lenin's Bolshevik faction and the rest of the party. Second, Lenin's revisions of the classical Marxist theory of revolution (see Chapter 16) came to include an important innovation: an alliance between factory workers *and peasants* to carry out a revolution. Marx had not seen the peasants as a revolutionary force.

### 1912: Formal Break in the Marxist Movement

A series of meetings, including the Stockholm Conference of 1907, took place to create a unified Russian Marxist party. Lenin was disturbed by these efforts, because they had the effect of submerging his Bolshevik faction in a majority unsympathetic to his views.

In 1912, Lenin called a conference of his followers at Prague. It resulted in a clear break between Lenin's faction and the other groups within Russian Marxism.

### Lenin's Theory of Revolution

In the years after 1905, Lenin developed his views on how revolution in Russia should be conducted.

He reached two important conclusions, both of which set him further apart from groups like the Mensheviks. He stated that the first of the coming revolutions, in which the old monarchical order would be overthrown, could be carried through by the workers and the peasantry alone. Although, according to Marxist theory, a bourgeois revolution to overthrow the monarch had to occur (see Chapter 16), in Russia the bourgeoisie was too weak to carry it out in Lenin's view.

Second, Lenin concluded that the government to emerge from this revolution would not be a government of the bourgeoisie. Instead it would be a temporary dictatorship of the workers aided by the peasantry.

Lenin used the word *dictatorship* loosely here. He meant a workers' and peasants' government that would be basically democratic and would permit capitalism to develop. This regime would quickly prepare the country for a full-fledged socialist revolution.

### Lenin's Growing Radicalism

Lenin's views on the revolution revised standard Marxism in a radical way. Lenin envisioned an alliance with the peasantry, who were seen in standard Marxism as a politically backward force. Moreover, Lenin was in favor of pushing the first revolution rapidly forward. Standard Marxism called for a long interval between the first revolution and the transformation of society through a second, socialist, revolution. Standard Marxism expected capitalism to develop fully and generate the seeds of its own destruction in the extended interval after the first revolution.

Lenin was to use these ideas as guidelines in 1917 (see Chapter 20).

## The Socialist Revolutionaries (SRs)

Since 1901, the Populist revolutionary tradition had been represented by the Socialist Revolutionary party. As revolutionaries tied to the peasantry, who made up the largest group in the population, the SRs were potentially a powerful force in radical politics.

### The SRs Compared with Marxists

The SRs differed from Marxists like the Mensheviks in several respects. They saw both the peasants and the factory laborers as exploited workers and thus as supporters of a future revolution. However, as noted previously, Lenin, the unconventional Marxist, held similar views on the possibility of cooperation between factory workers and peasants.

### The SR Program

The SR program focused on land reform. The party wanted a revolution that would overthrow the autocracy and place the land into the hands of the peasant communes.

Although industry would initially remain under private control, the SRs expected that the revolution as it developed would eventually end capitalist ownership. Privately owned factories were to be transformed into a system of workers' cooperatives.

### The Issue of Terror

Portions of the SR party were attracted to the old Populist tactic of terror. The unwillingness of other groups to go along with this method led to splits in the party.

### The Weakness of the SRs

The chief weaknesses of the Socialist Revolutionaries were their lack of a dynamic leader and of an organization linking them to the mass of the peasantry. In addition, the Stolypin reforms, which promoted privately owned farms, cut directly against the revolutionary hopes of the SRs. The party was weakened as well by revelations in 1908 that one of its leaders was a police agent.

# Economic Affairs

Following the Revolution of 1905, Russia continued to make economic progress, although at a more moderate pace than the breakneck expansion of the 1890s. Despite these advances, Russia remained the poorest of the Great Powers and economically one of the weakest of the world's industrialized countries.

The government no longer played the economic role that it had under Witte. Privately owned banks, aided by vast foreign loans, now directed most of the industrial growth. Russian industry continued to depend on large plants, run with a minimum number of trained engineers. The industrial system still relied upon advanced equipment brought in from more industrialized foreign countries.

## Foreign Affairs

The decade before the outbreak of World War I saw Russia clashing frequently with Austria-Hungary over the future of the Balkans.

Two factors contributed to a series of dangerous crises: the decline of Ottoman Turkey and Austria-Hungary's fears of fragmentation if its Slavic population joined such independent Balkan states as Serbia. On the Russian side, both the government and the Duma favored a foreign policy aimed at promoting Russia's influence and prestige.

**Russia on the Eve of World War I**

## The French Alliance

In the face of the growing power of Germany, Austria-Hungary's closest diplomatic ally, the ties between Russia and France tightened. A series of plans for joint action in the event of war led to Russian pledges for an early offensive westward against German territory.

## Treaty with Britain

In 1907, Russia came to an agreement with Great Britain over a number of longstanding issues. Conflicts over Persia, Afghanistan, and Tibet were settled through compromise. Britain had been Russia's most persistent competitor for imperial prizes in Asia. The agreement of 1907 thus freed the Russians to turn most of their energies to the Balkans.

## The Bosnian Crisis of 1908–1909

In the winter of 1908–1909, Russia came close to war with Austria-Hungary.

### Austrian Annexation of Bosnia-Herzegovina

The Austrians suddenly annexed the former Turkish provinces of Bosnia-Herzegovina in the fall of 1908. The Russians saw this action as a slap in the face. Previous negotiations between the Austrian and Russian foreign ministers had seemed to promise Russia an important concession in return for Austria's move. Specifically, Russia was to receive Austrian support for Russia's right to send warships through the Turkish Straits into the Mediterranean.

But the Austrians had acted unilaterally without compensating Russia. German support for Austria in the crisis forced the Russians into a humiliating diplomatic retreat. Despite Austria's expansion, Russia got nothing in return.

### The Serbian Issue

Serbia, Russia's chief Balkan ally, saw its interests threatened by Austria's action. Serbia felt itself squeezed between Turkey and an expanding Austria.

The Russian government feared a war for which it was not prepared if it supported Serbia against Austria. Thus, Russia was unable to support Serbia's call for compensation. As a result the crisis strained Russia's ties with Serbia.

### The Balkan Wars, 1912–1913

The Balkan Wars brought new collisions with Austria-Hungary. Turkey was deprived of most of its territory during the First Balkan War (1912–1913).

Austria, backed by Germany, prevented Serbia from acquiring ports on the Adriatic. Once again, Russia felt unready for war and thus unable to support its chief Balkan ally.

# The Arts: Silver Age

The decades preceding World War I saw a remarkable flowering of Russian culture that historians call the "Silver Age." Its achievements were less spectacular than those of the cultural "Golden Age" between 1820 and 1890 (see Chapter 15). Nonetheless, the Silver Age brought serious achievements in literature, music, and dance.

The era was characterized by a growing public for the arts within Russia and the declining force of government censorship. Much of Russian culture now acquired a substantial audience in the West.

### Anton Chekhov (1860–1904)

The best known Russian writer of the Silver Age, Chekhov wrote short stories and dramas. His most distinguished dramas, *The Three Sisters* and *The Cherry Orchard*, present sensitive psychological studies of the declining Russian gentry.

### Igor Stravinsky (1882–1971)

Russia's most important composer in the Silver Age, the young Stravinsky, impressed Western Europe when his ballet, *The Firebird*, was presented in London and Paris in 1910.

Stravinsky's work during this period drew heavily on the themes of Russian folklore.

### Sergei Diaghilev (1872–1919)

The artistic impresario Diaghilev presented *The Firebird* and other Russian works with his *Ballets Russes* ensemble to a series of Western European audiences in the pre–World War I years.

## Vekhi (Signposts)

An important indication of artistic diversity was the set of essays published in 1909 under the title *Vekhi*. These essays stressed the value of religion and culture. Contributions by the economist Peter Struve (1870–1944) and the philosopher Nicholas Berdiaev (1874–1948), for example, urged Russian intellectuals to turn away from their single-minded concentration on political change.

# The Debate over Russia's Future

The years preceding World War I brought substantial changes in Russian politics, economics, and society. The major historical question is whether or not these changes meant that Russia was headed toward internal stability.

## The Optimistic View

Some historians stress the fact that the old system had been altered enough after 1905 to permit continuing, peaceful change. For example, the autocracy was now limited, and the role of the Duma was likely to grow over time.

Moreover, the Stolypin reforms opened the way for the rise of a prosperous, politically loyal peasantry. In addition, the worst strains of early industrialization seemed to be over.

## The Pessimistic View

An alternative interpretation points to the continuing power of the tsar and his reluctance to consider serious political change.

More important, some historians note, the basic tensions in Russian society had not diminished. The mass of the peasantry was still discontented, and the growing mass of factory workers was becoming increasingly radical.

*Between 1906 and 1914, Russia had continued its economic development and moved haltingly toward a constitutional monarchy. Stolypin had shown that imaginative reform could be begun in the countryside.*

*Nonetheless, Russia's future remained uncertain. The monarchy*

*resisted real political change, while radicals like Lenin were com-
mitted to the overthrow of the existing system.*

*In international affairs, Russia was increasingly involved in a
dangerous rivalry with Austria in the Balkans.*

---

## Recommended Reading

Atkinson, Dorothy. *The End of the Russian Land Commune, 1905–1930*
(1983).

Bonnell, Victoria E. *Roots of Rebellion: Workers' Politics and Organizations in St. Petersburg and Moscow, 1900–1914* (1983).

Brooks, Jeffrey. *When Russia Learned to Read: Literacy and Popular Literature, 1861–1917* (1985).

Edelman, Robert. *Gentry Politics on the Eve of the Russian Revolution: The
Nationalist Party, 1907–1917* (1980).

Eklof, Ben. *Russian Peasant Schools: Officialdom, Village Culture, and
Popular Pedagogy, 1861–1914* (1986).

Emmons, Terence. *The Formation of Political Parties and the First National Elections in Russia* (1983).

Fuller, William C. *Civil-Military Conflict in Imperial Russia, 1881–1914*
(1985).

Healy, Ann. *The Russian Autocracy in Crisis, 1905–1907* (1976).

Hosking, Geoffrey. *The Russian Constitutional Experiment: Government
and Duma, 1907–1914* (1973).

Lieven, D. C. B. *Russia's Rulers under the Old Regime* (1989).

Lincoln, W. Bruce. *In War's Dark Shadow: The Russians before the Great
War* (1983).

McKean, Robert B. *St. Petersburg between the Revolutions: Workers and
Revolutionaries, June 1907–February 1917* (1980).

Manning, Roberta. *The Crisis of the Old Order in Russia: Gentry and
Government* (1982).

Meyer, Alfred G. *Leninism* (1957).

Miliukov, Paul. *Political Memoirs* (1967).

Oldenburg, S. S. *Last Tsar: Nicholas II, His Reign and His Russia*, 4 vols.
(1975–1978).

Perrie, Maureen. *The Agrarian Policy of the Russian Socialist-Revolutionary
Party: From Its Origins through the Revolution of 1905–1907* (1976).

Pinchuk, Ben-Cion. *The Octobrists in the Third Duma, 1907–1912* (1974).

Pipes, Richard. *The Russian Revolution* (1990).

Riha, Thomas. *A Russian European: Paul Miliukov in Russian Politics* (1969).

Robbins, Richard G. *The Tsar's Viceroys: Russian Provincial Governors in the Last Years of the Empire* (1987).

Robinson, Geroid Tanquary. *Rural Russia under the Old Regime* (1932).

Rossos, Andrew. *Russia and the Balkans: Inter-Balkan Rivalries and Russian Foreign Policy, 1908–1914* (1981).

Shanin, Theodor. *Russia as a "Developing Society": Turn of the Century*, vol. 1 (1985).

Shatz, Marshall S, and Judith Zimmerman, trans. and eds. *Signposts: A Collection of Articles on the Russian Intelligentsia* (1986).

Stavrou, Theofanis, ed. *Russia under the Last Tsar* (1969).

Stites, Richard. *The Women's Liberation Movement in Russia: Feminism, Nihilism, and Bolshevism, 1860–1930* (1978).

Thurston, Robert W. *Liberal City, Conservative State: Moscow and Russia's Urban Crisis, 1906–1914* (1987).

Wcislo, Francis William. *Reforming Rural Russia: State, Local Society, and National Politics, 1855–1914* (1990).

Weissman, Neil B. *Reform in Tsarist Russia: The State Bureaucracy and Local Government, 1900–1914* (1981).

Williams, Robert C. *The Other Bolsheviks: Lenin and His Critics, 1904–1914* (1986).

Wolfe, Bertram. *Three Who Made a Revolution* (1948).

# CHAPTER 19

## World War I (to the Start of 1917)

### Time Line

| | |
|---|---|
| June 1914 | Assassination of Archduke Franz Ferdinand |
| July 1914 | Austria declares war on Serbia |
| August 1914 | Germany declares war on Russia |
| | Russian defeat at Tannenberg |
| May 1915 | German-Austrian breakthrough at Gorlice-Tarnow |
| August 1915 | Formation of Progressive Bloc in Duma |
| September 1915 | Tsar Nicholas II takes command of Russian military forces |
| | International Socialist conference at Zimmerwald |

| April 1916 | International Socialist conference at Kienthal |
| June 1916 | Brusilov Offensive |
| November 1916 | Miliukov's "stupidity or treason" speech in Duma |
| December 1916 | Assassination of Rasputin |

*The war brought uncontrollable change to Russia. The most significant development was the unmanageable strain that the conflict put on the political, social, and economic system.*

*Russia suffered an early and catastrophic military defeat at the hands of the Germans at Tannenberg. This set a pattern for consistent Russian defeats in encounters with German troops.*

*In the political sphere, the war was marked by the failure of the monarchy and its ministers to direct the military effort adequately. Meanwhile, the major institution to gain prestige during the war was the Duma.*

*By the close of 1916, the country was in a severe crisis. For the average Russian, especially in the cities, every day brought shortages of food and fuel. For soldiers near the front, the war seemed a futile effort directed by inept military and political leaders.*

*The monarchy, in particular, suffered a catastrophic loss of prestige.*

# Origins of the War

## The July Crisis

In late June 1914, the assassination of Archduke Franz Ferdinand of Austria-Hungary by a Serbian terrorist created a crisis for Russia, just as it did for most of the other countries of Europe. Austria's intention of crushing Serbia endangered Russia's most valued ally in the Balkans. More important, the long series of diplomatic and military defeats Russia had suffered since the Crimean War (1854–1856) made it seem vital for the nation to assert itself at this critical moment.

### Germany's "Blank Check" to Austria

Germany pushed Austria forward into a confrontation with Serbia and Russia. The German government offered Austria full support for a bold policy toward Serbia even if this meant conflict with Russia. Thus, the government in Berlin was willing to risk a general European war to bolster Austria's position in the Balkans and to weaken Russia.

### The Austrians Declare War on Serbia

The Austrian government sent a deliberately harsh ultimatum to Serbia on July 24. They rejected the Serbian government's reply and declared war on Serbia on July 28.

## The Mobilization

Russia began to mobilize its forces, calling up reserves on July 30. The confrontation between Austria and Serbia made it necessary to prepare for action on the border with Austria.

Partly because the army had no plans for partial mobilization, partly because of pressure from Russia's ally, France, the mobilization was carried out all along Russia's western border. Thus, Germany could claim to be threatened by Russian preparations for war. A German demand that Russia cease to mobilize was rejected, and, on August 1, Germany declared war on Russia.

# The Military and Political Course of the War

## Russia's War Strategy

The Russian general staff, in agreement with France, expected to begin wartime operations against the Central Powers by the fifteenth day after mobilization. Russia pledged to take the offensive against Germany with two field armies either in East Prussia or toward Berlin. The Russians planned to send another four armies in an advance against Austrian territory.

## Russian Aid to France

The devastating German invasion of France in August 1914 led to French pressure on Russia to take the offensive in Eastern Europe as quickly as possible. Two poorly coordinated Russian armies, commanded by generals who did not cooperate with one another, advanced into East Prussia. By striking Germany from the East, the

Russians intended to disrupt Germany's offensive westward against the French.

## The Campaign of 1914

### *Defeat at German Hands*

In a preview of future combat against the Germans, Russia's forces in East Prussia were severely defeated at Tannenberg (August 26–29). The Russian advantage in manpower was not enough. Superior German leadership and a superior German system of transportation proved decisive. The Russians gave the Germans an additional advantage: Important Russian radio messages were sent uncoded and were intercepted by German operators. Thus, German commanders were able to anticipate many moves made by their Russian counterparts.

The Germans concentrated against the First Army, commanded by General Alexander Samsonov (1859–1914), which was surrounded at Tannenberg and cut to pieces. Soon afterwards the Second Army, commanded by General Paul Rennenkampf (1854–1918), was defeated at the Masurian Lakes and pushed back to Russian territory.

### *Success Against Austria*

Against Austrian forces, the Russians did better. They entered Galicia (Austrian Poland), capturing the Galician capital, Lemberg (Lvov), in early September and besieging the key fortress city at Peremysl.

## Political Trends of 1914

The Duma was sent home after meeting for a single day at the start of the conflict. It had voted a war budget with only a few dissents. Civilian authority, led by the aged Premier Ivan Goremykin, was overshadowed by the expansion of the military sphere. Large areas both near and removed from the fighting front came under military control. Thus, the conduct of civilian government was severely hindered from the beginning of the war.

## St. Petersburg Renamed

A few weeks after the beginning of the war, the Russian government renamed the country's capital Petrograd. The old name seemed too German for the tsar and his ministers. Petrograd, by contrast, had a patriotic Slavic ring to it.

## The Campaign of 1915

### *Gorlice-Tarnow and the Retreat from Poland*

Disaster struck in the spring of 1915. Fearing Russian advances into Austro-Hungarian territory, the Germans launched a series of offensives starting at Gorlice-Tarnow in May. By September, Russian forces had been forced to retreat from all of Russian Poland. The year ended with Germany and Austria occupying most of Imperial Russia's western provinces.

### *The Shell Shortage and Russian Morale*

The Russians, like all other belligerents, suffered from a shortage of ammunition in 1915. But the Russian army was undersupplied in a particularly harsh way. There was a shortage of rifles as large numbers of Russians were drafted in the winter of 1914–1915. In the Polish campaign, Russian artillerymen had only a few shells to fire each day to support the masses in the infantry. The collapse of morale started to become a severe problem.

## Political Trends of 1915

The clear ineptitude with which the government led the war effort aroused increasing unrest in the Duma. The liberal Cadet politician Paul Miliukov led in forming the "Progressive Bloc," a coalition of liberals and moderate conservatives. Following the summer calamity in Poland, Tsar Nicholas II left Petrograd to take personal command of the army.

But even liberals in the Duma were not yet demanding a Western-style government responsible to a majority in the Duma. They limited their ambitions to a call for a more competent set of ministers, a ministry that would have "the confidence of the nation."

The tsar fired a number of ministers in September, not in deference to the Duma's wishes but because they had opposed his assumption of the supreme military command. Still, inside the Duma, support for the war effort remained high.

## Foreign Relations

In May 1915, Foreign Minister Sergei Sazonov (1860–1927) received a pledge from Russia's British and French military partners that, following victory, Russia would acquire control of the Turkish Straits connecting the Mediterranean and the Black Sea. This was one of the most important and traditional goals of Russian foreign policy. Duma leaders like Miliukov were impressed with the prospect of such territorial gains.

## The Campaign of 1916

### The Brusilov Offensive

Russia found a capable leader in General Alexis Brusilov (1853–1926). His offensive, planned for the summer, began earlier in answer to French calls for help at Verdun and Italian calls for help in the face of an Austrian attack on the Trentino front.

Brusilov's effort made important progress against Austrian opposition, but the Russians were halted, then pushed back when German troops arrived to stiffen the Austrian defenses.

### German Advances: Romania and the Baltic

The military situation worsened in the last months of the year with Germany's successful invasion of Romania. Russia now had to stretch its resources to defend a vast new southwestern front along its border with Romania. German forces advancing northeastward along the Baltic coast were approaching the Gulf of Riga, only a short distance from Petrograd.

## Political Trends of 1916

Opposition to the existing political order now sharpened and spread widely. The Progressive Bloc hardened its demands, calling for a Western-style government with a limited monarchy and a cabinet responsible to a majority in the Duma.

### Miliukov's Speech

In a direct and unprecedented political attack, Miliukov gave an inflammatory speech to the Duma on November 14. In it he criticized

**Russia in World War I**

one government failure after another, asking "Is this stupidity or is this treason?"

### *Threats to the Tsar*

The year ended with rumors of impending coups to remove Nicholas II from the throne. The replacement of cabinet ministers had caused so much uncertainty and instability in the government that observers described the situation as "ministerial leapfrog." Hostility and suspicion of Rasputin (1868?–1916) as an evil influence on the imperial family led to his assassination on December 30.

*Rasputin.* Rasputin was a self-declared holy man who had entered the circle around the imperial family sometime after 1905. He seemed to have the power to treat the hemophilia from which Alexis, the heir to the throne, suffered. The empress was particularly impressed by him.

During the war, Rasputin's political influence grew. With the tsar at the front much of the time after 1915, Rasputin seemed to many observers to be manipulating the empress. In fact, he did have substantial success in placing his cronies in high ministerial positions.

## The Home Front

Total war brought a combination of devastating strains to Russian life. Fifteen million men were mobilized for the armed forces. This disrupted industrial production and, to a lesser degree, the production of food. Meanwhile the country's need for both increased. Soldiers needed a better diet than they had consumed as civilians; modern warfare required a huge production of military equipment. At the same time, a huge number of refugees from the fighting areas crowded into the cities of European Russia.

Russia had the least developed railroad system of any of the major powers of Europe, and the requirements of wartime pushed it to the breaking point. The loss of Russia's Polish provinces in 1915 deprived the country of some of its most industrialized regions.

Unlike governments in Britain and Germany, which also faced severe problems in the production of both food and industrial goods, the Russian government failed to adjust sufficiently. It did not expand its own powers to cope with the situation. Nor did it forcefully help private organizations to fill the new needs created by the war.

### Economic Strains

#### Industry

Many skilled workers were drafted for military service. The expansion of industry required factories to hire large numbers of women and children. Working hours were substantially increased, and many recently established health and safety measures were discarded.

On the whole, factory wages did not keep up with prices. The price of meat tripled between 1914 and 1916; the price of salt increased five hundred percent. Meanwhile, most factory workers saw their incomes only double.

### Agriculture

The rural areas of Russia had been overpopulated before the war. Thus, mobilization of millions of men from the peasant villages did not affect planting or harvesting, and food production continued in the countryside. But farm laborers were drafted from private estates near the large cities. These estates had provided much of the food on which the city population depended.

Peasants in the countryside were soon unwilling to sell their grain to the government. There were no consumer goods they could buy with their earnings. At the same time, the breakdown of the railroads made it difficult to ship food to northern cities like Petrograd and Moscow from farming regions in the south and the east.

### The Railroads

From the start of the war, Russia was hindered by its weak railroad system. Russia had only one-tenth of the railroad strength that Germany had constructed. Most of Russia's railroads, including the Trans-Siberian Railroad from central Russia to the Pacific and the line from central Russia northward to Archangel, had only one track.

The military took over much of the rolling stock (locomotives and freight cars) at the start of the war. The shipment of food and fuel to the cities for civilian needs became increasingly difficult.

### Food and Fuel Crisis

By late 1916, the populations of Petrograd and Moscow were colder and hungrier than at any time during the war. Only one-third the normal supply of food was now arriving from the outside. Factories and bakeries were being closed because of a lack of fuel.

## Public Organizations

### Special Councils

The war forced the government to permit individuals from outside its ministries and bureaucracy to help in running the war effort. The president of the Duma, Mikhail Rodzianko (1859–1924), got the consent of the tsar for such an effort in the summer of 1915. Eventually Special Councils were set up to deal with defense, artillery production, transport, food, and fuel.

The Councils formed a new institution in Russian life. Government ministers, Duma and State Council deputies, local officials, and even private citizens worked alongside one another.

### Central Military-Industrial Committee

Set up to help the Defense Council increase industrial production, this body was even more of a novelty. Because industrial leaders wanted working-class participation, the committee included workers' representatives from factories with 500 or more workers.

### Zemgor

In November 1915, the government permitted formation of a national organization (*Zemgor*) of local government institutions including the zemstvos (rural elected bodies) and municipal councils (November 1915). *Zemgor* aided war refugees and other civilians suffering from the disruptions brought by the war.

## Revolutionaries at Home and in Exile

### Lenin's Views

At the start of the war, Vladmimir Lenin, from his exile in Switzerland, took a position that other Marxists found too extreme. He began by condemning those Western as well as Russian Marxists who offered any support to their respective governments' war effort. But he went much further and argued that revolutionaries ought to use the dislocation caused by the war to pull down the existing order. He favored a Russian defeat in the war, since this would be an important step in opening the way to revolution.

### Zimmerwald and Kienthal

Lenin failed to get his views adopted at the two international socialist conferences that were held during the first years of the war: Zimmerwald (September 1915) and Kienthal (April 1916). However, his success in getting more support at Kienthal than at Zimmerwald was a sign that his ideas were spreading.

## Other Marxist Positions

Even Leon Trotsky, Lenin's collaborator in 1917, would not go as far as Lenin in hoping for Russia's defeat. At the opposite extreme, George Plekhanov, the founder of Russian Marxism, enthusiastically supported the war effort. Menshevik leaders like Julius Martov worked to end the war quickly and without victory for either side.

## Kerensky

Within the Fourth Duma, Alexander Kerensky (1881–1970) emerged as a fiery and vocal revolutionary leader. The leader of a peasant socialist party known as the Trudoviks, he first responded to the war by refusing to vote for the military budget in August 1914. Thereafter, he publicly criticized both the government's ministers and the imperial family for their disastrous leadership. Behind the scenes, he worked actively to overthrow the tsarist order.

*After two and a half years of warfare, Russia was seething with discontent. Military failures, economic hardship, and an increasingly unpopular and ineffective government made many observers expect some kind of drastic change in the near future. The most influential opponents of the regime within Russia, however, seemed to be Duma leaders like Miliukov who wished to change the leadership of the country in order to fight the war more effectively.*

*Still, even unwavering radicals like Lenin did not foresee that the entire monarchical system would collapse within a week in early 1917.*

## Recommended Reading

Abraham, Richard. *Alexander Kerensky: The First Love of the Revolution* (1987).

Deutscher, Isaac. *Trotsky: The Prophet Armed, 1879–1921* (1954).

Florinsky, Michael. *The End of the Russian Empire* (1931; reprint 1973).

Gatrell, Peter. *The Tsarist Economy, 1850–1917* (1986).

Gronsky, Paul P, and Nicholas J. Astrov. *The War and the Russian Government* (1929; reprint 1973).

Knox, Major-General Alfred W. F. *With the Russian Army, 1914–1917* (1921; reprint 1971).

Lieven, D. C. B. *Russia and the Origins of the First World War* (1983).

Lieven, D. C. B. *Russia's Rulers under the Old Regime* (1989).

Lincoln, W. Bruce. *Passage Through Armageddon: The Russians in War and Revolution, 1914–1918* (1986).

Neilson, Keith. *Strategy and Supply: The Anglo-Russian Alliance, 1914–1917* (1984).

Pares, Bernard. *The Fall of the Russian Monarchy: A Study of the Evidence* (1939).

Pearson, Raymond. *The Russian Moderates and the Crisis of Tsarism, 1914–1917* (1977).

Rutherford, Ward. *The Russian Army in World War I* (1975).

Schmitt, Bernadotte E., and Harold C. Vedeler. *The World in the Crucible, 1914–1918* (1984).

Showalter, Dennis E. *Tannenberg: Clash of Empires* (1991).

Siegelbaum, Lewis. *The Politics of Industrial Mobilization in Russia, 1914–1917: A Study of the War-Industries Committees* (1983).

Smith, C. Jay, Jr. *The Russian Struggle for Power, 1914–1917: A Study of Russian Foreign Policy During the First World War* (1956).

Stone, Norman. *The Eastern Front, 1914–1977* (1975).

Ulam, Adam. *The Bolsheviks: The Intellectual and Political History of the Triumph of Communism in Russia* (1965).

Washburn, Stanley. *On the Russian Front in World War I: Memoirs of an American War Correspondent* (1982).

Wildman, Allan K. *The End of the Russian Imperial Army: The Old Army and the Soldiers' Revolt (March–April 1917)* (1980).

# CHAPTER 20

## The 1917 Revolutions: March and November

### Time Line

| | |
|---|---|
| March 1917 | Demonstrations in Petrograd |
| | Tsar abdicates |
| | Formation of the Provisional Government |
| | Formation of the Petrograd Soviet |
| April 1917 | Lenin returns to Russia |
| May 1917 | Fall of Miliukov; formation of the First Coalition Government |
| | Trotsky returns to Russia |
| June–July 1917 | Kerensky Offensive |

| | |
|---|---|
| July 1917 | July Days |
| | Lenin escapes to Finland |
| | Finns declare autonomy |
| August 1917 | Formation of the Second Coalition Government |
| | Date set for election of Constituent Assembly |
| September 1917 | Kornilov Affair |
| | Kerensky arms the Bolsheviks |
| | Bolsheviks win control of Moscow and Petrograd soviets |
| October 1917 | Lenin returns to Petrograd |
| | Lenin wins approval for coup in Bolshevik Politburo |
| November 1917 | Bolshevik Revolution |

---

*Russia experienced two revolutions in 1917. In the March Revolution, the accumulated tensions of the war led to a popular uprising that overthrew the monarchy. The result was a weak government based upon the Duma.*

*The following months saw Russia's problems grow despite the change in government. Popular unrest and the presence of determined revolutionaries set the stage for a second revolution.*

*The November Revolution that followed turned out to be a crucial turning point in Russian history. Lenin's Bolshevik Party, claiming to represent the workers, soldiers, and peasants, overthrew the Provisional Government and set out both to transform Russia and to promote revolution throughout the industrialized world.*

## The Collapse of the Old Order

The Romanov dynasty collapsed with extraordinary speed in early March of 1917. Unrest in the capital city of Petrograd began with industrial strikes. These soon exploded into mass demonstrations that the government was unable to control.

Within a week, Nicholas II had abdicated, the monarchy had come to an end, and a Provisional Government drawn from members of the Duma was in power.

## Dating the Revolutions of 1917

In 1917 Russia was still using the Julian Calendar adopted in the reign of Peter the Great (see Chapter 9). In the twentieth century this put Russian dates thirteen days behind those of the Gregorian Calendar adopted in the West. Thus the first revolution of 1917 is referred to as the February Revolution (under the Julian Calendar) or the March Revolution (under the Gregorian).

Two names are also used for the second revolution of 1917 (see p. 276): the October Revolution (under the Julian Calendar) and the November Revolution (under the Gregorian).

## The March Revolution

Striking factory workers and housewives angry at food shortages staged mass demonstrations in Petrograd on March 8. The government tried to suppress the crowds with the police force, then with Cossacks, but these efforts proved insufficient.

### The Mutiny of the Military

Bringing in soldiers to crush the crowds was the last tool the government could use. If this failed for any reason, the authority of the government would be shattered. That is what happened.

When soldiers were called in on March 11, many of them refused to shoot. Some even joined the demonstrations.

The decisive moment for the revolution came on March 12. On that day most of the garrison at Petrograd joined the side of the demonstrators. The government no longer controlled its own capital.

### Formation of the Provisional Government

Duma deputies joined in the revolution. On March 12, some deputies defied a government order proroguing (i.e., adjourning) the Duma's session. These deputies formed a Provisional Committee on March 12.

Two days later, on March 14, the Provisional Committee chose a number of deputies to form the Provisional Government.

### *Formation of the Petrograd Soviet*

Looking back to the experience of 1905, leaders of the workers created a Petrograd Soviet on March 12. In short order, the rebelling soldiers of Petrograd were invited to send representatives to the Soviet.

### *Abdication of Nicholas II*

Nicholas heard the news of the unrest in Petrograd at his military headquarters at Mogilev. On his way back to Petrograd, he was stranded by railroad strikes at Pskov, the headquarters of the Northern Front. There he found he no longer had the support of his army commanders.

The tsar abdicated on March 15. When his younger brother, Grand Duke Michael (1878–1918), refused to take the throne, the monarchy ended.

## Post-Revolutionary Order: Dual Power

Following the collapse of the monarchy, no stable government developed to control and direct the country. Instead, there stood two centers of power: the Provisional Government and the Petrograd Soviet.

The Provisional Government claimed to speak for the entire Russian population. The Petrograd Soviet claimed to speak for the lower classes: the factory workers, the soldiers, and the peasantry.

The result was a period of "Dual Authority." Although the Soviet and the government cooperated for a time, the division of power and the rivalry between them created a highly unstable situation.

### Provisional Government

### *Origins*

The Provisional Government that took office in March consisted of former Duma deputies, most of whom came from the liberal parties of the Progressive Bloc.

The Provisional Government was linked to the Petrograd Soviet primarily by Alexander Kerensky, who was both vice-chairman of the Soviet and the government's minister of justice.

### Authority

The members of the Provisional Government had defied the government's orders to prorogue the Duma. But they had not been elected to run the country. Thus, the Provisional Government could not claim any legitimate authority to rule. It stood merely as a temporary body in office until a constituent assembly could be selected.

Following the March Revolution, the Provisional Government was most firmly based in the cities of Russia. It was generally accepted by educated and prosperous Russians. Many in these groups hoped that it would conduct the war against Germany more effectively than the tsar had done.

### Achievements of the Provisional Government

The new government moved quickly to end the harshness and political oppression that had characterized the tsarist system. The death penalty was abolished in both the military and the civilian court systems. Criminals were no longer punished by exile to Siberia. All official discrimination based on religion and nationality was ended.

### Weaknesses

The members of the Provisional Government lacked any effective police force, since the old police system had collapsed along with the monarchy. The authority of the government was never effectively established in rural areas.

The policies of the government soon alienated much of the population. It put off action on important questions until the Constituent Assembly could meet.

The Provisional Government refused to consider land reform; it insisted on continuing with the war; and it resisted the efforts of minority nationalities like the Finns and Ukrainians to move toward independence (see p. 272).

## Petrograd Soviet

### Origins

The Soviet emerged as the result of spontaneous action on the part of self-proclaimed representatives of the workers and soldiers. It was founded in part on the memory of the St. Petersburg Soviet of 1905 (see Chapter 17). Its leaders saw their first task to be the defense of the revolution against a counterattack from the political right.

### Authority

The Soviet had effective control over the capital and extended its authority over hundreds of soviets that developed throughout the country.

### Weaknesses

The Soviet was a large, unwieldy body of 3000 delegates. Procedures for admitting new delegates were uncertain.

### The Soviet Refusal to Exercise Direct Power

Initially, the Soviet's Executive Committee was willing to give conditional support to the Provisional Government. This cooperation was due, in large part, to the ideological views of the Soviet's leaders, among whom were Mensheviks like Iraklii Tseretelli (1882–1960) and Socialist Revolutionaries like Victor Chernov (1873–1952). In the pattern of classic Marxism adopted by George Plekhanov (see Chapter 16), they assumed that the fall of the monarchy had to be followed by the period of bourgeois (or middle-class) rule. Indeed, how could one imagine that the prerequisites for socialism already existed in Russia?

Thus they believed that they could not take power immediately after the March Revolution. Instead they had to wait, in opposition and for a prolonged period, until history was ripe for a second, workers', revolution. In the meantime, the bourgeois Provisional Government was appropriate for this stage of the revolution.

## Lenin and the Bolsheviks

The few Bolsheviks living in Petrograd around the time of the March Revolution reacted with uncertainty to the overthrow of the tsar. Their basic response was to support the Provisional Government just as the Petrograd Soviet was doing.

The revolution found most of Lenin's followers in exile abroad, like Lenin himself, or in Siberia. After Lenin's return to Russia in April 1917, the party took a position opposed to the Provisional Government. It demanded Russian withdrawal from the war, distribution of land to the peasantry, and workers' control over the factories.

## "Letters from Afar"

In his "Letters from Afar," written from his place of exile in Switzerland, Lenin sketched out plans for an armed rebellion to topple the Provisional Government.

## Lenin's Return

Lenin reached Russia via Germany. He could not leave Switzerland through France or Italy. As Russia's wartime allies, these countries were unwilling to allow him, a declared opponent of the war effort, to return home.

The Germans considered that Lenin, like other radicals they wanted to see back in Russia, would weaken the Allied war effort. However, to prevent him from subverting their own workers with his antiwar views, he was required to travel through Germany in a sealed train.

## Lenin in Russia: "The April Theses"

Lenin reached Petrograd in mid-April. He moved to get the Bolsheviks to adopt his policy against the war, and he also set out to take control of the Petrograd Soviet.

In his program for action, "The April Theses," Lenin presented his alternative to the extended two-stage revolutionary pattern of classical Marxism.

In a radical departure from traditional Marxism, Lenin insisted that Russia could go swiftly into the second stage of the revolution. He wanted the Soviet, as the representative of the working class, to take power immediately.

In fact, Lenin was looking to a second revolution under the leadership of his party. The Bolsheviks, he pledged, would carry out a program of "Peace, land, bread, and all power to the Soviets."

## Lenin's Hope for the Spread of Revolution

Lenin assumed that a Bolshevik revolution in Russia would spark similar revolutions in the other belligerent countries. He realized that

Russia was not an industrial country ripe for revolution in the pattern laid out by classical Marxism. But he believed that if Russia set off a chain of revolutions, Bolshevik governments elsewhere would assure the success of the revolution in Russia. He put his highest hopes on Germany.

## Failure of the Provisional Government

After a brief period of popularity, the Provisional Government fell into a series of crises. Two basic decisions helped to destroy its authority.

First, there was its decision to remain in the war. This continued the economic and social strain of the conflict. It also split the government and the Petrograd Soviet over the goals for which Russia was fighting. Was the war intended to expand Russian power and influence, or was it to defend the home of the Revolution?

The second decision was to put off serious domestic reform until a properly elected body representing the entire population could be brought together. This "Constituent Assembly" would have the authority that the Provisional Government lacked. In the view of Provisional Government leaders, decisions about domestic change belonged to the Constituent Assembly.

### "Order Number One"

The organization of the army was the first topic on which the Soviet put a radical stamp on the policies of the Provisional Government.

"Order Number One" was issued by the Soviet, and the Provisional Government decided that it had to be accepted. This order undermined military discipline by stating that units should elect soldiers' committees. Moreover, soldiers need not obey orders that conflicted with the policies of the Soviet.

### The First Crisis: Paul Miliukov's Expansionist Foreign Policy

The broader issue of the war itself came up in late April and early May. Paul Miliukov, foreign minister in the Provisional Government, tried to maintain Russia's prerevolutionary war aims. Specifically, he wanted Russia to receive territorial gains like Constantinople and the Turkish Straits. When these aims became known in April, street demonstrations forced Miliukov and like-minded ministers to resign.

## The First Coalition Government

A new government was formed in May. It had a bourgeois majority, but Kerensky was now joined by several other socialist ministers, including Chernov and Tseretelli.

During the months that followed, the policies of the government proved increasingly unpopular. Its authority began to decline sharply.

### *The Decision to Remain in the War*

The government's decision to remain in the war was politically catastrophic. It prolonged the strains of the conflict on both the military forces and the civilian population. It made it difficult to call together the Constituent Assembly or to address any of Russia's pressing problems.

Kerensky became the main advocate of remaining in the war. He believed that a Russian withdrawal would lead to a German victory against Russia's allies. This would be followed in turn by Germany's conquest of Russia and the obliteration of the revolution.

### *Postponement of Land Reform*

The government refused to sanction land reform until the Constituent Assembly met to deal with the issue. Meanwhile, peasants over much of the country seized land and found that no government authority existed to stop them.

### *Demands of the National Minorities*

The government failed to satisfy the demands of various non-Russian nationalities for freedom from central control.

Immediately after the March Revolution, the Finns regained their traditional autonomy, lost under Nicholas II in 1908, from the Provisional Government. The Finns tried to go further: In July 1917, they declared they would exercise full power over their affairs except in matters of foreign policy and military policy.'Led by Kerensky, the Provisional Government refused to agree and dissolved the Finnish legislature.

Meanwhile, the Ukrainians pushed even more vigorously for independence. A Ukrainian parliament (the *Rada*) emerged shortly after the March Revolution. By July, its demands for increased powers over Ukrainian affairs led to a virtual break with the Provisional Government.

A federal system might have eased tensions in both cases. Nonetheless, the Provisional Government insisted that only the Constituent Assembly could take such action.

### Plans for Constituent Assembly

There was a long delay before the government set a date for elections to the Constituent Assembly. The problems of conducting the war and dealing with other pressing issues diverted the government's attention from this action.

Some groups, like the Cadets, sought to put off elections, since they did not expect to make a good showing if the voting took place soon.

In August, the Kerensky government finally set a date for the elections in late November.

## Summer Offensive

The last Russian offensive of World War I took place in late June and early July 1917. Alexander Kerensky, war minister in the new Provisional Government, was the leading advocate of this measure.

The offensive gained some ground against the Austrians in Galicia. In the end it failed catastrophically when German reinforcements arrived. The Russian army, already weak and ill-disciplined, now deteriorated more rapidly than before.

### July Days

Street demonstrations, involving workers and radical-minded soldiers and sailors, erupted in Petrograd as the offensive broke down.

The top Bolshevik leaders hesitantly supported the masses in the streets, but they refused the call of the demonstrators to take power from the Provisional Government. They were fearful that, having taken power, they would not be able to keep it at this stage of events.

### Government Repression

The government had its best chance to crush the Bolsheviks at this point. The minister of justice, Pavel Pereverzev (?–?), released evidence that indicated Lenin was a German agent. The government thus regained the initiative. Loyal troops put down the unrest in the streets, and Bolshevik newspapers were forcibly closed.

Lenin went into hiding in Finland. Other leading Bolsheviks, now including Leon Trotsky, who had just joined the Bolshevik Party formally, were arrested.

### Formation of a Second Coalition Government

With the establishment of a Second Coalition cabinet, Kerensky now emerged as the undisputed strong man of the Provisional Government. From July onward, he held the position of prime minister combined at times with the portfolio of minister of war.

## Bolshevik Seizure of Power

Between the late summer and early November of 1917, the surrounding circumstances undercut the Provisional Government. Soldiers deserted the army in large numbers. Peasants went on seizing land. Hunger grew in the cities. The non-Russian minorities increasingly disregarded the edicts of the Provisional Government. The Bolsheviks recovered from their weakened political position.

### The Kornilov Affair

The Kornilov affair was a crucial event both in weakening Kerensky's government and in strengthening the Bolsheviks. Kerensky's dealings with Lavr Kornilov (1870–1918), the new commander-in-chief of the Russian army, alienated both conservatives and groups on the left.

#### Kerensky and Kornilov

The exact intentions of Kornilov and Kerensky, as well as their mutual relationship, remain highly controversial, with historians sharply divided in interpreting the Kornilov episode.

Kornilov wanted the government to crack down on dissidents and to restore order to the country, by force if need be. He may have had broader ambitions of becoming a military dictator. Kerensky may have agreed with a policy of domestic repression. He promised Kornilov to implement the general's ideas and encouraged Kornilov to hold his troops in readiness for a march on Petrograd to suppress unrest there.

Kerensky may have agreed to accept Kornilov as military dictator. In any case, Kornilov marched on Petrograd only to be denounced by Kerensky.

### Kerensky's Appeal to the Left

In order to help stop Kornilov, Kerensky turned to the Bolsheviks in two important ways. First, he released the Bolshevik leaders, including Trotsky, from prison. Second, he armed the workers' militia called the Red Guard, a group largely composed of Bolshevik sympathizers.

Kornilov's forces were stopped, and the general himself was captured.

## Disintegration of Kerensky's Authority

The Kornilov affair helped to discredit Kerensky. The military and political conservatives would no longer support him after he had humiliated the army's commander.

At the same time, groups on the Left pulled away from Kerensky because he refused to end the war or sanction land distribution. Moreover, he was stained by his earlier association with Kornilov's plans to put down the Left and restore order by force.

The Provisional Government and its leaders were now helplessly isolated.

### Trotsky and the Petrograd Soviet

The clearest sign of rising Bolshevik influence was in its establishing control over the Moscow and Petrograd soviets in September 1917.

The election of Leon Trotsky as chairman of the Petrograd Soviet was an indication of mass support for the Bolsheviks in Russia's most important city.

### Lenin's Role

Lenin, still in hiding and acting through letters, pushed the other eleven members of the party Central Committee to move to seize power. At first most of these Bolshevik leaders were reluctant to strike. Through his personal prestige and forceful persuasiveness, Lenin gradually won a majority to his position.

### Trotsky's Role

At the insistence of Trotsky, the insurrection was to take place under the cover of the coming Congress of Soviets in early November. Thus, the Bolsheviks could claim to be taking power under the authority of the Congress. They claimed to be pushing the Soviets to take power.

## Lenin's Outline of the Future Society

While in exile in Finland, Lenin had written a brief book about post-revolutionary society.

*State and Revolution* explained the need for a temporary dictatorship to follow the revolution. Old elements, hostile to the revolution, would remain on the scene and a proletarian (or workers') dictatorship was needed to repress them.

Lenin went on to describe the final stage of development after the revolution. As Friedrich Engels (1820–1895), one of the founders of Marxism, had put it, the state would "wither away." There would be a society of abundance and political freedom. No police force would be needed. Government itself would fade away, since there would be no social divisions or frictions to cause disorder.

## The November Revolution

While the government barely moved, the Bolsheviks executed a coup that took power easily in Petrograd.

### Petrograd

The coup was carried out under Trotsky's leadership starting on the night of November 6–7. The Red Guard militia seized the vital centers of life in Petrograd, like the telephone exchange.

The Provisional Government held out briefly in the old imperial Winter Palace. The Bolsheviks and their supporters captured the Winter Palace and imprisoned most of the leading figures of the Provisional Government on November 7. Kerensky managed to flee the capital.

### Moscow

The seizure of power by the Bolsheviks in Moscow was more difficult. For several days, there was bloody street fighting as military cadets and others defending the Provisional Government clashed with Red Guard units.

### The Provinces

The Bolsheviks established themselves mainly in the urban centers of the Russian-speaking areas. The countryside and regions inhabited by non-Russian minority peoples remained outside Bolshevik control.

## The New Government

### Lenin and Trotsky

Lenin was the prime minister in the new government established in November 1917. Trotsky took the position of commissar of foreign affairs.

### The SRs

A number of left-wing SRs joined the government, giving it the appearance of a coalition of the Left. The SR party had split during 1917. The party's left wing shared enough interests with the Bolsheviks over the need for peace and a program of land for the peasants to cooperate in forming a coalition government. Thus, the voice of the SRs on matters involving the peasants would influence government policy.

The alliance was a shaky one, however, and it lasted only until the Treaty of Brest-Litovsk (see Chapter 21). At that point, the SRs resigned in protest. Despite their call for peace in 1917, they objected to the harsh terms of the treaty and demanded the war against Germany continue.

## Interpretations of the Revolution

As the winners in 1917, the Bolsheviks presented an influential description of what had really happened. They claimed, in accordance with Marx's view of history (see Chapter 16), that their success had been an inevitable development resulting from the growth of a capitalist society in Russia. By the time they took power, they did in fact enjoy immense support among the population.

## The Position of Lenin

Alongside the claim that the revolution was inevitable, later Communist historians added the element of Lenin's brilliant and decisive leadership. This interpretation led to a difficult dilemma: If the revolution was destined to succeed, why did Lenin need to play a decisive role?

## Non-Communists' Interpretations

### The Role of Leadership and Circumstances

Many Western historians reject the claim that the Bolshevik November Revolution was inevitable. They point instead to the poor leadership of the Provisional Government and the helplessness of other political parties. In this view, the Bolsheviks won power, not because their victory was inevitable, but rather because of their political skills. The circumstances of war, famine, rural unrest, and national discontents set the stage for success. But a less determined leadership—in particular the absence of Lenin—would have meant failure.

### The Role of Chance and Accident

Some historians have denied that Lenin convinced the Central Committee to act or that the Bolsheviks actually planned a coup. In this view, the November Revolution was primarily a response to a clumsy effort by the Provisional Government to suppress the Bolsheviks. Thus, the takeover of key buildings was, at first, nothing more than a series of defensive actions by the Bolsheviks who took power without intending to do so.

*In the turmoil of war and domestic unrest, the various cabinets of the Provisional Government failed to solve Russia's pressing problems in 1917.*

*As the Provisional Government faltered, Lenin's Bolsheviks grew in influence, survived the defeat of the July Days, and struck successfully in the late fall. Their hold on power, however, seemed weak, even following the November Revolution.*

*Like the Provisional Government in 1917, the Bolsheviks now faced the desperate problem of escaping World War I. Beyond that, there was the dilemma of consolidating control over a country close to anarchy.*

---

## Recommended Reading

Abraham, Richard. *Alexander Kerensky: The First Love of the Revolution* (1987).

Carr, Edward Hallett. *A History of Soviet Russia: The Bolshevik Revolution, 1917–1923*, vol. 1 (1950).

Chamberlin, William Henry. *The Russian Revolution, 1917–1921*, 2 vols. (1935).

Daniels, Robert. *Red October: The Bolshevik Revolution of 1917* (1967).

Ferro, Marc. *October 1917: A Social History of the Russian Revolution* (1980).

Ferro, Marc. *The Russian Revolution of February, 1917* (1972).

Gill, Graeme J. *Peasants and Government in the Russian Revolution* (1979).

Hasegawa, Tsuyoshi. *The February Revolution: Petrograd 1917* (1981).

Katkov, George. *Russia 1917: The February Revolution* (1967).

Katkov, George. *Russia: 1917: The Kornilov Affair: Kerensky and the Breakup of the Russian Army* (1980).

Keep, John L. H. *The Russian Revolution: A Study in Mass Mobilization* (1976).

Kerensky, Alexander. *Russia and History's Turning Point* (1965).

Koenker, Diane. *Moscow Workers and the 1917 Revolution* (1981).

Medlin, Virgil D., and Steven L. Parsons, eds. *V. D. Nabokov and the Russian Provisional Government, 1917* (1976).

Pipes, Richard. *The Russian Revolution* (1990).

Rabinowitch, Alexander. *The Bolsheviks Come to Power: The Revolution of 1917 in Petrograd* (1976).

Rabinowitch, Alexander. *Prelude to Revolution: The Petrograd Bolsheviks and the July 1917 Uprising* (1968).

Raleigh, Donald J. *Revolution on the Volga: 1917 in Saratov* (1986).

Rosenberg, William G. *Liberals in the Russian Revolution: The Constitutional Democratic Party, 1917–1921* (1974).

Schapiro, Leonard. *The Russian Revolutions of 1917: The Origins of Modern Communism* (1984).

Smith, S. A. *Red Petrograd: Revolution in the Factories, 1917–18* (1983).

Sukhanov, N. N. Edited by Joel Carmichael. *The Russian Revolution, 1917* (1984).

Thompson, John. *Revolutionary Russia, 1917* (1981).

Trotsky, Leon. *History of the Russian Revolution*, 3 vols. (1932).

Ulam, Adam. *The Bolsheviks: The Intellectual and Political History of the Triumph of Communism in Russia* (1965).

Wade, Rex A. *Red Guards and Workers' Militias in the Russian Revolution* (1984).

Wade, Rex A. *The Russian Search for Peace, February–October 1917* (1969).

Wildman, Allan K. *The End of the Russian Imperial Army: The Old Army and the Soldiers' Revolt (March–April 1917)* (1980).

Wildman, Allan K. *The End of the Russian Imperial Army: The Road to Soviet Power and Peace* (1987).

# CHAPTER 21

## The New Regime (November 1917– July 1918)

## Time Line

November 1917  Decree on Peace

Decree on Land

Elections to Constituent Assembly

December 1917  Cadets outlawed

Armistice with Germany

Cheka organized

Peace talks begin at Brest-Litovsk

January 1918  Constituent Assembly dispersed

| February 1918 | Trotsky declares "no war, no peace" |
| | Renewed German offensive |
| | Capital moved from Petrograd to Moscow |
| | Separation of church and state |
| March 1918 | Treaty of Brest-Litovsk signed |
| | Bolsheviks become the "Communist Party" |
| | SRs leave the coalition government |
| May 1918 | Food requisitioning begun in the countryside |
| June 1918 | Large-scale industry nationalized |
| July 1918 | Execution of the imperial family |
| | First Soviet Constitution |

*In the first months following the November Revolution, Lenin's government strengthened its hold on power and addressed the crucial issue of removing Russia from the war.*

*The radicalism of the new regime became obvious as it eliminated the Constituent Assembly, attacked the church, and established a political police organization.*

## The Revolutionary Government

Between November 1917 and July 1918, Lenin and the Bolsheviks consolidated their control over the government and began to reshape Russian life.

An immediate problem for Lenin was to maintain Bolshevik authority against the threat of the Constituent Assembly. The new government consisted of Bolsheviks and a small number of Left SRs. A national election that brought a sharply different result would pose a direct threat to the revolutionary government.

### The Constituent Assembly

The government permitted the scheduled elections to the Constituent Assembly to take place in late November. The results were catastrophic for the Bolsheviks, and Lenin's government had to find a way to negate the elections returns.

### The SR Victory

Historians consider that the SRs won a striking victory in a generally fair election. While the Bolsheviks won twenty-five percent of the vote, a strong minority, the SRs won a clear majority of fifty-eight percent.

### The Repression of the Constituent Assembly

First, the Constituent Assembly was weakened by measures taken before it convened. Lenin stated publicly that the Constituent Assembly must accept the existing government. The Cadets, the leading middle-class party, were outlawed.

Second, the Constituent Assembly was intimidated when it met. Pro-Communist military forces surrounded the meeting place and jammed into the meeting room with loaded weapons. The military force guarding the assembly ordered the delegates to disperse after a single meeting.

### The Significance of Crushing the Constituent Assembly

Russia's wartime allies were shocked by Lenin's treatment of the Constituent Assembly. His actions made it clear that Russia was being run for an indefinite time by a minority dictatorship.

Along with Russia's moves to leave the war, the treatment of the Constituent Assembly led to Russia's growing isolation from its former allies.

## Economic Policy

### Peasant and Worker Power

The radicalism of the new government appeared in economic affairs. The seizure of land by the peasants, which had taken place spontaneously, received government approval. Factories were placed in the hands of workers' committees.

### The Results of Economic Radicalism

As a consequence, the country's weakened economy went through a further decline. Workers' control led to chaos and ineffectiveness in industry. In the countryside, government authority remained almost nonexistent, and the problem of getting peasants to bring food to urban markets became critical.

## The War on Religion

### Causes

The Orthodox Church was a prime target for the new government. Government hostility had several causes. Since the era of Peter the Great, the church had been a firm subordinate and supporter of the imperial government. Moreover, Marxist ideology proclaimed that religion in general was a device for repressing the working class.

### Attacks on Church Authority

The government passed a number of measures designed to weaken the church and to deprive it of its footholds in Russian life. Traditional church responsibilities like marriage and family relations were brought under state control. The official tie between church and state was ended (February 1918). Church land and property, including objects used in church rituals, were taken over by the state.

## The Cheka

The new government armed itself with a political police organization called the Cheka. The Cheka was established in December 1917 to deal with a threatened strike of public employees, but it soon became a nationwide organization intended to wipe out counterrevolutionary activities.

# Russia's Withdrawal from the War

One of the most radical steps taken by the new government was to remove Russia from the war. This action stirred up strong opposition to the Communist government among Russia's former allies, and it helped bring together domestic opponents of the government.

## The Need for Peace

The strain of the war on the population had been crucial in weakening the authority of the Provisional Government. Similarly, the Bolshevik pledge to withdraw Russia from the conflict had been an important factor in winning support for Lenin and his party. Therefore, a delay in bringing peace threatened to undermine the new government.

## The Decree on Peace

The first measure that the new government took in foreign affairs was to issue an appeal to all combatants. This "Decree on Peace" called for immediate negotiations to end the conflict and for a peace settlement "without annexations or indemnities." That meant a peace that would not involve changes in international borders or the forced payment of money from one country to another.

The Russian government was not able to get its allies to meet. Thus, negotiations began only between the Russians on one side, and the Germans and their allies on the other.

## The Armistice

The first agreement was to stop the fighting temporarily so that peace talks could take place. The "armistice" that suspended combat between Russia and Germany went into effect on December 6.

## The Location of the Peace Conference

The Russians wanted the negotiations held in Stockholm, the capital of neutral Sweden, where they hoped to appeal to world opinion through extensive newspaper coverage.

However, the Germans showed their control of the situation by insisting on meeting at Brest-Litovsk, the site of German military headquarters.

## Brest-Litovsk

### *Phase One (December 1917–January 1918)*

During the first weeks of negotiations, the Russians presented their established program of peace "without annexations or indemnities." The Germans responded by demanding that Russia transfer large areas of the former Russian empire to German control.

### *Phase Two (January–February 1918)*

The second phase of the negotiations was dominated by Leon Trotsky, the Russian commissar of foreign affairs. Trotsky attempted to slow the pace of the negotiations, hoping that revolution would break out in Germany

*"No War, No Peace."*    When he could delay no longer, Trotsky shocked the Germans with a declaration of "no war, no peace." This meant that the Russians would refuse to sign an unjust treaty, and they would also refuse to continue the war.

*The New German Offensive.*    The Germans responded to Trotsky by resuming their offensive eastward. They met no Russian resistance and soon approached key objectives like Petrograd.

### Phase Three (March 1918)

Lenin had the decisive role in convincing the Communist Party to agree to the terms offered by the Germans. He accepted the harsh provisions of the treaty for several reasons. First, he wanted to preserve Russia as the unconquered base for world revolution. Second, he looked forward to an eventual German defeat. Finally, he intended to evade the peace terms as far as possible.

### The Terms of the Treaty

The treaty put a heavy burden on Russia. The Communist government lost a vast stretch of territory from Russia's former western provinces. Nearly 1.3 million square miles of land were transformed into weak new states, including Estonia, Lithuania, and Latvia, that were nominally independent but actually under German control. Sixty-two million former subjects of the Russian empire were transferred from it.

The territory taken from Russia contained much of Russia's industrial and agricultural wealth. Moreover, Russia now had to supply Germany with food.

### Bukharin and the Radical Position

Lenin had to overcome the opposition of radical leaders of the Communist Party like Nicholas Bukharin (1888–1938) who wanted to continue the war despite Russian weakness. They presented one compelling argument: By accepting a peace treaty, Russia would be abandoning revolutionary workers in Germany, who might soon rise up if Germany was forced to continue fighting on the Eastern Front.

**Russia's Territorial Losses Following World War I**

The Communist radicals also suggested that the war might be continued by using small-scale guerrilla forces, since Russia no longer had a large, conventional army.

## The Consequences of Brest-Litovsk

Russia's departure from the war increased the government's isolation and hardened the feelings of its opponents, many of whom considered the treaty a disgrace and unpatriotic.

### Reaction of the Entente

Russia's former allies felt abandoned and betrayed at a time when Germany was about to start a furious offensive in France. Along with their distrust of Communism, they now wondered about Russian cooperation with Germany.

Entente leaders like President Woodrow Wilson of the United States now began to consider military intervention in Russia as a means of restoring Russia's participation in the war.

### Domestic Opposition

Within Russia, the peace settlement helped bring numerous groups together to try to overthrow the Communist government.

The SRs in the government resigned and formed a militant opposition party. At the same time conservatives and moderates came together in the Don region and in western Siberia to form anti-Communist coalitions.

## Deepening Radicalism (Spring–Summer 1918)

The new government, now composed entirely of Communists, pushed forward to tighten its control over Russia and to transform the country.

Several steps marked a new break with the past.

## The "Communist Party"

At Lenin's insistence, the official name of the Bolshevik Party was changed to the "Communist Party" in March 1918. Lenin had first raised the issue in "The April Theses" the previous year. The new name associated the Party with the militancy of the Paris Commune of 1871, which Lenin saw as an early example of workers taking up arms against a bourgeois state.

## "The War on the Village"

In order to get food for the cities, in May 1918 the government instituted a program of forced requisitions from the countryside. This was a policy the tsarist government had never undertaken seriously during the war. Now it was carried out with harsh effectiveness.

Lenin's government tried to enlist poor peasants to help seize food supplies held by their more prosperous neighbors. In the end, however, the seizures were carried out by forces, including the Red Army, that were sent into the villages from the outside.

## The New Constitution

In July 1918, the first Soviet Constitution was adopted. Supreme power was placed in the hands of the All-Russian Congress of Soviets, which was to be elected by rural and urban workers.

The Constitution restricted civil rights and the right to bear arms to members of the working class. Voting rights were given to urban and rural workers. Urban workers got far more power than rural ones: Every 25,000 city voters had one representative in the Supreme Soviet; in contrast, every 125,000 rural voters had one representative.

The Constitution specifically removed voting rights and the right to bear arms from the middle and upper classes. Priests and monks as well as former police officials were also deprived of these rights.

## The Role of the Communist Party

The Communist Party, which effectively governed the country, was not mentioned in the Constitution. But the fundamental Communist doctrine that the revolution had to be followed by "a dictatorship of the proletariat" was included. This was a tenet of traditional Marxism restated by Lenin in works like *State and Revolution*.

If Russia had to go through a prolonged dictatorship of the proletariat, this provided a justification for rule by the Communist Party. The Party, after all, was the highest representative of the proletariat and its interests.

## The Murder of the Tsar and the Imperial Family

The assassination of the imperial family marked another break with the past. Imprisoned in western Siberia, the tsar, his wife, and their children found themselves close to one of the fighting fronts in the growing civil war (see Chapter 22). It was possible they might be rescued by anti-Communist forces.

In mid-July 1918, local Communist leaders, acting on orders from Moscow, executed the entire family.

*By the summer of 1918, Lenin and his Communist Party had solved two major dilemmas. They had removed Russia from the war, and they had crushed the legal challenge posed to their power by the democratically elected Constituent Assembly.*

*Nonetheless, much of the country remained beyond the control of the revolutionaries. The rural population was increasingly hostile in the face of food requisitioning. Russia's departure from the war had come at the cost of painful concessions to Germany, and groups all over the political spectrum could now rally against the Communists and the Treaty of Brest-Litovsk.*

*By the early months of 1918 the polarization of Russian society, for and against the policies of Lenin's government, made civil war imminent.*

## Recommended Reading

Brovkin, Vladimir. *The Mensheviks after October: Socialist Opposition and the Rise of the Bolshevik Dictatorship* (1987).

Burbank, Jane. *Intelligentsia and Revolution: Russian Views of Bolshevism, 1917–1922* (1986).

Carr, Edward Hallett. *A History of Soviet Russia: The Bolshevik Revolution, 1917–1923*, vol. 2 (1951).

Debo, Richard. *Revolution and Survival: The Foreign Policy of Soviet Russia, 1917–18* (1979).

Deutscher, Isaac. *Trotsky: The Prophet Armed, 1879–1921* (1954).

Keep, John L. H. *The Russian Revolution: A Study in Mass Mobilization* (1976).

Kennan, George F. *Soviet-American Relations, 1917–1922. Vol. 1, Russia Leaves the War* (1956).

Leggett, George. *The Cheka: Lenin's Political Police* (1981).

Pethybridge, R. *The Spread of the Russian Revolution: Essays on 1917* (1972).

Pipes, Richard. *The Russian Revolution* (1990).

Radkey, Oliver. *The Elections to the Constituent Assembly of 1917* (1950).

Ulam, Adam. *The Bolsheviks: The Intellectual and Political History of the Triumph of Communism in Russia* (1965).

Wheeler-Bennett, John W. *The Forgotten Peace: Brest-Litovsk, March 1918* (1939).

# CHAPTER 22

## The Civil War Era
## (1918–1921)

### Time Line

| | |
|---|---|
| December 1917 | Creation of the Supreme Council of the National Economy |
| February 1918 | Red Army established |
| March 1918 | Treaty of Brest-Litovsk |
| | Trotsky becomes commissar of war |
| | Allied troops land at Murmansk |
| April 1918 | Japanese land at Vladivostok |
| May 1918 | Revolt of Czech Legion |
| July 1918 | SR revolt |

| | |
|---|---|
| August 1918 | White forces capture Kazan |
| | Assassination attempt on Lenin |
| September 1918 | Red Terror |
| | Omsk Directorate formed |
| | Red Army recaptures Kazan |
| November 1918 | Armistice ends World War I fighting |
| | Omsk Directorate overthrown |
| | Kolchak becomes Supreme White Commander |
| March 1919 | First Comintern Congress |
| | Eighth Communist Party Congress |
| | Kolchak takes offensive in Siberia |
| April 1919 | Kolchak offensive halted |
| May–October 1919 | Denikin offensive northward |
| June 1919 | Kolchak begins to retreat |
| October 1919 | White Armies under Denikin and Yudenich threaten Moscow and Petrograd |
| | Denikin retreats from Orel |
| | Yudenich retreats from Petrograd |
| January 1920 | Allied blockade ends |
| February 1920 | Peace with Estonia |
| | Kolchak executed |
| April 1920 | Soviets retake Azerbaijan |
| | Russo-Polish War begins |
| | Wrangel succeeds Denikin |
| May 1920 | Poles take Kiev |

| June 1920 | Wrangel offensive northward from Crimea |
| | Polish retreat from Kiev |
| July 1920 | Second Comintern Congress |
| August 1920 | Battle of Warsaw |
| October 1920 | Peace negotiations with Poles at Riga |
| November 1920 | Wrangel evacuates the Crimea |
| December 1920 | Soviets retake Armenia |
| February 1921 | Soviets retake Georgia |
| March 1921 | Treaty of Riga |

*The new Communist government of Russia had to win a fierce civil war that lasted for three years in order to establish its control. The Communists faced a diverse group of Russian opponents. These "White" forces received assistance from foreign interventionists, chiefly Russia's former World War I allies.*

*After a bloody, destructive struggle, the Communists were successful. Leon Trotsky created a disciplined and effective Red Army. The Whites failed to build an effective political movement or to follow a coordinated military strategy.*

*In this era of war, the Communist Party became increasingly dictatorial and centralized. Radical changes took place in Russian social, economic, and cultural life.*

## The Start of Armed Opposition

Military forces opposed to the new Soviet government began to gather soon after the November Revolution.

### The Volunteer Army

The first important military force on the White (anti-Communist) side was the Volunteer Army, which was formed in the Don Cossack region in early 1918.

### Left-Wing Opposition to the Army

Even though the army avoided features of the old imperial system, such as guards units and elaborate privileges for officers, members of the Communist Party still objected to Trotsky's force. Left-wing Communists called for an army based on the volunteer Red Guards with their elected officers. Another radical demand aimed at an army that would fight as guerrillas instead of in the conventional regiments formed by Trotsky.

Although Trotsky defended his position successfully at the Eighth Party Congress in March 1919, opposition to his military system lasted until the close of the war.

### The Red Army's First Success (Volga, 1918)

The new Red Army proved itself in a successful campaign against the Czechs.

In fighting on the Volga (August–October 1918) around Kazan and Simbirsk, the Czech army was defeated, then forced to retreat eastward along the Trans-Siberian Railroad line.

## The White Forces

The White forces faced two difficult problems. First, they were composed of a variety of political elements, ranging from conservative monarchists to liberals like the Cadets. Second, they were scattered around the outskirts of European Russia. The central areas, with the greatest concentration of people and cities, remained under the Communists.

### Political Unification

The Whites tried to form a united political front under Admiral Alexander Kolchak (1874–1920). The Omsk Directory, a coalition provisional government that included SRs and liberals, was overthrown in a military coup in November 1918. Thereafter, Kolchak was the official leader (or Supreme Ruler) on the White side, which operated from Siberian headquarters.

### Military Coordination

In 1919, the Whites planned to attack the Communist heartland in a coordinated assault from several different directions.

## 1919: Turning Point of the Civil War

During 1919, the White challenge to the Soviet government reached its peak. White armies attacked central Russia from three directions. The collapse of this attempt at a coordinated offensive effectually ensured a Red victory.

### Causes of the White Defeat

By the close of the year the White offensive failed disastrously. Several factors doomed the White effort.

**The Civil War at its Peak: The Battlefronts in Mid-1919**

### The Problem of Military Coordination

The White forces had not been able to coordinate their efforts, and the Red Army met the White attacks one at a time.

### Whites Failure to Win the Civilian Population

White leaders antagonized the peasant population and non-Russian ethnic groups by refusing to recognize the takeover of land by the peasantry or the nationalist ambitions of non-Russians. Thus, the flanks and rear areas of the White armies were insecure.

### The Problem of Distance

Finally, the vast distances White armies had to cover in order to reach the Soviet heartland created serious problems of supply and communication. For example, one of the White armies in the south attacking Moscow in the summer of 1919 moved 750 miles to reach its objective.

### Political Diversity

Even though conservative generals dominated the White side by 1919, the forces fighting the Reds contained groups lacking a common aim. In the south, for example, there was substantial friction between Cossacks in the Kuban and the White commander, General Anton Denikin (1872–1947).

## The Campaigns of 1919

### Kolchak and the Eastern Offensive

Admiral Kolchak was the first to attack. He began his advance westward toward Moscow and reached the Volga in April. However, his forces were stretched thin over vast areas. In addition, he was weakened by mutinies within his army and by the distrust of the peasant population in the regions he occupied.

Kolchak was forced to retreat in June 1919, when his collapsing army was driven back to eastern Siberia. In January 1920, Kolchak stepped down as the White commander-in-chief. The next month he fell into Communist hands at Irkutsk and was executed.

### Denikin and the South

Chances for a striking White victory still existed when General Denikin drove northward from the Ukraine in May 1919. But a determined Red defense of Tsaritsyn on the Volga kept Denikin from joining forces with Kolchak.

Denikin's offensive was weakened by opposition in his rear. He refused to compromise with Ukrainian nationalists. Peasant partisan forces under leaders like Nestor Makhno (1889–1934) also opposed him.

Denikin reached the city of Orel, less than 300 miles south of Moscow in October. By then, his overextended forces were struck by a decisive Red counterattack. Thus, Denikin, like Kolchak, was in headlong retreat in the late fall.

### Yudenich and the Baltic

The third prong of the White advance came closest to capturing a vital Soviet center. In October and November, General Nicholas Yudenich (1862–1933) led a combined White and Estonian force toward Petrograd.

As Yudenich seemed on the verge of capturing the birthplace of the revolution, Trotsky rushed to the scene to organize the city's defense. Meanwhile, however, Yudenich antagonized his Estonian allies and destroyed the stability of his rear by his insistence that Estonia remain a part of the Russian empire.

In the middle of November, Yudenich began his retreat westward.

## The Polish Threat

The successful defense of the Communist heartland brought the appearance of a Red victory in the Civil War. In early 1920, however, forces of the newly recreated Polish state attacked the Ukraine.

### Pilsudski

The Polish leader Josef Pilsudski (1876–1935) intended to use Russia's weakness to restore Poland as a major political and territorial power in Eastern Europe. He formed an alliance with the Ukrainian nationalist Simon Petliura (1876–1926).

### Polish Advance to Kiev

In late April 1920, Polish forces invaded the Ukraine and took Kiev. For a brief time, it seemed that Pilsudski would succeed in creating an enlarged Poland linked to a independent Ukrainian state under Petliura.

## Advance of Wrangel from the Crimea

The Polish threat permitted the White forces in the south to launch a final offensive. Their new commander, Peter Wrangel (1878–1928), had replaced Denikin in April 1920. Wrangel was a skilled military leader who also tried to win over the peasant population in areas controlled by the Whites.

Wrangel's attack succeeded as long as the Reds had to concentrate on the Polish threat.

## The Russo-Polish War

In June 1920, Soviet forces counterattacked at Kiev and compelled Pilsudski to retreat.

### Non-Communists Rally to Aid the Government

The Polish threat drew many non-Communists to help the Red side. Lenin's government thus received support, not for its radical policies, but as the defender of Russia against a traditional foreign enemy. For example, General Alexis Brusilov, the distinguished World War I commander, offered his services to the Red Army.

### The Advance to Warsaw

The Red Army swept westward into Poland. This advance raised the possibility that Communist revolutions in Eastern Europe might be stimulated and supported by Russian military power.

### Defeat in the West (August 1920)

In the Battle of Warsaw, Polish forces, aided by French military advisers, defeated the Red Army. As Soviet forces retreated, prospects for the spread of Communist revolutions westward faded for the immediate future.

### Treaty of Riga

The Poles found themselves too weak for a new advance into Soviet territory. Peace talks between the two sides began at Riga in October 1920. In March 1921, the Treaty of Riga drew a compromise frontier between Poland and Soviet Russia. It split both the

Ukraine and White Russia, placing portions of both under Poland's control.

## The End of Armed White Opposition

Once the Red Army had dealt with the Polish invasion, Wrangel's position was severely weakened. His relatively small army was pushed southward into the Crimea in early November 1920. The British fleet evacuated Wrangel's men and their families later that month. This ended all large-scale military opposition by the Whites against the Soviet government.

## Allied Intervention

Allied troops began to land in Russia in the spring of 1918. Foreign military forces like the British navy were a factor in the Civil War until Wrangel evacuated the Crimea in November 1920.

### The Basis for Allied Intervention

Historians agree that several factors played a role in bringing foreign forces into the course of events in Russia.

#### *Opposition to Communism*

Foreign leaders, primarily in Britain, France, and the United States, were hostile to the radical principles proclaimed by Lenin's new government. Some, like Winston Churchill, saw it as a threat to civilization. They noted that Lenin and Trotsky called for the spread of revolution to the advanced, industrialized countries of the West.

The dispersal of the Constituent Assembly and the murder of important figures from the Provisional Government in early 1918 increased foreign alarm over the course of Russian politics.

#### *The Pressure of World War I*

A more important immediate Western concern was Russia's departure from the war. Russia's former allies noted the vast concessions Lenin had made in the Treaty of Brest-Litovsk. These came at a time when the Germans were launching a dangerous final offensive in France.

Russia seemed to be under German influence. Vast stores of Allied war materials located at Russian ports were in danger of falling in German hands.

Some Allied leaders had vague hopes of setting up a Russian government that would bring Russia back into the war.

### Allied Rivalries

Landings by the Japanese at Vladivostok in April 1918 alarmed the American government. It seemed that Japan was using Russia's weakness in order to seize strategic points in northeastern Asia.

## The Course of Intervention

### Landings in Northern Russia (March–November 1918)

The first Allied intervention came in northern Russia. Beginning in March 1918, British, French, and American troops landed at Murmansk and Archangel.

Japanese landings at Vladivostok were followed by landings of American forces in August 1918.

### Allied Intentions

The motives for these first examples of intervention included concern for Allied war supplies located at the northern ports and Vladivostok. The desire to aid the escape of the Czech Legion was an important consideration. There were also false rumors that hordes of Germans taken prisoner in World War I had been sent to work in Siberia. They were reportedly running loose and threatening Russia's ports and the Allied supplies they contained. Such concerns combined to bring the American landing in Vladivostok.

## Postwar Allied Intervention

Following the November 1918 Armistice, Allied forces remained on Russian soil and Allied naval forces penetrated the Black Sea and the Baltic.

The most substantial Allied intervention took place in the year following the Armistice. At this time the principal motive for intervention was to help the White forces overthrow Lenin's government.

The most significant intervention came from the British side. British naval units supported the White campaigns along the Baltic and in the Black Sea. British forces from Persia occupied parts of the Transcaucasus.

At the close of the Civil War, as the White forces were defeated, British naval vessels evacuated the remnants of Wrangel's army from the Crimea (November 1920).

# The Home Front

The Civil War years saw massive changes in Russian life. Most historians consider the strains of this period to be an important factor in permanently shaping the Communist dictatorship. This view suggests that the Party and government became harsher and more dictatorial in order to survive and defeat the Whites.

## War Communism

During the Civil War, the government instituted a radically new economic system. It featured the nationalization of industry, a shift away from the use of money, and government regulation of industrial workers and peasant farmers.

### *Motives for War Communism*

Two motives combined to produce this system of "War Communism."

*The Ideological Motive.*    Many leaders of the Communist Party considered radical economic changes to be a logical part of the Bolshevik Revolution. They believed that now that Russia was no longer a capitalist country, its economy and society should be transformed along Marxist lines.

A spokesman for this view was Nicholas Bukharin. He had also joined the radical wing of the Communist Party in arguing against the Treaty of Brest-Litovsk.

*The Practical Motive.*    An even more influential motive was the need to place the country's limited resources at the disposal of the government in order to defeat the Whites and their foreign supporters.

### *Effects of War Communism*

*Industry.*    The new system eventually placed most of Russian industry under state control.

In December 1917 the Supreme Council of the National Economy was established to control industrial production. At first large firms, then most other private companies, came under government control.

*Agriculture.*    In order to assure food for the cities, the peasantry was made subject to compulsory grain deliveries. They were compelled to hand over their crops, keeping only a minimum amount determined by the government.

The government lacked the resources to compel peasants to join collective farms, although it launched a propaganda campaign to encourage them to do so. There was no substantial positive response. Even poor peasants preferred to farm individually or within the framework of the old commune. The government chose not to run the risk of further arousing peasant hostility and dropped the pursuit of collectivized agriculture.

*The Labor Force.*    Factory workers came under strict government control. Unions were transformed into organs by which the government directed the workers. Workers between the ages of sixteen and fifty could be conscripted to fill certain industrial jobs anywhere the government desired.

## Political Terror

In August 1918 Fanny Kaplan (1890–1918), a member of the SR party, wounded Lenin in an assassination attempt. The Communist government responded with a campaign of terror intended to repress and frighten opponents of the regime. Thousands of hostages were arrested throughout Soviet territory. The arrests were made on a class basis: Those arrested were mainly middle-class Russians and military officers.

Many of the hostages were executed at once. Five hundred were shot in Petrograd alone in the week after the attempt on Lenin's life.

The practice of taking hostages and executing large numbers of them continued throughout the Civil War. Some historians believe that 50,000 executions took place at the hands of the Cheka. The White forces used the same kind of terror campaign in regions under their control.

## Urban Life

The pressure of the war on the population was evident in the decline of the urban population. Workers fled the cities to return to the countryside where food was more available. The fuel shortage was also critical.

## The Greens

Rural opposition to the Communist government was widespread. Some historians describe the Civil War as a three-sided conflict among the Communist "Reds," the conservative "Whites," and the "Greens."

### Green Position

The term "Greens" refers to peasants who fought against both the Reds and the Whites. These peasants objected to the Whites as a group that would bring back the old landowners. They opposed the Reds because of such government policies as requisitioning of their crops.

### Nestor Makhno

The most significant Green leader was the peasant anarchist Nestor Makhno, who at the peak of his power led a peasant army of 50,000 men. Sometimes allied with the Reds against the Whites, Makhno remained independent of the government.

Makhno fought against Communist rule once the Whites had been defeated. Though he was forced to retreat to Romania in 1921, the extent of his support showed how deeply the peasant population was alienated from the government.

## Cultural Radicalization

Many of the writers who remained in Russia after 1917 supported the Communist Revolution for some time.

### Poetry

Poets like Alexander Blok (1880–1921), Sergei Esenin (1895–1925), and Vladimir Mayakovsky (1893–1930) wrote works hailing the arrival of the new era.

*Proletkult*

The most important new literary group was the Association of Proletarian Cultural and Educational Organizations (or *Proletkult*).

*Proletkult*, founded by Alexander Bogdanov (1873–1923), maintained that the revolution had to be supported by the creation of a proletarian culture. Some elements in *Proletkult* even insisted upon a complete break with past cultural traditions.

The radicalism and independent organization of *Proletkult* led Lenin himself to call for its subordination to the government.

# The Nationalities

During the Civil War, parts of the old Russian empire tried to break away from the control of the government in Moscow. In some cases, notably in the Baltic region, they succeeded. Most of the old empire, however, ended up as part of the emerging Soviet state.

## The Bolshevik Position

In 1917, Lenin's party used the slogan of national self-determination to undercut the Provisional Government. This seemed to mean that the non-Russian peoples who had lived under the tsars had the right to form independent countries.

After taking power, however, Lenin and his lieutenants effectively reversed this policy. They took the position that the decision to set up an independent state belonged to a nationality's working class, not to the population as a whole.

In practice, this meant that Moscow intended to retain areas like the Ukraine, claiming that the workers of the region wanted to remain part of the Soviet state.

## The Ukraine

The Ukraine was the largest and most important non-Russian region within the old empire. The Bolsheviks encouraged Ukrainian separatism in 1917 as a powerful blow against the authority of the Provisional Government.

### Subversion of Ukrainian Independence

In December 1917, the Communist government recognized the independence of the Ukraine. At the same time, however, a Russian sponsored Communist government was set up in the large industrial city of Kharkov in the eastern part of the Ukraine.

### The Ukraine in the Civil War

The Ukraine became one of the principal battlegrounds in the Civil War. Cities like Kiev changed hands repeatedly depending on the successes of the Reds or the Whites and their foreign allies.

With the defeat of Wrangel and the close of hostilities, most of the Ukraine was retaken by the Red Army. This meant that the region's future would be determined by decisions made in Moscow.

## Moslem Central Asia

The Moslem regions of Central Asia were likewise retaken by force and incorporated in the Soviet state.

Local armed resistance, conducted by Moslem tribal forces called *Basmachi*, began in 1917 and continued in regions like Turkestan until 1924.

## The Caucasus

The three main regions of the Caucasus—Georgia, Armenia, and Azerbaijan—set up independent states in the spring of 1918.

### The Caucasus in the Civil War

The three new states survived most of the Civil War. British forces arrived there from Persia, and the region was shielded from Moscow by White armies.

### Reconquest by Soviets

The end of the Civil War put this area within striking distance of the Russian government. Azerbaijan was retaken in April 1920. Following the war with Poland, Soviet forces renewed their pressure in the Caucasus. Armenia fell in December 1920, and Georgia in March 1921.

## Baltic Provinces

The areas of Estonia, Latvia, and Lithuania had been occupied by the German army during World War I. They were retaken by the

Russian Red Army in late 1918, following the November Armistice. But this action was not decisive.

### The Baltic Region in the Civil War

The Baltic region contained powerful nationalist groups anxious to break away from Russian control. Moreover, these regions were important strongholds for White forces during the Civil War. For example, the army of General Nicholas Yudenich operated from Estonia and, for a time, received help from Estonian nationalists.

The Baltic regions were also able to receive outside assistance from forces including the British navy.

### Independence

By the close of the Civil War, Russian military strength had not been great enough to overcome Baltic nationalism augmented by foreign assistance. Estonia, Latvia, and Lithuania became independent countries.

# Russia and the Outside World

During the Civil War years, Russia's Communist leaders were overwhelmed by their domestic difficulties. They saw the outside world primarily as a scene for future revolutions. Promoting revolution in the industrial countries was the most immediate goal. Help from these countries would immensely aid the Russian revolutionary government's prospects for survival.

## The First Comintern Congress

In March 1919, Lenin called together foreign Marxists who were sympathetic to the Bolshevik Revolution.

Traditional Marxists in Western Europe were reviving the Socialist International. That was an international organization of socialist parties founded in 1889; it collapsed at the start of World War I. Lenin, however, wanted to form a new, more radical organization of the world's Marxists.

His Comintern ("Communist International") aimed at overthrowing existing governments. Russia, the one country that had experienced a successful Marxist revolution, would aid the spread of such revolutions.

## The Second Comintern Congress

A larger gathering came together in Moscow in July 1920. By this time there were throughout the world forty-one Communist parties to send delegates to Russia.

This Congress strengthened Russian control over the international organization.

### The Twenty-One Conditions

The Comintern determined that only parties that met a set of twenty-one conditions could be accepted as Communist parties. These conditions required a party to be organized with the same disciplined hierarchy and militant doctrine that characterized the Russian Communist Party.

### Other Measures to Ensure Russian Control

Russian control over the Comintern was heightened by establishing Moscow as its headquarters. In addition, Russia's Communist Party was guaranteed a dominant influence on the Comintern's Executive Committee.

*The Civil War left Russia economically devastated. Parts of the old empire had broken away, the cities had undergone years of deprivation, and much of western Russia had been the scene of intensive fighting.*

*Nonetheless, the nation was under the control of the Communist Party. That control was strongest in the cities. The peasant population, which had broken loose from state supervision in 1917, remained an independent, and potentially hostile, force for the new regime.*

---

### Recommended Reading

Benvenuti, Francesco. *The Bolsheviks and the Red Army, 1918–1922* (1988).

Brinkley, George. *The Volunteer Army and the Allied Intervention in South Russia, 1917–1921* (1966).

Carley, Michael. *Revolution and Intervention: The French Government and the Russian Civil War, 1917–1919* (1983).

Carr, Edward Hallett. *A History of Soviet Russia: The Bolshevik Revolution, 1917–1923*, vol. 2 (1952).

Chamberlin, William Henry. *The Russian Revolution, 1917–1921*, 2 vols. (1935).

Davies, Norman. *White Eagle, Red Star: The Polish-Soviet War, 1919–20* (1972).

Erickson, John. *The Soviet High Command: A Military-Political History, 1918–1941* (1962).

Footman, David. *The Civil War in Russia* (1962).

Got'e, Iu. V. Edited by Terence Emmons. *Time of Troubles: The Diary of Iurii Vladimirovich Got'e: Moscow, July 8, 1917 to July 23, 1922* (1988).

Kenez, Peter. *Civil War in South Russia 1918: The First Year of the Volunteer Army* (1971).

Kenez, Peter. *Civil War in South Russia, 1919–1920: The Defeat of the Whites* (1977).

Kennan, George. *Soviet-American Relations, 1917–1922. Vol. 2, The Decision to Intervene* (1958).

Koenker, Diane P., William G. Rosenberg, and Ronald G. Suny, eds. *Party, State, and Society in the Russian Civil War: Explorations in Social History* (1982).

Leggett, George. *The Cheka: Lenin's Political Police* (1981).

Lehovich, Dmitry V. *White against Red: The Life of General Anton Denikin* (1974).

Lincoln, W. Bruce. *Red Victory: A History of the Russian Civil War* (1989).

Malle, Silvana. *The Economic Organization of War Communism, 1918–1921* (1985).

Mally, Lynn. *Culture of the Future: The Proletkult Movement in Revolutionary Russia* (1990).

Mayer, Arno J. *Wilson versus Lenin: Political Origins of the New Diplomacy, 1917–1918* (1959).

Mawsdsley, Evan. *The Russian Civil War* (1987).

Pipes, Richard. *The Formation of the Soviet Union: Communism and Nationalism, 1917–1923* (rev. ed., 1964).

Pipes, Richard. *The Russian Revolution* (1990).

Radkey, Oliver. *The Sickle under the Hammer: The Russian Socialist Revolutionaries in the Early Months of Soviet Rule* (1963).

Radkey, Oliver. *The Unknown Civil War in Russia: A Study of the Green Movement in the Tambov Region, 1920–1922* (1976).

Rigby, T. H. *Lenin's Government: Sovnarkom, 1917–1922* (1979).

Sakwa, Richard. *Soviet Communists in Power: A Study of Moscow during the Civil War, 1918–21* (1988).

Smith, Canfield F. *Vladivostok under Red and White Rule: Revolution and Counter-Revolution in the Russian Far East, 1920–1922* (1975).

Unterberger, Betty M. *America's Siberian Expedition, 1918–1920: A Study of National Policy* (1969).

Von Hagen, Mark. *Soldiers in the Proletarian Dictatorship: The Red Army and the Soviet Socialist State, 1917–1930* (1990).

# CHAPTER 23

## The NEP Era of the 1920s

## Time Line

| | |
|---|---|
| February–March 1921 | Kronstadt uprising |
| March 1921 | Tenth Party Congress |
| | Start of NEP |
| April 1922 | Treaty of Rapallo |
| | Stalin appointed Party General Secretary |
| May 1922 | Lenin incapacitated |
| December 1922 | Formation of the Soviet Union |
| January 1924 | New constitution put into effect |
| | Lenin's death |

| | |
|---|---|
| February 1924 | Diplomatic relations begun with Britain |
| October 1924 | Diplomatic relations begun with France |
| January 1925 | Diplomatic relations begun with Japan |
| October 1926 | Trotsky removed from Party Politburo |
| April 1927 | Chiang Kai-shek attacks Chinese Communists |
| May 1927 | Diplomatic relations broken off by Britain |
| December 1927 | Fifteenth Party Congress |
| | Trotsky expelled from Party |
| January 1928 | Stalin begins "extraordinary measures" against peasantry |
| October 1928 | First Five-Year Plan formulated |

*Between 1921 and 1928, the most visible feature of Russian life was a relaxation of harsh political controls. Much of the nation's social and economic life now developed under a loosened degree of government supervision.*

*Within the Communist Party, the era was more turbulent. Lenin fell seriously ill in 1922 and died in early 1924. These events set off a brutal succession struggle.*

*The signal for a relaxation of the wartime dictatorship came in 1921 with Lenin's call for a new economic policy. A controversy raged during the decade on continuing this new economic policy or replacing it with a government-directed program of rapid growth. Another bitterly contested issue concerned whether to attempt to spread the revolution to other countries or to concentrate on the construction of a new socialist order in Russia.*

*Within the Soviet Union, quarrels over the proper course for foreign policy, along with disagreements over economic affairs, promoted the rise and fall of those competing to succeed Lenin.*

# Unrest and Rebellion

### The Crisis of 1921

By the early months of 1921, the Communist government faced overwhelming difficulties. There was no longer a threat from White armies or foreign invaders, but the domestic situation had become critical.

The industrial system was in ruins. Even more important, peasant opposition to the government and the Communist Party now threatened to become unmanageable. The peasantry made up eighty percent of the population. Angry at the policies of War Communism—especially the confiscation of their crops and efforts to compel them to join collective farms—many were already in armed revolt.

### Kronstadt Mutiny

In late February 1921, unrest spread to the armed forces. Sailors at the Kronstadt naval base near Petrograd revolted. Many were conscripted peasants who had recently returned from leave to their native villages. The insurgents demanded free elections to the soviets and broad freedom for the peasantry to farm their land as they chose.

Commissar of War Leon Trotsky suppressed the revolt with Red Army units, and many of the rebels were executed immediately. Nonetheless, the revolt had erupted among military units that had been enthusiastically loyal to the Communist Party since 1917. It persuaded many Party leaders that they needed to reconsider their policy toward the peasantry.

### Tambov Revolt

Another sign of dangerous unrest emerged in Tambov province in central Russia. Here, peasant rebels formed an anti-Communist army numbering 40,000. Their rebellion broke out in the summer of 1920 and continued for an entire year. Moreover, by 1921, peasants were carrying out over 100 other rebellions against government authority.

## New Economic Policy

Although the New Economic Policy (NEP), as it became known, began as a series of concessions to the peasant population, it developed in a spontaneous fashion. Soon it had wider and unintended effects in other areas of economic life.

## Lenin's Change of Course

By the start of 1921, Lenin recognized the need to end the policies of War Communism that had stirred such a violent and dangerous response. The Kronstadt Rebellion helped him to overcome opposition within the Communist Party to a more moderate course.

At the Tenth Party Congress (March 1921), Lenin called for ''an economic breathing space.'' It was evidently not possible, he concluded, to create a new socialist system in a short period of time. In order to let Russia recover from years of war, the government had to loosen its controls over the peasant economy. A strong majority of the delegates to the Congress approved the change.

## NEP in Agriculture

Small private farming was now encouraged in a number of ways. Only a portion of a peasant's crop had to be delivered to the state; the rest could be sold on the open market. In addition, peasants could lease more land. In some circumstances, they could even hire laborers to help them farm.

Opponents of these sweeping concessions to the rural population sometimes referred to the NEP as ''a peasant Brest-Litovsk.'' This meant that just as in 1918 the Communists had been forced to make painful concessions in foreign affairs to Germany, so were they now compelled to compromise in order to maintain stability in Russia's countryside.

## NEP in Industry

In order to offer consumer goods to the peasantry, the government permitted the revival of many privately owned industrial companies.

The state retained control of the ''commanding heights'' of the Soviet economy, including banking and trade with foreign countries. Heavy industry was also kept under state control. But even heavy industry was reorganized, grouped into approximately 500 trusts and decentralized so that local factory managers had far greater authority than under War Communism.

# Soviet Society and Culture in the 1920s

## The Famine of 1921

The NEP era began with a disastrous famine in the Volga Valley. Drought struck at a time when agriculture was still disrupted as a result of the Civil War and War Communism. Between 3 and 5 million people starved to death.

Though the Soviet government was reluctant to seek outside help, Lenin encouraged the Russian writer Maxim Gorky to ask for aid from the West. A large-scale relief effort was mounted, including an American Relief Administration led by Secretary of Commerce Herbert Hoover.

## Religion

During the NEP era, the Orthodox Church faced a campaign of government sponsored atheism, a government-supported splinter religious body called "the Living Church," and sporadic persecution. The head of the Orthodox Church, the Patriarch Tikhon (1865–1925), was imprisoned in 1922–1923.

Although the official atheism of the Communist Party put the future of the church in doubt, a fragile compromise emerged. The government did not engage in mass persecutions of priests or churchgoers. By 1927, the Patriarch Sergei (1867–1944) had recognized the new government.

## The Arts

The NEP years formed a period of cultural creativeness in literature and film.

### Literature

Groups like *Proletkult* and *VAPP* arose to demand that literature be written only by workers or that literature be restricted to revolutionary themes.

As in the case of the church, Party leaders refrained from a frontal attack on non-Communist elements in the literary community. Communist writers were however encouraged, and many literary figures like Vladimir Mayakovsky (1893–1930) felt liberated and inspired by the Revolution. Nonetheless, it was still possible to write on nonpolitical themes. For example, Isaac Babel (1894–1941) in *Red Cavalry* could even describe the Civil War in realistic rather than heroic terms.

### Film

In film, the early works of directors like Sergei Eisenstein (1898–1948) reflected an emotional tie to the Revolution. *Strike* and *Battleship Potemkin* were glorifications of 1905. *Ten Days That Shook the World* romanticized the Bolsheviks of 1917 and satirized their enemies. But Eisenstein employed daring new film techniques, including *montage*, in which contrasting images (firing machine guns, scattering crowds) are shown in rapid succession. He saw no need to direct his work to the taste of the average worker or Party bureaucrat.

## The Soviet Federation

The population of the new Soviet state was as diverse as that of the old Russian Empire. Out of 140 million individuals, nearly half were non-Russian. Soviet leaders decided to deal with this ethnic mix by creating a federation.

### The 1924 Constitution

The Constitution set up the framework for a federal system, the Union of Soviet Socialist Republics (USSR). The federal government (the government of the USSR) was given sweeping powers: the control of foreign policy, military policy, and foreign trade; and the direction of economic planning. The republics comprising the Soviet Union received the powers not reserved for the federal government.

### Continuing Controls

The federal system was effectively limited by the power of the Communist Party, which formed a rigid political system linking the republics to Moscow. Moreover, the economic strength and size of the Russian Republic or RSFSR (which formed nine-tenths of the entire Soviet Union) made the Russian core the magnet drawing in the other republics.

### Cultural Freedom

The Soviet system promoted native cultures and the official use of native languages. This cultural freedom in such important areas as the Ukraine served to disguise and smooth the way for the political centralization that the Party imposed.

## The Secret Police

The secret police, renamed the GPU in February 1922, continued its wartime efforts to preserve a monopoly of power for the Communist Party.

### Political Prisoners

Menshevik and SR leaders were arrested, tried, and exiled in 1922. The system of labor camps for political offenders, founded during the Civil War years, remained in existence. Although the number of people confined remains uncertain, some historians believe there were several hundred thousand political prisoners in the 1920s. Thus, political repression on a large scale was evident even before Stalin's purges of the Party and the general population in the 1930s.

### Limits on Terror

In general, however, the 1920s did not witness anything like the political terror of the Civil War years or the sweeping arrests of the late 1930s. The average citizen who did not engage in open political opposition remained more or less free to pursue his economic and cultural interests.

## The Communist Party

The Communist Party went through several important changes between 1921 and 1928. It grew in size, and it increased its membership from the working class. Most important, it became a more tightly organized and disciplined body. Factions were officially outlawed, and the power of the Party administration, led by the General Secretary, expanded over individual members.

### The Purge of 1921

The Civil War years had vastly expanded the size of the Party. Lenin now ordered a purge of unreliable members who had entered the Party without fully accepting Bolshevik ideas. Party ranks were reduced from 567,000 in 1921 to 350,000 in 1924. Such purges gave the central leadership enormous control over the character of the Party itself.

### Democratic Centralism

By 1921, two groups—the Workers' Opposition and the Democratic Centralists—had emerged among Party leaders to promote their own policies. At the Tenth Party Congress (1921), such factions were formally banned.

Under a system of "Democratic Centralism," Party members remained free to discuss issues of policy that had not yet been formally decided. But they were not allowed to form pressure groups within the Party. Most important, once the Party had adopted a policy, all members were expected to support it.

With the Party increasingly under Stalin's control, the theoretical right to offer alternatives to his policies became useless in practical terms. The bar on forming factions meant that any effort to organize against Stalin's wishes could be labeled contrary to the Party line.

### Lenin Enrollment

Between 1924, and 1926, the size of the Party increased to more than 1 million members. Carried out in honor of the recently deceased revolutionary leader, this "Lenin Enrollment" changed the composition of the Party. Newly recruited members were primarily factory workers, but the percentage of peasants and members of the armed forces in the Party also grew.

### The Politburo

Created on the eve of the November Revolution and then abolished, this inner council of the Party for policy making had consisted of Lenin and his closest collaborators. It was reconstituted at the Eighth Party Congress (March 1918). By the start of the NEP era its members included Lenin, Trotsky, and Stalin, and it was becoming the most powerful decision-making body within the Party.

## The Secretariat

Created in 1919 to help administer the Communist Party, this body increased in importance after Joseph Stalin (1879–1953) was appointed General Secretary of the Party in April 1922.

Through the Secretariat, Stalin had wide power to control the appointment of Party officials throughout the Soviet Union. He was able to place his supporters in key positions everywhere in the Party apparatus. This proved a crucial advantage for him in the succession struggle that followed Lenin's death.

# The Succession Struggle

## Lenin's Illness and Death

In 1922, Lenin held the position of chairman of the council of people's commissars or head of the Soviet government. In fact, his personality and prestige made him the uncontested leader of both the Soviet government and the Communist Party.

In the spring of 1922, Lenin suffered the first in a series of strokes. By the end of the year, he was transformed permanently into an invalid.

Lenin died in January 1924. Well before that point, some of the most prominent figures in Soviet political life had moved to become his successor. Individuals did this primarily in two ways: First, they built up their own power positions, often by forming alliances with other leaders. Second, they tried to block the ascendancy of other candidates for Lenin's role.

## The Main Contenders

### Trotsky

Leon Trotsky seemed to enjoy numerous advantages as Lenin faded from the scene. A brilliant speaker, writer, and theorist, he had been Lenin's chief lieutenant during the November Revolution and the Civil War. In 1922, Lenin twice offered to make Trotsky his deputy (as vice-chairman of the council of ministers) in the government. Moreover Lenin encouraged Trotsky to oppose the ambitious General Secretary of the Communist Party, Joseph Stalin.

Trotsky had no talent for the political maneuvering that was now required. Moreover, his arrogant manner offended many Party members. He was hurt as well by the fact that he was a latecomer to the Bolshevik Party, which he had joined only in 1917. His military work in the Civil War raised questions about his ambitions to become a Bonapartist dictator backed by the army.

At crucial points in the succession struggle, Trotsky was unable to act decisively. He refused Lenin's offer of the crucial government post in 1922. The following year, at the Twelfth Party Congress, he held back from an effort to crush Stalin politically as Lenin wanted him to do.

Finally, Trotsky's policy of "permanent revolution" (see p. 324) turned out to be far less appealing to Party members than Stalin's alternative of "socialism in one country."

### Stalin

Stalin did not seem to be an impressive candidate to succeed Lenin. His work in 1917 and during the Civil War did not equal what Trotsky had done. He had no reputation as a writer, speaker, or theorist. His most valuable talent seemed to be an untiring ability to run the bureaucratic organizations in the government and Party.

Stalin's crucial advantage lay in controlling the administrative structure of the Party. This permitted him to place his supporters in key Party positions and to dominate the Party's local organizations. When an opponent like Zinoviev tried to present his views to the Fourteenth Party Congress in December 1925, Stalin's supporters were numerous enough to shout him down.

### Other Contestants

The upper ranks contained a handful of prominent individuals who had been Lenin's associates long before 1917.

*Zinoviev and Kamenev.*    Grigory Zinoviev (1883–1936) was the Chairman of the Comintern and the head of the Petrograd Soviet. Lev Kamenev (1883–1936) was one of Lenin's deputies at the top of the government of the USSR and the head of the Moscow Soviet. Both were politically vulnerable because of their opposition to

Lenin's plans for the November Revolution. Neither had Trotsky's charisma and stature as a theorist or Stalin's administrative talents.

*Bukharin.*    Nicholas Bukharin was a younger figure with considerable stature as a theorist, who was popular within the Party. He was the foremost defender of the NEP policy and, in general, called for a program of moderate economic change based upon the consent of the peasantry. Nonetheless, Bukharin lacked the political energy and determination to fight vigorously for the right to succeed Lenin.

## Shifting Alliances

Between 1924 and 1929, the top leaders of the Party formed a complex series of political alliances. These alignments were intended to put each of the various leaders in a commanding position and to bar the succession to contenders each found objectionable.

### Stalin and the "Troika"

Stalin showed himself unmatched in maneuvering within such a political environment. At the time of Lenin's death in early 1924, he had formed a three-way alliance (or "Troika") with Zinoviev and Kamenev, on the left wing of the Party leadership. It was based on the antipathy of all three toward Trotsky. Together they effectively isolated Trotsky in the crucial period in which national leadership first became open.

### Stalin and the Right

At the close of 1925, the maneuvering entered a second phase. Now Stalin joined representatives of the Party's moderate wing—Bukharin, Alexei Rykov (1881–1938), and Mikhail Tomsky (1880–1936)—to crush Zinoviev, Kamenev, and Trotsky.

At the start of 1928, Stalin was powerful enough to break with this "Politburo Right" in order to pursue a course of agricultural collectivization. By playing various leaders off against one another over the past four years, he had weakened, neutralized, or eliminated all of his competitors.

## The Economic Debate

The struggle to succeed Lenin took place against the background of a sharp debate over how to develop the Russian economy. While agriculture made rapid progress under the NEP, industry grew more slowly. For many Party leaders, the position they took on economic planning helped determine their allies and enemies in the political succession struggle.

### Bukharin and the Right

One group in the Party advocated a program of gradual industrial growth. Bukharin, the spokesman for this group, expected peasant prosperity to stimulate the demand for industrial goods. Hence he held that the government should intervene in only indirect ways to boost industry. For example, it should encourage state factories to cut the price of manufactured goods in order to attract peasant buyers. It should encourage well-off peasants to deposit their savings in banks run by the state. In this way, the peasants would grow more wealthy. Then their wealth would be placed voluntarily at the state's disposal for future industrial growth.

Another member of the Party who seemed to favor the continuation of the NEP and a program of gradual industrial growth was the General Secretary of the Party, Joseph Stalin.

### The Left Opposition

A second group within the Party, whose members included Trotsky and the economist Evgeny Preobrazhensky (1886–1937), rejected a gradual industrialization based on the voluntary help of the peasantry.

The Left insisted on a leap forward. The government was to take over industrial expansion; the peasantry must be controlled, and the government had to squeeze resources from well-off peasants (or *kulaks*) to finance speedy industrialization. But even the Left rejected the idea of forced collectivization.

## "Permanent Revolution" versus "Socialism in One Country"

The contest between Trotsky and Stalin in part took place in the area of ideology. Each presented a view of how the revolution in Russia would develop and connect with revolutions in the rest of the world.

### Trotsky's Theory

Trotsky presented a theory of "permanent revolution." Russia with its peasant majority and its primitive economy could not carry its revolution to a successful conclusion alone. In order to build a Communist society, it would have to spread the revolution to more advanced countries. Communism in these advanced countries would then aid the more backward Russians.

### Trotsky's Failure

Trotsky's revolutionary optimism did not seem to match the facts. Efforts to promote revolution in other countries, in Germany in 1923, for example, failed dismally. More important, Trotsky's policy was a recipe for constant friction with the major nations of the outside world.

### Stalin's Winning Argument

Stalin presented an attractive theory of "Socialism in One Country." He insisted that Russia could consolidate and develop the revolution within its own borders. There was no need to depend on revolutions made abroad by foreigners. There was no need for the exhausted Russian people to waste energy and resources to promote such revolutions. Thus, he appealed to Russian pride and nationalism. Equally important, he appeared to offer leadership that would concentrate on domestic reconstruction.

### Stalin's Triumph

The Fifteenth Party Congress, held in December 1927, brought the final triumph of Stalin and his supporters. The Politburo now contained a majority of Stalin's followers. Under Stalin's direction, the Congress expelled numerous supporters of Trotsky and other foes of Stalin from the Party.

### The Exile of Trotsky

Another sign of Stalin's domination over the Party was the exile of Leon Trotsky. He was sent to Alma Ata, close to the Chinese border, in January 1928. In January 1929, he was forced into exile abroad and was never permitted to return.

## Foreign Policy

Soviet foreign policy was shaped by the failure of the revolution to spread to other countries. The defeat of the Red Army in Poland in 1920 was a sign that both Eastern and Western Europe were becoming more stable. Thus, Soviet Russia had to develop relations with the outside world on a very different basis from the revolutionary optimism that had followed the 1917 November Revolution.

## Goals

The first aim of Soviet foreign policy became to reestablish diplomatic relations with and trade ties to the major powers of Europe. This strategy was intended to help protect the new Soviet state from a further wave of military intervention. Russian leaders also hoped it would open the way for foreign economic assistance.

At the same time, however, Soviet Russia remained determined to aid the spread of revolution in both the advanced and the less developed countries of the world.

## Russia's Situation

### Advantages

Russia benefited from the war weariness and economic disruption other countries felt after World War I. The major powers of Europe had no desire for further military intervention against Russia. Several, including Britain and Germany, thought that renewed relations with Russia would help restore their injured economies.

Germany was the principal loser in World War I and thus a diplomatic outsider like Russia. Some officials in Berlin thought that Germany would benefit diplomatically by renewed ties to Moscow. Thus Germany was the first major country to grant official diplomatic recognition to the Soviet government.

### Disadvantages

Russia still faced distrust from other countries. Many political leaders in Europe feared Russia's intention of spreading revolution. A second source of friction was financial. Lenin's government refused to recognize the huge international debts incurred by earlier Russian governments. Embittered investors insisted that the Soviet government settle such claims. This was especially the case in France, from which the Russian government had borrowed huge sums before 1917.

## Tools of Foreign Policy

Since Soviet foreign policy had two sets of goals, one short term and one long term, Soviet leaders used two different organizations in carrying out their foreign relations.

### *Narkomindel*

The Soviet government developed a conventional system of ambassadors and consulates to represent its interests in foreign countries. Leading this apparatus was a government ministry, the Commissariat for Foreign Affairs (or Narkomindel). It was the *Narkomindel* that carried out the policy of restoring and maintaining normal diplomatic relations with other countries.

### *Comintern*

The effort to spread revolution was carried out by the Comintern. Technically the Comintern was not part of the Soviet government; it was the international organization of Communist parties with headquarters at Moscow. But since the only Communist Party in power was the Soviet Party, the Comintern was dominated by Soviet leaders and served as the revolutionary counterpart to the *Narkomindel*.

## Chicherin

The Soviet foreign minister during the 1920s was Georgi Chicherin (1872–1936). A former tsarist diplomat and a former Menshevik, he had joined the Bolshevik Party only in 1918. Never a policymaker, he performed brilliantly in carrying out policies set by Party leaders like Lenin.

## The Genoa Conference

The Russians were invited to the economic conference held at Genoa in April 1922. The Genoa Conference was intended to promote European economic recovery, and even the outcast countries Russia and Germany were invited to attend. Chicherin represented the Soviet government.

### *Soviet Tactics at Genoa*

The Soviet delegation played on German fears of being burdened with additional penalties as a result of losing the war. The Soviets managed to persuade the Germans not to avoid a formal tie with Russia in hopes of getting better relations with the countries of Western Europe.

### The Treaty of Rapallo

The Rapallo agreement (signed in a suburb of Genoa on April 16, 1922) broke the pattern of official diplomatic isolation for Soviet Russia. The German government extended official recognition to the Communist government of Russia, and the two countries agreed to exchange ambassadors. In addition, the treaty set up the framework for Russo-German economic and military cooperation. Claims for war reparations between the two countries were canceled.

## End to Diplomatic Isolation

Other major countries soon established formal diplomatic links with Moscow. The British and French governments each sent an ambassador to Moscow in 1924. Japan followed in 1925. Ties with Germany were strengthened by a new treaty in 1926. In several cases, the Russians were able to get trade agreements and short-term economic credits from foreign nations.

By the close of the decade, the United States was the only major country that had not formally recognized the Soviet government.

## Diplomatic Defeats

### Great Britain

The most striking defeats in conventional diplomacy came as a result of Soviet Russia's revolutionary intentions. For example, in 1927, the British government broke off diplomatic relations for several years, claiming that the Russians were promoting revolution within Britain.

### Germany

The activities of the Comintern led to even more serious disasters. The German Communist Party, encouraged by Comintern leaders including Zinoviev, tried to seize power in 1923. Their revolt was crushed by the German army.

## China

An even greater calamity took place in China four years later. The Comintern encouraged the Chinese Communist Party to cooperate with the nationalist and non-Communist Kuomintang Party. Joseph Stalin and other Soviet leaders thought that the revolution in China would come in stages. First, a "united front" of Communists and nationalists would form a centralized government and expel foreign imperialists. A proletarian revolution would then follow.

Instead, the nationalist leader Chiang Kai-shek ended the alliance in April 1927. His forces killed thousands of Communists in Shanghai and destroyed the influence of Chinese Communism for years to come.

*During the 1920s, Soviet Russia had begun to recover from the trials of war and revolution. A moderate economic policy set the tone for an era in which revolutionary change seemed to be put aside. Even the bitter struggle within the Party to see who would succeed Lenin had been a war of words and political maneuvering, not bloodshed.*

*Reestablishing formal relations with the major nations of the outside world (except the United States) was a major achievement of the NEP era. The competing policies of promoting revolution in other countries and conducting conventional relations with existing governments had seen the first fail, the second succeed.*

*By the close of the 1920s, however, Stalin had consolidated his control of the Communist Party and the question of how to push the country forward economically was becoming a pressing one. With dictatorial power in his hands, the man who had succeeded Lenin now moved to transform the country and its society.*

---

## Recommended Reading

Avrich, Paul. *Kronstadt 1921* (1970).

Ball, Alan M. *Russia's Last Capitalists: The Nepmen, 1921–1929* (1987).

Chase, William J. *Workers, Society, and the Soviet State: Labor and Life in Moscow, 1918–1929* (1987).

Cohen, Stephen F. *Bukharin and the Russian Revolution: A Political Biography, 1888–1938* (1973).

Daniels, Robert. *The Conscience of the Revolution: Communist Opposition in Soviet Russia* (1960).

Deutscher, Isaac. *The Prophet Unarmed: Trotsky, 1921–1929* (1959).

Erlich, Alexander. *The Soviet Industrialization Debate, 1924–1928* (1960).

Fainsod, Merle. *Smolensk under Soviet Rule* (1958).

Fink, Carole. *The Genoa Conference: European Diplomacy, 1921–1922* (1984).

Fischer, Louis. *The Soviets in World Affairs: A History of the Relation between the Soviet Union and the Rest of the World, 1917–1929* (1951).

Getzler, Israel. *Kronstadt, 1917–1921: The Fate of a Soviet Democracy* (1983).

Kenez, Peter. *The Birth of the Propaganda State: Soviet Methods of Mass Mobilization, 1917–1929* (1985).

Lewin, Moshe. *Lenin's Last Struggle* (1968).

Lewin, Moshe. *Russian Peasants and Soviet Power: A Study of Collectivization* (1968).

Maguire, Robert A. *Red Virgin Soil: Soviet Literature in the 1920s* (1968).

O'Connor, Timothy. *Diplomacy and Revolution: G. V. Chicherin and Soviet Foreign Affairs, 1918–1930* (1988).

O'Connor, Timothy. *The Politics of Soviet Culture: Anatolii Lunacharskii* (1983).

Radkey, Oliver. *The Unknown Civil War in Soviet Russia: A Study of the Green Movement in the Tambov Region, 1920–1921* (1976).

Tucker, Robert. *Stalin as Revolutionary, 1879–1929: A Study in History and Personality* (1973).

Tumarkin, Nina. *Lenin Lives! The Lenin Cult in the Soviet Union* (1983).

Ulam, Adam. *Expansion and Coexistence: The History of Soviet Foreign Policy, 1917–1967* (1968).

Uldricks, Teddy J. *Diplomacy and Ideology: The Origins of Soviet Foreign Relations, 1917–1930* (1979).

Von Hagen, Mark. *Soldiers in the Proletarian Dictatorship: The Red Army and the Soviet Socialist State, 1917–1930* (1990).

# CHAPTER 24

## The Stalin Revolution
## (1929–1939)

## Time Line

January 1928    First "emergency" grain confiscations

Fall 1928    Crisis in food deliveries

November 1928  First Five-Year Plan (1928–1933) begun

April 1929    Five-Year Plan formally adopted by Sixteenth Party Conference

November 1929  Bukharin removed from Politburo

Forced collectivization begins

December 1929  Stalin authorizes liquidation of *kulaks*

| | |
|---|---|
| March 1930 | Retreat from collectivization: "Dizzy with Success" article |
| Fall 1930 | Resumption of forced collectivization |
| December 1932 | Early conclusion of First Five-Year Plan |
| 1932–1933 | Famine in the Ukraine |
| January–February 1934 | Seventeenth Party Congress ("Congress of Victors") |
| February 1934 | Second Five-Year Plan adopted (1933–1937) |
| July 1934 | Founding of NKVD |
| August 1934 | Establishment of Socialist Realism |
| December 1934 | Assassination of Sergei Kirov: Start of "Great Purge" |
| January 1935 | Trial of "Moscow Center": Zinoviev and Kamenev |
| August 1935 | Stakhanov labor triumph |
| August 1936 | First Moscow "show" trial: Zinoviev and Kamenev |
| September 1936 | Yezhov replaces Yagoda as head of secret police |
| December 1936 | New Constitution |
| January 1937 | Second Moscow "show" trial: Radek |
| 1937–1938 | Completion of collectivization |
| June 1937 | Purge of military leaders |
| March 1938 | Third Moscow trial: Bukharin, Rykov, Yagoda |
| | Third Five-Year Plan begun |
| | Study of Russian made compulsory throughout the Soviet Union |
| December 1938 | Beria replaces Yezhov as head of secret police |

*Following Stalin's rise to dictatorial power, the Soviet Union underwent three basic and sweeping changes. First, agriculture was collectivized, a process that altered the lives of a majority of the Russian population. A second change took place in industrial affairs: The government carried out a program of rapid industrialization.*

*Finally, government and Party control spread into the life of every citizen. The most dramatic manifestation of this was the great purge of the 1930s that struck at all levels of society. Its most notable accusations were directed at major Communist Party leaders.*

## Totalitarianism

Some historians consider the Soviet system created by Stalin by the close of the 1930s to be an example of "totalitarianism." The term describes a political system in which power is concentrated at the top and in which the population is totally mobilized to carry out a vast transformation of society. No institutions, such as independent political parties or labor organizations, are permitted to stand between the dictatorial government and the individual citizen. The mobilizing process includes widely applied police terror, striking many and threatening everyone. It also involves the use of propaganda to rally the population to carry out vast national goals.

It is uncertain that Stalin achieved such total control over Soviet life. Of necessity, he had to rely on local subordinates to implement his plans. Nonetheless, the Soviet experience, along with the era of the Nazis in Germany, seems to be a clear example in the twentieth century of a totalitarian system.

## Collectivization

At the close of the 1920s eighty percent of the nation's people lived as peasant farmers. Thus, the collectivization of agriculture profoundly affected the Soviet population.

Collectivization ended land holding both by individuals and by the peasant commune. When completed it placed the entire rural population and agricultural production under the direct control of the government.

## The Grain Crisis of 1928–1929

The NEP system had permitted peasants to farm with relative freedom. After 1921 the government had tried to induce peasants to join collective farms voluntarily, but only a small minority had done so.

Relations between the government and the peasantry worsened starting in 1928. The immediate issue was the unwillingness of many peasants to bring their grain to market. They hoped to withhold the grain until they could receive a higher price for it. Such actions raised a number of challenges to the country's leaders, including the powerful Communist Party Secretary Joseph Stalin.

### The Problem of Feeding the Urban Population

The refusal of peasants to market their grain right after the harvest meant that the government could not obtain enough to provide food to urban areas.

### The Problem of Industrial Growth

Since the peasants continued to control the grain they harvested, the government could not rely on a steady flow of income from exporting grain. This hindered its efforts to buy vital materials abroad, such as modern equipment to aid in the process of forced industrialization (see p. 337).

### The Problem of Asserting Political Leadership

By the winter of 1928–1929, Stalin had defeated his rivals within the Communist Party. He was now strengthening his dictatorship over the entire country.

If the peasantry retained control over the agricultural system, the Party and the government would have no choice but to bargain with them. Issues like the price of food and the amount of food available for export would therefore remain beyond the government's authority.

Thus, a secure dictatorship could not be set up without bringing the rural portion of the population under control.

## Revolution in the Countryside

Beginning in early 1928, Stalin struck at the freedom of peasant agriculture. At first the campaign to place the entire peasant population under state control was carried out with delays and hesitation. However, the process intensified sharply in late 1929.

### *"The Urals Method"*

Stalin toured Siberia and the Urals in early 1928. He gave an initial sign of his future policy toward the peasantry at this time, ordering grain stores to be seized from the wealthier peasants in these areas.

### *Agriculture under the First Five-Year Plan*

A direct attack on the freedom of the peasantry was missing in the First Five-Year Plan, adopted in April 1929. The plan called for only a gradual process of collectivization.

### *The Shift to Forced Collectivization*

Suddenly, in November 1929, Stalin and his lieutenants ordered massive, forced collectivization.

The change included seizing the land of better-off peasants (the *kulaks*) and compelling entire villages to enter collective farms. Many *kulaks* were imprisoned or forced into exile in distant parts of the Soviet Union.

Local officials were put under pressure to speed the pace of collectivization. By early March 1930, more than half the peasant households had entered collective farms.

### *Peasant Resistance*

The government claimed that collectivization was largely a voluntary effort on the part of the peasant masses. In fact, resistance took place on a massive scale.

Two forms of resistance were especially dangerous for the government. First, peasants slaughtered their animals rather than lose them to the collective farms. Second, the destruction of seed grain and the unwillingness of peasants to work within the collective farms meant that the spring crop might not be planted in 1930.

### *The Pause: "Dizzy with Success"*

Stalin retreated from his policy in March 1930 in an article in the Party newspaper, *Pravda*, entitled "Dizzy with Success." Here he called for a halt in collectivization, blaming local officials for their harshness in carrying out the government's wishes.

Many peasants responded to Stalin's apparent retreat by leaving the collective farms.

## The Resumption of Collectivization

By the end of 1930, the government renewed the process of collectivization. Peasants were forced into the collective farms. The government used a number of methods against those reluctant to obey. Such methods included harsh taxes on individual farmers, threats of arrest, and even attacks by the Red Army and military units of the secret police.

By the end of the Second Five-Year Plan in 1937, ninety-three percent of the country's peasant households were under the collective farm system. The entire process had been chaotic and violent.

For the first time in Russian history, the central government obtained efficient and direct control over the rural population. Thus, while the level of farm production fell, the grain the peasants produced was at the disposal of the government.

### *The Great Famine*

Large-scale famine took place in the Ukraine in 1932 and 1933. In part, the famine was the result of poor harvests. But Stalin and his lieutenants deliberately seized grain in the affected areas.

Thus, starvation was inflicted on millions of peasants as a result of government policy to crush resistance to collectivization. Estimates of the death toll vary considerably since outside observers were not permitted into the famine region. Some historians have questioned whether the number of victims actually went into the millions. But others have estimated that between 5 and 10 million peasants died in this tragedy.

### *The Growth of the Police State*

Placing eighty percent of the population into forced service in collective farms required a basic change in national life. The system could be kept up only by expanding the powers of the government and of the secret police. Thus, both collectivization of agriculture and the need to maintain the system promoted a police state.

# Industrialization

The second development that transformed life in the Soviet Union was a program of rapid industrialization. The process was carried out according to plans set down by the government. It featured the expansion of heavy industry, led by the production of iron, coal, and electric energy.

Stalin formulated the new policy and drove it to completion. Now that he controlled the Party and the government, he shifted from his position of the 1920s when he had favored a moderate pace of industrial growth.

The economy of the Soviet Union thus moved forward according to a series of five-year plans. These were designed to make the country into an industrial power in a short period of time.

## The First Five-Year Plan

The plan was put into effect in August 1929. It was intended to expand existing industries, to create new industries, and to relocate industrial centers away from vulnerable frontier areas.

The plan was officially completed, ahead of schedule, at the close of 1932.

### Successes of the Plan

According to Soviet statistics, there was a vast increase in the production of machinery and electrical equipment. New industrial centers were set up in the Urals and southern Siberia. Completely new kinds of industry, aviation and synthetic rubber, for example, were begun.

The Soviet Union was now able to maintain industrial expansion and defense production without depending on importing foreign machinery.

### Failures of the Plan

The plan did not meet its goals in producing iron, steel, coal or consumer goods. Moreover, while the level of production went up in many areas, the quality of the goods produced was often unsatisfactory.

## The Second Five-Year Plan

The Second Five-Year Plan had the same basic objectives as the First. It too featured the expansion of heavy industry, notably the production of metals and machine tools.

New features reflected concern over a future war and lessons learned from the First Five-Year Plan about the weakness of Soviet transportation. Thus the new plan stressed improvements in the railroads. In particular, expansion of the Trans-Siberian Railroad helped preparation for a future conflict against Japan.

Tension with Germany as well as Japan led to a new emphasis on the manufacture of weapons of war.

The Second Five-Year Plan was declared completed, ahead of schedule, in 1937.

### Successes of the Plan

The plan resulted in expanded steel production and the creation of a new automobile industry. There was a vast expansion in the output of machinery and electric power.

As the new workers in industry became increasingly skilled, Soviet factory labor became far more efficient than it had been before the Second Five-Year Plan.

### Weaknesses of the Plan

Once again, the targets for consumer goods were not met. The results of the plan fell short of planned increases in the production of oil and coal as well.

## The Soviet Union as an Industrial Power

The overall result of the first two five-year plans was a vast increase in Soviet industrial strength. Heavy industry expanded enormously; the new centers of production were established in secure areas like Siberia. The country no longer depended on foreign countries for most industrial goods.

The industrialization drive was accompanied by a major propaganda campaign. It tried to draw a parallel between industrialization and the sacrifices and heroism of the Civil War years. It also held out the promise of a more powerful and more prosperous country in the future. Thus, while industrialization included enormous hardships for the population, accompanied by a tightened dictatorship, it also aroused a degree of popular enthusiasm.

The dramatic leap forward brought major changes in Soviet society (see p. 343).

# The Purges

Stalin's reshaping of Soviet life was held in place by a brutal police state and the application of terror.

Soviet Russia had been a dictatorship under the effective control of a single political party since the end of the Civil War. Following 1929, however, the power of the secret police and the number of its victims expanded enormously.

The peasantry were the first to feed the brutal change. For most Russians outside the villages, the violence of collectivization was not evident until the mid-1930s. Then, high-ranking members of the Communist Party itself were tried and punished as traitors.

## Early Purges

Soon after the start of the First Five-Year Plan, a number of engineers and other technical experts were tried as saboteurs.

### *Charges against Technical Experts*

In the late 1920s, such experts working in the mining and transportation industries were accused of sabotaging the development of the Soviet economy.

### *The Bases for the Trials*

There were two basic purposes for these trials of technical experts who did not belong to the Communist Party. First, the trials provided an explanation to the public for the failures and bottlenecks in carrying out the First Five-Year Plan. Second, the elimination of older experts opened positions for newly trained young Communists.

## The Secret Police

In 1934, the secret police apparatus was reorganized and expanded. Its new title was the NKVD.

## The Murder of Kirov

A turning point in the use of political terror arrived with the murder of Sergei Kirov (1888–1934).

Kirov was a high-ranking Party official who had emerged as a critic of Stalin's dictatorship at the Seventeenth Party Congress in early 1934. He was assassinated in December 1934 under mysterious circumstances. Most historians think his death came as a result of Stalin's orders.

## The "Great Purge"

Starting with Kirov's death, the Soviet Union entered a four-year period characterized by mass terror. In this "Great Purge," the secret police no longer restricted their arrests to actual or potential opponents of the regime. They now struck at large numbers of Soviet citizens who had no inclination to oppose the system. Part of the government's goal was to stock a system of slave labor.

Most striking of all, purges were now directed at high-ranking Party officials. These accused individuals were often judged after public "show trials," featuring implausible confessions delivered by the defendants.

### "Kirov's Assassins"

An initial sign of the new policy was the response to Kirov's death. Approximately half a million Soviet citizens were arrested and imprisoned for their alleged responsibility in murdering Kirov. Thus, the purges reached unprecedented proportions.

### The Moscow Center

A second indication of a new trend were the arrests of Grigory Zinoviev (1883–1936) and Lev Kamenev (1883–1936). Both were distinguished old Bolsheviks and leading collaborators with Lenin.

At their trial in January 1935, the NKVD accused them of membership in "the Moscow Center," an organization allegedly implicated in the assassination of Kirov.

Each was sentenced to a prison term of ten years.

## The Moscow Trials

Three trials held in Moscow from 1936 to 1938 were shocking highlights of the purges. The first two involved distinguished figures who had been identified with the left wing of the Communist Party. The final trial struck at individuals tied to the right wing.

The trials featured apparently voluntary confessions by the accused. In the early trials, they admitted to organizing domestic opposition, including terrorist groups. As the trials continued, the major charges leveled at the accused consisted of working for foreign enemies of the Soviet Union.

### 1936 Trials

In August 1936, Zinoviev, Kamenev, and several other leading Communists were tried. They were accused of such crimes as involvement in the Kirov murder and plotting to kill Stalin. The trial was open to some foreign observers and included confessions by the defendants, who were convicted and executed.

### 1937 Trials

In early 1937, Karl Radek (1885–1939) and a number of lesser figures were tried and convicted of domestic subversion and plotting with foreign governments.

Radek received a ten-year prison sentence and later died in Siberia. Most of the others, convicted partly on Radek's testimony, were executed.

### 1938 Trials

In March 1938, leaders of the right wing of the Party, including Nicholas Bukharin (1888–1938) and Alexei Rykov (1881–1938), were tried and executed. Also tried at this time were a number of leaders of the non-Russian republics, as well as Henrik Yagoda (1891–1938), the deposed leader of the NKVD.

## The Purge of the Military

In June 1937, the purges took a new direction. This time they struck at leading figures in the military high command. These leaders were not put on public trial. Instead they were arrested and executed in secret proceedings.

Notable victims of the military purge included the chief of general staff, Mikhail Tukhachevsky (1893–1937).

The scope of the purge was so great that many of the most experienced military leaders, from senior to junior levels, were executed or imprisoned. Some historians estimate that 35,000 officers were victims of the purge.

### The Stalinization of the Communist Party

Besides terrorizing the population, the purges also reshaped the Communist Party. Its most important founding leaders were accused of heinous crimes and then executed. Even loyal supporters of Stalin were replaced and executed.

Seventy percent of the Central Committee members chosen at the 1934 Party Congress were purged. The crowd of delegates that gathered at the 1939 Party Congress contained almost no one from the Congress that had met in 1934.

### Causes of the Purges

Historians do not agree on a single reason for the purges. Some stress Stalin's personality, suggesting that his brutal and suspicious nature reached the level of bloodthirsty insanity. They believe that his paranoid tendency made him strike in particular at prestigious older members of the Party like Bukharin and Zinoviev. Others see the purges as a bloody effort by Stalin to consolidate his power. His purpose, they suggest, was to eliminate not only real opponents but also those who might become his enemies. Certain historians consider this motive to be linked to the growing threat of war with Nazi Germany. Since war would bring immense domestic strains, Stalin did not wish to have potential enemies around to conspire against him.

### The New Dictatorship

Some historians consider the governing system that resulted from the purges to be a police-state dictatorship with totalitarian features (see p. 333). That means that the Communist Party itself had lost its power, and the Soviet Union was being run by Stalin and the NKVD. Terror was being employed against the population to carry out and to maintain vast social and economic changes.

# The New Society

At the close of the 1930s, the shape of Soviet society was far different from what it had been in the NEP era. Much of the rural population had been swept into collective farms. But millions of Soviet citizens had been drawn out of the countryside to the new industrial cities.

At the close of the 1930s, one-third of the population lived in cities, many of which, like the industrial city of Magnitogorsk in the Urals, were newly built.

## The Workers

The factory workers of the Soviet Union were placed under harsh restrictions during the era of the five-year plans. The government obtained the authority to assign workers to specific jobs and specific locations. Unauthorized absence from work was harshly punished.

### The New Wage System

In the 1930s, workers were increasingly paid on a piecework basis. This meant that an individual's earnings were directly tied to the amount he or she produced. The difference in wages between skilled and unskilled workers was widened.

Many historians note that Stalin's industrialization program thus used some of the harsh methods employed in capitalist societies during their early industrialization.

### The Passport System

In another restriction designed to heighten control over the workers, the government restored the tsarist passport system. Starting in December 1932, all residents of cities needed an internal passport. It served as an official identity card, and it was required for any travel between cities. It had to be renewed every five years.

Peasants did not receive such a passport. Thus, they could travel only with the advance consent of the authorities.

### Stakhanovism

An important method for increasing production was "Stakhanovism." This meant using the performance of an outstanding worker to set the normal production quotas for a large number of individuals.

The term comes from the highly publicized actions of coal miner Alexis Stakhanov (1905–1977). In August 1935, Stakhanov set a new production record, mining 102 tons of coal in a single shift.

It must be noted that Stakhanov had the advantage of using new equipment. He also had several helpers at his side. Nonetheless, his achievements were cited by the government as justification for raising industrial goals throughout the Soviet Union.

## The Cultural Revolution

The 1930s brought enormous changes in Soviet intellectual life. The relative freedom of the NEP era in the arts and education now ended.

### Schools

The Soviet Union established a traditional school system featuring strict discipline and a heavy dose of political indoctrination. This policy represented a substantial shift from the educational experiments and "progressive education" of the NEP era.

The level of popular literacy increased in the 1930s, reaching eighty-one percent by 1939. At the same time, however, higher education was devastated by the purges as thousands of faculty members were arrested.

### The Arts

The arts were placed under firm political control. The governing ideal was "Socialist Realism." This doctrine linked artistic merit to the purpose of transforming society. Thus, a novel or poem or piece of music was valuable if it glorified the revolution and the new society being created in the 1930s.

Under "Socialist Realism," art had to be simple, direct, and easily understood by the man in the street. The officially approved art produced in this era can also be seen as the kind of art personally pleasing to the dictator, Joseph Stalin.

## Non-Russian Nationalities

The most important trend in dealing with the non-Russian peoples of the Soviet Union was an attack on "bourgeois nationalism." This meant that the cultural freedom and hopes for some political autonomy that had been permitted ethnic minorities in the NEP were crushed.

### *Russification*

In 1938, study of the Russian language was required throughout the Soviet Union. The government and the Communist Party promoted the idea of loyalty to a "Soviet nation." In practice this meant proclaiming the superiority of Russian culture as a model for all the peoples of the Soviet Union.

### *The Ukraine*

Events in the Ukraine show how Russification was applied in a crucial area.

The Ukraine was the most heavily populated and the most economically important of the non-Russian regions. Resistance to collectivization had been particularly heavy there.

The leadership of the Communist Party and local government leaders in the Ukraine were purged on several occasions, notably in 1933 and again in 1937–1938. The purges were extended to wipe out cultural leaders from local universities and the Ukrainian Academy of Sciences.

*The Bolshevik Revolution of 1917 had brought about basic political changes in Russian life. The years from 1929 onward brought a second, more sweeping revolution.*

*As the decade ended, Soviet Russia possessed the basis for a modern, industrialized society. Wielding the weapon of the secret police, Stalin held dictatorial control over the Soviet people.*

---

## Recommended Reading

Brown, E. J. *The Proletarian Episode in Russian Literature, 1928–1932* (1971).

Conquest, Robert. *The Great Terror* (1968).

Conquest, Robert. *The Harvest of Sorrow: Soviet Collectivization and the Terror-Famine* (1986).

Davies, R. W. *The Industrialization of Soviet Russia, Vol. 1: The Socialist Offensive: The Collectivization of Soviet Agriculture, 1929–1930* (1980).

Davies, R. W. *The Industrialization of Soviet Russia, Vol. 2: The Soviet Collective Farm, 1929–1930* (1980).

Davies, R. W. *The Industrialization of Soviet Russia, Vol. 3: The Soviet Economy in Turmoil, 1929–1930* (1989).

Dunham, Vera. *In Stalin's Time: Middle-Class Values in Soviet Fiction* (1976).

Fainsod, Merle. *Smolensk under Soviet Rule* (1958).

Fitzpatrick, Sheila. *Education and Social Mobility in the Soviet Union, 1921–1934* (1979).

Getty, J. Arch. *Origins of the Great Purge: The Soviet Communist Party Reconsidered, 1933–1938* (1986).

Ginzburg, Evgeniia S. *Journey into the Whirlwind* (1967).

Ginzburg, Evgeniia S. *Within the Whirlwind* (1981).

Gunther, Hans, ed. *The Culture of the Stalin Period* (1990).

Hollander, Paul. *Political Pilgrims: Travels of Western Intellectuals to the Soviet Union, China, and Cuba, 1928–1978* (1981).

Katkov, George. *The Trial of Bukharin* (1969).

Lewin, Moshe. *Russian Peasants and Soviet Power* (1968).

Mandelshtam, Nadezhda. *Hope Abandoned* (1974).

Mandelshtam, Nadezhda. *Hope against Hope: A Memoir* (1970).

Medvedev, Roy A. *Let History Judge: The Origins and Consequences of Stalinism* (rev. and exp. ed., 1989).

Millar, James R. *The Soviet Economic Experiment* (1990).

Nove, Alex. *Economic Rationality and Soviet Politics, or, Was Stalin Really Necessary?* (1964).

Rassweiler, Anne D. *The Generation of Power: The History of Dneprostroi* (1988).

Reiman, Michal. *The Birth of Stalinism: The USSR on the Eve of the "Second Revolution"* (1987).

Siegelbaum, Lewis H. *Stakhanovism and the Politics of Productivity in the USSR, 1935–1941* (1988).

Starr, S. Frederick. *Red and Hot: The Fate of Jazz in the Soviet Union, 1917–1980* (1983).

Thorniley, Daniel. *The Rise and Fall of the Soviet Rural Communist Party, 1927–39* (1988).

Tucker, Robert C. *Stalin in Power: The Revolution from Above, 1928–1941* (1990).

Tucker, Robert C., ed. *Stalinism: Essays in Historical Interpretation* (1977).

Viola, Lynn. *The Best Sons of the Fatherland: Workers in the Vanguard of Soviet Collectivization* (1989).

Von Laue, Theodore. *Why Lenin? Why Stalin? A Reappraisal of the Russian Revolution* (2nd ed., 1971).

Vucinich, Alexander. *Empire of Knowledge: The Academy of Sciences of the USSR, 1917–1970* (1984).

# CHAPTER 25

## Foreign Policy in the 1930s

## Time Line

July 1930      Litvinov replaces Chicherin as commissar of foreign affairs

September 1931   Japan invades Manchuria

December 1932   Soviet Union reestablishes relations with Nationalist Chinese government

January 1933     Hitler takes power

November 1933   United States recognizes Soviet Union

January 1934     German-Polish Nonaggression Treaty

September 1934   Soviet Union joins League of Nations

| | |
|---|---|
| May 1935 | Soviet treaty with France |
| | Soviet treaty with Czechoslovakia |
| July–August 1935 | Seventh Congress of Comintern |
| March 1936 | Hitler invades Rhineland |
| November 1936 | Anti-Comintern Pact (Germany, Italy, Japan) |
| August 1939 | Soviet victory in Outer Mongolia |
| | Hitler-Stalin Pact |
| September 1939 | Invasion of Poland |
| | Armistice with Japan |
| November 1939 –March 1940 | War with Finland |
| June 1940 | Germany defeats France |
| July 1940 | Incorporation of Baltic states into Soviet Union |
| November 1940 | Molotov's visit to Berlin |
| April 1941 | Germany invades Yugoslavia |
| | Soviet Neutrality Treaty with Japan |

*The most important factors shaping Soviet foreign policy during this period were the threats posed by Japan and Nazi Germany.*

*Stalin responded to German power by joining the League of Nations (1934) and seeking alliances against Hitler. In the end, however, the Soviet Union signed a nonaggression pact with Nazi Germany in 1939.*

*New frictions soon developed between the two countries, chiefly over the control of Eastern Europe. By the spring of 1941, Hitler was preparing an assault on the Soviet Union. Stalin still hoped to postpone a break with Germany.*

# The Far East (1930–1933)

### Relations with Japan

The most important issue embittering relations between Japan and the Soviet Union was Tokyo's expansionist policy in the Chinese province of Manchuria. This friction reached a climax when Japanese troops invaded Manchuria at the close of 1931.

### Relations with China

The need to obtain assistance against Japan led Moscow to reestablish diplomatic relations with Chiang Kai-shek's Nationalist government in China (December 1932).

### Relations with the United States

The Soviet government also hoped for American support against Japan. Promises to settle American financial claims against Russia and to avoid spreading revolutionary propaganda in the United States cleared the way for the establishment of diplomatic relations in November 1933.

# The Rise of Hitler in Europe

Relations between the Soviet Union and Weimar Germany remained good at the start of the 1930s. Both countries benefited from economic and military cooperation.

### Sixth Comintern Congress

#### Guidelines

This congress (July–September 1928) established an important set of policy guidelines for relations between the Comintern and foreign political developments. At Stalin's insistence, cooperation between Communist parties and non-Communist parties of the Left was rejected.

#### The Early Soviet Attitude toward Hitler

When Hitler's movement began to grow in Germany during the Depression years after 1929, Stalin's guidelines for the Comintern blocked cooperation between German Communists and German Socialists against Hitler. Stalin thought that, by arousing domestic resistance, a Nazi government would actually help open the way for the inevitable Communist revolution.

## Litvinov's Diplomatic Policy

Maxim Litvinov (1876–1951) took over as commissar of foreign affairs from the ailing Chicherin in the summer of 1930. The new commissar, a veteran Bolshevik, had close ties to the West. He had lived in England for a decade before and during World War I. He was Jewish and was married to the daughter of an important English literary family.

Litvinov carried out a policy of improving relations with Russia's Western neighbors. Moscow signed nonaggression pacts with countries like Poland and the Baltic republics in 1931 and 1932 as it became more likely Hitler would gain control of Germany. These pacts offered some protection against future German expansion.

At the same time, the Soviets were able to concentrate their attention on the growing problems with Japan.

## Soviet-German Tensions

Hitler took power in Germany at the close of January 1933. He was on record, in his book *Mein Kampf*, in favor of German expansion into Russia. Moreover, the Nazi dictator had also crushed the German Communist Party shortly after seizing power. In January 1934, Hitler signed a nonaggression pact with Poland. This seemed a clear sign that he was not concerned with having good relations with the Soviet Union, since Poland was considered unfriendly to the Russians.

Stalin showed his concern at the German threat by a willingness to seek alliances with capitalist countries such as Britain and France.

## Membership in the League of Nations

An early sign of the new trend in Soviet policy came with Moscow's entry into the League of Nations in the fall of 1934. Previously, the Soviets had criticized the League as a tool for capitalist and imperialist countries.

Litvinov enthusiastically praised the League and its policy of collective security.

## Anti-German Alliances

Links with several European countries seemed to offer Russia future assistance against Germany. But these agreements turned out to be limited ones, and their implementation depended upon a solid desire of all other European countries to cooperate against Germany.

### Treaty with France

An important sign of new Soviet initiatives to bolster security against German attack took the form of an alliance with France. Signed on May 2, 1935, this treaty pledged the two countries to consult on common action in case one of them was attacked in Europe.

The tie was weakened, however, by the absence of detailed joint military planning. Moreover, it was hard to see how Soviet Russia could help France against Germany since several Eastern European countries stood between Russian and German territory.

### Treaty with Czechoslovakia

Soon after signing its treaty with France, Soviet Russia made a similar agreement with Czechoslovakia. The Czechs were France's ally as well. The agreement, however, contained a crucial weakness for the Czechs: It provided that Russia would aid Czechoslovakia only if France did so first.

### Shift in the Comintern

At the Seventh Comintern Congress (July–August 1935), the organization changed its position of 1928. Communists were now encouraged to participate in "popular front" organizations with non-Communists to combat the threat of Fascism.

## The Rhineland Crisis (March 1936)

Stalin found a clear sign of France's unwillingness to stand up to Hitler in the spring of 1936. Hitler defied France and Britain by moving his armed forces into the demilitarized zone along the Rhine River in western Germany. This action violated the Treaty of Versailles, and, more important, it shifted the military balance in Europe in Germany's favor.

# The Spanish Civil War

Soviet intervention in the Spanish Civil War, which broke out in July 1936, added to the difficulties of forming a solid alliance against Hitler. The Soviets sent men and weapons to back the Loyalist forces against rebels led by General Francisco Franco. Franco had the support of Hitler and Mussolini, and he threatened to overthrow a Spanish government in which the Communist Party and other groups of the Left participated.

### Split between Russia and the West

Britain and France were suspicious of Soviet intentions in Spain. By refusing to intervene they also hoped to keep the conflict from leading to a general European war.

### Russia's Failure in Spain

Russian intervention in Spain was complicated by the presence of several radical factions of the Left, including anarchists and followers of Trotsky. Stalin pursued a policy of only limited assistance to the Loyalists. This helped prolong their resistance, but it could not prevent Franco's success by early 1939.

### Effects for International Relations

In all, the effects of the war heightened Western suspicions of the Soviet Union and stirred Soviet concerns about the willingness of Britain and France to fight Hitler.

# The Far East (1936–1939)

The Soviet position in the Far East was threatened at the same time that dangers increased in Europe.

### Anti-Comintern Pact

In November 1936, Germany and Japan signed a pact to cooperate against Communism. One year later, Italy joined in to form a three-way "Anti-Comintern Pact." Meanwhile, in July 1937, Japan went to war with China, strengthened its position on the Asian mainland, and soon clashed with Soviet armed forces on the Soviet-Manchurian border. The overall effect of these events was to link the enemies of the Soviet Union in Europe and Asia and to confront Soviet forces with a direct military challenge in the Far East.

### Undeclared War with Japan

The most serious military collisions with Japan came in the summer of 1939 on the borders of Outer Mongolia. The possibility that Germany might use its tie with Japan to help settle tensions in the Far East may have helped pave the way for the Hitler-Stalin agreement of August 1939 (see p. 356).

## The Czech Crisis and the Munich Conference

By the late summer of 1938, the Soviet Union faced the possibility of war with Germany.

### Hitler's Demands

Hitler's annexation of Austria in March 1938 had moved Germany's borders 400 miles closer to Soviet territory. Hitler's demands for territorial concessions from Czechoslovakia created a serious crisis for all the major European powers.

### Repercussion of the Munich Pact

At Munich in September 1938, Italy, France, and Britain agreed to German demands. The Soviet position suffered substantially from this outcome. Germany was now moving eastward with no apparent opposition from Britain and France. It probably appeared to Stalin that the Western powers were encouraging Hitler to attack the Soviet Union.

Prospects for Anglo-French cooperation against a German threat dimmed further given the fact that the Soviet Union was not even permitted a place at the Munich conference.

## Hitler-Stalin Relations

The diplomatic world changed drastically in March 1939 when Hitler violated his own pledges at Munich and seized all of Czechoslovakia. Britain and France now sought allies in Eastern Europe, establishing treaties with Poland and Romania.

## Warming of German-Soviet Relations

In public statements, both Stalin and Hitler dropped hints that they would consider better relations between their countries. At the Eighteenth Party Congress in March 1939, for example, Stalin disclaimed any Soviet intention to protect British and French interests. The Soviet Union, he said, wanted better relations with all countries.

## Fall of Litvinov

On May 2, Maxim Litvinov was replaced as commissar of foreign affairs by Viacheslav Molotov (1890–1986). This change was an important signal that the Soviet Union was considering closer ties to Germany. Litvinov had been anathema to Germany both as a Jew and as a symbol of Soviet efforts to ally with the Western democracies.

## Negotiations with the West

A product of Litvinov's policy was a round of talks among Russian, British, and French representatives during the summer. Several factors, however, made these talks seem fruitless. Only relatively low level negotiators had been sent by London and Paris, raising doubts about the seriousness of Western intentions.

## The Issue of Eastern Europe

Moreover, the Soviet government insisted on the right to send troops into Eastern Europe by passing through Poland and Romania and the right to protect the Baltic states. These were provisions the West found objectionable and difficult to impose on independent states in Eastern Europe.

## The Agreement with Germany

The Soviet government found no such hesitation on the part of Berlin. Talks between the Soviet and the German government had been going on since the fall of 1938. From the start of August 1939,

Hitler pushed for an agreement in order to clear the way for his planned attack on Poland.

### Nonaggression Pact

On August 23, the two foreign ministers, Joachim von Ribbentrop and V. Molotov, signed a set of documents in Moscow. The documents declared a policy of nonaggression between the two nations and began a program of economic cooperation.

### The Secret Protocol

The centerpiece of the Russo-German agreement was a secret protocol on Eastern Europe. It split the region into a German and a Russian sphere, with Poland west of the Vistula to go to Germany and Poland east of the Vistula to go to Russia. Moscow got control of Estonia, Latvia, and Bessarabia. Germany received Lithuania.

## Invasion of Poland

Soviet forces entered Poland in September 17. The Germans had begun their advance into Poland from the west on September 1. The delay in starting the Russian advance may have been a result of large-scale conflict between Soviet and Japanese forces on the Manchurian-Mongolian border in late August and early September. General Georgi Zhukov (1896–1974) defeated the Japanese at Khalkin Gol and secured an armistice by mid-September.

## Revision of the Hitler-Stalin Pact

The German advance into Poland proceeded beyond the line of the Vistula into regions assigned to Soviet control. An additional agreement, signed on September 28, redivided Eastern Europe. Germany obtained additional territory in Poland, and the Soviet Union received the right to control Lithuania.

## Economic and Military Cooperation

The Soviet Union became a crucial source of raw materials for the German war economy. Since Hitler faced an Allied blockade, he relied heavily on oil and iron ore from Stalin. In an effort to maintain friendly ties, Stalin continued deliveries right up to the moment of the German attack in June 1941.

Due to the Hitler-Stalin pact, the Germans felt secure in concentrating their forces in the West for offensives in the spring of 1940. Germany enjoyed spectacular successes, notably the quick defeat of France.

## The Breakdown of the Alliance

Both Germany and the Soviet Union moved to expand their areas of control in Eastern Europe after the fall of Poland. The Soviets, for example, quickly forced Lithuania, Latvia, and Estonia to accept Russian military bases.

The maneuvering of the two countries in Eastern Europe brought war between them closer in two ways. It created mutual fears and suspicions. It also gave the Germans a chance to see the military weakness of the Soviet Union.

### *Winter War with Finland*

Unlike the Baltic states, the Finns refused Soviet demands for territorial changes. On November 28, 1939, the Soviet Union attacked.

*Finnish Resistance.* The Finns resisted Russian advances in Karelia and central Finland with startling success. The picture of Russian defeats against a country with an army of only 200,000 men encouraged Hitler to think that Germany would have no difficulty invading the Soviet Union. Moreover, Moscow's aggression against Finland provoked widespread criticism throughout the world. In December 1939 the League of Nations expelled Russia as an aggressor.

*The Conclusion of the Russo-Finnish War.* In March 1940 the war ended with a Soviet victory, won at the expense of heavy casualties. The peace treaty brought 16,000 square miles of Finnish territory into the Soviet Union in order to strengthen the western border. A second consequence of the war was a crash program to modernize and reorganize the battered Soviet armed forces.

### *The Baltic (Summer 1940)*

To match German gains in Western Europe, Stalin used the Red Army to occupy Estonia, Latvia, and Lithuania in June 1940. The three formerly independent countries were made part of the Soviet Union the following month.

### The Balkans (Summer 1940)

Competition between Germany and the Soviet Union grew rapidly in the Balkans by the middle of 1940. Stalin forced Romania to give up Bessarabia and Northern Bukovina in June. Hitler responded in August by forcing the Romanians to sign over portions of their territory to Hungary and Bulgaria, both German allies.

### Molotov's Visit to Berlin (November 1940)

The Soviet foreign minister visited Berlin in the fall of 1940 in an unsuccessful effort to settle differences between the two countries. The Russian envoy refused German suggestions that Moscow direct its expansion southward toward the Indian Ocean. Molotov stressed Soviet concern about German intentions in Eastern Europe.

Following the visit, Hitler concluded that it was time to plan for an attack on the Soviet Union in 1941.

# The Far East (1939–1941)

## Easing of Tensions with Japan

A bright spot in the conduct of Soviet foreign policy appeared in relations with Japan. The Soviet military victory in Mongolia in the summer of 1939 helped to persuade Japan to shift the direction of its expansion to Southeast Asia. The likelihood of war with the United States was a further incentive for the Japanese to improve relations with Moscow.

## Soviet-Japanese Treaty

A Soviet-Japanese nonaggression pact was the result in April 1941. Powerful Soviet forces remained in the Far East, but the lessened threat of war with Japan allowed Stalin some freedom to concentrate his preparations on a war with Germany.

*Soviet foreign policy from 1930 to 1941 produced several sharp changes of direction. After seeking to join a diplomatic front against Hitler and after fighting an undeclared war against Japan, Stalin moved toward better relations with both of these dangerous neighbors.*

*The Soviet Union managed to remain an observer, rather than a participant, in the early part of World War II in Europe. But the speed and decisiveness of Hitler's victories had been alarming. Growing tension between Germany and the Soviet Union in Eastern Europe now raised the possibility that Stalin would soon be drawn into the conflict.*

## Recommended Reading

Cattell, David. *Communism and the Spanish Civil War* (1956).

Chew, Allen F. *The White Death: The Epic of the Soviet-Finnish Winter War* (1971).

Coox, Alvin. *The Anatomy of a Small War: The Soviet-Japanese Struggle for Changkufeng-Khasan, 1938* (1977).

Coox, Alvin. *Nomonhan: Japan against Russia, 1939* (1985).

Craig, Gordon, and Felix Gilbert, eds. *The Diplomats, 1919–1939* (1953).

Haslam, Jonathan. *Soviet Foreign Policy, 1930–33: The Impact of the Depression* (1983).

Haslam, Jonathan. *The Soviet Union and the Struggle for Collective Security in Europe, 1933–39* (1984).

Hilger, Gustav, and Alfred G. Meyer. *The Incompatible Allies: A Memoir-History of German-Soviet Relations, 1918–1941* (1953).

Hochman, Jiri. *The Soviet Union and the Failure of Collective Security, 1934–1938* (1984).

Jakobson, Max. *The Diplomacy of the Winter War: An Account of the Russo-Finnish War, 1939–1940* (1941).

McKenzie, Kermit E. *Comintern and World Revolution, 1928–1943: The Shaping of Doctrine* (1963).

Ulam, Adam. *Expansion and Coexistence: A History of Soviet Foreign Policy, 1917–1967* (1968).

Weinberg, Gerhard. *Germany and the Soviet Union* (1954).

# CHAPTER 26

## World War II (1941–1945)

### Time Line

| | |
|---|---|
| June 1941 | Germans invade Soviet Union |
| September 1941 | Russian forces surrender at Kiev |
| December 1941 | Battle of Moscow |
| July 1942 | Germans capture the Crimea |
| August 1942 | Start of Battle of Stalingrad |
| November 1942 | Soviet counterattack at Stalingrad |
| February 1943 | German Sixth Army surrenders at Stalingrad |
| May 1943 | Abolition of Comintern |
| July 1943 | Battle of Kursk-Orel |
| September 1943 | Metropolitan Sergei elected patriarch |

| November–December 1943 | Teheran Conference |
| --- | --- |
| August–October 1944 | Warsaw uprising |
| February 1945 | Yalta Conference |
| April 1945 | Soviet attack on Berlin |
| May 1945 | End of war in Europe |
| August 1945 | Soviet Union declares war on Japan |
| | End of war in Far East |

*World War II stands as one of the great turning points in the history of the Soviet Union. The Soviet system survived its greatest test since 1917. As a result of the war, Soviet power was planted in Eastern and Central Europe.*

*During this period, the country went from diplomatic ties with Germany to become a key part of the anti-German Allied coalition. Although relations with the United States and Britain were sometimes strained, the wartime coalition held together and achieved victory in 1945.*

*All aspects of Soviet life felt the impact of the war. The population suffered enormous casualties and massive destruction of property.*

## The Course of the War

The war began with crushing defeats for the Soviet Union in 1941 and 1942. Nonetheless, distance, supply problems, and the harsh climate combined with Soviet resistance to prevent a decisive German victory.

In December 1941, the Soviet Army counterattacked at Moscow, administering the first serious defeat the Germans had known on land since the start of World War II.

German victories continued in 1942. But by the closing months of the year, the Soviets had mounted a counterattack at Stalingrad. The Battle of Stalingrad lasted more than six months, and the Soviet victory turned out to be the pivot of the war on the Russian front.

The Germans were able to renew their offensive on a large scale in 1943 at Kursk. But they never grasped the initiative again. For the final two years of the war, Soviet forces advanced steadily. After retaking all the lost Soviet territory, they advanced into Eastern Europe. In the spring of 1945, they reached Berlin.

## The Campaign of 1941

Stalin had received numerous warnings of Hitler's aggressive intentions from his own agents and from foreign intelligence agencies, including the British. Nonetheless, the war in the east began on a gigantic scale with a surprise German attack. On the morning of June 22, 1941, more than 150 German and satellite divisions struck. They advanced in three army groups over a huge battle line that stretched more than 1000 miles from the Baltic to the Black Sea.

One German army group struck northeastward toward Leningrad. A second advanced eastward against Moscow. The third moved southeastward toward Kiev and the Ukraine.

### Initial Defeats

The major consequence of the first months of fighting was the failure of the Soviet forces. The German attacks proceeded without interruption for several reasons.

First, Stalin had not allowed an effective defensive system to be set up along the border. He apparently believed that extensive defenses along the frontier with Germany would antagonize Hitler and would help to provoke a German attack. Second, the purges of the 1930s had deprived the Soviet army of most of its best and experienced senior leaders. Third, the Soviet forces were still in the middle of a basic reorganization that had begun after their poor performance in the Winter War against Finland. Finally, Stalin's orders to hold territory at all costs led to disastrous encirclement of Russian armies. The most significant example of this was the loss of Kiev (September 1941), where the Germans captured 600,000 Soviet troops.

### Hitler's Errors

In August Hitler decided to divert much of his strength into the Ukraine. Other German units were sent northward to attempt a quick seizure of Leningrad. This dispersion of German military power delayed the striking of a powerful blow directly at Moscow.

### Slowing of the German Advance

By October, Soviet resistance was more effective and coordinated. The rains and early snows that month also helped to slow the German advance.

### The Battle of Moscow

The Battle of Moscow in December 1941 marked the shift of initiative to the Soviet side.

Fresh troops were brought from Siberia to strike at the Germans. Meanwhile, harsh winter weather made it difficult for German tanks to maneuver. The forested terrain around Moscow also slowed the German advance. Finally, the Germans were exhausted after advancing and fighting since June.

The command of the defense was given to Georgi Zhukov (1896–1974), a senior general who had enjoyed success against the Japanese in the 1939 border conflict. Under Zhukov, the Soviet forces stopped the German advance.

## 1942: The Turning Point

The second year of the war began badly for the Soviet side, but it ended with the Germans in a desperate situation at Stalingrad.

In the spring, the Germans easily defeated an offensive by Stalin's force at Kharkov. The Germans then resumed a sweeping advance, similar to those of 1941, eastward across the Ukraine.

The Soviets could not prevent the loss of the Crimea. Nor could they stop the German advance to the Volga and to the oil fields of the Caucasus.

In late 1942, however, Soviet forces attacked the vulnerable flanks of the German forces at Stalingrad (formerly Tsaritsyn).

### Initial Russian Defeats

In May 1942, the Soviet army went on the offensive in an effort to retake Kharkov. Stalin had insisted on an effort to recapture this important industrial center.

The effort failed disastrously. The Germans followed their victory here with the capture of the Crimea (July 1942). Then they advanced eastward toward Stalingrad and southeastward toward the oil fields of the Caucasus.

### The Battle of Stalingrad

*First Phase (September–November 1942).*    The tide of the war began to favor the Russians at Stalingrad. The German advance reached the outskirts of the city in September 1942. But the Germans could not exploit their superiority in tank warfare within a large, industrialized city.

The Germans only slowly overcame heavy Russian resistance. By early November, however, they had taken most of the city.

*Second Phase (November 1942–February 1943).*    In late November Soviet forces attacked to the west of the city. General Nicholas Vatutin (1901–1944) and General Constantine Rokossovsky (1896–1968) broke through the German lines from the north. General Andrei Eremenko (1892–1970) then struck from the south.

The German Sixth Field Army under General Friedrich von Paulus was cut off. Hitler refused to permit attempts at a retreat, and von Paulus was forced to surrender in early February 1943.

The victory at Stalingrad showed that Soviet forces could defeat the Germans in the fighting conditions of the eastern front.

### The Siege of Leningrad

The German offensive of 1941 had brought Hitler's forces to the outskirts of Leningrad. The city remained under siege from August 1941 to January 1944. Hundreds of thousands of the city's citizens starved to death; the heaviest loss of life due to lack of food came during 1942.

The city survived due to the determination of its citizens and the existence of a precarious winter supply route across the ice on Lake Ladoga.

The siege was the longest to take place anywhere during World War II. The exact Soviet death toll is uncertain, but it probably reached 1 million.

### 1943: Beginning of the Soviet Advance

During 1943, Soviet forces blocked a final German effort to regain the initiative. Following their victory at Kursk, Stalin's troops began a steady advance westward. By the close of 1943, the Soviet offensive had retaken the Ukraine.

### The Battle of Kursk

The Germans attacked at Kursk in early July 1943. With large numbers of tanks, they hoped to split the Soviet front and capture Moscow.

The Russians had several advantages, including high morale and confidence after their success at Stalingrad. Moreover, Soviet military intelligence had obtained information on the time and place of the German advance.

The Russians absorbed the German attack with a vast defensive line over 60 miles deep. They followed with an effective counterattack at Orel, north of Kursk, which threatened the German rear.

### The Mediterranean and the Eastern Front

Due to the Allied landing in Sicily in July 1943, Hitler was forced to suspend operations at Kursk. His reserves were sent from the eastern front to meet the new threat in the Mediterranean.

### Soviet Offensive Westward

Following Kursk, Soviet forces moved westward to free large areas lost to Germany earlier in the war.

Kharkov was recaptured (August 1943), followed by Smolensk (September 1943) and Kiev (November 1943).

By the end of the fighting in 1943, Soviet troops had reached the line of the Dnieper.

## 1944: The Advance into Eastern Europe

During 1944, Soviet forces recaptured the remainder of Soviet territory taken by the Germans.

When Soviet forces advanced into Eastern Europe a new element entered the war. The stage was now being set for future conflicts with Russia's allies over this region.

### Expelling the Germans

By June 1944, most of the Soviet territory held by Germany during the war was back in Soviet hands.

The long siege of Leningrad was ended by the arrival of Soviet troops in January 1944. The Crimea was recaptured in May.

### The Entry into Eastern Europe

Starting in early 1944, Soviet forces moved beyond their own borders. Finland, fighting alongside Germany, was invaded in June and left the war in September.

Parts of the Baltic states—Estonia, Latvia, and Lithuania—were occupied in August.

### Poland

The largest and most important country in Eastern Europe was Poland. Soviet troops crossed the border into Poland in January 1944.

Despite an uprising in August of the Polish underground in Warsaw, the Soviet army halted outside the Polish capital until October. This event led to accusations that Stalin's government deliberately betrayed the non-Communist Polish leadership in order to smooth the way for Communist control in that country.

An alternative explanation claims that the Soviet forces outside Warsaw were exhausted and lacked the supplies and equipment needed to advance into the city.

### Other Advances in Eastern Europe

In August, the Soviet army captured Bucharest, the Romanian capital, and the Romanian oil fields at Ploesti. That same month, Soviet advances forced Bulgaria, another of Germany's allies, to drop out of the war.

By the end of 1944, Soviet troops had entered Yugoslavia, Hungary, and eastern Czechoslovakia.

## 1945: Victory in Europe and the Far East

The final campaigns of the war in Europe brought Russian forces to the center of the continent. No Russian ruler since Alexander I in 1815 (see Chapter 13) had held as much control over European lands as did Stalin in mid-1945.

A series of giant offensives on the eastern front began in January and continued until the German surrender on May 7.

Soviet forces entered the Far Eastern war against Japan on August 8, two days after the United States dropped an atomic bomb on Hiroshima.

Soviet troops conducted a swift advance into Manchuria before the fighting in the Far East ended on August 14.

### Assault on Germany

In the middle of January 1945, four Soviet army groups attacked on a vast front stretching from the Baltic Sea to the Carpathian Mountains.

There were spectacular gains in the northern sector. Warsaw fell on January 17, and Cracow was taken on January 19. Soviet troops reached Frankfurt on the Oder on February 10, and Danzig was occupied on March 30.

Meanwhile, in the south, Budapest was occupied on February 13, and a German counterattack in Hungary was beaten off in early March. Vienna fell to the Soviets on April 13.

### The Final Offensive in Europe

The assault on Berlin began in mid-April. The city was encircled on April 25. That same day Soviet and American troops met at Torgau on the Elbe River. This juncture established a belt of Allied territory stretching across Germany.

Soviet forces captured Berlin on May 2, and the war in Europe ended five days later.

### Victory in Manchuria

In the Far East, Soviet forces entered the war against Japan on August 8. Under the command of Marshal Alexander Vasilesky (1895–1977), several Soviet armies advanced into Manchuria from Mongolia, Vladivostok, and Khabarovsk.

The Soviet advance quickly defeated Japan's Kwantung Army. When the war ended, the Soviet Union occupied northern China and the northern part of the Korean peninsula.

# The Soviet Union under German Occupation

The German invading forces held large portions of the Soviet Union for nearly three years.

Initially, German troops received a friendly welcome from the civilian population in many areas. Nonetheless, German confusion and brutality toward Soviet civilians resulted in their loss of opportunities to shake the Soviet system.

The occupying forces maintained the collective farm system. They treated prisoners of war with great brutality. Moreover, the Germans carried out the systematic murder of the Jewish population in areas under German control.

## The Vlasov Movement

During the war, the Germans made an effort to form a Soviet force to fight on their side. The effort centered on General Andrei Vlasov (1900–1946).

Vlasov was a Soviet general captured by the Germans in 1942. He was permitted to plan the formation of a non-Communist Russian government and an anti-Soviet Russian army.

### Hitler's Opposition

Fearful of arming enemy nationals, Hitler blocked the formation of Vlasov's army until late 1944. At that time only two divisions were set up, and these made no contribution to the German fighting effort.

### Execution of Vlasov

Vlasov was captured by the United States Army at the close of the war. He was handed over to Soviet authorities and executed in 1946.

## The Partisans

Partisan bands began to form behind the German lines immediately after the start of the war.

### Origins of the Partisan Movement

Some partisan bands were organized around military units cut off by the German advance. Most bands, however, were formed from the civilian population, starting in early 1942. By that time, the brutality of the occupation toward the civilian population had become clear.

### Non-Russian Partisans

Some partisan bands in non-Russian areas like the Ukraine maintained their independence despite efforts by the Soviet army to control them.

At the close of the war, non-Russian partisan bands sometimes refused to disarm and disperse. They formed armed forces that now fought the Soviet army, sometimes for years, after the war's official end in May 1945.

# The Diplomacy of the War

## Early Negotiations

The German attack drastically changed the Russian position in the diplomatic world. The Soviet Union went from being Hitler's ally to becoming a vital part of the anti-Hitler coalition.

The Soviets now received large amounts of assistance from the United States and Britain. Stalin played an important role in Allied negotiations over the conduct of the war and the shape of the postwar world.

### Lend-Lease

In September 1941, the United States extended the Lend-Lease Act to the Soviet Union. This allowed the Americans to send massive quantities of aid to further the Soviet war effort.

During the early years of the war, trucks, food, and medical supplies were the most important items sent under Lend-Lease. At that time, the Soviet Union faced difficult shortages of goods partly as a result of the German occupation of industrial areas.

### Second Front

An important issue complicating the anti-German alliance was the problem of a "Second Front." This meant a front in Europe where the Allies could fight the Germans on land and take pressure off the Russian front.

Stalin repeatedly noted that the Soviet Union was bearing the brunt of the war against Germany. For example, in June 1941 the Russians had faced 145 German divisions while the Allies had opposed only three German divisions in North Africa at that time.

Stalin insisted that the Soviets needed help in the form of a direct Allied attack on the Germans in Western Europe.

American and British campaigns in North Africa (1942–1943) and Italy (1943–1944) did not satisfy the Soviets. It is likely that Stalin believed that the Allies were deliberately delaying a second front, until the Soviet war effort had worn down the Germans.

## The Issue of Poland's Territorial Settlement

Another difficult issue was the question of territorial changes, especially concerning Polish land, to take place following the war.

## Early Diplomatic Moves

In early negotiations with the British, Stalin demanded the return of Polish lands that he had gotten in 1939 as Hitler's ally. The issue was explosive, because the Western allies wanted to maintain good relations with both the Soviet government and the Polish government in exile.

In May 1942 the Soviets and the British signed an initial treaty on postwar territorial changes. At the request of the United States, the problem of the western border of the Soviet Union was left unmentioned.

## Crisis of 1943

The Allied powers had a major crisis in 1943 over Soviet-Polish relations.

### *The Accusation*

The Germans claimed to have found the bodies of thousands of Polish officers in the Katyn Forest near the Russian city of Smolensk. According to the Germans, the Poles had been prisoners of the Soviet Union, and had been murdered and buried by Soviet authorities in 1940.

Since both Poland and the Soviet Union were allied to the Western powers, the controversy threatened to undermine the alliance against Nazi Germany.

### *Attempt at Investigation*

The Polish government in exile, located in London, asked the Red Cross to investigate the alleged atrocity. The Soviets refused to permit this and broke off diplomatic relations with the Poles.

### Recent Evidence and Admissions of Guilt

In the late 1980s and early 1990s, the Soviet responsibility for the murder of the Poles was completely established. Russians who took part in the massacre were interviewed and told their story. Moreover, the Soviet government under Mikhail Gorbachev (see Chapter 30) admitted that the Poles were murdered under Stalin's orders.

## Abolition of the Communist International

In May 1943, Stalin declared that the Communist International (or Comintern), which had existed since 1919, was now abolished.

The move was consistent with the Soviet wartime effort to play down the revolutionary tradition in Communism. The Communist International had been established to promote the spread of Communist revolution. Its abolition seemed to indicate that the Soviet Union would be a reliable partner of its Western allies in shaping the post-war world.

## Allied Conference at Teheran

The first summit conference to bring Stalin together with British Prime Minister Winston Churchill and American President Franklin Roosevelt was held in November and December 1943. The Allied leaders met at Teheran, the capital of Iran.

### Soviet Advantage

The conference took place against the background of Soviet victories on the eastern front. The Germans had been defeated at Stalingrad and Kursk, and they were now retreating westward.

### Agreements at Teheran

At Teheran the Allies took the important decision to establish a second front. There would be an Anglo-American invasion of France in the spring of 1944. The Soviets promised to attack on the eastern front at the same time.

The Americans and the British agreed "in principle" to let the Soviet Union keep the Polish territory it had seized in 1939.

## Allied Conference at Yalta

The second and final meeting attended by Stalin, Churchill, and Roosevelt took place at Yalta, in the Crimea, during February 1945.

### Soviet Advantages

Once again, Stalin could negotiate from a position of strength. The Soviet advance in Eastern Europe had continued, and the final offensive to take Berlin was about to begin.

Moreover, the leaders of the United States and Britain were anxious to bring the Soviets into the Far Eastern war against Japan.

### Decisions on Eastern Europe

Roosevelt and Churchill gave their consent to Stalin's demands for territory from Poland. The Soviet Union would receive the Polish lands it had held between 1939 and 1941.

In return, Poland was to receive territory along its western border with Germany. This meant that Poland would be pushed toward good relations with the Soviet Union in order to protect itself against German retribution.

In general, the Western allies seemed to accept Soviet supervision of Eastern Europe in the coming postwar era.

### Decisions on Germany

The allies agreed to divide Germany into four zones of occupation. There would be a zone for each of them as well as one for France. Berlin would also be put under four-power occupation.

### Decisions on Japan

The Soviet Union agreed to join the war against Japan once Germany had been defeated.

In return, the Soviets were to receive Japanese territory: the southern half of Sakhalin Island and the Kurile Islands.

## Allied Conference at Potsdam

The final summit among the Allied leaders took place at Potsdam outside Berlin in July and August 1945.

### Tensions among Allies

The meeting demonstrated growing tensions among the Allied powers. Changes in leadership in both the United States and Britain gave Stalin the advantage of being the senior figure present. Harry Truman had become president of the United States in April 1945, following the death of Franklin Roosevelt. Clement Attlee replaced

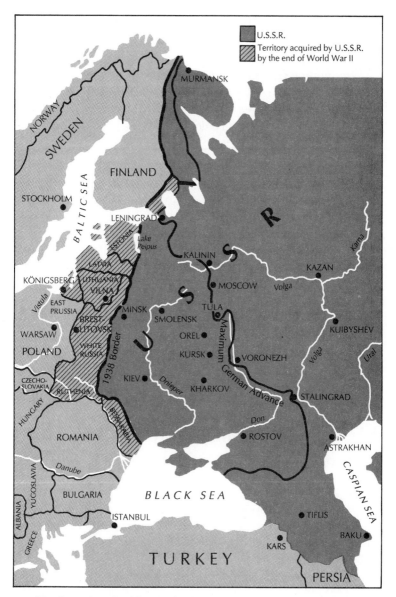

**Territory Acquired by the Soviet Union at the Close of WW II**

Winston Churchill in the middle of the conference. Attlee's Labor party had just defeated Churchill's Conservatives in Britain's national elections.

### Decisions on Germany

The conference set up the postwar occupation government for Germany. It also followed Soviet wishes in awarding German territory along Poland's western border to the Poles.

# The Communist Party

The war brought massive expansion of the Party. The Party also regained some of the status it had lost in the 1930s when Stalin created his police dictatorship.

## New Party Members

Almost 9 million people joined the Party during the war. Most of them were members of the armed forces, and many were engineers or other highly educated individuals.

## New Prestige for the Party

Communists were needed to staff key positions in expanding areas of the economy and the military system. Communists made up a large proportion of the individuals decorated for bravery in the armed forces.

# Soviet Society

The wartime years brought substantial changes in Soviet life. The harsh dictatorship of the 1930s was loosened in an effort to build popular support for the war effort.

The government revived traditional nationalism and reconstructed the Soviet army on pre-1917 lines. Both the church and the intellectual community got a degree of freedom that had vanished after the NEP era of the 1920s.

## Wartime Culture

The government relaxed the harsh censorship of the 1930s, and writers devoted both literature and journalism to the topic of the war.

Some works even criticized poor Soviet military leadership in the early stages of the war. This was the theme of *The Front*, a play by Alexander Korneichuk (1905–1972) published in 1942.

### Glorification of the Past

Many works looked back to the heroes of the Russian past. Earlier defenders of Russia against outside invasion, such as Alexander Nevsky and General Mikhail Kutuzov (1745–1813) of the Napoleonic era, were glamorized.

### Renewed Censorship

By 1943, there were early signs that the government was again tightening its control of literature.

In one important incident, satirist Mikhail Zoshchenko (1895–1958) was criticized for failing to incorporate patriotic ideals in his work.

## The Church

The Soviet government adopted a more sympathetic attitude toward organized religion during the war. This was another step in appealing to the population to rally behind the defense of the nation.

Orthodox churches were permitted to reopen, and the antireligious propaganda campaign begun in the early 1930s was played down.

In September 1943, Stalin personally received church leaders in the Kremlin. He permitted the church to pick a new patriarch, thereby filling a vacancy that had existed since 1925.

## The Military

A traditional military system dating from the era before the revolution was restored. Thus, much of the revolutionary coloration the army had possessed since its founding in 1918 was removed. In October 1942, for example, Stalin established a system of "one-man command" at all levels. This freed military leaders to give orders without first seeking the approval of political officials (commissars). The political officials had been placed in the military since the Civil War to assure the loyalty of the commanders (see Chapter 22).

Stalin himself took military rank and became a marshal of the Soviet army. Individual military commanders like Marshal Zhukov were presented to the public as national heroes.

Many features of the new system seemed deliberate devices to revive memories of the tsarist era. These included extensive privileges for officers, cadet schools to train future leaders, and even elite guards units.

# The Soviet Union in 1945

## The Population

### Casualties of War

The Soviet Union lost more people than any other participant in World War II. Older Soviet estimates indicated that 20 million Soviet citizens died, about half of them civilians. More recent figures released by the Soviet government speak of 27 million dead.

Losses to the population included millions who were weakened and had their lives cut short by harsh conditions during the war. Because of wartime casualties, there were far more women than men in the postwar population.

### Glimpses of Other Countries

Large numbers of Soviet citizens got a look at foreign countries during the conflict. These included prisoners of war, laborers conscripted by the Germans, and members of the victorious Russian armies that fought in Eastern and Central Europe in 1944 and 1945.

### The Jews

The Soviet Jewish population suffered particularly severe losses during the war. Most Jews lived in parts of the country that were occupied by the Germans.

Jews were wiped out in large numbers as victims of a deliberate German policy of extermination. About sixty percent of the Soviet Union's Jewish population perished during the war.

## International Status

The Soviet Union's newly powerful role in world affairs was its most crucial change to result from the war.

### The Situation at the Start of the War

Before the outbreak of war in 1939, the Soviet Union had been only one of a number of powerful European countries. It had been confined to the eastern fringe of the continent. Moreover, it was threatened by two powerful enemies: Germany and Japan.

### The Situation at the Close of the War

In late 1945, the Soviet Union was the most powerful European country. It occupied Eastern and Central Europe, and it faced no danger from any other European state.

In the Far East, the crucial facts were the collapse of Japan and Soviet gains of territory in the last days of the war.

These conditions gave the Soviet Union both new security and unprecedented influence.

### The Problem of the United States

The most important check on Soviet power was the strength of the United States. The Soviets faced American forces in Europe and Asia.

Moreover, American power had grown even more spectacularly than Soviet power during the war. The United States had suffered only small losses in manpower compared to the Soviet Union, while its economy had expanded dramatically.

The final days of the war had seen the United States use its atomic bombs. These were powerful tools of war over which the United States held a complete monopoly.

## Stalin as War Leader

Stalin's achievements as the wartime leader of the Soviet Union were publicized at home both during and after the conflict. Much of his political reputation came to depend upon his supposed triumphs in this area.

### Early Failures

Historians consider Stalin largely responsible for the disasters at the start of the war. In 1941, he had refused to allow his armed forces to deploy for the coming German attack. Apparently he clung to the idea that, by demonstrating his continuing willingness for friendly relations with Germany, he could somehow prevent or delay a German attack.

Stalin did not make any public statements for almost two weeks after the start of the war. Some reports indicate that he may have suffered an emotional collapse.

### Later Effectiveness

Stalin is credited by historians with maintaining order and discipline in the Soviet Union during the disastrous retreats of 1941 and 1942. He was also able to choose highly capable military leaders like Zhukov. Some commanders who had been purged in the 1930s were even called back into uniform from labor camps.

While Stalin cannot be credited with great military skills, he pursued an effective policy of rallying the population against the invader. To that end, he was willing to loosen features of the dictatorship he had created in the 1930s.

In the field of diplomacy, Stalin succeeded in obtaining enormous territorial gains for the Soviet Union by the close of the war.

#### *Recent Soviet Views*

In the era of *perestroika* (see Chapter 30), Soviet revisionist historians have stressed Stalin's indifference to human life in waging the war. They believed he caused many Soviet military men to die needlessly.

*The war ended with the Soviet Union physically devastated but politically and militarily powerful. Soviet losses in blood and wealth were enormous. Nonetheless, Soviet power was now established in Central Europe and Eastern Asia. Moreover, as a key participant in the wartime coalition, the country was in a powerful position to influence the postwar world.*

*The war had also brought a new flexibility in Soviet political life. The Russian people had been asked to fight for their country rather than for Communism.*

*At the war's conclusion, one question to be answered was how the Soviet Union would use its new international role. Another question was whether domestic liberalization would continue or be reversed.*

## Recommended Reading

Adamovich, Ales, and Daniil Granin. *A Book of the Blockade* (1983).

Andreyev, Catherine. *Vlasov and the Russian Liberation Movement: Soviet Reality and Émigré Theories* (1987).

Armstrong, John A. *Soviet Partisans in World War II* (1964).

Bialer, Seweryn, ed. *Stalin and His Generals: Soviet Military Memoirs of World War II* (1969).

Clemens, Diane Shaver. *Yalta* (1970).

Cooper, Matthew. *The Nazi War against Soviet Partisans, 1941–1944* (1979).

Craig, William. *Enemy at the Gates: The Battle for Stalingrad* (1972).

Dallin, Alexander. *German Rule in Russia, 1941–1945: A Study of Occupation Policies* (rev. ed., 1981).

Erickson, John. *Stalin's War with Germany, Vol. 1: The Road to Stalingrad* (1975).

Erickson, John. *Stalin's War with Germany, Vol. 2: The Road to Berlin* (1983).

Kochina, Elena. *Blockade Diary* (1990).

Linz, Susan J., ed. *The Impact of World War II on the Soviet Union* (1985).

Lucas, James S. *War on the Eastern Front, 1941–45: The German Soldier in Russia* (1982).

Lyons, Graham, ed. *The Russian Version of the Second World War: The History of the War as Taught to Soviet School Children* (1983).

McCagg, William O. *Stalin Embattled, 1943–1948* (1978).

Mastny, Vojtech. *Russian's Road to the Cold War: Diplomacy, War and the Politics of Communism, 1941–45* (1979).

Nekrich, Alexander M. *"June 22, 1941": Soviet Historians and the German Invasion* (1968).

Paul, Allen. *Katyn: The Untold Story of Stalin's Polish Massacre* (1991).

Pavlov, Dimitrii V. *Leningrad 1941: The Blockade* (1965).

Salisbury, Harrison E. *The 900 Days: The Siege of Leningrad* (1969).

Seaton, Albert. *The Russo-German War, 1941–1945* (1970).

Seaton, Albert. *Stalin as Warlord* (1976).

Werth, Alexander. *Russia at War* (1964; reprint 1984).

Zawodny, J. K. *Death in the Forest: The Story of the Katyn Forest Massacre* (1962).

# CHAPTER 27

## The Late Stalinist Period
## (1945–1953)

### Time Line

| | |
|---|---|
| February 1946 | Stalin's remobilization speech |
| March 1946 | Churchill's "iron curtain" speech |
| March 1947 | Truman Doctrine announced |
| June 1947 | Marshall Plan announced |
| June 1948 | Relations broken between Stalin and Tito |
| June 1948–<br>May 1949 | Berlin blockade |
| April 1949 | NATO organized |
| August 1949 | Soviets explode atomic bomb |

| June 1950–<br>July 1953 | Korean War |
|---|---|
| October 1952 | Nineteenth Communist Party Congress |
| January 1953 | Arrests in ''Doctors' Plot'' |
| March 1953 | Death of Stalin |

*During the period after World War II, Stalin ended the relatively relaxed control the dictatorship had practiced during the conflict. In a second major development, cooperative relations between the Soviet Union and the United States, its chief wartime ally, broke down. The Cold War soon followed.*

*Soviet relations with the outside world were also affected by the development of a bloc of satellites in Eastern Europe and by the successful Communist revolution in China.*

*Friction with the United States arose over the future of Eastern Europe and Germany. The more restrictive regime at home became evident with a crackdown on the intellectual community and the establishment of a new five-year plan.*

## Consequences of the War

The gains of the war had been substantial, but they had come at a fearful price. The Soviet Union regained almost all of the land lost by the collapse of the tsarist empire in 1917. In addition, Moscow exercised effective control over most of Eastern Europe. But Russian casualties had been enormous—more than 20 million lives lost according to some estimates—and Russia's industrial economy had been devastated.

## Postwar Repression

Stalin pursued a policy of reimposing harsh controls over Soviet life. Groups that had allegedly behaved badly in the war were one target. Groups that had escaped unbroken Soviet control, by becoming prisoners of war or by receiving greater freedoms as a result of government policy between 1941 and 1945, were another.

## Former Prisoners of War

Large numbers of Russians who had become German prisoners now returned to the Soviet Union, sometimes against their will. The government met them with deep suspicion, and many were punished for their wartime experiences by being imprisoned again once they had returned home. The Soviet government considered a Soviet soldier who had been captured or a Soviet citizen who had been forced to work for the Germans as an individual who had committed treason.

## The Non-Russian Nationalities

During the last years of the war, several ethnic groups had been deported en masse as punishment for supposedly cooperating with the Germans. Thus, by war's end the Crimean Tatars, for example, found themselves exiled to Central Asia and Kazakhstan.

The postwar period brought intensified control to the Ukraine, where the invading Germans had initially been welcomed by much of the population. The first Ukrainian reactions to the Nazi invasion are understandable, given the Ukrainian experience of collectivization and famine in the 1930s.

## The Anti-Western Campaign

Stalin set the tone of the postwar period in a radio address of February 1946. He pointed to the danger of war with the capitalists of the West and asked for new sacrifices from the Soviet population.

### The Intellectual Community

An attack on the intellectual community followed, starting in the summer of 1946. Contact with the West by Soviet citizens and even exposure to Western ideas were condemned. Soviet writers and composers, who had enjoyed substantial latitude during the war, were now compelled to follow the guidelines of Socialist Realism.

### The Role of Zhdanov

Andrei Zhdanov (1896–1948) took the lead in the assault on the intellectual community. He was a longtime lieutenant of Stalin and had been in charge of the Communist Party apparatus in Leningrad. Zhdanov seemed to be Stalin's handpicked successor.

## Economic Life

A return to the harsh policies of the 1930s took place in economic life as well.

### Agriculture

In the countryside, an agricultural system based on the collective farm was reemphasized. One of Stalin's principal lieutenants, Nikita Khrushchev (1894–1971), was placed in charge of agriculture. One of his policies was to bring together collective farms in the form of rural cities (*agrogoroda*).

### Industry

In industry, the techniques of the 1930s returned, with harsh punishment for absenteeism.

An important source for the raw materials needed to reconstruct Soviet Russia was Eastern Europe. Materials first arrived in the form of reparations drawn from Germany. Soon, the Soviet Union benefited from one-sided trade agreements drawn up with the satellite states of Eastern Europe.

### Fourth Five-Year Plan

Begun in 1946, the new five-year plan was designed to repair the damage of the wartime years and to set the stage for future growth. Like the earlier five-year plans, it stressed the development of heavy industry at the cost of gains in agriculture or consumer goods.

Combined with restored political controls, the five-year plan demonstrated Stalin's desire to return to the system by which he had ruled the Soviet Union in the 1930s.

## The Cold War

The most significant development in Soviet relations with the outside world was the breakdown of the wartime alliance and the resulting confrontation with the United States.

### Interpretations of the Start of the Cold War

Historians have disagreed sharply in evaluating the motives of both sides and in assessing responsibility for the "Cold War." One view holds that Stalin tightened his control over Eastern Europe and Russian-occupied Germany as a base for future expansion into Western Europe. Another interpretation suggests that the Soviet leader was primarily interested in protecting his own borders with a buffer zone of satellite states along the western border of the Soviet Union.

The absence of information concerning the decisions taken in Moscow during the first years after the end of World War II makes it difficult to settle this issue. Meanwhile, some historians in the West have accused American leaders, including President Harry Truman, of heightening tensions by a belligerent policy toward the Soviet Union.

### Beginning of Friction with the United States

A number of specific issues resulting from the military victory in World War II led to heated disagreements between the Soviet and Western governments. One issue was the future of Eastern Europe: Would the populations there be permitted to recover from the war on their own, or would they be dominated by the Soviet Union? Western leaders soon found that the Soviet Union was determined to play a dominant role in Eastern Europe.

A second issue was the future of Germany: Was it to be permanently divided and occupied, or would the Germans be allowed to move toward political and economic recovery?

### The Sovietization of Eastern Europe

#### Soviet-Occupied Countries

Soviet control in Eastern Europe began with the successful military campaigns of the Red Army against the forces of Nazi Germany. By V-E day, Russian troops occupied Poland, Czechoslovakia, Romania, Hungary, and Bulgaria. Between 1945 and 1948, these countries were brought into a "Soviet bloc," separated from the rest of Europe by what Winston Churchill called an "iron curtain."

#### Communist-Dominated Governments

Under Soviet influence, several countries, including Hungary, Poland, and Czechoslovakia, established coalition governments in which native Communists played a dominant role. In the years following the war, Soviet pressure in these countries brought Communist governments to power.

### Communist Societies

The societies of Eastern Europe were reshaped as well. Agrarian reforms confiscated large estates and gave the land in small portions to individual peasants. The government took over large businesses. Soviet patterns in culture and education (Socialist Realism in art, for example) were established.

## The Threat of Soviet Expansion

Western countries first responded to the threat of Soviet expansion in the Middle East and the Mediterranean.

### The Crisis in Azerbaijan

The Russians occupied Azerbaijan, an area of northern Iran along the Soviet border, during World War II. When they tried to set up permanent control in northern Iran in 1946, the United States and Britain objected forcefully. Facing a possible military reaction from the Western powers, Stalin pulled out.

### Soviet Pressure on Greece and Turkey

In Greece, Communist guerrillas had played a major role in resisting the German and Italian occupation during World War II. In a civil war following 1945, Communist forces seemed headed for success. In Turkey, Greece's neighbor to the east, the government faced Soviet demands for military bases in the strategic area around the straits connecting the Black Sea and the Mediterranean.

### The Truman Doctrine

In March 1947, the American government, led by President Harry Truman, moved to block these communist threats. Military and economic aid went to both Greece and Turkey as part of a "Truman Doctrine" designed to prevent the spread of Communism.

## The German Question

The most bitter point of confrontation between the Soviet Union and the West came in Germany. The defeated enemy of World War

II had been divided into four zones of occupation: American, British, French, and Russian.

Cooperation between the Western Allies and the Soviet Union broke down over such issues as reparations that would transfer factories and other valuable property from Germany to Russia. The larger issue was who would control the future of Germany, once Europe's most powerful nation.

### The Berlin Blockade

In June 1948, the Soviet Union directly challenged Western power in Germany. Berlin, located 110 miles deep in the Soviet zone, was divided into American, British, French, and Russian sectors. The Russians now blocked road and rail traffic from the Western sectors of Germany to the Western zones of Berlin.

By pressuring the West in Berlin, Stalin could hope to achieve two primary goals. One was to get Western acceptance of the new territorial and political system he had imposed on Eastern Europe. Secondly, he could humiliate the West in German eyes, setting the stage for Soviet domination over all of Germany.

### The Berlin Airlift

The West responded by supplying Berlin by air. This avoided a direct military confrontation with Russian forces. It also showed the superior strength of Western air power.

### NATO

Another response to the Soviet challenge was the formation of a military alliance to defend non-Communist Europe. Led by the United States, a Western defense system (the North Atlantic Treaty Organization or NATO) was set up in April 1949.

In May 1949, in the face of the successful Berlin airlift and the formation of NATO, the Soviet Union lifted the blockade of Berlin.

### The Marshall Plan

Along with the formation of NATO, the Marshall Plan prevented the spread of Soviet power beyond the Iron Curtain. In June 1947, George Marshall, the American Secretary of State, outlined a program of American aid for Europe's economic recovery.

### Soviet Rejection

Marshall Plan aid was open to all European countries. After brief hesitation, the Soviet Union refused to participate, as did the satellite governments of Czechoslovakia and Poland. Apparently Stalin feared both economic contact with the West and economic dependency on the United States.

### The Impact of the Marshall Plan

The aid that flowed to non-Communist Europe soon restored high levels of economic production. This recovery undercut the appeal of even powerful Communist parties, such as those in France and Italy.

## Cominform and COMECON

The Soviets responded to American initiatives with moves designed to tighten Moscow's ties with Eastern Europe and Communist parties outside the Soviet Union. A Communist Information Bureau (or Cominform) was set up in October 1947 to coordinate the work of Communist parties.

COMECON, a body designed to coordinate the economic ties between the Soviet Union and the satellites of Eastern Europe, was formed in January 1949. Its founding document declared the hostility of its members to the Marshall Plan.

## Yugoslavia

The first sign of Soviet difficulty in maintaining control over the Communist governments of Eastern Europe came in Yugoslavia.

The position of the Communist Party, led by the partisan hero Marshal Tito (1892–1980), differed from that of Communist parties elsewhere. Yugoslav Communists had led an effective resistance movement against German occupation, and they had received extensive support directly from Britain and the United States during the war. Yugoslav resistance forces, not the Russian army, liberated the country at the close of the war.

### Collapse of Relations with Tito

Stalin's efforts to impose the same controls on Yugoslavia that worked well elsewhere exploded in his face. Tito objected to Russian exploitation of the Yugoslav economy. He opposed Stalin's attempts to place Soviet agents in charge of crucial positions in the Yugoslav army and the Yugoslav Communist Party.

In June 1948, Stalin moved against Tito. He got the Cominform to condemn Tito and his followers, and he called for Tito's overthrow. Neighboring Soviet satellites like Bulgaria mobilized their armies and placed them on the Yugoslav border.

### Tito's Defiance of Stalin

Nonetheless, Tito survived. His success was due to his dictatorial control over his own country, aided by patriotic support of his population against Russian domination. Tito also found former wartime allies, notably the United States, willing to send him economic and military help.

### Purges in Eastern Europe

Stalin's failure to transform Yugoslavia into a docile satellite raised the danger that other Communists in Eastern Europe would imitate Tito.

Starting in 1949, the leaders of Communist parties in Eastern Europe were eliminated as Stalin tried to root out potential Titos elsewhere. In Hungary, for example, Foreign Minister Lazslo Rajk (1909–1949) was executed in June 1949, and a purge of the entire Hungarian Communist Party soon followed.

## Relations with Communist China

Communist leaders in China like Mao Tse-tung also pulled away from Stalin's leadership.

### Stalin's Policy toward Chinese Communism

During World War II, Mao had accepted Russian advice and refrained from attacking the non-Communist Chinese government of Chiang Kai-shek. Stalin also aimed at postwar cooperation between the Soviet government and Chiang. Thus, he pushed the Chinese Communists to continue their truce with Chiang's nationalists.

### The Chinese Revolution

The Chinese Communists ignored Stalin's directives. Between 1946 and 1949, they waged an effective partisan war against

Chiang's forces. By the close of 1949, Mao's government controlled the Chinese mainland. Chiang had fled to the island of Taiwan.

## New Russo-Chinese Relations

The long-range implications of the successful Chinese revolution were enormous. Now two vast and powerful countries had Communist governments. Moreover, the Chinese leaders had their own program for building a Communist society. This featured a rapid transformation of life in China, far more rapid a change than the one Russia had experienced after 1917.

Thus, a Communist China posed a dangerous challenge to Stalin. It showed that the Russian model of Communism need not be followed in all countries or in all circumstances. The potential for rivalry and even hostility between China and the Soviet Union was obvious.

### Mao's Visit to Moscow, 1949–1950

One factor above all restrained the development of Chinese-Russian tensions. In the aftermath of civil war, Mao's government needed outside economic help. Given China's diplomatic isolation, that help could come only from the Soviet Union.

During the winter of 1949–1950, Mao visited Moscow. Russian officials deliberately avoided treating him as an honored guest. Mao was not permitted to meet with Stalin for several weeks, a clear signal that the Russians would not treat him as an equal.

### Demand for Chinese Concessions

The Chinese received Russian aid, but only in modest amounts. In return, Mao had to grant the Soviet Union important military and economic concessions, such as the right to draw oil from the Chinese province of Sinkiang. It remained uncertain how long the Chinese would accept a status similar to that of the satellite states of Eastern Europe.

## The Korean War

Cold War tensions increased in the late 1940s and the early part of the next decade.

### North Korean Invasion

In June 1950, a North Korean army that had been trained and equipped by the Soviet Union crossed the 38th parallel and invaded South Korea. Although there is uncertainty about the precise decisions taken in Moscow, it seems likely that Stalin hoped a united Communist Korea would provide him with some influence over a potentially powerful postwar Japan.

### United Nations Intervention

The United Nations condemned the invasion. United Nations forces, under an American commander and with a large American contingent, recovered most of South Korea even though Chinese Communist forces entered the war in the fall of 1950.

The Soviet delegate had walked out of the United Nations Security Council in January 1950 to protest the exclusion of Communist China from the United Nations. Thus, the Security Council resolution to intervene in Korea was not blocked by a Soviet veto. Some historians believe the Russians were surprised and immobilized by the rapid United Nations response to the invasion. The attack took place on June 25, and the resolution to intervene passed on June 27.

### Communist-U.S. Military Conflict

The Korean War marks the first direct military conflict between Communist forces and American troops since the close of World War I. Truce negotiations began in July 1951, but the fighting in Korea did not end until after Stalin's death.

## The Soviet Union as an Emerging Atomic Power

The international situation grew even more dangerous when the Soviet Union tested its first atomic bomb in August 1949. Stalin had ordered a crash program to build an atomic bomb immediately after the American atomic attacks on Japan in 1945. The American monopoly on atomic weapons had lasted only four years.

In the first part of the 1950s, the Soviet Union built hydrogen bombs as well. Thus, Cold War confrontations between the Soviet Union and the United States raised the possibility of massive loss of life on both sides through nuclear war.

# Stalin's Last Years

Stalin's efforts to dominate Soviet life continued, and even intensified, during the closing part of his life. He ordered giant building projects. In such fields as biology and linguistics, he prescribed scientific theories that matched his views on how the world would move forward to a Communist society.

His desire to smash political dangers regardless of their origins led Stalin to strike in a number of directions. For example, he conducted an "anti-Zionist campaign" that seemed a prelude to an unlimited wave of persecution of the Soviet Jewish population.

## Nineteenth Party Congress

In October 1952, the Soviet Communist Party met in its first congress since 1939. The proceedings seemed to mark Stalin's lieutenant Georgi Malenkov (1902–1988) as the dictator's selected heir; Malenkov gave the main report to the Congress.

### Fifth Five-Year Plan

The Congress also approved the Fifth Five-Year Plan. Like its predecessors, it stressed the growth of heavy industry at the expense of agriculture and consumer goods.

### Changes in Party Structure

Stalin had the Congress approve changes in the highest levels of the Party's structure. Governing bodies like the Party's Central Committee Secretariat were expanded or merged. Younger men, including Leonid Brezhnev (1906–1982), were promoted into these governing organs. In this way, the power of Stalin's small circle of Party lieutenants was weakened.

## "Doctors' Plot"

During the Congress, rumors flew that a mass purge, similar to the Great Purge of the 1930s, was likely to take place soon. One sign of a renewed hunt for traitors came in January 1953. Nine doctors, most of whom were Jewish, were arrested for murdering high-ranking Soviet leaders like Andrei Zhdanov. This appeared to be the prelude to the deportation of the Jewish population, or possibly the prelude to a campaign of arrests and terror directed against the entire Soviet population.

## The Death of Stalin

In the midst of widespread concern about a new reign of terror, the Soviet population received the news that Stalin had died on March 5, 1953. The dictator had dominated Soviet life for decades. For the Soviet people and the outside world, it was difficult to imagine what a new (and perhaps different) kind of Soviet leader might be like.

*Stalin's final years had been remarkably active ones. He had reasserted tight, dictatorial control over Soviet society. At the same time, he established Soviet control over Eastern Europe. The triumph of Mao Tse-tung in China seemed an indication of Communism's dynamic expansion.*

*But the picture was a mixed one. The Soviet Union now faced an aroused adversary, the United States. Eastern Europe saw the emergence of a Soviet regime hostile to Moscow in Yugoslavia. China's willingness to remain in a position subordinate to the Soviet Union was uncertain.*

## Recommended Reading

Bethell, Nicholas W. *The Last Secret: The Delivery to Stalin of over Two Million Russians by Britain and the United States* (1974).

Brzezinski, Zbigniew. *The Soviet Bloc* (rev. and enl. ed., 1967).

Conquest, Robert. *The Nation Killers: The Soviet Deportation of Nationalities* (1970).

Conquest, Robert. *Power and Policy in the USSR: A Study of Soviet Dynasties* (1961).

Gaddis, John L. *Russia, the Soviet Union, and the United States: An Interpretive History* (1978).

Gaddis, John L. *The United States and the Origins of the Cold War* (1972).

Hahn, Werner G. *Postwar Soviet Politics: The Fall of Zhdanov and the Defeat of Moderation, 1946–1953* (1982).

Joravsky, David. *The Lysenko Affair* (1970).

Kaplan, Cynthia. *The Party and Agriculture: Crisis Management in the USSR* (1987).

Levin, Nora. *The Jews of the Soviet Union since 1917: Paradox of Survival*, 2 vols. (1988).

McCagg, William O. *Stalin Embattled, 1943–1948* (1978).

Medvedev, Zhores. *The Rise and Fall of T. D. Lysenko* (1969).

Nekrich, Alexander M. *The Punished Peoples: The Deportation and Fate of Soviet Minorities at the End of the Second World War* (1978).

Pelican, Jiri, ed. *The Czechoslovak Political Trials, 1950–1954: The Suppressed Report of the Dubcek Government Commission of Inquiry* (1971).

Shulman, Marshal. *Stalin's Foreign Policy Reappraised* (1963).

Ulam, Adam. *Expansion and Coexistence: The History of Soviet Foreign Policy, 1917–9167* (1968).

# CHAPTER 28

## The Khrushchev Years
## (1953–1964)

### Time Line

| | |
|---|---|
| March 1953 | Death of Stalin |
| | Khrushchev becomes Party Secretary |
| June 1953 | Berlin uprising |
| July 1953 | Beria deposed and executed |
| | Armistice in Korean War |
| March 1954 | ''Virgin Lands'' scheme begun |
| October 1954 | Treaty between Soviet Union and China |
| February 1955 | Malenkov resigns as prime minister |

| | |
|---|---|
| May 1955 | Warsaw Pact formed |
| June 1955 | Khrushchev visits Yugoslavia |
| July 1955 | Geneva summit conference |
| | Austrian peace treaty |
| February 1956 | Twentieth Party Congress and the "Secret Speech" |
| | Sixth Five-Year Plan begins |
| June–October 1956 | Reforms in Poland |
| October–November 1956 | Hungarian uprising |
| June 1957 | Defeat of "anti-party group" |
| October 1957 | Launching of *Sputnik* |
| March 1958 | Khrushchev becomes premier |
| November 1958 –March 1959 | Berlin crisis |
| September 1959 | Khrushchev visits the United States |
| May 1960 | U-2 incident and Paris conference |
| August 1961 | Berlin Wall erected |
| October 1961 | Twenty-Second Party Congress |
| October 1962 | Cuban missile crisis |
| July 1963 | Test ban treaty |
| October 1964 | Khrushchev forced from office |

*Stalin's death was followed by a series of striking changes in Soviet domestic and foreign policy. The atmosphere of terror characteristic of the pre-1953 police state faded. Industrial and agricultural policies were altered to make life more tolerable for the average Soviet citizen. The new Soviet leaders made substantial efforts to reduce Cold War tensions.*

*There was a vigorous struggle to succeed Stalin in which Nikita Khrushchev emerged the winner. But Khrushchev made it clear that he was opposed to Stalin's abuses of power.*

# The Rise of Khrushchev

Following Stalin's death, two significant developments took place within the Soviet Union. First, the group of Stalin's subordinates who now took control of the country initiated a series of reforms that diminished the harshness of the Stalinist dictatorship. The second development was a fierce competition for power among the members of the new "collective leadership."

## The Idea of Collective Leadership

Following Stalin's death, the Party Presidium (formerly the Politburo) emphatically stated the need for "collective leadership" rather than the control of a single individual. This indicated the predictable fear of the Soviet leaders that one of them would emerge to dominate and threaten the others.

## Post-Stalin Reform

Within a month after Stalin's death, the government took steps to show that the old system of police terror and economic deprivation was being changed.

### Reversal of the "Doctors' Plot"

Beria, the head of the secret police, announced that there had been no "Doctors' Plot," and the surviving defendants were released. This action indicated that the police terror on which Stalin's power had been based was being curtailed.

### Food and Consumer Goods

Meanwhile, Malenkov (1902–1988), the head of the government, announced that more food would be made available to the population. Moreover, the production of consumer goods would increase in the next several years.

## The Succession Struggle

Stalin's positions in the Party and government were divided among several of his lieutenants. The individuals who now obtained key positions were the leading contenders to succeed Stalin.

### Malenkov's Position

Georgi Malenkov had been Stalin's closest assistant in the dictator's last years. He was the effective head of the Communist Party at the time of Stalin's death. He now took the position of premier (or prime minister) of the government as well. Almost immediately, the other Soviet leaders compelled Malenkov to give up his position at the head of the Party.

### Khrushchev's Position

Nikita Khrushchev (1894–1971) was the head of the Communist Party in Moscow province and a member of the Party Presidium. He was also the Party's leading specialist in agricultural affairs.

Within a week after Stalin's death, Khrushchev took over the leadership of the Soviet Communist Party from Malenkov. He formally received the post of First Secretary of the Party several months later.

### Beria's Bid for Power; His Fall

Lavrenty Beria (1899–1953) had been the head of the secret police since 1938 and was a member of the Party Presidium. He was the first big loser in the struggle for power.

As head of the secret police, Beria controlled the most powerful and highly organized body in the country. Moving quickly to expand his base of power, he presented himself as a reformer in the areas of agriculture and policies toward the non-Russian nationalities. His apparent success alarmed his competitors.

In July 1953, Khrushchev, with the help of the military, deposed Beria. The former secret police leader was probably executed immediately.

An important effect of Beria's execution was to put a permanent limit on the power of the secret police. Unlike the situation in the Stalinist era, the secret police now came under the control of the Party.

### Khrushchev versus Malenkov

The fall of Beria left Khrushchev and Malenkov as the main competitors for supreme power. Their rivalry was largely fought out in the area of economic policy.

*Malenkov's Bid for Power.* Malenkov tried to widen his support by advocating a shift from industrial production to consumer goods. He was handicapped by a number of factors. His position as head of the government turned out to be less powerful and prestigious than the position of Party leader that he had been forced to give up. Moreover, as Stalin's closest subordinate, he was identified with the terror and economic hardships of the old system.

*Khrushchev's Bid for Power.* Khrushchev had the advantage of holding the position of First Secretary (the leader) of the Communist Party. He was also strengthened by his role in eliminating Beria.

Most important of all, Khrushchev had dramatic and early success in improving agricultural production. He increased the output of the collective farms, for example, by offering rewards for better production.

In 1954, Khrushchev initiated a policy of increasing the amount of land in the Soviet Union to be used for food production. In his policy of cultivating "virgin lands," he extended agriculture to north Kazakhstan and west Siberia. The early results were spectacular. The harvest of 1953 had been particularly bad. The harvest of 1956 was the best since the Bolshevik Revolution in 1917.

*Khrushchev's Victory.* Malenkov submitted his resignation as premier in February 1955. He was replaced by Nikolai Bulganin (1895–1975).

Although Bulganin was an important Party official and a leading government administrator, he presented no challenge to Khrushchev's stature as the leader of the Soviet system.

*Malenkov's Party Position.* As a member of the Presidium, Malenkov remained a high-ranking Party official. This was significant in two ways. First, it showed that a Soviet leader could now fail in a try for supreme power and remain safe and unpunished. It was a sign that the political system was losing some of its old brutality.

Moreover, Malenkov remained in a relatively strong position from which he could mount a future attack on Khrushchev.

# New Trends in Foreign Policy

The leaders who took over after Stalin's death also established new policies in Soviet foreign relations.

A main theme of the new foreign policy was an effort to reduce Cold War tensions with the United States. Meanwhile, the Soviets made a major effort to bridge their differences with the Communist leadership in Yugoslavia.

### The Korean Armistice Negotiations

The Korean Armistice of July 1953 was an early sign of improved relations between the Soviet Union and the United States. During negotiations the Soviets encouraged the Chinese to reverse their position that prisoners of war held by United Nations forces be returned to their own country. Under the new agreement, the prisoners themselves (mainly Chinese) would decide whether or not to return to Communist China.

### The Geneva Summit

A major breakthrough in East-West relations occurred at Geneva in July 1955. Khrushchev met American President Dwight Eisenhower for their first summit conference. Also present were Prime Minister Anthony Eden of Great Britain and Premier Edgar Faure of France.

### The Austrian Peace Treaty

At the summit conference the two leaders signed the Austrian peace treaty. It provided for the withdrawal of all foreign troops from Austria and the establishment of Austrian neutrality.

The treaty involved the first withdrawal of Soviet forces after World War II from any area of Europe. It also indicated that additional issues separating the Soviets and the Americans might be settled by high-level negotiations.

### Reconciliation with Tito

Khrushchev reversed Stalin's policy of open hostility toward Tito's Yugoslavia. In June 1955, the Soviet leader visited the Yugoslav capital of Belgrade. It was a public symbol of Soviet willingness to accept Tito's claim that Yugoslavia need not follow the Soviet model of building a Communist society.

Tito's example served to loosen ties between Moscow and the Communist satellites. The satellite countries of Eastern Europe could now claim, for example, that they too had the right to construct Communism in ways appropriate for their countries rather than adhere strictly to the Soviet model.

### The Warsaw Pact

On the other hand, the formation of a military alliance between the Soviet Union and the East European satellites tightened Moscow's power. The Warsaw Pact, signed in May 1955, provided for a coordinated defense of Albania, Bulgaria, Czechoslovakia, East Germany, Hungary, Poland, and Romania under Russian command. The Soviet Union now had firm legal justification for continuing to station its forces in several Eastern European countries.

# Khrushchev in Power (1956–1959)

Between 1956 and the end of 1959, Khrushchev survived crises at home and in Eastern Europe. Moreover, his authority grew with his apparent successes in scientific competition with the United States and in improving the Soviet economy.

### Twentieth Party Congress (February 1956)

The Party Congress of February 1956 was the first to meet following the death of Stalin. It approved the Sixth Five-Year Plan as well as significant changes in Soviet ideology.

#### Ideological Shifts

Khrushchev presented the novel view that Communist and non-Communist societies could compete within a framework of "peaceful coexistence." This reversed the traditional view that armed

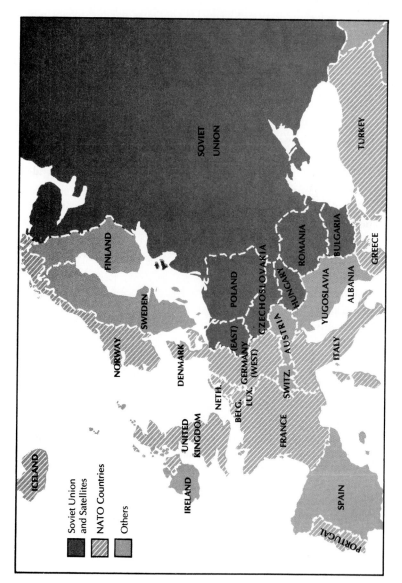

**Communist and Non-Communist Europe in the Era of Khrushchev**

conflict between countries like the United States and the Soviet Union was inevitable in the long run.

Khrushchev also presented the concept that different countries could move from capitalism to socialism in their own way. Thus, Yugoslavia, for example, need not follow the Soviet model.

### The Secret Speech

The most important ideas presented at the Congress came in a speech Khrushchev delivered on the final evening. It was given to a closed session attended by the Congress's delegates.

*Khrushchev's Denunciation of Stalin.*    Khrushchev stunned his audience by criticizing Stalin in a way not heard in public since the 1920s. In particular, he condemned the crimes that Stalin had committed against the Party and its members and his murder of innocent Communists in the purges of the late 1930s. He likewise denounced Stalin's cult of personality and his incompetent leadership in the early stages of World War II.

*Motives for the Secret Speech.*    Historians remain divided over why Khrushchev gave his explosive speech. One motive may have been to discredit Stalin's rule by terror, since he believed such a method was no longer useful.

It is possible that Khrushchev was responding to pressure from within the Communist Party. The Party was still the key organization in the Soviet Union. Many of its leaders wanted assurances that the Party would never again be injured as it had been under Stalin.

The speech also allowed Khrushchev to present himself as a bold and enthusiastic reformer. He made himself appear a more attractive figure than Stalinist conservatives like Molotov and Malenkov, who remained present as his potential rivals.

*The Limits of the Secret Speech.*    Khrushchev did not, however, criticize the Communist system even though it had allowed a criminal like Stalin to take and hold supreme power. Similarly, he presented no condemnation of the human cost of collectivization or planned industrial growth.

### Eastern Europe

The death of Stalin encouraged the populations of Eastern Europe to show their discontent with Soviet control. When news spread concerning Khrushchev's secret speech of February 1956, the push for change in Eastern Europe intensified. The speech shattered the notion that the Soviet Communist Party was infallible. By criticizing Stalin, Khrushchev had severely undermined the authority of Stalinist leaders in Eastern Europe.

### The Berlin Uprising (June 1953)

In June 1953, workers in East Berlin protested against work conditions. Their revolt was suppressed, but it indicated the possibility of more popular uprisings in Eastern Europe.

### Reform in Poland

Popular unrest in Poland began in June 1956, a few months after Khrushchev's secret speech, when factory workers demonstrated in Poznan. The next stage in Poland's push for change came in October. Wladyslaw Gomulka (1905–1982), a Communist leader with a reputation for defending Polish interests against the Soviet Union, became head of the Communist Party in Poland. He quickly pledged to create a more democratic brand of Polish Communism.

Khrushchev was unable to force a Polish retreat despite the threat of Soviet military intervention.

### Revolution in Hungary

The push for change took a more radical turn in Hungary in 1956. There were demonstrators in late October in support of the Poles. These led to the creation of a new government under Imre Nagy (1896–1958). Like Gomulka in Poland, Nagy was a Communist with a reputation for liberalism and defending his country's interests against Moscow.

After considerable fighting between Hungarians and Soviet forces, Khrushchev withdrew the Soviet army in late October. But Soviet troops returned in early November to suppress Hungarian resistance.

### Comparison of Events in Poland and Hungary in 1956

The Soviets proved to be willing to permit reformers to remain in power in Poland but not in Hungary.

One reason was the greater difficulty involved in subduing Poland by force. Poland was the largest satellite in Eastern Europe, with the most sizable population.

A second reason was the relative moderation of the change in Poland. Gomulka pledged to maintain Communist control and to remain in the Warsaw Pact. In contrast, Nagy followed a more radical policy. Non-Communist parties emerged in Hungary, and several non-Communists joined Nagy's government. Moreover, Nagy declared that Hungary would leave the Warsaw Pact and take a neutral position in international affairs.

## The Anti-Party Plot (June 1957)

The revolts in Eastern Europe weakened Khrushchev's position among many Communist Party leaders at home. In addition, his push for domestic reform—more consumer goods, better prices paid to collective farmers, release and rehabilitation of political prisoners—aroused opposition among Party conservatives.

### Leaders of the Opposition

The leading opponents of Khrushchev were individuals closely tied to the Stalinist system. Malenkov, Molotov, and Kaganovich directed the efforts of Party conservatives to overthrow Khrushchev.

### Prelude to the Crisis

Khrushchev sharpened opposition to his leadership by his calls for increasingly radical change. In the first months of 1957, he planned to cut down the power of the central economic ministries. Much of their authority would be transferred to regional economic councils. Such a change threatened the position of important Party officials in Moscow.

Khrushchev also called for a vast expansion of the food supply. He claimed dramatically that the Soviet Union would soon surpass the United States in producing meat, milk, and butter. Such ideas seemed wildly impractical, and they increased Khrushchev's reputation for embarking on dangerous changes.

### Khrushchev's Victory

Khrushchev's opponents (the "anti-Party group") attempted to remove him from power in June 1957. They won over a majority of the Communist Party Presidium and demanded his resignation.

Khrushchev fought back successfully. He demanded that the issue be settled by the Party's Central Committee, where he had enough support to carry the day. His survival depended on the regional Party leaders who were heavily represented in the Central Committee. He also received important support from the military. For example, Marshal Zhukov provided military aircraft to fly Khrushchev's supporters to Moscow to attend the meeting of the Central Committee.

### The Aftermath of the Crisis

Several significant developments followed Khrushchev's success. The leaders of the anti-Party group, including Malenkov, were deprived of their positions in Moscow and sent to minor posts far from the capital. The fact that they were allowed to survive indicated that Khrushchev wished to avoid a return to Stalinist terror.

Khrushchev consolidated his authority by filling the Presidium with his personal followers and protégés, including Leonid Brezhnev.

Khrushchev replaced Bulganin as premier in March 1958. He now held top posts in both the Party and the government. The claim that the country was still under a collective leadership was now dropped.

### The Peak of Khrushchev's Authority

Historians consider Khrushchev's power and prestige at their greatest level in the years immediately following the defeat of the anti-Party group. His opponents had been defeated. His policies, like the Virgin Lands scheme, were popular and seemingly successful.

### Sputniks

In October and November 1957, the launches of two Soviet space satellites—*Sputnik I* and *Sputnik II*—inaugurated man's exploration of space.

The successful launching of the world's first space satellite heightened Khrushchev's personal prestige. It also established the Soviet Union as a world leader in science and technology.

## Khrushchev in Decline (1959–1964)

From the late 1950s onward, Khrushchev faced a series of difficult problems at home and abroad. His failures, combined with his reputation for making policy in a foolish and erratic manner, opened the way for a powerful coalition of leaders determined to oust him.

## Foreign Policy Crises

Under Khrushchev the Soviet Union clashed with two other major nations. Within the Communist world, the Chinese led by Mao Tse-tung challenged Soviet leadership. Meanwhile, relations with the United States also created unmanageable problems.

### Clash with China

*Refusal of Military Assistance.*    The leaders of Communist China openly disapproved of Khrushchev's attacks on Stalin. A second source of friction developed after the *Sputnik* launches. The Chinese wanted Soviet military assistance in taking the Chinese Nationalist stronghold of Taiwan, and Khrushchev's refusal strained Soviet-Chinese relations.

*Differences over Communist Ideology and Leadership Rivalry.* The larger issue causing friction between the Soviets and the Chinese was a serious set of differences over how to build a Communist society. Closely tied to this question was the rivalry between the two countries as to which would serve as the recognized leader of Communist parties throughout the world.    The Chinese rejected Khrushchev's view that Communism could triumph over capitalism without war. The Chinese claimed that they could survive and triumph in a nuclear war. Khrushchev challenged this view.

The Chinese also claimed that their domestic policies were leading rapidly to the final goal of a Communist society. Thus, Communist China had advanced beyond the Soviet Union and deserved to be recognized as the foremost Communist nation in the world.

### Escalating Tensions

In 1960, the friction between China and the Soviet Union became obvious. Khrushchev publicly attacked Mao, and the Chinese leaders responded vigorously. Soviet technical experts, who had been helping the Chinese since 1949, were abruptly called home.

Tensions increased over Chinese criticism of Khrushchev's policies in the Cuban missile crisis (see p. 407–408) in 1962. That same year the Soviets backed India in its border war with China.

The Chinese bitterly criticized Khrushchev for being overly friendly to the United States. For example, they strongly condemned the Soviet leader for signing a nuclear test ban treaty with Washington in July 1963.

### The Berlin Wall

Despite Khrushchev's moves toward lowering tensions with Washington, Soviet relations with the United States were often difficult. It is possible that Khrushchev hardened his policies toward the United States as a result of criticism from the Chinese.

Berlin was the most obvious point at which American and Soviet interests clashed. The city itself symbolized the struggle for control of Germany and Central Europe.

Starting in 1958, Khrushchev demanded repeatedly that the Western powers leave Berlin. In 1961, the crisis reached its peak. East German authorities, clearly following Khrushchev's wishes, built a wall separating East and West Berlin. This stopped East German refugees from escaping via Berlin. The loss of professionals and skilled workers was crippling the economy of East Germany. The erection of the wall also seemed part of a new campaign to force the Western powers out of the city.

### The Cuban Missile Crisis

The most serious confrontation between the Soviet Union and the United States took place over Cuba. Since Cuban leader Fidel Castro (1926–) had come to power in 1959, relations between Cuba and the Soviet Union had grown closer. In 1962, Castro openly proclaimed his ties to Marxism and Leninism.

*Confrontation.*    In the fall of 1962, Khrushchev placed in Cuba offensive missiles capable of launching nuclear weapons. This was a direct challenge to the United States. It was also a way of challenging China's claims to be the most militant and effective leader of Communists throughout the world.

*Outcome.*    President John F. Kennedy's administration responded to the Soviet actions by establishing a naval blockade of Cuba. A full-scale American invasion of the island seemed likely. These developments raised the possibility of war between the United States and the Soviet Union.

In the face of American demands Khrushchev reversed himself and removed the missiles. In return the American government promised not to invade Cuba.

*Reactions.*    The Chinese responded to the crisis by criticizing Khrushchev in several ways. They attacked him for his recklessness in putting the missiles in Cuba. Then, they attacked him for his cowardice in giving in to the Americans and withdrawing the missiles.

On the other hand, relations between Moscow and Washington improved. There were several actions signaling a desire by both sides to avoid another such crisis. For example, a direct communications link (or "hot line") was set up between Washington and Moscow. Moreover, the two countries agreed to stop testing nuclear weapons in the atmosphere.

## Domestic Problems

Khrushchev suffered obvious and embarrassing failures at home. The economy failed to reach the goals he had set, notably for food production. Meanwhile, Khrushchev alienated important groups by his radical plans for reorganizing the Communist Party and the government.

### Crisis in Agriculture

Starting in 1959, the Soviet Union experienced a series of bad harvests. The goals of surpassing the United States in food production were shown to be unrealistic. Moreover, Khrushchev's earlier successes in setting up the Virgin Lands scheme turned out to be of no value over the long run. The newly opened lands suffered soil erosion and could not be farmed regularly.

The clearest sign of agricultural crisis came in 1963. Following a poor harvest, the Soviet government had to buy huge quantities of grain from foreign countries, including the United States and Canada.

### The Party and the Government

Khrushchev deeply offended Party members by requiring that Party personnel in important committees be rotated regularly. He also called for dividing the Party into two structures. One would direct agriculture, the other, industry. The two systems would be placed under the control of the First Secretary of the Party.

Khrushchev set out equally radical plans for restructuring the government. These involved restoring economic planning to agencies in Moscow, thus reversing the decentralizing reforms of 1957.

Whatever the merits of these proposals, they threatened the privileges and sense of stability of most of the country's leaders.

### Military Expenditures

Khrushchev's policies of economic reform included reductions in the Soviet armed forces, notably the army's ground forces. In 1960, he announced a reduction of military manpower from 3.6 to 2.4 million men. Hundreds of thousands of officers were released from service. By becoming civilians they were deprived of real material advantages and a privileged status in Soviet society.

Khrushchev thus lost the political support of the military that had been important to his survival in the 1957 crisis.

### The Twenty-Second Party Congress (October 1961)

*Economic Program.*   A sign of Khrushchev's continuing desire for change came in the economic program he presented at the Twenty-Second Party Congress. The dramatic program he offered can also be seen as an effort to distract attention from the country's economic problems at that time.

Khrushchev outlined plans for surpassing per capita production in the United States and achieving prosperity for all Soviet citizens by 1970. By 1980, he expected to approach the abundance set down by Marx for a completely achieved Communist society.

Khrushchev thus opened himself to bitter criticism as it became clear these utopian goals could not be achieved.

*Stalin's Body Moved.*   By decision of the Congress, Stalin's body was removed from Lenin's tomb, where it had rested since 1953. Thus Khrushchev's campaign to lower the prestige of Stalin's memory continued.

The great dictator's body was placed in a modest grave near the Kremlin wall among other dead Soviet leaders. Unlike the other graves, Stalin's burial plot was not even decorated with a bust.

# Khrushchev's Fall

Khrushchev's failure in Cuba had undercut his prestige among the topmost leaders of the Party. His apparently reckless reorganization schemes and the continuing food crisis made his rivals determined to act.

### The Plot

Khrushchev was deposed in October 1964. He was confronted by a hostile majority in the Presidium and forced to resign. He no longer had the support of lower-ranking officials to whom he had appealed with success in 1957.

### The Aftermath

Khrushchev was permitted to remain in Moscow until his death in 1971. His peaceful retirement, like that of Malenkov after 1957, was another sign that the system had moved away from the murderous brutality of Stalin's days.

# The Growing Freedom of Soviet Writers

The period following Stalin's death brought important changes in Soviet culture. The most significant development was the growing freedom of Soviet writers.

### The Thaw

An early novel indicating hopes for a happier future now that change appeared possible was *The Thaw* by Ilya Ehrenburg (1891–1967). It was soon followed by a work strongly critical of the bureaucracy, *Not By Bread Alone* by Vladimir Dudintsev (1918–).

### Pasternak

Another important novel that departed from Stalinist norms was *Doctor Zhivago* by Boris Pasternak (1890–1960), who was also a renowned poet. When Pasternak was awarded the Nobel Prize for Literature in 1958, he was subjected to harsh condemnation by the Soviet government and threatened with exile. He informed the Nobel

Prize committee that he could not accept the honor due to the reaction he had encountered in his own country.

## Solzhenitsyn

A crucial example of greater literary freedom was the publication of *One Day in the Life of Ivan Denisovich* by Alexander Solzhenitsyn (1918–) in 1962. The book was a picture of forced labor in the Stalinist era, and it was published with Khrushchev's personal permission. Khrushchev evidently hoped such literary works would strengthen his campaign to discredit Stalin.

*The period from 1953 to 1964 had brought a substantial degree of liberalization to Soviet life. The Communist Party retained dictatorial power, but the days of mass terror were over. Leaders like Malenkov and Khrushchev pursued policies designed to appeal to Soviet consumers.*

*In foreign affairs, the Soviet Union continued to hold its authority over Eastern Europe, even though a pattern of active resistance had become evident in Poland and Hungary. Relations with the United States had led to several dangerous crises. By 1964, however, the ties between the two countries were marked by peaceful competition and a degree of cooperation.*

*The most dramatic change had taken place in relations with China. The mutual hostility of Chinese and Soviet leaders and their competing claims to serve as a model for Communists everywhere created a new arena of conflict for the Soviet Union.*

## Recommended Reading

Breslauer, George. *Khrushchev and Brezhnev as Leaders: Building Authority in Soviet Politics* (1982).

Brown, James F. *The New Eastern Europe: The Khrushchev Era and After* (1966).

Chotiner, Barbara A. *Khrushchev's Party Reform: Coalition Building and Institutional Innovation* (1984).

Cohen, Stephen F., Alexander Rabinowitch, and Robert Sharlet. *The Soviet Union since Stalin* (1980).

Crankshaw, Edward. *Khrushchev: A Career* (1966).

Crankshaw, Edward. *The New Cold War: Moscow and Peking* (1963).

Dinerstein, Herbert. *The Making of a Missile Crisis: October 1962* (1976).

Frankland, Mark. *Khrushchev* (1967).

Gibian, George. *Interval of Freedom: Soviet Literature During the Thaw, 1954–1957* (1960).

Gunther, John. *Inside Russia Today* (1958; rev. ed., 1962).

Hyland, William, and Richard Shrylock. *The Fall of Khrushchev* (1968).

Johnson, Priscilla, and Leo Labedz, eds. *Khrushchev and the Arts: The Politics of Soviet Culture, 1962–1964* (1965).

Khrushchev, Nikita. *Khrushchev Remembers* (1970).

Khrushchev, Nikita. *Khrushchev Remembers: The Last Testament* (1974).

McCauley, Martin, ed. *Khrushchev and Khrushchevism* (1987).

Medvedev, Roy A., and Zhores A. Medvedev. *Khrushchev: The Years in Power* (1976).

Micunovic, Veljko. *Moscow Diary* (1980).

Nove, Alec. *Stalinism and Afterward* (1975).

Rush, Myron. *Political Succession in the USSR* (2nd ed., 1965).

Salisbury, Harrison. *War between Russia and China* (1969).

Solzhenitsyn, Alexander. *The Oak and the Calf: Sketches of Literary Life in the Soviet Union* (1980).

Tatu, Michel. *Power in the Kremlin: From Khrushchev to Kosygin* (1969).

Zinner, Paul. *Revolution in Hungary* (1962).

Zinoviev, Alexander. *The Radiant Future* (1981).

Zinoviev, Alexander. *The Yawning Heights* (1979).

# CHAPTER 29

## The Brezhnev Era
## (1964–1982)

### Time Line

| | |
|---|---|
| October 1964 | Collective leadership established under Brezhnev and Kosygin |
| September 1965 | Economic decentralization plan adopted by Party Central Committee |
| January 1966 | Tashkent conference |
| February 1966 | Trial of Sinyavsky and Daniel |
| March–April 1966 | Twenty-Third Party Congress |
| June 1967 | Summit conference at Glassboro, N.J. |

| | |
|---|---|
| July 1968 | Andrei Sakharov publishes *Thoughts on Progress, Peaceful Coexistence, and Intellectual Freedom* |
| August 1968 | Invasion of Czechoslovakia |
| November 1968 | Brezhnev doctrine proclaimed |
| March 1969 | Large-scale warfare between the Soviet Union and China along Amur-Ussuri River |
| September 1970 | Soviet moon landing |
| March–April 1971 | Twenty-Fourth Party Congress |
| 1971–1975 | Ninth Five-Year Plan |
| May 1972 | Nixon-Brezhnev summit conference in Moscow |
| | SALT I agreement signed |
| June 1972 | Large-scale Soviet grain purchases from the United States |
| February 1974 | Solzhenitsyn expelled from the Soviet Union |
| November 1974 | Ford-Brezhnev summit conference in Vladivostok |
| July 1975 | Joint space project (*Soiuz*) with United States |
| July–August 1975 | Helsinki Security Conference |
| June 1977 | Brezhnev named Chairman of Supreme Soviet |
| October 1977 | New Soviet constitution adopted |
| April 1979 | Formal cancellation of Soviet-Chinese alliance |
| December 1979 | Invasion of Afghanistan |
| January 1980 | Sakharov exiled to Gorky |
| | United States' boycott of Moscow Olympics |
| August 1980 | Solidarity trade union legally established in Poland |
| October 1980 | Kosygin resigns as premier |

December 1981    Martial law established in Poland

November 1982    Death of Brezhnev

---

*The leaders who deposed Khrushchev deliberately set out to govern the Soviet Union in a measured, undramatic fashion. Even though a single figure, Leonid Brezhnev, eventually dominated the system, the era from 1964 to 1982 was marked by caution and stability.*

*The most significant development of this period was the deepening economic crisis. Evident in both agriculture and industry, Soviet economic problems made the country increasingly dependent on advanced Western countries like the United States for technology and even for food.*

*Paradoxically, the Brezhnev years produced a massive expansion of Soviet military strength, including a large, modern navy. During this period, Soviet diplomatic contacts and influence likewise grew, notably in Africa and the Middle East.*

*A notable development within the Soviet Union was the emergence of a dissident community that included world-famous writers and scientists. Thus, criticism of the Soviet system was louder and more widely heard than at any time since the 1920s.*

## The Ascendancy of Brezhnev

Khrushchev was replaced by a collective leadership. One of its members, Leonid Brezhnev, eventually emerged as the dominant figure.

The era of Brezhnev, like the Khrushchev years, differed politically from the Stalinist period. Brezhnev, even at the peak of his power, remained basically the senior leader among a group of powerful Party officials.

### The New Leaders

#### *Brezhnev*

Leonid Brezhnev (1906–1982) rose to prominence as a protégé of Khrushchev, especially during the years after 1953. He served under

Khrushchev in World War II and then led several regional branches of the Soviet Communist Party.

Brezhnev's major achievement before 1964 was in directing the Virgin Lands scheme (see Chapter 28) during its early, successful years.

With the fall of Khrushchev, Brezhnev took the key position in the Soviet system by becoming the First Secretary of the Communist Party.

### Kosygin

At first Alexei Kosygin (1904–1980) seemed equal in significance to Brezhnev. A veteran government official, Kosygin took over the post of premier (head of the government) following Khrushchev's fall from power.

### Suslov

A third figure who played a key role in deposing Khrushchev was Mikhail Suslov (1902–1982), the Communist Party's expert in ideology. His prominence in the Party and government following Khrushchev's fall has caused some historians to refer to a period of rule by *troika* (group of three of leaders) until 1971.

## Brezhnev in Power

Brezhnev used his base as leader of the Party from 1964 to overshadow both Suslov and Kosygin.

### 1964–1971: Consolidation of Authority

In the first seven years following the ousting of Khrushchev, Brezhnev's relative importance grew. He received the prestigious title, dating from the Stalin era, of Party General Secretary (1966). The following year, he was the dominant figure during the celebration of the 1917 Revolution's fiftieth anniversary.

At first Brezhnev confined his statements to Party affairs. But he soon made his views known on foreign policy and economic issues.

Nonetheless, Kosygin played an important role in foreign policy. For example, it was he, not Brezhnev, who met with American President Lyndon Johnson at Glassboro, N.J., in 1967. This was the first Soviet-American summit since the Khrushchev years.

At the Twenty-Fourth Party Congress in 1971, Brezhnev placed his personal supporters in control of the Politburo. As the Executive Committee of the Communist Party since 1917, the Politburo (called the Party Presidium from 1952 to 1966) was the key decision-making body in the Party. Brezhnev's domination of the Politburo enabled him to control the Party from that point on.

### 1971–1980: Predominance

During this period, Brezhnev held the center of the stage in Soviet political life. He became the chief spokesman for Soviet foreign policy. Thus, he represented the Soviet Union at summit conferences with American presidents Richard Nixon, Gerald Ford, and Jimmy Carter.

In 1977, Brezhnev took the post of Chairman of the Presidium of the Supreme Soviet. This made him the first Soviet leader to serve as both head of the Communist Party and chief of the Soviet state.

Kosygin faded into the background, and his public role diminished. Until his resignation due to ill health in 1980, Kosygin, the nation's highest-ranking economic expert and premier, seemed mainly occupied in running the government bureaucracy.

### 1980–1982: Decline

For the last several years of his life, Brezhnev suffered from a number of crippling diseases. During his declining years, policy decisions came in part from Constantine Chernenko (1911–1985), veteran Party leader whom Brezhnev had selected as his successor. Another important leader operating behind the scenes as Brezhnev became a mere figurehead was Yuri Andropov (1914–1984), former head of the KGB (secret police).

## Domestic Affairs

Brezhnev and Kosygin stressed their willingness to abandon radical developments begun in the Khrushchev years. The new leaders instead presented an image of stability and conservatism.

They avoided dramatic declarations of impending changes and predictions of future successes. For example, they made no bold promises and predictions of future Soviet prosperity as Khrushchev had done.

## New Policies

### Collective Leadership

The new leaders' first step was to pledge that they would operate a collective leadership. This stood in contrast to the prominent position Khrushchev had occupied after 1957. Other moves away from the Khrushchev pattern quickly followed.

### Reversal of Party Division

Khrushchev's startling proposal to divide the Party into agricultural and industrial branches was dropped in late 1964.

### "Stability of Cadres"

A key theme of the new leadership was to reassure Communist Party leaders at all levels that their positions were secure. Thus, the opposition that Khrushchev had stirred up within the Party was replaced by broad support.

The slogan "stability of cadres" emphasized the leaders' desire that Party officials enjoy job security. In practice, it came to mean that middle level officials were assured of holding their positions and their privileges indefinitely.

### Collective Farms

Khrushchev's campaign to make collective farms into state farms, in which the farmers would be employees like workers in a factory, was also abandoned. A sign of confidence in the traditional collective farms system was the restoration of private plots of land.

## Economic Affairs

A crucial development during the Brezhnev era was the Soviet Union's growing economic difficulties. Despite efforts at reform, the system remained heavily centralized and inefficient. Most important, it suffered from a declining rate of growth.

Economic life featured a massive military build-up. The construction of a large, ocean-going navy was clearly a response to Soviet weaknesses demonstrated during the Cuban missile crisis. But the cost of such military expansion drained the Soviet economy and led to a critical situation by the time Brezhnev died in 1982.

During the Brezhnev years signs of continuing economic problems and new crises appeared in both agriculture and industry.

By the close of the Brezhnev era, the Soviet economic system seemed to be in a period of stagnation. In 1982, the rate of growth in the economy was the lowest since the end of World War II.

### Initial Reforms

In its early years, the new leadership tried to decrease the role of central planning. Using the ideas of economist Evsei Liberman (1897–1983), Kosygin promoted the installation of market forces (supply and demand) and local initiative.

Opposition from the Party bureaucracy soon brought these efforts to a halt.

### Ninth Five-Year Plan

Reform currents were visible as late as 1971. The Ninth Five-Year Plan (1971–1975) marked a change in industrial policy. It put more emphasis on expanding the production of consumer goods than in the growth of heavy industry. This was a major shift from the pattern that had existed since the late 1920s.

### Problems in Agriculture

The agricultural system consistently failed to produce enough to feed the population. Crop failures, such as the one in 1972, led to food shortages and the need to buy large amounts of food abroad.

Productivity on collective farms remained low. Only the private plots, cultivated by individual farmers and their families, proved to be an exception.

In the 1980s, Soviet exports of oil and gold went to pay for increasingly large purchases abroad of food.

### Problems in Industry

The production of industrial goods stagnated as well. The problem had traditionally involved a labor shortage and low productivity per worker. By the 1970s new elements entered the picture, such as Soviet backwardness in automating factories and in using computers.

*The Failures of Central Planning.*    Economists consider the Soviet dilemma in the Brezhnev era to be in part the result of central planning. The centrally managed economy was slow to adopt innovation, continuing to produce unnecessarily large quantities of material like steel. Bottlenecks in one part of the system could paralyze production in many sectors. Goods were often produced at greater cost than the price for which they could be sold abroad.

In general, the absence of the need to produce for a competitive market meant that Soviet industry manufactured unneeded goods at excessive prices.

### Soviet Standard of Living

From 1953 to the early 1970s, the standard of living in the Soviet Union had gradually risen. Popular attitudes, conditioned to hardship by the 1930s and the World War II years, became more optimistic with this slow but steady progress. From the mid-1970s onward, however, the standard of living leveled off and for much of the population even began to decline. By the close of the Brezhnev period, the Soviet Union had the lowest standard of living of any of the late twentieth-century industrial leaders.

### The Military Build-up

An important area of growth in the economy was in military production.

The Brezhnev era saw the Soviet Union in a heated arms race with the United States. The American superiority at the time of the Cuban missile crisis in categories like intercontinental missiles now disappeared. The Soviet navy was expanded into a force capable of operating all over the world.

But Soviet military production operated from a relatively weak industrial base. Some economists believe that in the years from 1964 to 1982 as much as twenty-five percent of the Gross National Product of the Soviet Union was devoted to the manufacture of weapons and the space program.

The Soviet Union failed to reach the moon before the American *Apollo* crew landed in July 1969. Nonetheless, the unmanned Soviet space program had notable successes. In September 1970, for example, a Soviet space ship landed on the moon. Using robots, it took samples of moon dust with which it returned to earth. In November, a second unmanned mission arrived with a robot-operated "moon buggy" (*Lunakhod*) that was launched to travel on the moon's surface.

## Halt to De-Stalinization

One of the first serious changes to occur in domestic affairs after 1964 was an end to public attacks on Stalin's reputation. The new leaders seemed to believe that such attacks undermined the entire system under which the Communist Party led the nation. They may also have been more comfortable with Stalin's repressive methods than Khrushchev had been during his years in power.

### Stalin's Role in World War II

The first signs of a more positive attitude toward Stalin began in the spring of 1965. Celebrations of the twentieth anniversary of victory in World War II featured pictures of Stalin and references to his skilled wartime leadership.

### 1966 Party Congress

Prior to the March–April 1966 Party Congress, rumors spread that Brezhnev and Kosygin were about to rehabilitate Stalin formally. Foreign Communists along with Soviet intellectuals and scientists like Andrei Sakharov (1921–1989) openly opposed such a step.

At the Congress, no formal rehabilitation took place. Nonetheless, speeches by Soviet leaders reemphasized the need for orthodox ideas and strong Party discipline. Kosygin, for example, praised the economic transformation that had taken place in the 1930s.

Such remarks were a clear sign of approval for many of Stalin's practices.

### Stalin's Grave

In June 1970, Stalin's modest grave outside the Kremlin (see Chapter 28) was decorated with a bust of the late dictator. This appeared to be an additional sign that Khrushchev's successors were anxious to preserve Stalin's reputation.

### Absence of Police Terror

But even leaders sympathetic to Stalin could not restore the old system. A clear sign of the new situation was the absence of mass terror conducted by the secret police. Even in dealing with open dissidents (see p. 427), the harsh repression employed did not compare to the massive bloodshed of the 1930s.

# Foreign Affairs (1964–1979)

For the first decade and a half after 1964, the new leadership pursued a foreign policy similar to that of the Khrushchev years. Key elements included growing tensions with Communist China and continuing efforts to maintain Soviet control in Eastern Europe. These years also saw a tentative détente with the United States. Détente meant an improvement of relations, featuring efforts to avoid military confrontation, to settle differences through diplomacy, and to build closer trade ties.

## Relations with China

Relations between the Soviet Union and Communist China continued to deteriorate after 1964. Traditional antagonisms between Russia and China combined with ideological differences between the two major Communist countries to produce armed conflict in 1969.

### Traditional Problems

The countries clashed over the ownership of territory seized from China by the tsarist government in the nineteenth century. At a time of Chinese weakness, the Russians had taken the Maritime Provinces of Siberia and large areas in Central Asia.

The Russians, on the other hand, felt a longtime fear, heightened perhaps by memories of the Mongol conquest, of a powerful Asian neighbor.

### Communist Rivalries

The Chinese criticized the Soviet variety of Communism, insisting that Chinese-style Communism was a more useful model for the underdeveloped parts of the world. The Chinese also rejected the Soviet abandonment of Stalinism and the Soviet shift toward peaceful coexistence with the West.

Chinese dependence on Soviet economic and technical assistance since Mao's forces took power in 1949 irritated the leaders in Beijing. Khrushchev's refusal to provide Mao with weapons resulting from the Soviet space program (see Chapter 28) increased Chinese bitterness.

### Fighting in 1969

Border clashes went on between Soviet and Chinese forces during the early years of the 1960s. In the spring of 1969, massive fighting broke out, especially along the Ussuri River in Manchuria.

The Soviet forces won a clear-cut military victory in the 1969 encounters. But the border remained extremely tense after the fighting had died down, and relations between the two countries continued to be severely strained. Large portions of the Soviet armed forces had to be placed permanently along the Chinese border.

## Relations with the United States

Soviet relations with the United States improved in the decade and a half following 1964. Despite strains caused by the war in Vietnam and the Soviet invasion of Czechoslovakia (see p. 424), the early 1970s brought a relaxation of tensions.

### Moscow Summit of 1972

In May 1972, President Richard Nixon visited Moscow. In talks between the American president and Leonid Brezhnev, the two leaders agreed to limit armaments and to cooperate in easing international crises.

The summit discussions led to plans for a joint space project (the *Soiuz* mission) in 1975. The summit also had a practical result in the SALT I treaty.

### SALT I

The SALT (Strategic Arms Limitation) I treaty, signed in May 1972 and then ratified by the United States Senate, placed a ceiling on military resources including intercontinental ballistic missiles and missile-launching submarines. It also limited the antiballistic missile systems each country could construct.

## Helsinki Agreement

A further sign of better East-West relations was the success of the international Helsinki Conference in 1975. The agreement reached at Helsinki fell into three categories or "baskets." The first dealt with European security issues, including the recognition of existing boundaries. The second dealt with trade and technical ties between

### Afghanistan

The Soviet invasion of Afghanistan in late 1979 was particularly significant. It involved the first military advance in decades undertaken by the Soviet Union outside the borders of the Communist world.

#### *Motives for the Invasion of Afghanistan*

It is still uncertain why Soviet troops moved into Afghanistan at this time. Afghanistan was under the control of a shaky pro-Soviet government.

The Soviet action may have been due to fears that a radical Islamic government, similar to the one already installed in Iran, might take power. Such a regime would threaten the stability of Soviet Central Asia with its Moslem population.

Another possible motive was the desire of the Soviet Union to establish a base for further advances toward the Persian Gulf and the Indian Ocean.

#### *The War in Afghanistan*

The conflict in Afghanistan developed into a prolonged and bloody guerrilla war. Soviet forces and their Afghan allies controlled the major cities and the chief highways. Afghan guerrillas, supported by numerous countries, including the United States, maintained control of the countryside.

At the time of Brezhnev's death, the war remained in full swing. It was marked by huge casualties among the Afghan population and the flight of millions Afghan refugees to Pakistan. As a result of the war the Soviet military suffered steady losses and the Soviet economy came under increased strain.

#### *Effects of the Invasion on U.S.-Soviet Relations*

The most important diplomatic consequence of the Soviet invasion in 1979 was a sharp and unfriendly turn in American policy toward Moscow. President Jimmy Carter's government responded by sponsoring a boycott of the 1980 Moscow Olympics and by limiting American grain sales to the Soviet Union.

SALT II, signed with the United States in 1979, failed to win enough support to be ratified by the American Senate. This treaty would have set equal ceilings for the number of nuclear missile

### Andrei Sakharov

A leading figure among intellectuals critical of the political system was the noted scientist Andrei Sakharov. His book *Thoughts on Progress, Peaceful Coexistence, and Intellectual Freedom* (1968) was a plea for the Soviet Union to end the Communist Party's monopoly on power. Sakharov wanted a new political system based on the liberal principles and multiparty systems of the West.

In 1980, Sakharov was exiled to the provincial city of Gorky as a result of his criticism of the Soviet invasion of Afghanistan.

### Solzhenitsyn

Alexander Solzhenitsyn (1918–) was the Soviet writer best known outside his own country. A former political prisoner during the Stalin years, Solzhenitsyn wrote novels like *Cancer War* (1968) and nonfiction like *The Gulag Archipelago* (1974–1978) that were critical of Communism and the Soviet government. He received the Nobel Prize for Literature in 1970.

In 1974 Solzhenitsyn was exiled from the Soviet Union after publishing abroad the first volume of his study of Soviet prison camps, *The Gulag Archipelago*. This work was an unprecedented, profound, and fundamental condemnation of the entire Soviet system. Solzhenitsyn rejected the notion that there was such a thing as "Stalinism." In his view, the events of Stalin's era were part of Lenin's legacy. The Communist system had perpetrated unspeakable crimes against its own people, and Solzhenitsyn demanded the punishment of individuals still alive who were accomplices in Stalin's crimes.

### Psychiatric Terror

The Brezhnev government frequently imprisoned dissidents in mental hospitals for alleged psychiatric reasons. Such individuals were subjected to torture through chemicals under the guise of medical treatment. By claiming that such individuals were mentally ill and in need of "medical care," the Brezhnev government isolated dissidents and frightened potential dissidents. Moreover, ideas critical of the Soviet system were officially labeled the products of deranged minds.

A notable example of a political dissident placed in a psychiatric hospital was General Peter Grigorenko (1907–1987).

Some historians note that even psychiatric punishment represented a more restrained treatment for dissidents than the imprisonments and executions of the Stalinist era. Dissidents such as Vladimir Bukovsky (1942–) vigorously dispute this. They argue that psychiatric punishments not only were worse, but in theory could last forever.

## Ethnic Minorities

During the Brezhnev era, the non-Russian population of the Soviet Union grew in numbers and in a willingness to press claims for influence. For example, a low birthrate in European Russia and a far higher one in Central Asia meant that a growing percentage of the population now consisted of Moslems.

### Non-Russian Minorities

Representatives of ethnic minorities now became more outspoken. They criticized such trends as the dominant role of ethnic Russians in governing throughout the Soviet Union. The government responded by imprisoning vocal defenders of minority rights like the Ukrainian Viacheslav Chornovil (1938–).

### The Jews

The Jews were a notable example of a traditionally repressed minority now seeking greater rights. Starting in the early 1970s, the Soviet government permitted substantial Jewish immigration from the Soviet Union to destinations like Israel and the United States.

*The Brezhnev years left a mixed legacy. Relations with the United States had grown warmer in the era of détente, then returned to distrust and hostility. Soviet military power had grown in a spectacular way, but the country's standard of living was sinking in the midst of a general economic crisis. Soviet influence had been projected into much of the Third World, but unsolvable problems had arisen in both Poland and Afghanistan.*

*Brezhnev had achieved a high level of popularity within the Communist Party by assuring the security and privileges of its cadres.*

*The major issue facing the country in late 1982 was whether Brezhnev's cautious and unimaginative policies would continue under future leaders.*

## Recommended Reading

Alekseeva, Liudimila. *Soviet Dissent: Contemporary Movements for National, Religious, and Human Rights* (1985).

Amalrik, Andrei. *Involuntary Journey to Siberia* (1970).

Amalrik, Andrei. *Will the Soviet Union Survive until 1984?* (rev. and exp. ed., 1981).

Azrael, Jeremy. *Managerial Power and Soviet Politics* (1966).

Bialer, Seweryn. *Stalin's Successors: Leadership, Stability and Change in the Soviet Union* (1980).

Bloch, Sidney, and Peter Reddaway. *Psychiatric Terror: Russia's Political Hospitals* (1977).

Brown, Archie, and Michael Kaser, eds. *The Soviet Union since the Fall of Khrushchev* (1978).

Bukovsky, Vladimir. *To Build a Castle: My Life as a Dissenter* (1978).

Carrère d'Encausse, Hélène. *Decline of an Empire: The Soviet Socialist Republics in Revolt* (1979).

Cave, Martin. *Computers and Economic Planning: The Soviet Experience* (1980).

Cohen, Stephen F., ed. *An End to Silence: Uncensored Opinion in the Soviet Union* (1982).

Dornberg, John. *Brezhnev: The Masks of Power* (1974).

Freedman, Robert O., ed. *Soviet Jewry in the Decisive Decade 1971–1980* (1984).

Garton Ash, Timothy. *The Polish Revolution: Solidarity, 1980–82* (1983).

Gelman, Harry. *The Brezhnev Politburo and the Decline of Détente* (1984).

Hammond, Thomas. *Red Flag over Afghanistan: The Communist Coup, the Soviet Invasion, and the Consequences* (1984).

Holloway, David. *The Soviet Union and the Arms Race* (1983).

Kaiser, Robert. *Russia: The People and the Power* (1976).

Oberg, James E. *Red Star in Orbit: The Inside Story of Soviet Failures and Triumphs in Space* (1981).

Pipes, Richard. *Survival Is not Enough: Soviet Realities and America's Future* (1984).

Pipes, Richard. *US-Soviet Relations in the Era of Détente* (1981).

Pipes, Richard, ed. *Soviet Strategy in Europe* (1976).

Rothberg, Abraham. *The Heirs of Stalin: Dissidence and the Soviet Regime* (1972).

Shatz, Marshall. *Soviet Dissent in Historical Perspective* (1980).

Shipler, David. *Russia: Broken Idols, Solemn Dreams* (rev. ed., 1989).

Simis, Konstantin M. *USSR: The Corrupt Society: The Secret World of Soviet Capitalism* (1982).

Smith, Hedrick. *The Russians* (1976).

Tokes, Rudolph L., ed. *Dissent in the USSR: Politics, Ideology, and People* (1975).

Ulam, Adam. *Dangerous Relations: The Soviet Union in World Politics, 1970–1982* (1983).

Valenta, Jiri. *Soviet Intervention in Czechoslovakia, 1968: Anatomy of a Decision* (1979).

Voslensky, Michael. *Nomenklatura: The Soviet Ruling Class* (1984).

Wesson, Robert. *The Aging of Communism* (1980).

# CHAPTER 30

## 1982–1991: From
## Stagnation to Revolution

### Time Line

November 1982  Death of Brezhnev

Andropov becomes General Secretary of Soviet Communist Party

January 1983  Anticorruption drive

September 1983  Soviets shoot down KAL plane off Sakhalin

February 1984  Death of Andropov

Chernenko succeeds Andropov as General Secretary

| | |
|---|---|
| March 1985 | Gorbachev succeeds Chernenko as General Secretary |
| November 1985 | Geneva summit with President Reagan |
| February–March 1986 | Twenty-Seventh Party Congress |
| March 1986 | Yeltsin becomes member of Politburo |
| April 1986 | Nuclear disaster at Chernobyl |
| October 1986 | Reykjavik summit with President Reagan |
| December 1986 | Sakharov released from internal exile |
| | Ethnic riots in Kazakhstan |
| February 1987 | Competitive elections for some local soviets |
| October 1987 | Yeltsin removed from Politburo |
| November 1987 | Gorbachev publicly condemns Stalin's crimes |
| December 1987 | Washington summit conference between Reagan and Gorbachev |
| February 1988 | Ethnic violence breaks out in Armenia and Azerbaijan |
| May–June 1988 | Moscow summit: Reagan visits Moscow |
| October 1988 | Gorbachev becomes president of the Soviet Union |
| November 1988 | New presidential system and Congress of People's Deputies adopted |
| | Estonian Communist Party declares supremacy of Estonian laws |
| December 1988 | Gorbachev offers unilateral Soviet military reductions |
| | Earthquake in Soviet Armenia |
| February 1989 | Soviet troops complete withdrawal from Afghanistan |
| March 1989 | National elections including nonparty candidates |

|  | Gorbachev calls for dismantling of collective farm system |
|---|---|
| April 1989 | Massacre of demonstrators in Georgia |
| June 1989 | Gorbachev abandons "Brezhnev doctrine" |
| Fall 1989 | Collapse of Communist governments throughout Eastern Europe |
| December 1989 | Lithuanian parliament approves multiparty system |
| February 1990 | Civil War in Azerbaijan; Soviet troops occupy Baku |
|  | End to Communist Party's political monopoly |
| March 1990 | Free elections in East Germany |
|  | Lithuania declares independence |
| July 1990 | Lithuania agrees to postpone independence |
|  | Twenty-Eighth Party Congress |
|  | Yeltsin and other liberals resign from the Communist Party |
| August 1990 | Gorbachev and Yeltsin agree on 500-day plan for transition to market economy |
| October 1990 | Gorbachev presents plan for more gradual economic reform |
| January 1991 | Soviet forces attack communications centers in Lithuania |
|  | Gorbachev picks conservative Valentin Pavlov as Soviet prime minister |
| May 1991 | Law passed permitting free travel and emigration for Soviet citizens by 1993 |
| June 1991 | Yeltsin wins popular election to presidency of Russian Republic |
| August 1991 | Coup by conservative leaders; Gorbachev arrested by plotters |

| | |
|---|---|
| | Yeltsin mobilizes Moscow population to resist coup |
| | Gorbachev returns to Moscow, resigns as General Secretary of Communist Party |
| | Activities of Communist Party suspended in most Soviet republics |
| September 1991 | Estonia, Latvia, and Lithuania become independent states |
| | Leningrad renamed St. Petersburg |
| | Centralized government replaced by voluntary agreement among now sovereign republics |
| | Ten former Soviet republics agree to set up common market |
| October 1991 | Yeltsin presents radical plan for Russian Republic's transition to market economy |

*The era following the death of Brezhnev can be divided into three remarkably different periods. Between 1982 and 1985, the Soviet Union remained under frail leaders incapable of pursuing a policy of change even as the nation's problems deepened. Economic decline and continuing tension with the United States were the two most obvious difficulties.*

*Beginning in 1985, the Soviet Union acquired a new kind of leader who brought extraordinary change. Mikhail Gorbachev overturned what had seemed permanent features in the Soviet system in both domestic and foreign affairs.*

*At the same time, dramatic changes developed from below. As Gorbachev loosened political controls, for example, vast numbers of Soviet citizens took on active and unprecedented political roles. Non-Communist political parties were one sign of this political awakening. So too were mass public demonstrations and, in the extreme case, armed ethnic rebellions.*

*In the summer and fall of 1991, events moved with dramatic speed. A clumsy coup carried out by Party conservatives ousted*

*Gorbachev for a few days, then collapsed. In the aftermath, the entire centralized system that had governed the Soviet Union for more than seven decades disintegrated. The country's economic crisis deepened, most of the fifteen republics that had made up the Soviet Union quickly declared independence, and the authority of the Communist Party dissolved. The Communist era in Russian history had seemingly ended, and the shape of the future was uncertain.*

# The Andropov Interlude (1982–1984)

Brezhnev was succeeded by Yury Andropov (1914–1984), the former head of the KGB. By this time, the problems of the Brezhnev era had become critical.

Nonetheless, the most important element in Andropov's period of power turned out to be his failing health. In 1983, he stopped appearing in public. His young protégé, Mikhail Gorbachev, gained substantial influence as a tentative reform program got underway.

## The Rise of Andropov

From 1967 to mid-1982 Andropov was the head of the KGB. During Brezhnev's last months, Andropov left the KGB to take the leading position in the Communist Party Secretariat.

As Brezhnev neared death, Andropov outmaneuvered Constantine Chernenko (1911–1985), whom Brezhnev had chosen as his favored successor. Andropov undercut Brezhnev's influence by charging several of Brezhnev's subordinates with corruption and by leaking information about the old leader's failing health.

## Domestic Policies

Apart from his own health problems, several other factors prevented Andropov from moving boldly in domestic affairs. For one thing, he lacked the support Brezhnev had drawn from middle-level Party leaders. Moreover, Chernenko and his followers in the Politburo remained a powerful barrier.

### *Economic Reform*

Andropov's recipe for Soviet economic stagnation centered on making the existing system work more effectively. He insisted that the population work harder. Beginning in January 1983, he tried to implement this idea by using the police to arrest people illegally absent from their jobs.

It is possible that Andropov hoped to carry out more sweeping changes. If so, his poor health and the opposition of conservatives in the Politburo kept him from doing this.

### Political Change

Andropov gradually promoted younger figures to replace some of the aged members of the Politburo. With the aid of Mikhail Gorbachev, a young leader who had been a member of the Politburo since 1978, he replaced large numbers of Party leaders at the regional level.

## Foreign Policy

Brezhnev had left behind a series of foreign policy crises. These included the war in Afghanistan, anti-Soviet feelings in Poland, and serious distrust between the United States and the Soviet Union.

### Afghanistan

Under Andropov's leadership, the Soviet Union continued to prosecute the bloody, stalemated war in Afghanistan.

### Poland

Similarly, Andropov brought no changes in Soviet-Polish relations. He backed the system of martial law imposed by General Jaruzelski.

### Relations with the United States

The ties between the Soviet Union and the United States remained strained between 1982 and 1984.

In response to Soviet medium-range SS-20 missiles installed in the Soviet Union and Eastern Europe under Brezhnev, the United States now moved to place similar weapons in Western Europe.

In September 1983 the Soviet military shot down a Korean civilian airliner that had gone off course into Soviet air space en route from the United States to Japan. All 269 people aboard were killed. This event created a serious crisis. The United States government accused the Soviets of murder. Moscow responded by claiming that the plane had been engaged in a spy mission.

### The Role of Gorbachev

Gorbachev's power grew substantially in the Andropov years. This fact was particularly striking, since his reputation should have been weakened by the failures of the agricultural system for which he was responsible. Gorbachev seemed to face an uncertain political future, but Andropov's patronage was decisive in helping the young leader.

## The Chernenko Interlude (1984–1985)

Andropov's brief era at the top of the Soviet system led to an even shorter interlude under Constantine Chernenko. Elderly and physically frail, Chernenko did little more than stand as a figurehead for a year.

The Chernenko interlude is significant in showing the continuing conservatism of much of the nation's leadership.

### The Rise of Chernenko

Chernenko was a longstanding political lieutenant under Brezhnev. He had no independent political reputation, and he stood for a return to the conservatism and stagnation of the period prior to 1982.

A majority in the Politburo chose Chernenko to succeed Andropov rather than picking the more dynamic and independent Gorbachev. It appears that Gorbachev's supporters obtained some concessions in return, including an agreement that Gorbachev would succeed Chernenko.

### Trends under Chernenko

The foreign policy pursued under Chernenko was basically the same as that undertaken by Andropov. Relations with the United States remained cool, the war in Afghanistan continued, and no movement for reform was permitted in Eastern Europe.

In domestic policy, Chernenko seemed uncomfortable with any suggestion that change was needed in areas like economic affairs.

**The Role of Gorbachev**

During the Chernenko year, Gorbachev presented himself as an advocate of new, progressive methods in economic life. He thus linked himself to reforming trends begun under Andropov but now blocked by the Chernenko faction.

# The Gorbachev Phenomenon

When Mikhail Gorbachev (1931–) took power in March 1985, two basic changes quickly became evident. First, the Soviet Union was now led by an energetic, bold, and imaginative figure. There could have been no greater difference in style than the one between Gorbachev and the elderly and ailing leaders of the past decade and a half.

Second, the Soviet system became the object of an unprecedented wave of reform. Proclaiming the need for political "openness" (*glasnost*) and economic "restructuring" (*perestroika*), Gorbachev changed the direction of both foreign and domestic policy.

One change stands out as even more spectacular than a change in policy: By 1990, Gorbachev had ended the monopoly on power held by the Communist Party ever since the Bolshevik Revolution. The effect was to open the way for a multiparty system.

### Gorbachev's Rise to Power

#### *Background*

Gorbachev was a regional Party official from Stavropol in the northern Caucasus. Trained in Moscow as a lawyer (an unusual background for a Soviet leader), he returned home and rose in the local Communist Party network.

#### *Period in Moscow (1978–1985)*

In 1978, Gorbachev became the Central Committee secretary responsible for agriculture. In 1980, he joined the Politburo as a full member.

Two features marked Gorbachev's career in Moscow from 1978 to 1985. For one thing, he was only forty-nine when he joined the Politburo. This made him the youngest figure within the highest ranks of the Party: The average age of the Politburo's members was over seventy. Second, Gorbachev avoided the blame for the agricultural failures that took place over this period, although he was the Politburo member in charge of agriculture.

## Consolidation of Power

### Control of Party

Within a year after becoming Party General Secretary, Gorbachev placed several of his supporters in the Communist Party Politburo and the Party Secretariat. In each case, he now controlled a key organ of the Party.

By the middle of 1987, Gorbachev had replaced the majority of the key officials in the Communist Party's regional organizations.

### The Ouster of Romanov

Gorbachev's chief rival, Grigory Romanov (1923–), head of the Leningrad branch of the Communist Party, was forced out of the Politburo in July 1985.

# New Trends in Domestic Policy

Gorbachev enjoyed striking success in a number of areas. He departed from the tradition of earlier Soviet leaders by encouraging a frank examination of the country's history and its current problems. He also carried out a series of radical political changes.

At the same time, serious difficulties emerged. Ethnic unrest flared up in various forms. Political opposition developed: Some criticized Gorbachev for too much reform, and some criticized him for too little. The Soviet economic decline worsened.

## Glasnost

Gorbachev set the stage for the reform of institutions by encouraging a new attitude. Government officials, journalists, and ordinary citizens were encouraged in outspoken criticism of Soviet life.

### Freedom for Sakharov

In December 1986, by freeing Andrei Sakharov (1921–1989) from exile Gorbachev sent a clear signal that even prominent dissenters would not be persecuted for their views. Sakharov had been sent to the provincial city of Gorky in 1980 as punishment for criticizing the invasion of Afghanistan.

### Glasnost and History

This policy of candor included a reexamination of Soviet history, including Stalin's crimes. Gorbachev and other high officials took the lead in criticizing actions like forced collectivization.

Prominent victims of Stalin like Nicholas Bukharin were publicly rehabilitated.

### Glasnost and Soviet Disasters

A new honesty on the part of Soviet leaders also appeared concerning natural disasters. After a delay, Gorbachev officially announced the nuclear accident at Chernobyl in April 1986. There, a nuclear power station suffered a catastrophic accident, sending radiation over a large area of the Soviet Union, Poland, and Scandinavia. Two years later, the Soviet government permitted massive foreign coverage of the December 1988 Armenian earthquake and the ensuing relief effort.

## Political Reforms

Spectacular changes took place in Soviet political life. Independent organizations, including rudimentary political parties, began to appear in both Russian and non-Russian parts of the country. Within the government, important new practices and institutions emerged.

### Competitive Elections

Starting in February 1987, elections to some local soviets involved competition among rival candidates.

### New Institutions

Gorbachev established a new legislative system. A Congress of People's Deputies, consisting of 2250 members, was elected in March 1989. In several hundred of the electoral districts, genuinely competitive electoral contests took place.

Under the new system, the Congress chose the smaller Supreme Soviet (with 542 deputies). The system also included a powerful presidency with the president elected by popular vote.

Gorbachev had already taken the presidency in October 1988. He thereby established a new power base located in the government rather than the Communist Party. At the same time, he remained head of the Communist Party.

### The End of the Communist Party's Political Monopoly

In February 1990, the Communist Party, followed by the Congress of People's Deputies, accepted Gorbachev's suggestion that the Party's monopoly on political power be ended.

Non-Communist candidates quickly won control of the city governments in Moscow, Leningrad, and Kiev.

## Ethnic Unrest

Gorbachev found it hard to control and channel the desires of non-Russian peoples within the Soviet Union. Ethnic groups took the policy of *glasnost* as a sign they were free to express their grievances openly. Scenes of massive crowds demonstrating, sometimes violently, in one region of the Soviet Union stimulated ethnic groups elsewhere to do the same.

Two elements posed particular problems. First, some interethnic hatreds threatened to explode into regional civil wars. Second, ethnic minorities called for sweeping changes in the Soviet system. Several even demanded the right to leave the Soviet Union entirely.

### Armenia and Azerbaijan

The most significant example of local interethnic violence developed in the Transcaucasus. Between 1988 and early 1990, Christian Armenians and Moslem Azeri Turks clashed in continually more bloody confrontations.

The immediate issue was the status of an Armenian enclave in Azerbaijan. The larger issue was longstanding ethnic and religious hostility between Armenians and Turks.

In January 1990 Soviet armed forces intervened to stop the bloodshed, especially in the Azerbaijani capital of Baku.

### The Baltic States

The greatest ethnic challenge to the political order came in the Baltic states. There, national feelings were particularly strong, fed by memories of independent statehood before World War II.

The Estonians, Latvians, and Lithuanians were embittered at their economic exploitation by the Soviet state. The tensions were heightened by the settlement of large numbers of Russians in the region after 1945.

### *Lithuania Declares Independence*

Lithuania led the way in open opposition to Moscow. Mass meetings in 1988 featured the display of the old national flag and the singing of the old national anthem.

In December 1989, the Lithuanian parliament ended the political monopoly of the Communist Party in Lithuania. Then, in March 1990, the Lithuanians declared their independence and confronted Gorbachev with a crisis of the first order.

A temporary Lithuanian retreat followed in the summer of 1990. But Gorbachev soon faced a choice in the Baltic states between holding the region by force or permitting the move toward independence to reach completion.

## Domestic Opposition

The set of changes encouraged or permitted by Gorbachev drew increasing opposition from a variety of political opponents.

### *Political Conservatives*

Opposition elements emerged from existing institutions. Conservatives in the Communist Party, the military, and the KGB objected to the pace of reform. Military critics were particularly vocal in criticizing the collapse of Soviet power in Eastern Europe (see p. 447).

Within the Party Politburo, Egor Ligachev (1920–) emerged as a center of opposition to much of Gorbachev's domestic program.

### *Radical Conservatives*

Other opposition elements developed, due in part to the loosening of political controls initiated by Gorbachev.

Radical nationalism appeared in the Russian parts of the Soviet Union. The organization *Pamiat* (Memory) and even monarchist groups emerged, sometimes with anti-Semitic features, to criticize both the Communist Party and Gorbachev's reforms.

### Liberal Critics

Gorbachev also faced opposition for moving too slowly. Critics noted that he maintained the Communist Party in a predominant position and proceeded too cautiously in economic reform (see p. 446). He was also criticized for setting up the powerful post of president and occupying it himself.

Notable critics were Andrei Sakharov and Boris Yeltsin.

*Sakharov.*    Until his death in 1989, Sakharov emerged in the new Supreme Soviet as a major opponent of Gorbachev's plan for the powerful office of Soviet president.

*Yeltsin.*    Boris Yeltsin (1931– ) was a former ally of Gorbachev, expelled from the Politburo in October 1987. He became president of the Russian Republic in 1990, called for sweeping domestic reforms, and established himself as Gorbachev's chief political rival.

In the summer of 1990, Yeltsin left the Communist Party. He pressed Gorbachev to agree to a program of speedy economic reform, featuring a shift to a market economy. Gorbachev first assented, then, in October, backed away.

Yeltsin's prestige as a spokesman for reform and as a popular leader rose sharply in June 1991 when he was elected president of the Russian Republic in a free and hotly contested election.

## Economic Difficulties

Gorbachev's efforts to shift the centralized, planned economy to a new basis resulted in his most significant failure. By the early 1990s, both the industrial and agricultural sectors were in sharp decline. Food shortages in the winter of 1990–1991 made the crisis obvious to the entire population and endangered Gorbachev's hold on political power.

### Agricultural Reform

Gorbachev moved from a position of support for collective farming in 1985 to increasingly radical alternatives. In 1988 he opened the possibility of putting land in the hands of private groups through long-term leases.

By the start of 1989, Gorbachev seemed ready to abandon collectivized agriculture entirely. He now promoted a gradual transition to private farming for at least part of the rural population.

### Industry and Prices

The basic problem for Gorbachev was how to move away from an inefficient, centrally planned system of production and distribution. He remained reluctant to accept various proposals for a rapid shift to a market economy. To a certain extent, Gorbachev seemed ideologically committed to retaining much of the old economic order. In practical terms, removing controls and direction from industry meant huge price rises that were certain to arouse popular discontent. In general, Gorbachev was unwilling to abandon the system under which the state owned most of the factories and related businesses.

At the Twenty-Seventh Party Congress in early 1986, Gorbachev promoted the idea of radical economic reform based on decentralized planning and the elimination of price control by the state.

During the last years of the 1980s, Gorbachev wavered over the proper policy to adopt. In one important instance, he first favored, then criticized, groups of Soviet citizens who formed private cooperatives to run such businesses as restaurants.

## New Trends in Foreign Policy

The hallmark of Gorbachev's foreign policy was to play down hostility between the Soviet Union and the capitalist world. The requirement for a defensive bastion in Eastern Europe was dropped.

Gorbachev implemented these policies by cooperating with the United States over a wide range of issues such as arms control. He permitted popular insurgencies to topple Communist governments throughout Eastern Europe.

Gorbachev also offered unilateral cuts in the size of the Soviet armed forces and the removal of offensive necessities, including equipment to bridge rivers, from Eastern Europe.

### Summit Diplomacy

Gorbachev met with American President Ronald Reagan on four occasions, starting in Geneva in 1985. The major theme of the discussions was arms control.

Gorbachev's new thinking on Soviet military needs was reflected in an agreement with the United States in December 1987 on the mutual destruction of warheads for intermediate-range ballistic missiles.

### Withdrawal from Afghanistan

Gorbachev's policy toward Afghanistan marked a clear departure from the views of Brezhnev, Andropov, and Chernenko.

In May 1988, the Soviets began a withdrawal of their combat forces from Afghanistan. The withdrawal was completed in February 1989. In October 1989, Foreign Minister Edvard Shevarnadze publicly condemned the invasion.

### Nonintervention in Eastern Europe

In the final months of 1989, change in Eastern Europe reached hurricane proportions. A stunning series of developments took place whose rapidity and momentum no one had anticipated.

The Soviet leadership refused to intervene while traditional Communist regimes were overthrown from East Germany to Romania. This represented the abandonment of a policy of maintaining satellite states to the west of the Soviet border dating back to the close of World War II.

### The Collapse of East Germany

The most striking development was the fall of the regime of Erich Honecker (1912–) in East Germany. In the summer of 1989, the Hungarians set the stage for dramatic change all over Eastern Europe by opening their border with Austria. In short order, the system of Soviet satellites that had existed for more than forty years crumbled.

Thousands of East German refugees passed through Hungary's open borders to the West. This struck a fatal blow at the East German government. The authorities in East Germany tried desperately to maintain their control by liberalizing measures, notably opening up the Berlin Wall. As massive crowds demonstrated in Leipzig and other East German cities, Communist power disintegrated. In the end, a non-Communist government came to power following elections in March 1990. The way now opened to the reunification of East and West Germany.

*The Implications of the Soviet Policy.*   The course of events would have been drastically different if Gorbachev had followed the policy of his predecessors, who had maintained docile East European Communist governments even at the cost of using armed force.

If Gorbachev had chosen to intervene with force, he would have endangered his new ties with the West. Such an adventure would have destroyed the goodwill he had engendered by his disarmament proposals and his withdrawal from Afghanistan. Moreover, the use of force offered no assurance of success in holding down Eastern Europe. Finally, the deepening economic crisis in the Soviet Union compelled Gorbachev to concentrate on domestic problems.

Permitting Eastern Europe Communist regimes to fall following the protests of their own citizens signaled a new Soviet attitude that there was no need to fear an attack by NATO through this region. Thus, Gorbachev's policy toward countries like East Germany and Poland was based on the view that détente had brought a permanent change in East-West relations.

# The Crisis of 1991

The political order in the Soviet Union collapsed with dramatic suddenness in the late summer of 1991. As the date approached for the signing of the Union Treaty, which would have ratified a sweeping shift of authority from the central government to the Soviet republics, Party conservatives attempted to seize power. The coup was unsuccessful. In its aftermath, the pillars of the old order collapsed.

The activity of the Communist Party was now suspended through much of the country. The power of the secret police (KGB) was curtailed. Most spectacular of all, most of the republics that had made up the Soviet Union declared independence.

### The Coup

The coup was launched by well-known Party conservatives like Boris Pugo (1937–), the Soviet Union's minister of the interior, and Vladimir Kryuchkov (1924–), the chairman of the KGB. Gorbachev was arrested at his vacation home in the Crimea, and the coup leaders announced that he was leaving office due to his health problems.

## Yeltsin Leads Opposition to the Coup

Resistance to the coup was centered in Moscow where Boris Yeltsin, supported by massive popular demonstrations, defied the coup leaders. The plotters failed to seize Yeltsin and were unable to find support in the armed forces or among KGB troops. Within three days the coup failed.

## The New Order

The failed coup served as a signal and stimulus for sweeping change. Gorbachev resigned as General Secretary of the Communist Party, and Party activities were suspended in the Russian Republic and most other parts of the Soviet Union.

Some symbolic changes indicated popular pressure for a new political order: Leningrad was renamed St. Petersburg; the statue of Felix Dzerzhinsky (1877–1926), founder of the Soviet secret police, was torn down in Moscow; the prerevolutionary Russian flag was prominently displayed.

### *The Breakup of the Soviet Union*

The Baltic states of Latvia and Estonia immediately announced their independence, joining Lithuania, which had declared itself independent in 1990. In early September 1991, by which time the new republics had received diplomatic recognition from many foreign countries, the Soviet central government formally accepted their independent status.

The wave of declarations of independence did not stop with the Baltic republics. Within a few days, they had been joined by Belorussia, Georgia, and the Ukraine. Most of the other fifteen republics soon followed.

### *The Shift in Political Authority*

The key political trend in late 1991 seemed to be the virtual collapse of Soviet central institutions and the flow of power to the republics. This meant that the most important leader on the scene was now Boris Yeltsin, the leader of resistance to the August coup and the president of the largest and most important of the republics.

*The September Agreement.*    A transitional system was set up in early September. It was designed to provide a framework for the independent republics to cooperate temporarily in political and economic affairs. It featured a State Council composed of the Soviet leader, Mikhail Gorbachev, and the leaders of the individual republics. The new system also included a loosely defined committee for economic affairs and a new legislative body. The Congress of People's Deputies voted to accept this makeshift government, then voted itself out of existence.

### The Shape of the Future

The fall of the Communist Party and the collapse of the Soviet central government in the weeks following the August coup created a situation filled with uncertainty.

#### *Economic Crisis*

No quick solution seemed available for the deepening economic crisis. Food shortages and possible famine were the immediate difficulties facing the peoples of the former Soviet Union. Late 1991 saw escalating inflation and a sharp decline in industrial production. Over the longer run, there was a pressing need to reshape the entire economy. Reform proposals centered on replacing the old centralized system with some kind of market economy and transforming collectivized agriculture into a system of private ownership.

Any transition was likely to be painful, but the collapse of the old order made change imperative.

#### *Political Crisis*

The political future of the areas that had made up the Soviet Union was also uncertain. The spread of civil liberties and political rights had helped to create the popular forces that defeated the August coup. It was not clear, however, whether popularly elected leaders like Yeltsin could restore order and deal with pressing problems like the economic crisis. Moreover, in some of the former republics, such as those in Central Asia, old Communist elites remained in power.

*Threats of a New Coup.*    Rumors in November 1991 that a new coup might take place in Russia were a sign of popular discontent.

*Relations among the Former Soviet Republics.*    There was further uncertainty about how the former Soviet republics would deal with one another. It seemed unlikely that a strong central government would reemerge to tie them together. Political analysts speculated that a loose confederation of independent republics, modeled on the British Commonwealth, was the most likely form for a future relationship. But the size and power of the Russian Republic remained a problem. There would surely be difficulty in getting areas like the Ukraine, with strong memories of repression by authorities in Moscow, to restore any close link with the Russians.

### Ethnic Unrest

The ethnic problems that had exploded in the late 1980s seemed certain to continue. Even within the newly independent republics there were numerous minority groups. Often these peoples themselves wanted self-rule, like the Moslem inhabitants of the Chechen-Ingush region within the Russian Republic. Moreover, millions of ethnic Russians were now located outside the borders of the Russian Republic. It was an open question how the authorities in Moscow would respond if they thought those Russians were being subjected to discrimination and repression.

## Communism: An Episode in Russian History

Historians now face the need to think of the Communist era, starting in 1917 and seemingly at an end in 1991, as an episode in Russian history. That means we need to consider how much it borrowed from the Russian past. Did Stalin's rule, for example, constitute a continuation of the old autocracy? Was Stalin a modernized version of Ivan IV?

Thinking of Communism as an episode also means thinking what its legacy will be for the future. For example, did the Communist success in establishing collectivized agriculture and centrally planned industry make Soviet Russia a modern nation by the standards of the twentieth century? Or did that success in fact place Soviet Russia hopelessly behind the rest of the world economically?

## The Russian Past and the Future

The Russian people in 1992 face three pressing problems. The first is the need to create a viable modern economic system. Both agriculture and industry must take new forms. By the standards of the late twentieth century, that kind of system cannot be based upon the central government's detailed control and planning. But the Russian past presents a pattern of economic progress, especially in industry, taking place only under such government direction. Is it now possible to create in Russia a hitherto unknown kind of economic system, based on free enterprise, to open the way to a more prosperous future?

A second problem is ethnic relations. The Russian state has been a multiethnic one for centuries. It has traditionally operated on the basis of central control exercised by ethnic Russians. Is it now possible for the peoples of the former Soviet Union to cooperate on a new basis without the arbitrariness and coercion of the past?

Finally, one must ask what political forms will emerge and become established. The aftermath of the August coup saw the triumph of democratic forces, a novel element in Russian history. Will democratic institutions and democratically elected leaders prove able to deal with the pressing problems that Communist leaders like Brezhnev found unmanageable? If not, will Russia turn once again to autocratic rule?

*The extent of change brought on in the Gorbachev years was immense in comparison to the Brezhnev years and the interlude from 1982 to 1985. Gorbachev quickly demonstrated that he was unwilling to maintain the political status quo. But he had also shown himself reluctant to abandon completely the framework of Soviet life constructed since 1917: notably the Communist Party and state ownership of land and factories.*

*As the Gorbachev era extended into the 1990s, the Soviet leader was challenged from several sides. Liberals like Yeltsin urged him to go faster, and Party conservatives objected to the changes that were already occurring. Within Soviet society, the spread of political rights and open discussion eroded the old order from below.*

*The failed coup of August 1991 opened the gates for swift and revolutionary change. The old order, based upon the rule of an elite Communist Party and a federal system dominated by ethnic Russians, collapsed with dramatic suddenness. The peoples of the former Soviet Union now found themselves living within the wreckage of an old and discredited system. There were hopes for a new democratic order and a reformed economy, but there was also deep concern that the transition to them would be long, painful, and, in the end, unsuccessful.*

## Recommended Reading

Bialer, Seweryn. *The Soviet Paradox: External Expansion, Internal Decline* (1986).

Bialer, Seweryn. *Politics, Society, and Nationalism inside Gorbachev's Russia* (1989).

Bialer, Seweryn, and Michael Mandelbaum, eds. *Gorbachev's Russia and American Foreign Policy* (1988).

Brumberg, Abraham, ed. *Chronicle of a Revolution: A Western-Soviet Inquiry into Perestroika* (1990).

Byrnes, Robert F., ed. *After Brezhnev: Sources of Soviet Conduct in the 1980s* (1983).

Cohen, Stephen. *Sovieticus: American Perceptions and Soviet Realities* (exp. ed., 1986).

Cohen, Stephen, and Katrina vanden Heuvel. *Voices of Glasnost: Conversations with Gorbachev's Reformers* (1989).

Crouch, Martin. *Revolution and Evolution: Gorbachev and Soviet Politics* (1989).

Daniels, Robert V. *Is Russia Reformable?: Change and Resistance from Stalin to Gorbachev* (1988).

Desai, Padma. *Perestroika in Perspective: The Design and Dilemmas of Soviet Reform* (1989).

Doder, Dusko. *Shadows and Whispers: Power Politics inside the Kremlin from Brezhnev to Gorbachev* (1986).

Doder, Dusko, and Louise Branson. *Gorbachev: Heretic in the Kremlin* (1990).

Feher, Ference, and Andrew Arato, eds. *Gorbachev: The Debate* (1989).

Goldman, Marshall. *Gorbachev's Challenge: Economic Reform in the Age of High Technology* (1987).

Gorbachev, Mikhail S. *Perestroika and Soviet-American Relations* (1990).

Hosking, Geoffrey. *The Awakening of the Soviet Union* (1990).

Hough, Jerry. *Russia and the West: Gorbachev and the Politics of Reform* (2nd ed., 1990).

Kaiser, Robert G. *Why Gorbachev Happened: His Triumphs and His Failure* (1991).

Laqueur, Walter. *The Long Road to Freedom: Russia and Glasnost* (1989).

Laqueur, Walter. *Stalin: The Glasnost Revelations* (1990).

Lewin, Moshe. *The Gorbachev Phenomenon: A Historical Interpretation* (exp. ed., 1991).

Mandelbaum, Michael, ed. *The Rise of Nations in the Soviet Union: American Foreign Policy and the Disintegration of the USSR* (1991).

Medvedev, Roy, and Guiletto Chiesa. *Time of Change: An Insider's View of Russia's Transformation* (1989).

Medvedev, Zhores A. *Andropov* (1983).

Miller, William Green, ed. *Toward a More Civil Society? The USSR under Mikhail Sergeevich Gorbachev* (1989).

Morrison, John. *Boris Yeltsin: From Bolshevik to Democrat* (1991).

Nagorski, Andrew. *Reluctant Farewell* (1985).

Nove, Alec. *Glasnost in Action: Cultural Renaissance in Russia* (1989).

Smith, Hedrick. *The New Russians* (1990).

Tatu, Michel. *Mikhail Gorbachev: The Origins of Perestroika* (1991).

Tsipko, Aleksandr S. *Is Stalinism Really Dead?* (1990).

White, Stephen. *Gorbachev in Power* (1990).

Yeltsin, Boris N. *Against the Grain: An Autobiography* (1990).

Zacek, Jane, ed. *The Gorbachev Generation: Issues in Soviet Foreign Policy* (1988).

# Index

# McGraw-Hill's College Core Books Series

If you liked this book, you might be interested
in other history volumes
in our College Core Books series.
Ask for them at your local bookstore.
If they are not available,
mail the coupon to McGraw-Hill, Inc.

**AMERICAN HISTORY BEFORE 1877**
Order Code 057539-8 / 057595-9 $9.95

**AMERICAN HISTORY SINCE 1865**
Order Code 067426-4 / 067452-3 $9.95

**ENGLISH HISTORY**
Order Code 067437-x $11.95

**MODERN EUROPEAN HISTORY**
Order Code 067453-1 $9.95

**RUSSIAN HISTORY**
Order Code 028649-3 $11.95

**WESTERN CIVILIZATION TO 1648**
Order Code 015395-7 / 015623-9 $9.95

**WESTERN CIVILIZATION SINCE 1600**
Order Code 015396-5 / 067454-x $9.95

| ORDER CODE | TITLE | QUANTITY | $ AMOUNT |
|------------|-------|----------|----------|
|            |       |          |          |
|            |       |          |          |
|            |       |          |          |

LOCAL SALES TAX _____

$1.25 SHIPPING/HANDLING _____

**TOTAL** _____

NAME _____
(please print)

ADDRESS _____
(no P.O. boxes please)

CITY _____ STATE _____ ZIP _____

ENCLOSED IS ☐ A CHECK ☐ MASTERCARD ☐ VISA ☐ AMEX ( ✓ ONE )

ACCOUNT # _____ EXP. DATE _____

SIGNATURE _____

*MAIL PAYMENT & COUPON TO:*
**MCGRAW-HILL, INC.**
*ORDER PROCESSING S-1*
*PRINCETON ROAD*
*HIGHTSTOWN, NJ  08520*

*OR CALL:*
**1-800-338-3987**

MAKE CHECKS PAYABLE TO MCGRAW-HILL, INC.  PRICES SUBJECT TO CHANGE WITHOUT NOTICE AND MAY VARY OUTSIDE U.S.  FOR THIS INFORMATION, WRITE TO THE ADDRESS ABOVE.